D1500269

The Library Paraprofessional

Dedicated to my parents,
Ruth Ann and Leonard Lief

The Library Paraprofessional

Notes from the Underground

TERRY RODGERS

McFarland & Company, Inc., Publishers
Jefferson, North Carolina, and London

ACKNOWLEDGMENTS: Thanks to all my contributors, named and anonymous, alive and dead, particularly my two interviewees.

Thanks to my mother for reading and editing my manuscript. Thanks to my family and friends for being patient with my crazed exclamations of "I'll never finish this! I have no time!" and encouraging me.

Thanks to Maggie Collins for being my island of sanity at work. Thanks to Linda McNamara and Gail Rizzo for enduring daily onslaughts of interlibrary loan requests.

Thanks to Bill Katz, Dorothy Harth, and to my mother for urging me to try to get my master's thesis published.

British Library Cataloguing-in-Publication data are available

Library of Congress Cataloguing-in-Publication Data

Rodgers, Terry.
    The library paraprofessional : notes from the underground /
Terry Rodgers.
        p.   cm.
    Includes bibliographical references (p.   ) and index.
    ISBN 0-7864-0222-9 (library binding : 50# alkaline paper) ∞
    1. Library technicians—United States.   2. Library science—
United States.   I. Title.
    Z682.4.L52R63   1997
    023'.3—dc20   96-26371
                                                                   CIP

Manufactured in the United States of America

McFarland & Company, Inc., Publishers
    Box 611, Jefferson, North Carolina 28640

Table of Contents

Introduction

In library literature, articles abound on CD-ROMs, online systems, search strategies, and bibliographic utilities. There are use surveys and pseudo-"scientific" studies. Authors have much to say on the subjects of funding, management, problem patrons, burnout among librarians, latchkey children, community outreach, budgets, indexing and abstracting, collection development, bibliographic instruction (BI), cataloging, and book and periodical jobbers. Censorship is a concern, as is copyright adjudication. Pieces on library architecture, rare books, acid-free paper, book preservation, the Internet, school libraries, media materials, librarians' salaries, conferences, and the mission of the library are all accorded space in professional journals. Every imaginable problem peculiar to librarians—that is, library school graduates—has been minutely covered, from the image they project to their vaunted professionalism.

But the greater number of employees in any given library are the so-called nonprofessional workers, i.e., those not holding the master of library science (MLS) degree. These workers, who in the United States are estimated to comprise from 50 to 85 percent of the library field, have been largely neglected: "overlooked, underpaid, and unappreciated," not only in the institutions they uphold, but in library literature, where coverage has been scant (Weibel, "I"; Kopp 102; Wolcott; Wakefield & Martin 9; Dyckman 77; Oberg, "Emergence" 102). Lorna Toolis has termed library assistants "invisible people," and so they are, despite their numbers. Indeed, Line and Robertson muse that "in the past less attention seems to have been given to staff than to book selection, cataloguing or binding" (161).

Since the mid–twentieth century, non–MLS workers have been variously termed "library clerks," "library assistants," "library specialists," "library technical assistants," "library associates," "library aides," "nonprofessionals," "paraprofessionals," "paralibrarians," "preprofessionals," "mini-librarians," "nonprofessional librarians," "support professionals," "quasi librarians," "subprofessionals," and even "librarians." Whatever the terminology, these workers account for most of the work and little of the pay and prestige in libraries ("Support Staff"; Oberg, "Emergence" 104; Ferguson, "Through" 93). Significantly, most

1

non–MLS-holding personnel of whatever variety have come to call themselves "*support* staff" because they supply the underpinnings without which a
library could not operate. Toolis writes,

> [I]f the non-supervisory library workers were all to disappear the library would
> grind to a halt within a week at most, the system having choked to death on the
> small tasks which are not important taken one by one, but without which the
> library cannot function. By comparison, most libraries could run for weeks, if not
> months without librarians [19].

Along very similar lines, a branch library head of my acquaintance once candidly exclaimed with amazement and chagrin that the library could go along
for months without a director—even without librarians.

"Support staff" is a more dignified appellation for the non–MLS-holding (and increasingly, MLS-holding) worker than "nonprofessional," a more
commonly used but somewhat pejorative older term. "Library assistant" is a
very old title, and still in general use. Both of these terms will be used in this
book, as will "paraprofessional" ("para" for "beside" or "around"). The newest
favored buzzword for library support staff, or paraprofessionals, is "library
associates," as propounded by the maiden issue of *Associates: The Electronic
Library Support Staff Journal.* (Anderson-Story has objected to "para": "[W]e
are *associates* with others who perform library work, not *supporters* of or those
who work *around* those who do library work" [Simmons, "Welcome"; emphasis added].) "Clerk" is an old and still widely used job title, but like "nonprofessional," it is inaccurate and somewhat pejorative; a vast number of people
in the clerical category are really performing (without acknowledgment) at a
much higher level, sometimes professional duties. In 1991, the *World Book*-
ALA/SCOLE project admitted:

> Ironically the continuing blurring of librarian and paraprofessional responsibilities
> that varies from library to library but is a clear trend, and which would seem to indi-
> cate respect for paraprofessional abilities, often exacerbates the issue, particularly
> in those library functions where librarians and paraprofessionals perform similar or
> identical tasks…. Paraprofessionals know they are doing work done previously by
> librarians who were typically paid more and whose positions had more status in the
> organization. They resent this if, as is often the case, commensurate pay increases,
> participation in decision making…, and increased potential for advancement do not
> accompany the increased or expanded duties ["Issue Paper #4"].

They also agreed that "paraprofessional positions are often classed with lower
paid clerical workers," their increased responsibilities glossed over by mis-
leading terminology, which gives no inkling of the knowledge or skill involved
in performance of their work (*World Book*–ALA "Issue Paper #5").

Castelyn, speaking for the library field worldwide in its bewilderment over
appropriate terminology for "support staff," claims, "Real progress would be
made if an acceptable collective title could be found … but a great many minds

have already been applied, with minimal success, to the finding of an acceptable alternative to the title of 'library assistant,'" and all the other terms (159–60). Recurring bouts of discussion on this subject are common on Libsup-l, the support-staff listserv on the Internet. One commentator from this source believes "librarian" should be used for library employees without specific education in library work, and that "master librarian" should be the term for advanced degree holders. But her thinking was prefigured by Charles Robinson as early as 1968, reflecting the duration of the problem and the way that history has repeated itself in the field of librarianship (Ravdin; Robinson, "Promise" 3759).

"By and large, the first ones to meet and deal with problems or patrons will be [the] staff of non-professionals," writes Miletich, "[the] first line of defense against time-robbers and energy-wasters" (39). Therefore they are often mistaken by the uninstructed public for librarians, are often indistinguishable from librarians, indeed are often *acting* as librarians (Veaner, "Continuity" 8; Hoffman 8; Schuman; Hobson et al.; Wolcott; Harris, *Librarianship* 28-9, 47, 138; and others too numerous to mention). Concern for the public's putative "misapprehension" over which library worker is the "librarian" keeps the fuss over terminology alive, and reflects a larger reality which has plagued the field since Day One, namely, the question of whether professional and clerical duties are clear-cut enough to warrant maintaining the class distinctions present in the nation's libraries between "professional" and "nonprofessional."

"The *role* [emphasis added] of the paraprofessional ... is as old as librarianship itself," wrote Charles Evans in his ground-breaking overview of the paraprofessional in history ("Evolution" 64; emphasis added). It was the librarian's effort to distance, nay, divorce, herself from the menial aspects of her job—so that she might be viewed as a "professional"—that gave rise to the type of worker now termed "nonprofessional." Kranz refers to the "clear trend to downshift what were formerly professional ... responsibilities to paraprofessionals" (89). While his reference was to cataloging practices, the "trend" to which he refers has affected every area of library work, and his words echo those of many other commentators.

Downshifting, or what Veaner calls "off-loading," has been occurring at an escalating rate for the past thirty years, an indirect homage, really, to paraprofessional capabilities and an accolade to the "born librarian," as well as a sad commentary on the status of libraries in the eyes of funding bodies (Veaner & Ackerman, "1985 [I]" 223).

Underscoring the increasingly thin line between MLS-holding librarians and non–MLS-holding support staff is that, ironically, most of support staff's professional problems "mirror the problems of librarians" (Oberg, "Paraprofessionals and the Future" 10). Most frequently the much-scrutinized "overlap" in work responsibility and pay comes between the highest level of nonprofessional (non–MLS-holding) staff and the lowest level of professional (MLS-bearing) staff, but it can extend much farther.

To wit, in 1993, Lynch and Lance coauthored an article based on statistics formulated by the Federal-State Cooperative System for Public Library Data (FSCS), in which they admitted that "only 41.1 percent of public libraries had qualified [i.e., MLS-bearing] librarians in 1990" (204). This figure appears to have plummeted from comparable FSCS statistics reported in 1989, in which 61.9 percent of librarians in responding libraries held the MLS (Podolsky 22). And this 61.9 percentage is down from the 63 percent of public librarians holding the master's in 1983 (from *Library Human Resources: A Study of Supply and Demand*, cited by Greiner, "Role" 76).

Today there are by conservative estimate at least 42,000 non–MLS-holding library employees in the United States. The *Occupational Outlook Handbook* claims 71,000 in 1992, but Kenady insists the figure has been even larger: in 1982 she found the figure to be "nearly 190,000" (Martinez, "In" 8; *America's Top...* 230; Kenady 1). According to the Federal-State Cooperative System, full-time public library paras alone numbered over 73,186 in 1990 ("over" because not all libraries responded to the FSCS with their figures), up from 49,283 in 1987 (Lynch & Lance 204; Rubin, citing Lynch, 19). If one stretches the definition of "paraprofessional" to include *all* non–MLS library workers—non–MLS-holding library directors, non–MLS-holding professional library specialists, volunteers, and student workers—employed in libraries, this figure is arguably higher, more like 86,941 and up, since only 21,305 workers (20 percent) of 108,246 library workers have the MLS in the nation's public libraries alone (Lynch & Lance 204).

Kenady's 190,000 figure may be more accurate than the other figures, or it may simply indicate that the job market has become tighter since 1982—though the increase in Lynch's public library figures belies this notion. It may also, in addition to including clerical staff from all other types of library, have included part-time workers. ALA stated in its *World Book–ALA Goal Award Project on Support Staff* circa 1991: "We do not know the number of part-time paraprofessionals ..." ("Issue Paper #4"). The larger figures undoubtedly also include, as indicated, so-called "non-librarian professionals" and non–MLS-holding library directors.

Mark Mentges, alluding to the mists surrounding accurate support-staff statistics, laments "the lack of a comprehensive national list of paraprofessionals" (14). This lack has more than once necessitated the sending of survey instruments not directly to support staff, but to or through library administrators, thus generating fear of honest reply among staff and producing a low response rate. Thus it seems likely that many of the surveys of support staff involving impressive statistical findings, but based on a low response rate, are omitting important points of view. They may, in fact, be obscuring the true picture, rather than revealing it.

Low pay is endemic among paraprofessionals. One study, conducted in Alabama, found that "75% [earn] less than the U.S. per capita income" (Fitch 317); a comparable situation exists in Britain, where a typical library assistant is paid "less than the European Community Poverty Level" (Thapisa, "Work" 35). Reflecting, I believe, a national reality, Dorothy Jones' 1989 survey of paras and the introduction of computer technology into their workplaces found that 55 percent of respondents have experienced increased responsibilities and have been expected to assimilate often elaborate new computer protocols without seeing an increase "in even one paycheck" (443). Indeed, a tremendous increase in workload is another invisible component of the modern paraprofessional's life, following massive budget cuts in the early 1990s. For example, in 1994, Cathleen Palmini conducted a survey of the impact of computerization on support staff in an academic setting in Wisconsin. One of her respondents agreed that computerization allowed her to get more work done, but stated that she had suffered an almost 600 percent increase in work since the advent of automation in her department (124).

In addition to being numerous, ill-paid, and overworked, paraprofessionals are mostly women. Over time and in different locations, the proportion of female paraprofessionals has fluctuated between 74 and 93 percent.* Early in the history of library literature, in 1895, a library assistant delineating the unfairnesses already inherent in her profession declared: "I believe that *she* is the impersonal pronoun in library science" (One Who Isn't, 241).† Anita Schiller speaks of female librarians as the "disadvantaged majority" of the library field, but that description may be more truly applied to female clerical and technical staff, who receive even less of every emolument than librarians.

The escalating overlap of job duty between MLS-holding librarians and non–MLS-holding support staff is so all-pervasive—despite efforts over the past 100 years to sort it all out—that the ongoing debate over what tasks should be done by whom, and the effort to maintain a rigid class structure in the libraries of America, is nothing more than comedic. Certainly the so-called job overlap, or role-blurring, or misapprehension of clerk for librarian, is not "dangerous," as Larry Oberg maintains, echoing older commentators, or a "serious transgression," as McCulley and Ream would have it ("Role" 235; Shores 240; McCulley & Ream, "From").

We all work for libraries, often doing the same job, paraprofessionals as

---

*Mort: 80 percent female in her survey, in 1992, p. 46; Hildenbrand: 80–85 percent female in 1983, p. 384; Azad: c. 74.2 percent female, for his paraprofessional sample, in 1978, p. 83; Presthus: 80 percent female, for both groups, in 1970, pp. 45, 48; Bryan: 91 percent of professionals; 93 percent of "subprofessionals" female, in 1952, p. 29.

†Therefore, instead of the English-language convention of making the third-person singular male in cases of non-specificity, I, like the anonymous "One Who Isn't," will use the feminine third-person singular throughout this book.

committedly and knowledgeably as librarians. The whole squirming, snake-like mess which these warring factions have compounded is really best described by the term "library workers"—librarian and clerk alike. It was the term of choice for early writers describing library employees. The Victorians had many ideas that the field would have done well to keep; this is one. "Library worker," then, will be a term I use in the following pages as freely as any of the other buzzwords, because of its stolid egalitarianism.

"The chimera of librarianship is the paraprofessional," wrote Rosanna Miller in 1975. With seven years of clerical library work behind her and a newly minted MLS to her credit, Miller wrote perceptively because she straddled the much-discussed "chasm" between clerk and librarian (551). Like the Chimera, the "para" is a composite, a patchwork. She may be a mere high-school graduate, or a holder of multiple advanced degrees, including the bachelor of arts, one or more subject master's, the Ph.D., and even the MLS. The para, or clerk, or nonprofessional (terms I use interchangeably because terminology is extremely inexact across the land) may be ordinary; she may be extravagantly intelligent; she may be unaspiring; she may be vauntingly ambitious. The nonprofessional may work at any level of proficiency, and at any job known to the library field, from clerk to director.

In many specialized libraries, from the start of modern American librarianship, applicants with subject specialties have been preferred over applicants trained in library school, simply because it is easier for a highly educated person to acquire library skills than it is for a person with library skills to become highly educated. "[C]atch your specialist," advised Rathbone in 1915, "and then make a librarian of him" ("Requests" 117). In 1923, before library schools had been squeezed into university contexts, Williamson quoted one candid university librarian on the subject of training:

> "The best reference people I have met in my own experience are not library school graduates but university-trained people who have somehow gone into library work[;] ... I ... have made a known scholarly attainment the basis of selection. I would rather have such people with an imperfect knowledge of library technique, than the best trained technician who lacks university training and some graduate study..." [*Training ... Service* 95].

Lynch and Lance cry out against the "almost 60 percent" of the nation's library directors who do not hold the MLS (206). But for over 100 years, educated people intimately associated with the well-being of libraries all over the country have been functioning—sometimes with vast distinction—in the direction and running of the nation's libraries, and the necessity of holding an MLS degree to do so is thus greatly in question.

Ironically, as the number of "professional" librarians declines in the United States, the number of paraprofessional workers holding the MLS, as well as other advanced degrees, is increasing. The uncomfortable presence of intelligent and eager—and often formidably degreed—paraprofessionals in the field caused Allen Veaner, in his widely discussed article, "Continuity or Discontinuity ...," to sketch what he sees as a threat to the professionalism of the field: "Highly educated employees in support staff roles feel dead-ended, embittered and frustrated, their talents and abilities far surpassing the challenge of their job assignments. In some cases employees on their own seek out more challenging work in the library, distorting existing job classification systems" (3).

In many instances, his portrait is exact. Barbara Conroy, reviewing the status of staff in the electronic library, credits paraprofessionals with frequently being "the first skilled library personnel in new areas such as outreach, audiovisual services, and automated circulation" (91). Gisela Webb mused that "[i]n many cases, highly skilled and eager paraprofessionals have exhibited more creativity and risk taking in assuming new responsibilities than professionals who have difficulties in letting go of comforting, but routine tasks" ("Educating" 113).

Moreover, their numbers have increased steadily since the 1960s. For instance, Braden et al. and Eskoz each conducted separate surveys—Braden one and Eskoz two—covering the years between 1977 and 1987, on the degree of support-staff involvement in cataloging. Where Braden et al. found 1.6 percent of her 121 respondents acknowledging support staff performing original cataloging in 1977, Eskoz found two of her 40 respondents admitting, in her later survey, that support staff did *all* "original descriptive cataloging," and that "adaptive cataloging" responsibilities were shared, by 1987, in 90 percent of respondent libraries by both paraprofessionals and professionals (Braden et al. 139; Eskoz 389). Joseph Rosenthal had remarked as early as 1969, in his study of five university libraries, that "[t]o a greater or lesser degree, original cataloging (especially descriptive work) of monographs is assigned to nonprofessionals" (326). Spyers-Duran averred as early as 1977 that "eighty to ninety-five percent of all cataloging is now performed by non-professional staff ..." (Braden et al. 149). In astonishment, Eskoz exclaims:

> The majority of departments involve both professionals and support staff at this level. Braden's 1977 study shows figures between 43 and 47 percent; among 1983-84 participants nearly two-thirds used both, and by 1986-87 three-fourths of the participants did so. Few have relied solely on support staff for all adaptive cataloging; interestingly, all three surveys, covering a ten-year span, show almost the same percentages throughout: 1977 reports 13 percent, while both the later surveys show 15 percent—this in spite of the near-universal agreement that the quality of cataloging in cooperative online networks has improved over the past decade [389].

Holley in 1981 maintained that "some libraries are asking whether a library science degree is necessary for most cataloging positions" (91).

Today, 92 percent of ARL libraries responding to Oberg et al.'s 1992 survey on support-staff responsibilities assign paraprofessionals copy-cataloging responsibilities, and 51 percent assign original cataloging to their skilled "nonprofessionals" (also see Appendix B). In addition, 36 percent assign subject analysis and classification to paras (Oberg et al., "Role" 224). This leap in "professional" responsibility for "nonprofessional" staff has occurred in other areas of library work as well, as we shall see.

Not only has the number of paraprofessionals increased in librarianship over the past 30 years, and their increase in professional duties been duly noted by current commentators, but observers see this joint trend continuing (Eskoz 382). In 1994 one authority in the field, Larry Oberg, stated matter-of-factly, "I foresee an *unprecedented increase* [emphasis added] of paraprofessionals ... [; Technology will permit] paraprofessionals to perform at much higher levels, including administration" (G. Flagg et al., "In" 719; emphasis added). Roma Harris, too, in her disturbing discussion of technology and libraries, warned, "Even those who are most optimistic about the new technologies acknowledge that in their vision of the future the direct service role formerly played by reference librarians will be deprofessionalized as nonprofessional staff assume primary responsibility for most patron contact" (*Librarianship* 131). In fact, she continues, "Many of the service roles played by librarians in the past will, in future, be taken over by paraprofessionals and clerical workers" (*Librarianship* 142). Robbins goes further:

> [M]any of the core functions of libraries, cataloging, classification, acquisitions, basic reference, etc., are presently and may be in the future more predominately assigned to support staff, while library role definition, selection of services to be offered, and management of these services, will become the key professional functions [17].

This redistribution of function will take place against the expectation that libraries will retain 60 to 80 percent of extant staff throughout the next decade and despite the fact that "the number of library workers has actually decreased in the United States since the mid-1980s" (Harris, *Librarianship* xiv). The strong implication is thus that the "new blood" will be paraprofessional (St. Lifer & Rogers, "ULC" 112). In fact, at a 1991 Rutgers Symposium, Charles Robinson "raised the roof by saying that he could staff a library with mostly technical assistants" (*Education* 68).

Today the intelligent and capable among support staff are striving, on the basis of proven ability, to enter the ranks of librarians without the MLS, even as librarians, hoping for a better lot, have striven to shed the stigma of clericalism throughout librarianship's brief modern history and to don the cloak of professionalism in the public eye. The inescapable fact is that librarianship is comprised of a lot of repetitive tasks, not particularly difficult to learn—clerical, technical, and intellectual—and it *is* a service industry, at base, if in fact it is what we know as librarianship, and not management—or denial. These tasks may as well be divided equitably amongst the entire library staff, whose intelligence-quotient range does not really show extreme variation, despite the persisting airs of librarians.

Usually, though far from always, the big sticking point for paraprofessionals or support staff aspiring to higher status is that they do not hold "the questionable passport" of the MLS (Miller, "Paraprofessional" 551). This dearth usually serves as an excuse for the atrocious salary most of them receive, and for a very real role as scapegoat in the library field: nonprofessionals are the means by which a "professional" librarian exorcizes the vastly clerical nature of her work, to appear better both to herself and to the world at large, which throughout the past hundred years has typically questioned her professionalism. Yet the MLS as a measure of professionalism is increasingly seen as bogus, by librarians as well as clerks. A study of Louisiana libraries, for example, uncovered a willingness on the part of 41 percent of respondent public libraries to see paras promoted to librarian positions, and 57 percent of these claimed the MLS would not be a prerequisite (Timberlake & Boudreaux 165).

The presence or absence of the MLS is in the realest sense irrelevant to the professionalism of the serious library worker, and serves as an excuse for nothing. It is a very weak way to adjudge the professionalism of a library-bound employee, and I speak here both as a long-term "clerk" observing MLS-holding librarians and as a bearer of the MLS. This view is held by many librarians, as well as support staff. For instance, Joy Greiner, a veteran professor at the University of Southern Mississippi's library school, claimed in 1990, "The requirement for a master's degree in library science in a professional public library position may be negotiable" ("Non-M.L.S." 209).

Libraries and librarians do not need to flourish at the expense of a valuable group of employees, the support-staff workers, who have labored as obscurely and lovingly as any unsung librarians to serve the institution of libraries throughout the twentieth century.* It is time to be fair to the many gifted so-called non-professional library workers, especially those with longevity and innumerable skills acquired on the job; to give them an equal voice in library governance and in the world; and to accord them the salaries they deserve.

In the early years of librarianship, years of experience were equated with years of schooling in placing an employee. And today the practice continues. For example, "professional" Library of Congress staff, who arguably provide the nation its standard for library cataloging, are, as often as they are MLS-holders, simply bright, attentive people with bachelor's degrees, subject training, and experience in the field—and no MLS (Hiatt 123-4). They undergo

---

*For example, library assistant Anita Mull bequeathed $442,203 and a collection of 216 music boxes valued at over $12,000 to the Miami-Dade Public Library in 1989 (Goldberg, "Endowment").

essentially the same course of training to become the nation's catalogers (*ibid.* 126). There is no reason—especially since computer advances outdate every person's training in a matter not of years, but more often of months—not to revert to this notion of experience being the equal of a certain number of hours spent in library-school classrooms.

The huge majority of the librarians I have spoken with over the years, when faced with my clamor about the MLS, admit that when fresh out of their respective library schools, they had felt utterly at sea in their first jobs. Quite simply, *they learned librarianship on the job.* In Alvarez's *Library Boss*, P. Hearne, a Pennsylvania library director, writes, apropos a piece on clerical and professional library workers: "[T]he MLS is only a ticket to on the job training which prepares most librarians to move into management and administration positions." He insists, "I have yet to find an enthusiastic, dedicated, experienced, non-degreed staff member who could not, with the proper guidance, perform most professional tasks" (211). "What stands between librarians and support staff," avers Judy Orahood, quoting Mary Bolin, "is 'a year or two of not particularly demanding graduate school, and then access to more information and more opportunities.'"

In 1992 I attended what I thought was going to be a fiery paraprofessional conference, but which turned out to be a tiresomely hokey stress-management session. I was appalled to hear grown women, veterans in their fields, all no more nor less intelligent than the many librarians I have known, standing to state their names, their titles, and the degree of their professional education, then uttering shamefacedly, one after the other, the same words: "Only on-the-job training." A few had the MLS; none had the LTA degree. I wondered what could be wrong with on-the-job training, since in the early years of modern American librarianship, the feeling of many prestigious commentators was that apprenticeship was, if not the only way to train, one valid way, or one necessary component of the way to train. Justin Winsor, a nineteenth century luminary, when asked "how best to acquire a knowledge of library work," replied succinctly, "By doing it" (R. L. Davis 180). As late as the 1960s, during a veritable burgeoning of in-house training programs, apprenticeship was the *de facto* mode of training for support-staff members who amounted in some places to 75 percent of personnel (Donahugh; Muller 225). The number of paraprofessionals trained on-site far exceeded the number trained by two-year colleges, even in these programs' brief vogue.

From the start, intelligent people have proven they could easily evolve into hyper-competent librarians, and have publicly conceded this. Commentators at the Fifth Session of the Portland Conference, 1905, were the first in a long line of librarians to urge this point of view, to wit: "The born librarian will not need a school to teach him principles of classification—put him into a library, and he will take to them as a duck to water ... ("Portland" 167). Brand points out that early in modern library history—at the turn of the twentieth century and before—"[i]n librarianship, the argument that the 'best librarians are born not made' was used to justify men without professional education in leadership positions" (394). Vann credits Lloyd Pearsall Smith with articulating this credo—*Custos librorum nascitur, non fit*—at the 1876 Conference of Librarians (4). Frederick Crunden, at the Portland Conference in 1905, during which this concept was discussed, observed sensibly: "[T]here were librarians before there were library schools ... ("Portland" 169). "It may well be doubted that the power in librarianship exercised by such men as Jewett and Poole, Winsor and Lloyd P. Smith, will ever owe its existence to library school training," insisted one record of an ALA meeting ([Meeting] 299). Although this argument is not voiced as orthodoxy today, it holds very true still; one has only to note the number of non–MLS-holding scholars who have smoothly been given charge of the nation's finest libraries—Billington, Boorstin, MacLeish, Healy, Gregorian, and LeClerc, to name a few—and performed like pros (De Gennaro).

Even non–MLS-holding library workers who are *not* scholars—the more than 50 percent who in fact run the nation's libraries today—have obviously been hired under some very similar presumption. Lynch and Lance regard this as an appalling problem requiring remediation. I don't share their concern. Line and Robertson very reasonably observe:

> Pressures on staff expenditure have led to more delegation, as a result of which the definition of professional and non-professional duties is changing. What used to be done by a fully qualified librarian with a degree may now be done by someone with fewer or no qualifications. It would be interesting to compare the prophecies of disaster made by librarians ten years ago with what has actually happened. Undoubtedly some services have suffered, but very few libraries are giving significantly poorer services on the whole today than they were doing, with many more staff, ten years ago. Somehow, productivity has been increased [162].

Moreover, a recent survey conducted by the ALA in 599 libraries of all sorts across the nation swore that "[m]ore than 90% of library users ... are satisfied with the services at their local library—with about three-quarters (74%) claiming to be very or extremely satisfied" ("Users"). Obviously the field's increasing reliance on paraprofessionals has not caused a diminution or compromise of professionalism at any point. The public, as we have noted, perceives all library workers as "librarians," and in effect is entirely correct in its perception.

It is time that we were consistent across the board. If librarians are born, not made, which may in fact be quite true, we must eschew this Orwellian some-animals-are-more-equal-than-others scenario.* So-called *non*-professionals are

*As an explanation and excuse for withholding the title of "librarian" from library assistants not meeting her high unarticulable standards, Black in 1918 merely fussed, "Librarianship is a queer intangible thing" (Black 200).

often as professional as MLS holders. Many were hired 15 to 25 years ago because of their intelligence: they were "college graduates ... with good scholastic records ... [possessed of an] interest in and knowledge of books ... [and an] ability to work well with people ... [with] ample amounts of initiative, imagination and maturity" (Donahugh 9). Others were high school graduates and middle-aged women returning to the work force with two-year technical degrees from community colleges. As a reward for being this talented and this educated, they could expect to receive a tad more than half the salary of newly graduated MLS holders (Evans, "Library" 22). There were other commentators, like McDiarmid, who hedged their bets over the new breed of paraprofessional. They urged a slightly dimmer, less ambitious type of recruit. We see both types of para in today's libraries, the results of recruitment methods based on these two divergent schools of thought on "nonprofessional" utilization. Yet despite the clearly articulated, and often contradictory, presumptions under which paraprofessionals were being recruited (they should be, in effect, smart, yet stupid; cheap, but of the best quality, since they were hired to replace "about half" of the librarians then employed), smug commentators of the time could actually write, without compunction and with sweetly stupid irony: "This could be the beginning of a career with opportunities unlimited" (Evans, "Library" 22; Knight 5).

Today, most of these workers are still wondering about the "unlimited" part. On the basis of personal professionalism, proficiency, aptitude, education in other specialties, or intelligence, and, increasingly, actual possession of the MLS, many such employees should have been monetarily rewarded and promoted without restraint to the top of the field, regardless of sex, degree, and type of formal education, or any other extraneous consideration; yet they continue to languish in severely underpaid positions with little official recognition of their expertise. In fact, they are often forced to remain there because librarians, fearful of their capacities, deny them access to wider library practice. But Alvarez makes a strong case for giving the talented clerical worker the key to the highway:

> I recall too many wonderful library staff members—both professional and clerical employees—who had more than their share of imagination, enthusiasm, common sense, dedication, and the other positive virtues ... everything, in fact, but a year of library school training. There are thousands of such individuals working in our libraries. We mustn't ever let their lack of professional training—which grows less and less important with every additional year of experience they have in the library—blind us to all they have to offer and are capable of doing if we are smart enough to give them the opportunity [*Library* 210–11].

In 1989, a *Library Journal* article heralded the coming "Issues of the Nineties." Three problems concerned the editors: the shortage of adequately trained librarians, the dearth of continuing education for both professional and nonprofessional staff in the face of "proliferating technology," and the "new constituency of 'paraprofessionals' ... organizing to seek opportunity and to define its role in libraries" ("Career Development" 52).

I submit that training programs and continuing education programs—preferably conducted *on-site* and (over more extensive periods of time than are now apportioned) for *all* library workers by traveling consultants/trainers—are necessary for any employee who intends to pursue a lifelong calling in the field. I also submit that the MLS, as it is currently issued, is an expensive, redundant, and pretentious joke, largely worthless in preparing the uninitiated for competence in mainly practice-based disciplines like librarianship or information brokering. Further, its intellectual content—Asheim's presumably invaluable "core curriculum"—is most often, though not always, "mickey mouse" ("Education of"; anonymous MLS candidate, Albany). Training programs for technicians need somehow to be merged with the best (i.e., most relevant) of what is now taught in library schools, namely, reference, technology, cataloging, and preservation; the curriculum needs to be far more practice-oriented; the professoriat—or itinerant trainer—needs to be far more in touch with what actual libraries face. A broad-based and continuously pursued background in sciences, humanities, the arts, and business should be encouraged in all library workers, rather than attainment of the somewhat parochial MLS.

Most of all, what the field needs is candid acknowledgment that on-the-job training—apprenticeship, in effect—has been a major and ongoing (though undercredited) fact of library life for over 100 years. Sheila Intner, for example, remarks with refreshing candor, "I ... recognize that there are ... libraries in which the training afforded to catalogers is nearly equal if [not] superior to the formal coursework offered in library schools" (6). Despite the field's flirtation with Library Technical Assistant (LTA) programs in two-year colleges in the 1960s and 1970s, on-site, in-house training is as alive and well today as at any point in the past. "We seem to have returned in a significant way," considered Robbins-Carter, "to the pre-twentieth-century condition when virtually all of the education for the *skill* level of librarianship takes place within our libraries" ("Reaction" 311).

Apprenticeship is as firmly entrenched now as it was in the early days of modern American librarianship, from the Library of Congress down to the minutest rural library. One has but to regard the plethora of articles on in-house training programs even today (e.g., Anderson & Huang; Gavryck; Hiatt; Hudson; Kranz; Landrum; Nevin; Preece; H. Sager; etc.), not to mention in the past (e.g., Daniels; Gebhard; Gross; Walker), and the frequent reference to "mentoring" as an important process in recruiting bright new faces (Harris; Massey, "Mentoring"; and others), to understand that *de facto* apprenticeship is still the unofficially preferred method of training both for paraprofessionals and, given the inadequacy of most graduate library programs, most professionals as well. Oberg and colleagues in their recent study of 467 academic libraries ("Role" 228), note that

> 84% of the Carnegie respondents offer orientation to new staff members, and 78% offer workshops and other in-house training programs. The corresponding percentages for the ARL libraries are 97% in both cases.

Ironically, the reason for the modern demise of college-based library training for both the paraprofessional and the graduate library student was adumbrated by Lester Asheim, that staunch supporter of the "core curriculum" and of the basic pro/non-pro status quo. In 1968, during the second COLT conference, Asheim remarked that "librarians ... would rather have a four-year graduate with no training whatsoever than a two-year graduate with some basic library skills" (*Progress* 9).

Has much changed from then until now? In their 1993 textbook for training paraprofessionals for reference service, McDaniel and Ohles note that some reference departments suffer "a lack of subject expertise" and counsel that one way to augment professional services, in effect, is "to hire people without library degrees but with valuable subject area knowledge." Certainly it is no coincidence that two sentences later they write, "Ideally, paraprofessionals should be hired only to complement, not replace, professional librarians, but, regrettably, this is not always the case" (2, 3). Such thinking has, for obvious reasons, been with the field from the first, as we have seen. Because the pragmatic approach works, it has become established. But it works best for hiring institutions. It does not work well for the smart paraprofessional specialist, who is paid dirt for her services and cannot see library work as a career. Therefore, within paragraphs, McDaniel and Ohles are covering the perennial issue of high turnover among paras (4). Still, the message inherent in this presentation—something along the lines of "hire the bright, train them your way, *pay them as professionals*, and forget the MLS..."—does not penetrate administrative ears.

Today, many LTA programs are defunct, and graduate library schools have closed in dramatic numbers, while many more are moribund. These circumstances make the 1990s a good time to contemplate what schooling for librarians should comprise, and whether this schooling is best accomplished within colleges and universities, many of whom have terminated library programs because, among other reasons, of their lack of academic relevance. With the nation's economy flagging, it may be time not only to jump up the quality and quantity of on-the-job training, but also to pursue aggressively the development of distance-education programs targeting library and information workers, and to implement the use of peripatetic trainers, who would reach both urban and rural libraries with the latest technological know-how.

In 1968, Asheim's *Library Journal* article "Education and Manpower for Librarianship" (I would substitute "Womanpower") included the following comment from a librarian: "I believe that each occupational category is essential to providing library service, and that there are no degrees of essentiality" (Paul Howard in Asheim, "Education and" 1109). I also believe avenues through library echelons should be far more fluid than they presently are, somewhat in the way they were in the Enoch Pratt Library of the 1920s and 1930s, and in other more pragmatic and fair systems (Coplan). Despite librarians' constant insistence on their professionalism, they really are not doctors, or lawyers, or any other species of true professional (in the sense of long years of study in qualified schools being absolutely necessary for adequate performance).

And with Roma Harris I believe library workers should "[press] society to assign greater value to those very characteristics that give their profession a female identity," and to eschew self-blame (*Librarianship* 74). She understands that "the alternative to imitating the male world, that is, trying to revalue women's work, is not easy," but urges the members of "female-intensive" fields "to join together with others in the women's movement, in other words, to recognize that theirs is a shared problem—one that goes beyond occupational boundaries and which reflects instead the gendered nature of the workplace" (*ibid.* 97). She also, radically, urges the ALA to become a feminist organization (*ibid.* 117).

All library workers today should strive to politicize themselves, to lobby for the institution of libraries, or to write strongly their opinions on the field (Garbacz). The traditional pyramidal form of library governance needs to become far "flatter," mostly to accommodate reality, but also to move forward more equitably and efficiently, with faces of library workers all focused in one direction: towards the survival of the beloved library. One way or another, the great library shakeup will occur, and is occurring. Each library worker has to decide where she or he will stand.

I live for the day when teamwork among peers becomes the defining characteristic of libraries, replacing its stodgy, encumbering hierarchical structure and its insufferable, baseless snobbery. For better or for worse, this is no longer the Victorian era; over and over again—ever since the French Revolution, in fact—the need for a more equitable social structure has impinged on the American polity. From militant rappers to striking nurses, the message is delivered unrelentingly. It is largely ignored, thus making us probably the angriest democracy in the world.

Instead of the traditional pyramidal hierarchy, participatory management, the "web" style of management, or the more recent TQM movements should be the rule in libraries (Hoerr; D. Sager; Wakefield & Martin 9). All library workers should be cross-trained and frequently rotated to obviate boredom and institute equity. The sheer fun of being immersed in books and myriad other library materials, operating complex machinery in the pursuit of information, and serving the public as a team of peers in this unique and free way should emerge from the current acrimony and grudgingness between "professional" and "nonprofessional," and from the artificial opposition of "librarianship" to "information science" (Gorman, "Bogus").

"Apprenticeship" should cease being a term under stricture. When a combination of intelligence, aptitude, performance, and *extent* of education—experiential or academic—replaces possession of the MLS as the criterion for library work, then libraries might at last be the fine educational settings they should be, "life support for a democratic form of government," staffed by polymathic, generous, democratic, relaxed, humanistic, and good-natured practitioners—different from each other, but all equal, all professional (Schwartz 1731).

Then again, is professionalism necessarily and exclusively the proper goal? Perhaps what should be more assiduously pursued, rather than squelched, in this field should be *amateurism*. An "amateur" is someone with "marked fondness, liking, or taste" for something, a "devotee," an "admirer" (*Webster's Third New International Dictionary* 65). All library employees should love learning, and should be known to love learning. An openly demonstrated love of the life of the mind—including far more abundant and scholarly publications originating from library workers, on a great range of subjects, than are presently evident—might earn them more respect in the world's eye than empty insistence on an all but invisible "professionalism" based on artificial segregation of seemingly identical workers and attainment of the MLS. This reputation, once earned, might finally put to rest all the silly nattering about "image" that has plagued library literature for decades—evidence of massive personal insecurity, if nothing else. The current demise of library schools in fact is often seen as the fault of the schools themselves, which for a variety of reasons covered below have stalled in giving clear voice to the appropriateness and, in particular, the scholarliness of their mission—namely, their academic professionalism—to their parent institutions.

An increase in scholarly publications of distinction and love of learning, combined with computer expertise, would guarantee respect to library workers in the eyes of funding bodies. Computers are the great levelers, the great democratizers. With Line and Robertson, I hold that it is "not so much whether libraries can afford staff development, but whether they can afford to go on as they are, using staff ineffectively" (175)—and, I might add, in all too many institutions, condescendingly, demeaningly, and cruelly. Ex-ALA president Patricia Glass Schuman puts it more starkly: "[W]e ignore [support staff issues] at the peril of our libraries and our profession" ("Librarians").

Line and Robertson posit that

> the traditional division into professional and non-professional duties in libraries has not been helpful. It has led to rigid demarcation lines.... It is encouraging that the Library Association [British] ... is to redefine professional and non-professional duties. The pity only is that the distinction has to be codified at all [170-71].

I agree fully with these men, traveling library "consultants" (trainers), and am certainly not the first to state this view, as this book will make abundantly clear. Because the message just never seems to get through, despite reiteration, I bring a fiercer conviction to this fray than many politer commentators. I wish to bring their very immediate voices to the field's attention again. Despite the undoubted insufficiencies of this book, I stand behind it, as much an authority as anyone else in librarianship. I hope I do not ultimately have to leave this field because its deficiencies prove terminal.

Librarians' cynical use—especially in the earliest years of modern American librarianship and again over the past few decades—of paraprofessionals as foils, in a vain and enraging attempt to appear more "professional" in comparison with them, is truly inexcusable. Moreover, the public's continuing obliviousness to which of the library's workers are "professional" would indicate this ploy has in any case failed.

Librarianship is being queried and challenged and threatened from any number of quarters in the 1990s, and sometimes rightfully. The gauntlet thrown down by this book constitutes, I believe, one of the rightful challenges. Given the history of paraprofessionals in library history, "professional" and "nonprofessional" are two of the most iniquitous and hypocritical words ever to have entered the lexicon of Libraryland.

Mary Niles Maack's brief essay, "Toward a History of Women in Librarianship: A Further Critical Analysis with Suggestions for Further Research," concerning the lacunae in the field of research on women librarians' contributions to librarianship, was particularly humbling to me in what I now consider to be my infant researches. Her mention of the dearth of oral interviews touches on my concern with the enormous number of individual paraprofessional voices waiting to be heard in the field of librarianship. Lurking and querying on the Internet and monitoring the conversations which take place on the Libsup-l listserv (a Net library support-staff group almost 2,000 subscribers strong), and stumbling across the many short but percipient letters (for the most part unindexed) in professional library journals, have made me burn to delve deeper into the library paraprofessional's experience through these and other means. Researcher Johannah Sherrer, remarking on survey participants' responses in a written section designed to ascertain most and least liked library tasks, confessed that "more [could] be learned from these pages of narrative than from the 550 pages of computer statistics..." (20).

Therefore, I will liberally quote people no library "scientist" has ever heard of: obscure paraprofessionals speaking on issues which comprise the substance of this book. Surely the people best qualified to speak about paraprofessionals and what it is they actually do—or suffer—are the paraprofessionals themselves, or those who work closely enough with them to have realized that they are peers (Rais 819).

In the main, with few exceptions, these paraprofessionals have preferred to remain anonymous. This preference is not a new development. Ruth Miller, working in 1990 with staff members to "brainstorm" about the better running of the Indiana State University Libraries, recommended that groups including support staff be comprised only of support-staff members "so that any comments perceived as dangerous or subversive were heard only by peers, not by supervisors" (13). Fear seems to be rampant in discussions of paraprofessional woes, even among librarians discussing them sympathetically (for example, the author of "A Personnel Formula," who preferred anonymity to notoriety). Are librarians so insecure that they seek bloody reprisals for what they perceive as threatening or insubordinate statements from underlings or colleagues? One can only infer that they are. They have set up an atmosphere over the past 100 years which has prohibited fearless, attributed expression of unorthodox ideas among all but the most prominent, and therefore, most protected. Such unseemly dread underscores the extreme hierarchical rigidity in library governance that this book deplores. Fear governed the responses of most of the paraprofessionals I queried about permission to use their names after quotations. "Anonymous," I found, was not only "a woman," but quite likely a support-staff member. She made her appearance in the earliest days of modern library work, e.g., "Anonymous," "Assistant," "Librarian," "Visitor," "Traveller," "One Who...."

The pages that follow will detail and document, from the extant literature, the generalizations and asseverations I have made. I have also included, in appendices, two interviews with paraprofessionals who typify certain problems non–MLS-holding workers face as depressing quotidian realities.

PART I:
THE PSYCHOLOGICAL TEXTURE OF TODAY: THE PLIGHT OF THE MODERN LIBRARY PARAPROFESSIONAL

1. The Last
35 Years: Overview

There are those who suggest that the roles of librarians and paraprofessionals have changed sufficiently to require a complete overhaul of our professional and personnel models. Suffice to say this is a controversial proposal. Some librarians are threatened by these changes, others welcome them. The same is true with paraprofessionals [ALA/SCOLE, *World* "Issue Paper #9"].

Evans called the paraprofessional presence a "disturbing element" ("Evolution" 64). Professional slighting of the "disturbing" paraprofessional contribution to librarianship has been more the rule than the exception for more than thirty years. Yet slighting, unsurprisingly, has done nothing to make the problem vanish. Paraprofessionals do not endure this unprofessional mistreatment meekly, as increasing union activity, formation of paraprofessional associations, or surly letters and small testimonies in magazines attest. Up until recently, however, they have been less active on their behalf than one would have expected, given their accomplishments, perhaps because the more active and pragmatic "clerks," like Owen (below) have given up and gone on to secure the MLS, and perhaps because of burnout and turnover (see Dyckman 81). In any case—and I shall try to uncover the many factors at work in clerkdom—this quietness has its roots in librarianship as well: "'I'm appalled at how professionals are willing to settle for undercompensation, let alone the paraprofessionals,'" stated Creth incredulously at the 1994 Annual Conference in Miami (G. Flagg et al., "In" 719). Librarians have long endured inequity and humiliation at the hands of the public, their boards of directors, and the entrenched gender system, and these tangled problems bear looking into.

"[Paraprofessionals] have grown in importance and have secured a place for themselves in libraries since [the late 1950s]," wrote Evans, in his surprisingly fair appraisal of the clerk-librarian conundrum ("Evolution" 64). Certainly this observation, penned in 1979, attains the quality of understatement today, given the developments of the past fifteen years. Technologies and their myriad protocols are chiefly to blame for the small difference today between clerk and librarian, other than what is enforced in rigid library systems by librarians with vested interests to protect (giving rise to directions like, "Don't answer that question, even if you know the answer: refer the patron to the librarian"). In the past, librarians were trained for a relatively steady state of affairs, for cataloging, for reference work, with perhaps a new circulation gizmo entering the scene, perhaps a new kind of bookshelf; and clerks, sensibly, were hired to see to the maintenance of files, the issuing of books, the typing of cards, and the binding of books and magazines. Today, there are Computers.

Computers are everywhere, and they change constantly, constituting what Lowry terms a major "paradigm shift," comparable to the development of the book format, the invention of moveable type, the nineteenth century mechanization of book publishing, the advent of the typewriter, or the development of cataloging systems (237). Computers constitute a quantum leap in communicational and informational potential, not only for librarianship, but for the whole civilized world. Twenty years ago, OCLC was a wonder. Ten years ago, local library systems were happy finally to be on a LAN (local area network) with sister libraries in their immediate area. With Internet, information access has gone global. Now librarians struggle to catch up with non–MLS-holding techies, and—embarrassingly, for all those who would dream that they were "professional"—even the self-taught, computer-wise homeless (Kleiner; Buthod, re: the Seattle Public Library).*

Meanwhile, clerks and library technicians, many with LTA certificates, have for over thirty years been increasingly charged with the running and maintenance of computer-based library technology. In many but not all libraries they are in charge of numerous public-service points totally on their own recognizance (viz., circulation and interlibrary loan). Non-MLS (and even MLS-holding) support staff perform a wide range of duties, from filing and shelving, and circulating and returning books—those duties traditionally the sole province of the lowly library clerk—to cataloging (both copy and original), performing complex tasks in automated settings, setting these automated settings up, collection development (selecting, ordering, and processing books and other materials), overseeing name-authority control in on-line systems, staffing reference desks, attending conferences (though usually at their own expense), running ILL (interlibrary loan), reserve, and circulation departments, supervising staff, conducting bibliographic instruction, and running whole libraries (Gillen; Files; Dyckman 83; Fehlman & Verma; Sarkodie-Mensah 8; Mace, "Creighton" 15; Bishop 15; Euster [2]; Weil; Liptak,

*In Seattle, publicly available terminals offering Internet access gave scores of homeless and unemployed men the opportunity to develop and hone their skills to such an extent that librarians began asking *them* for help with Internet questions. Some of these men also landed jobs because of their acquired expertise.

"Paralibrarians"; Kathman & Felix 202). These non-clerical duties, of course, have hitherto been thought to be the prerogative of librarians, but librarians have, over the years, too often abdicated and disdained—"off-loaded"—these and other responsibilities as being too routine, mundane, and "unprofessional" (Veaner & Ackerman, "1985 [I]" 223; Walton & Botero 49).

Additionally, because most libraries face budget constraints and because of a putative shortage of librarians (Heim et al. 149; Berry, "Other"), boards of directors and personnel departments often hire any sharp person who is able to do the job and who, bearing no MLS, can be had for a song. At an ACRL (Association of College and Research Libraries) Personnel Administrators and Staff Development Officers discussion group in 1993, Allen Veaner was reported to have said in effect that "[i]f librarians did not have programmatic responsibility, there would be no difference between librarians and support staff" ("ACRL Personnel" 3). Administrative eyes are averted from any special, unacknowledged, and certainly monetarily unrewarded gifts these people bring to the job and, in fact, must summon to perform their jobs satisfactorily, as in even the most menial clerical work anywhere across the nation (as evidenced, for example, in Teiger & Bernier's "Ergonomic Analysis of Work Activity of Data Entry Clerks in the Computerized Service Sector Can Reveal Unrecognized Skills").

They have served on reference desks in conjunction with librarians "for decades, … mostly without significant restriction" (Oberg et al., "Rethinking Ring" 145). And as we have seen, they are increasingly involved in the more complicated protocols of cataloging. The result is that they are often a jump ahead of librarians who are caught up in traditional book-based reference services, writing reports, and attending meetings, and who have lost touch with the day-to-day functioning of the units they nominally head (e.g., Webb, "Educating" 117). Kemp observed, "In many situations, support staff know things about the system … that department heads do not know—or cannot remember without having to relearn" (38).

At best, in this age of accelerated change in technologies, clerk and librarian are learning procedures at the same time, or being forced to learn them—since they are expected to utilize them to do their work—at their own pace alone, where libraries will not be troubled to train workers adequately or even to train them at all. "Challenges and opportunities seem to be multiplying exponentially in this technological/information age," urges Cromer. "All library staff members, degreed and non-degreed alike, are constantly training to make good use of newly-developed and newly-acquired tools." Stone sensibly pointed out as early as 1971, "The best library education and training can become obsolete in five years, or less, unless the librarian makes a very determined effort to continue his education" ("Introduction" 1). The same holds true of support staff. I would not hesitate to say that in my observations of library workers, it is the few, rather than the many, who make this effort to enhance their technological prowess. Hence, there is lots of room for native intelligence to come into play, as in the early days of modern American library history, because now, as then, adequate training programs are few and far between, because of the field's failure to accommodate aggressively the continuing-education needs of staff, particularly support staff.

Training is obtained hugger-mugger. "'In our profession we have paid attention to the MLS degree, which is obtained in 12-18 months out of a 30-year life of a librarian,'" stated ULC's (Urban Libraries Council) Executive Director Rodger. She goes on, "'While our professional attention has been on this fairly small proportion of workers in libraries, we have no sustained programs for keeping current or upgrading skills for'" the "majority of a library's employees, those without the MLS degrees" (St. Lifer & Rogers, "ULC" 112). When the meager workshops do occur, in desultory fashion, according to each separate library's whim, they are cursory and usually in arrears of the advent of the machine, which people have meanwhile struggled to learn on their own with at best token support from the parent institution. One indignant support-staff member, addressing the sketchiness of ongoing training for library workers, called for reformation of "the incredible scam of 1-day 'continuing education' workshops that cost millions and teach little" (Libsup-l correspondent, Dec. 14, 1994). Paraprofessionals in Dorothy Jones' survey found computer training to be no more than "adequate" or "moderately good" (440-1). Lukewarm responses led her to conclude that there was much room for improvement in training plans. There is not only room for improvement, but reason for alarm. Wanden claims that "one-third of the technical skills of U.S. workers will become obsolete this year [1995]." In the OCLC Online Computer Library Center Pacific alone, she claims, she and her co-workers receive "nearly one thousand calls a month from library staff" requesting computer support (29).

Paraprofessionals and clerks performing at a paraprofessional or professional level, but not being re-graded accordingly, contend with many of the same problems today that their counterparts have battled in the past, but now support staff are more numerous and more political, and paraprofessionalism (like clericism before it) in librarianship is an established concept, as it was not twenty-five years ago. Librarians may have learned to lament that they were ever quick to get into the labeling game. Labeling a group of people gives them an identity, a sense of solidarity against perceived foes.

Pearson characterized library support staff as the spokes in the library wheel, with librarians at the hub and materials at the rim. "As the spokes," she declared, "we technicians hold and support the entire wheel." Unlike real spokes, however, support staff have never really been credited—in money or respect—for the strength or visibility of their position. Toolis, as we have seen, has called support staff the "invisible" people of the library field. What needs to be examined is why these "invisible people" are accorded such minute consideration compared to other important issues in professional library journals. What stake have librarians had, over the past hundred years, in erasing these workers? Whatever the goal, their efforts have never been entirely successful, as we shall see.

Part of the reason paraprofessionals have never been totally erased is that librarians themselves insist on discussing them for a number of reasons, usually because of librarian-related difficulties (e.g., there are not enough clerks, or we can substitute bright clerks for librarians, or there are too many uppity clerks). So from time to time their cloud of invisibility evaporates and a semi-lucid picture swirls from the mists. Though writings on the class of people now termed "support staff" appeared intermittently throughout the 1980s and before—notably in the 1960s, and before that, in the late nineteenth and early twentieth centuries, albeit inferentially—recently there has been a veritable renaissance of interest in these lower-echelon "knowledge workers" (Flanagan citing Berkley 493; Veaner, "Paradigm" 394-5). Ed Gillen, an active and prolific paraprofessional advocate, and others call this renaissance "The Library Support Staff Movement" (Libsup-l posting, June 1995). "An angry rumble is rising" from Libraryland's "invisible people": the twentieth century reincarnation of the Chimera is once again breathing flames (Dyckman 82; Toolis 19).

Both the enhanced educational background and the increased number of paraprofessionals now working, conjoined with the upsurge of a variety of computer technologies and a burgeoning feminist awareness in library literature, underlie this renaissance. The roots of paraprofessional competence are buried deep in the history of all library work, which has always attracted a certain number of high-grade amateurs into its ranks, bookish and interested in promoting the book. These roots are entwined inexorably around the development of modern librarianship, not only in the United States, but, because free public libraries are so much a part of America's contribution to global culture, throughout the rest of the world as well.

Generally these overwhelmingly female workers lack both an MLS and the remuneration sufficient to send them through library school (or even remuneration sufficient to subsist upon), problems which have shadowed women career library workers since the late 1800s, when librarianship was trying to establish itself for increasing numbers of emancipated women not only as a profession, but as a women's profession, as were the fields of education and nursing. Unfortunately, at present as in the past, the MLS is usually the only easy way to achieve the accolade of professionalism and a salary commensurate with the title of librarian. However, the ever-increasing numbers of nonprofessionals who work in and run libraries, the controversy surrounding the quality of the MLS degree, and the closing of many of the nation's library schools may change this requirement.

A very great irony is that most of those who today we would call "librarians" in the late nineteenth century and into the twentieth century were known as "library assistants"; only the chief executive was the "librarian," a practice commentators like Veaner would like to see reinstituted. Moreover, in some libraries, librarians had nothing to do with the selection of books: the board of directors chose them. In one library, the librarian performed janitorial as well as clerical jobs and hotly defended himself in a newspaper as both clerk and janitor, claiming in effect that he knew his place. In another library, the janitor himself was authorized to circulate books (Evans, "Evolution" 70-3).

Nonprofessional but eminent academics from fields other than librarianship have held head-of-library positions in large, prestigious libraries throughout the late nineteenth and the entire twentieth century, from the Library of Congress to academic libraries to a whole host of small rural public libraries. Librarians of Congress from MacLeish to Boorstin have failed to hold the wondrous MLS, and have performed more than adequately—have outperformed MLS-holding librarians, in fact.

Thus another wrinkle in the MLS/non–MLS holder saga has always been the unofficial preference for educated specialists over mere MLS-holders. Increasingly, non–MLS-holding specialists are hired, mostly in special or research facilities, for professional positions in libraries where possession of the MLS is optional, but advanced study in other areas is mandatory. These people often enjoy higher salaries than MLS-holders, and further bring into question the value of the MLS as a prerequisite for library work (Detlefsen; Trumpeter).

Despite the articulations of library literature, the great majority of silent but active library administrators, true to the ALA's and Melvil Dewey's vision of "the Best Reading for the Greatest Number and [or "at"] the Least Cost," continued to take the path of least resistance against current library dogmas. In the earliest years of modern library work in America, they hired any woman educable to do the inordinately clerically burdened work of the field, and paid her practically nothing. It seemed to make no difference to most of these mean-minded administrators whether these workers bore a college degree. Income was predicated less on education than on sex. When Williamson, aghast at the state of the field, made it unfashionable to rely upon non-college-educated help for librarian work, administrators hired more librarians with the BLS. Sneakily, however, they continued to recruit training-class products for professional work; then, in later years, they hired graduates with the MLS, but paid them the same low rates they had by that time established for BLS-holders and training-school graduates (Bryan 63).

Librarians after Williamson were unwilling to redesign the field so that viable career tracks existed for both librarian and clerk, because they could squeak by without doing so. The more intelligent of the field's prospective recruits were unwilling to expend great amounts of money on graduate-level library schooling and then settle down to jobs consisting mostly of clerical work and paying practically nothing. So administrations hired whatever clever transients they could attract to fill their gaps and called them "clerks," in accord with Williamson's precepts, but made no energetic attempt ever to fashion a paying career for this very necessary type of library worker. These employees were expected to be intelligent and cheerful, but were paid less than a skivvy's wage. Moreover, though they were branded as clericals, a sizable and ever-growing number of them were taking on professional responsibilities, so that over the next 20 years "clerk" became a label both inaccurate and demeaning, in those cases when clerks were really acting no differently from librarians. Classifications were very amorphous.

Hence, by the time Presthus, in 1970, made his observations on the trends in the field, what he called the "anomalous presence" of the paraprofessionals was well-established; what's more, like their librarian coworkers, they were already disillusioned (24). The library field suffered a constant high turnover rate among clericals (e.g., N. White 567; Kinzer 220 & 222, and many others too numerous to itemize).

Andy Rooney once referred to writers of over-long letters as "bright nuts." Bright nuts—humanistically oriented, highly educated but vocationally unfocused, unconventional, and sometimes coruscatingly astute—were ever the surreptitious targets of Libraryland's recruiting efforts. When libraries hired bright nuts, they got something for nothing—a tempting prospect. Intelligent clerks (those who did not go on to become librarians) became, next to underfunding, one of the field's biggest problems. But in fact library administrators fashioned this problematic state of affairs, primarily through desire to save money, secondarily to compensate for flagging numbers of librarians in the field, and only tertiarily because librarian "professionalism" needed a boost. A 1971 public library directors' poll found that

> an average of 83 percent of ... directors of large public libraries now say that a person who hasn't been to library school can be trained to fill [standard professional library] positions. Almost 19 out of 20 directors say an "untrained person" can head a circulation department, while 85% say he or she can be trained to do reference work, 82% say the same thing regarding the running of a branch library, and 70% see no reason why such an individual couldn't become a good children's librarian. Some readers may be surprised that more directors think it possible to run a branch library without library school training than to be a children's librarian without it [Alvarez, *Library* 175].

In response to this perceived danger, middle-level librarians swiftly distanced themselves from clerks—now acting as paraprofessionals—setting up what even today is referred to as "the great divide": "'[W]ithin the library an artificially wide distinction is made between "academic" and "non-academic" staff, which is reflected neither in personal qualifications nor in the demands of the job,'" remarked one of Thapisa's British library assistants ("Burden" 141). The ALA was put on its mettle. It frantically scrambled about and belatedly, considering the endless controversy over the quality of education needed for librarianship and the professionalism question which had absorbed writers in the field since the late nineteenth century, "[i]n 1970 ... endorsed the principle of the master's degree as the basic requirement for employment as a librarian" (Harris, *Librarianship* 114).

In 1964, Elizabeth Cooper was to worry about the "growing rift between clerical and professional staff in many libraries," evolving out of "[o]ur constant emphasis and stress on the word 'professional'": "The non-professional worker who has the word crammed down his throat a dozen times a day, loses in self confidence, gains in belligerence and is altogether out of step." Naturally, this snobbery rankled. It still rankles, and is one of the most persistent characteristics of the librarian-staff relationship, unjustified by superior personal or, often, even educational qualification. Recently, one indignant paraprofessional, enraged by the "arrogance and pomposity" of a *Virginia Librarian* editorial attacking a proposed name change for the journal which would have made the title reflect more exactly the multiplicity of the VLA's membership, fumed,

> I do not have nor will I ever have an MLS. The reason for this is in good part the result of thinking like theirs. I have been in the "library business" for 23 years[;] before that I was a school teacher. I am as well educated as any "professional" that I know, but it is as if my degrees mean nothing to these people. In some instances over the years, I have felt nothing but pity for some that felt they walked on water because of this MLS degree. Do I have a bad attitude? Maybe yes, maybe no, but elitists always leave me with a bad taste in my mouth [Pat Scott, Libsup-l posting, July 17, 1995].

On the other hand, an embattled librarian spat out, cross with Berry's controversial "The Other 'Librarians'": "I know some of the paraprofessionals Berry mentions who are simply ambitious, envious, dissatisfied, and uneducated bureaucrats who want the easy way to parity"[;] "[p]rofessionals are better educated, as a rule, and deserve better pay than nonprofessionals" (Wiener). And of course there *are* paraprofessionals who are dim, lazy, incompetent, or unqualified. Unfortunately, however, there has always been a similar large number of librarians who could only be classed as functional philistines working in libraries all over the country, today as in the '60s—in fact, as always. The numbers of déclassé library workers who should be in fields other than librarianship are equally distributed throughout the professional and paraprofessional ranks.

Nettlefold determined, in 1989, that writing about the clerical library worker peaked in 1968 (531). In America alone, no fewer than 110 articles appeared in the most prominent journals between 1967 and mid–1969, most devoted to the issue of library-technician training (Held 35-36). But there has been a recent resurgence of written interest, because, more than ever, vast numbers of mostly long-term, now "graying" non–MLS-holding employees (the "uncommitted" young paraprofessionals of yesteryear at whom Presthus looked askance [24]) are being expected to perform the work of librarians. Disappointed in their failure, over the past 30 or so years, to garner the recognition and remuneration due them, and emboldened by the large number of paraprofessional organizations they have created over the same period, they now publish periodicals of their own, and articles in professional journals, just like librarians. And, like them, in a form of perpetual motion, wanting recognition of their professionalism, wanting to shed mere "clerical" duties, they shunt their more trivial duties away from themselves and onto others. So there is a constant devolution of tasks downward. These days, students and volunteers are carrying the load once delegated to clericals. Linda Owen, COLT President, gives a good description of the way library work is always being shifted down:

> If you took a look at the work flow in my department today as compared to 5 years ago, you would see major changes. Some came from changes in the technology we use to catalog and manage work flow. Others came from decreases in staff. A major change has been in who does what. We depend on students to do aspects of the work that once only a FTE [(full-time employee)] was allowed to do. The staff no longer does anything that a student can be trained to do with some supervision. That also means the staff now does work that used to be done by higher level staff or work created by the need to train and supervise students in higher level tasks or that created by the need to manage automated databases. It goes on and on. The benefit of this is that the work the staff does is more challenging and interesting. The drawback is the concept of the level of responsibility increasing is not accepted by administration so we stagnate at the old job classification. Since I do not see this changing anytime soon, I have chosen to work with organizations that may have an impact on the future of the profession and to go on with my education. I will probably have to move out in order to move up. I need to prepare to do so.
> Maybe the young workers of today who do only that which the job requires are correct. That is what they are hired to do. That is what they are paid to do. To do more is to accept the fact that exploitation of the worker is acceptable [posting on Libsup-l, April 28, 1995].

Volunteers, increasingly relied on to perform services in libraries too strapped to afford even paid non–MLS help, are also becoming a force to be reckoned with, albeit mainly by those members of the library community—both MLS-holding and paraprofessional—who cannot afford to work in libraries without being paid. A boon to libraries in need, they are, inadvertently, a further threat to library workers seeking a dignified wage for library work, and a further nail in the coffin of library "professionalism." For if volunteers can do the work of profession and paraprofessional alike, what hope is there for ever attaining a professional wage scale for any of us? Unbenefited part-time and contract workers also threaten salaried library workers by lowering the standard of pay painstakingly won, usually by unions, over the years.

Support staff are not unaware of the inequities of regard and salary that burden them as they have been asked to assume more of the duties of librarians, nor of the increase in automation and the ensuing need for an ever-higher level of sophistication and, often, degree of training/education required for their work. The effort to sort out differences between the two classes of library worker is ultimately circular, or maybe like a Moebius loop, again and again coming back on itself. Roma Harris, in her intelligent discussion of the "erosion" of librarianship, which like nursing and social work is a service, client-oriented profession, observes that the quest for higher, i.e., "professional," status in librarianship results in an endless struggle to climb the managerial ladder, and thus an inevitable move away from direct service to clients, the library's *raison d'être* (*Librarianship* 18, 39, 58). Consequently, "'[a]ctivities in direct pursuit of the organizational goal occur mainly at the lower levels,'" where paraprofessionals cluster (Simpson & Simpson in Harris, *Librarianship* 39).

> The irony in all this, of course, is that on the one hand, the female-intensive professions are castigated for their failure to exhibit "professional" attributes. Yet, on the other hand, when nurses, social workers, and librarians actively pursue the model exemplified by the traditional male professionals, they are rebuked for abandoning their clients [*Librarianship* 52].

My favorite metaphor for this debacle is the tigers in "The Story of Little Black Sambo" who chased themselves into butter trying to attain the more enviable parts of each other and were then eaten in great delight by Sambo's whole family over pancakes. Is there a cautionary message here somewhere? I hope so.

A great irony is that this population, so demeaned as paraprofessionals or clerks, constitutes a large percentage of the people who go to library school, earn the MLS, and miraculously, Pinocchio-like, become real, live professional librarians. In fact, MLS candidates are actively recruited from this group, "the most fruitful source of new students," with "roughly 50% of the MLS candidates surveyed in 1988 (the most recent data) ... having worked in libraries or currently doing so" (Kreitz 237; Harris, "Mentoring"; Para 12; Meiseles & Feller; Berry, "Other"; ALA/SCOLE, *World* "Issue Paper #6"). Student library workers (usually pages) also constitute a rich source of library-school candidates (C. Jones 16).

Just as researchers have recently recommended paying attention to paras, paras have begun paying attention to themselves. Over 1,900 library paraprofessionals participate in an active listserv on the Internet—Libsup-l—devised by Mary Kalnin of the University of Washington (Andrew & Gillen; figure from University of Washington ListProcessor, August 1995). Here, discussions rage on every aspect of the paraprofessional dilemma, and anything of interest in libraries is at some point touched on, from funding cuts to spots of interest in cyberspace.

COLT Newsletter, a publication on paraprofessional issues, throve from

1968 to 1989, keeping support staff workers abreast of current developments. As it ceased, *Library Mosaics: A Magazine for Support Staff in Libraries, Media and Information Centers*, began. As Katz rightly observed, the publication is "ambitious and fills a need." In 1994, restless members of NYSLAA (New York State Library Assistants' Association), notably Ed Gillen, urged forward by Mary Kalnin, pioneered the first e-journal (electronic journal) for paraprofessionals: *Associates: The Electronic Library Support Staff Journal*, circulation varying from 1,700 to 1,900 worldwide in its first year, circa 2,200 subscribers from 32 countries in its second (Simmons, "Editorial"; Simmons, "Support"; Simmons, "From"). Indiana-based *Support Report*, relatively unknown, enjoys a modest circulation in the Midwest and Canada ("Ruth"). An earlier publication, *Women Library Workers Journal* (*WLW Journal*), had seemed promising as a democratizing forum for both librarians and support staff, and certainly its terminology was desirable. In fact, though, like many promising titles purporting to deal with women library staff members, it dealt almost exclusively with issues pertinent to librarians. Close to its final hour, however, it declared an interest in a wider range of issues, foremost of which was support staff (Dumars, "Women" 14; Eaglen).

Perhaps because traditional trade unions have a poor track record with library support staff (Kusack 37-39), paraprofessionals as far back as the early 1970s began forming statewide library-assistant organizations, and more than half the states now have them ("Nonprofessionals Organize"; Lechner, "Benefits" 11). They have persuaded the American Library Association to grant them their own investigative committees: for example, the Education for Support Staff Issues Subcommittee of the Standing Committee on Library Education (SCOLE), the Membership Initiative Group (MIG) for Library Support Personnel, and the Library Support Staff Interests Roundtable (SSIRT), formed in 1993 (Lechner, "Idea" 23; Martinez, "Of"; G. Flagg et al., "Midwinter" 263; Martinez, "Give" and "MIG"; Gillen, "Challenges").

Library technicians and media assistants, often bearing two-year training certificates, can join the aforementioned ALA-affiliated national association called the Council on Library/Media Technicians, or COLT, which publishes a modest list of materials on technical support staff. In addition to these groups associated with ALA, there is the Southeastern Library Association Paraprofessional Association Roundtable (PART), and the nascent New England Library Association (Support Staff Interests). The Association of College and Research Libraries (ACRL), also, has a task force on Paraprofessionals in Academic Libraries (Timberlake). In 1994, the president of the Association for Library Collections and Technical Services (ALCTS), Jennifer Younger, established a Task Force on the Continuing Educational Needs of Paraprofessionals ("Task").

Support staff, in their necessary new militancy, object to the pejorative prefixes "non-" or "sub-" affixed to "professional" in their job titles and are increasingly insisting, *vis-à-vis* librarians' contrary insistence, on their professionalism. Paraprofessionals and clerks, overwhelmingly female—a study of striking Yale University employees revealed that 82 percent of the bargaining unit were women—are no longer merely part-time workers supplementing a husband's income and performing a species of polite but effete social work in their spare time (Kusack 23-4). Rebutting the myth of the "unstable" woman worker, Lipow et al., in their devastating report on the state of the gender war at Berkeley in 1971, noted of clerical and library assistant workers that

> the length of time women remain employed in these positions is frequently 10, 20, 25 years....To argue that women want to spend 20 years at demanding, often tedious, work for "pin-money" is a poor rationalization for the perpetuation of low wages [6].

Confirming Lipow, recent interchange on Libsup-l concerned the "graying" of these same employees. Many are "lifers" in their particular library or library system, and many more would be, thus obviating the legendary high turnover rate, if pay, prestige, and promotional opportunities were in proportion to the work they do. Palmini, in a survey published in 1994, confirmed that 60 percent of responding support staffers in Wisconsin had served in their respective libraries for over ten years; one-third of these had served over fifteen; 17 percent of these had served over twenty (120).

At present, because of the low regard in which support staff are held, job turnover is "three times as great as among librarians," and much of everybody's time is needlessly spent training new recruits (Halsted & Neeley 63). For example, as the impetus behind developing their admittedly meritorious computer-based training units, Bayne et al. cited a turnover rate of 30 to 40 percent per year at the University of Tennessee, Knoxville, as recently as 1994 (81). This problem is a testimony to librarians' continued willful opacity over support staff's unwillingness to be treated like so many donkeys. Thus, not unreasonably, Neal postulates that "a high turnover rate may be a sign of poor personnel practices and wasteful management of human resources" (99). There is no incentive to remain in jobs with low pay and no promotional ladder, especially in the presence of librarians who may actively scorn one's very being, other than the negative one of being glad to have any job in the face of shrinking full-time employment and impending national fiduciary disaster.

Most libraries do not provide for continuing education—"six out of ten libraries spend less than one percent of their personnel budgets on staff development"—or training towards librarianship, which is extremely costly (St. Lifer & Rogers "ULC" 112). As an example of that cost, consider Syracuse University, a private institution with a library school in New York, which charged $406 per graduate credit in Fall 1993, but $456 in 1994, and estimated expenses "for a single graduate student in 1992-93" as $20,436, and in 1994-5 as only $18,729 but with "some additional expenses to consider" (Syracuse University packets, 1992-3 [p. 22]; 1994-5 [p. 23]). If one commutes to a cheaper school, the costs of the commute—physical, psychological, and monetary—then have to be factored into the total cost. Either way, the burden is overwhelming if one's salary has not climbed over $20,000 per year during the time one is struggling through school, usually working full-time, and typically laboring to raise a family as well. Pay raises for paras have of course not even begun to keep pace with the rise in the national cost of living, nor with raises in the larger American work scene; much less have they been sufficient to cover such a large leap, in one year, as Syracuse's per-credit costs.

"Adjusted for inflation, wages for most Americans have stagnated for two decades," asserted a recent *Commonweal* editorial. We are now beholding the "widest gap between rich and poor since 1947," it continues ("It's" 3). Certainly, most support staff workers living on their salary alone, especially the ones at the lowest end of the paraprofessional pay spectrum (who would be the most likely to seek schooling as a way out of their terrifying poverty), would think twice before seeking matriculation at a private university, or even a state-supported school, if any kind of commute were involved. Graduate studies of any sort are very daunting pursued outside of working hours, and—especially in library science—often over long distances, because of the nationwide paucity of master's programs (Longsworth 842; Maguire; Paris, "Dilemma" 24; Vavrek, "Educating" 8).

But aggressive ongoing training is really justified by the ever-changing automation scene, in which support staff are willy-nilly very much involved, and because of increasing reliance on paraprofessionals to staff reference desks and to assume supervisory/management tasks. Perhaps this training would best be implemented by peripatetic library trainers, rather than by individual library employees usually vainly attempting to become appropriately educated on their own.

Finally, librarians themselves question the value of the MLS as it now stands, the "scientificalness" of library "science," the viability of library graduate programs (many have ceased and many more are unaccredited), and their own "professionalism" (Paris; Plaiss; White, "Pseudo, Pts. I & II"). In the letter columns of periodicals like *American Libraries* and *Library Journal*, invective flows between embattled librarians intent on preserving the perquisites and prestige of their turf and outraged paraprofessionals, who perform the jobs of librarians but are *sans* MLS and hence *sans* honor and money (e.g., Lamont; Masek; Dumars, "Peeved"; Sakers).*

---

*And even between MLS-holders. For example, a typical interchange—this one on inclusion of nonprofessional librarians in SLA in 1969:

Samuel Sass in a riposte to a fellow librarian's opinion: "I am in full agreement with Neil that we should 'include all fellow librarians and documentalists,' but if he is willing to accept as 'fellow librarian' any dopey clerk whom some employer decides to call a librarian, I am not" ("After the Afterthoughts").

I have forborne to tell to any extent my own tale of clerical woe because I find the broad outlines covered in the literature; however, I think much of the impetus for and rancor behind this book is epitomized in an oft-made and emblematic witticism with far-reaching implications habitually uttered by a retired, well-regarded librarian and library supporter. Her watchword for the library staff who issued her books to her was, "Clerks are jerks."

(cont.)   Riposte to a riposte by Neil Van Allen: "Sam's appellation of 'dopey clerk' applied more directly to a few of the degree-carrying professional librarians I know than it does to...[a stellar non-MLS-bearing woman librarian Van Allen has been describing] and to many other[s] like her who are doing truly professional jobs of running small libraries ....I am willing to accept as 'fellow librarian' anyone working in the field" (Van Allen).

2. Deprecation

[T]here are MLS who think support staff just stepped off the "Moron Express" ... [Diane Farber, Libsup-l poster, September 1995].*

Julia Pettee wrote prophetically in 1904, "[I]f the assistant and the librarian stand off and critically take each other's measure, material will be found to keep this subject ever with us" (584). And such material there certainly is. Echoing her today, Lucy Schweers of the Colorado Library Association believes that "if you focus negatively on the line between librarians and paralibrarians and look for problems, the lines will get stronger and the problems more pronounced," a fallacy I do not condone (Liptak, "Lucy" 12). Burying our heads in the sand, as we have done for 100 years, in the polite hope that the "line" will disappear is akin to believing that justice will always prevail. It is a naive, though genteel, set of mind more appropriate—if appropriate at all—to quainter times. We can only hope that if we air a brief history of librarians' rudeness to "nonprofessionals" they will at least think twice before unleashing further instances of unwarranted incivility and elitism.

From the earliest days of librarianship, commentators pointed the finger at "lack of harmony between the assistants and the librarian" (McMillan 412). In 1989, Bunge cited "tensions between professionals and nonprofessionals" as a major source of stress in libraries ("Stress" 95). Even the American Library Association conceded that paraprofessionals' myriad problems "are aggravated by the perceived, and sometimes quite genuine, negative attitude displayed toward them by librarians" (ALA/SCOLE, *World* "Issue Paper #10"). But Gary Kopp criticized the ALA itself for demoralizing "nonlibrarian staff" in not "giving credit where credit is due," citing the slogan: "Your Right to Know: *Librarians* Make It Happen [emphasis added]." Reference-desk paras in 1986 complained of suffering "varying amounts of arrogance" from librarians (Montag 36). As recently as 1995, the more thoughtful commentators have denounced the library field's need to "mistreat" support staff (Berry, "Professional").

*Diane Farber is fair-minded, wishing me to note that many MLS-holders "*do* recognize our value ... and give us the respect we deserve." But, she notes, of the pro/"nonpro" "war," there's "still a long way to go."

Many library workers of all grades have decried this continuing class feud—Goss calls it "class bias"; Dougherty and Diane Turner a "schism"—perpetrated largely by "librarians" upon their perceived underlings (Goss 48; Dougherty, "Personnel" 112; D. Turner, "Professional"). Resistance within the ranks to elitism in Libraryland accounted for the formation of the first library unions. In New York City, the Library Employees' Union arose to "consistently and fearlessly [fight] the un–American spirit of caste amongst librarians" ("Report of" 512). The degree of success this resistance enjoyed was obviously low indeed, for in 1953, a "low man on [the] organization chart" records his surprise at learning that "there is a caste system in libraries separating the professional librarians from the clerical and maintenance employees" (Bauer 37). "Caste," with its byzantine overtones, is defined as "a system of social stratification more rigid than a class and characterized by hereditary status, endogamy, and social barriers rigidly sanctioned by custom, law, or religion" (*Webster's Third New International Dictionary* 348). Fatzer theorizes:

> Universities are virtual caste systems, and librarians are not immune to this snobbery.... As librarians have sought acceptance as colleagues by faculty, many have regrettably done so by adopting the less attractive attitudes of faculty and ironically visiting upon other library staff the sort of disdain with which faculty have traditionally viewed librarians. This is particularly destructive of the morale of paraprofessionals, who see themselves today [1990] performing tasks which those same librarians performed a decade ago.... In an eerie sort of deja vu, paraprofessionals are now struggling to obtain a measure of respect and acceptance from librarians, just as librarians before them fought to win the respect of the academic faculty [161].

"Librarians have been taught from library school to separate themselves from the lesser (in terms of professionalism) forms of workers, i.e., support staffs," insists Rush Miller ("Support" 357). He wrote this in 1988. Not that much earlier, it was customary practice in public libraries to discourage clerks from fraternizing with pages, and librarians from fraternizing with clerks. Larry Oberg, well-known support-staff advocate, also suffered the consequences of this prejudice in an academic setting. In the 1960s California State Library segregated clerical from professional workers in the lunch room, where they were prohibited from occupying the same table. Oberg, then a clerk, and his future wife, a professional librarian, challenged the rule by sitting together and later marrying ("Paraprofessionals and the Future" 8). Where he worked, the policy was stated; in most places, the policy is unwritten, but understood. Oberg's story certainly is an instance of what one of Thapisa's respondents referred to as librarian/assistant "apartheid" (Thapisa, "Burden" 141). Such apartheid is alive and well today, though probably in fewer institutions than in the 1960s: "We have two break rooms, one for professionals and one for the rest," recounts one participant of a 1991 45-focus-group study conducted by ALA/SCOLE (*World* "Issue Paper #4").

Rush Miller, in an ambivalent article dealing with the relationship of the two groups, refers to the breach between the two groups as a "chasm." "The width and depth of this gulf varies from library to library, but every library has one," he maintains, an observation unfortunately corroborated on all sides (357). Recent library-school graduate Elizabeth Beere has taken metaphors of divisiveness the furthest, remarking upon a veritable "abyss" between paras and pros (Berry, [profile]).

Other commentators on librarian/paraprofessional disunity have used a term normally heard in discussion of women's inability to penetrate the topmost ranks of industry: "glass ceiling." "Unfortunately, the exclusion of the paraprofessional from 'professional' activities is not uncommon in most academic libraries," write two support-staff members, one a Ph.D. candidate, the other busy on her master's:

> For the paraprofessional, the lack of career advancement and educational opportunities, exclusion from the decision making policies, task forces, and committees has not only supported the "glass ceiling" theory, but, in turn, the library has missed an opportunity to use their personnel on the front-line to create a better, more efficient system. It cannot be argued that the academic library is not a meritocracy—structured by merit and performance alone. The power structures of most libraries are heavily determined by an artificial barrier [Romine-Weyandt & Weyandt].

Why do so many librarians affect a "superior attitude" towards clerks (Billings & Kern 176)? Surveyed library assistants in Britain speak of a "them and us'" attitude; one worker complained of being termed a "junior" by a librarian years younger and less experienced than she. Another queried, "Does the process through library school produce an elitist, uncaring, unsympathetic librarian?" (Russell, "Professional" 302-3). Martell cites as one of the problems in academic libraries the desperate "elitism that fosters status differentials within the library between professional and nonprofessional employees..." ("Nature" 113). "Clerks don't *do* bibliographies," pronounced one visibly annoyed academic librarian to a clerk in his employ, although she had—unaware of this commandment—over the past three years in her respective jobs, put together four very extensive ones, three for librarian colleagues, one for an exhibit.

Thus, next to the very low pay library clerical workers receive for performing often extremely stressful, complicated, and professional jobs, and problem patrons, librarians' condescension and jibes rankle most (Appendix A). "[O]ne of the more unethical behaviors in which all too many professional librarians engage is the denigration of paraprofessional librarians," remarked Burgin and Hansel (66). Ex-paraprofessional Ann Boyer exclaims, "[T]he desire of some professional librarians to more clearly differentiate themselves from paraprofessionals can be seen as a process of 'othering.'" "Othering" is synonymous with "reification" (the making of somebody into a thing) and usually is a necessary first step in the damaging of another creature. "[A]long with many fine librarians there is a representative number, often semi-literate, [who] ... are willing and eager to demonstrate their kill techniques on ... nonprofessional workers," remarked one M.A.-bearing "nonprofessional" (Grady). "Killing," of course, is a way of neutralizing the perceived danger of another. Educated and competent paraprofessionals threaten librarian co-workers, who sense that their "inferiors" may enjoy intellectual development which vies with or exceeds their own. Librarians are also aware that in many workplaces, paraprofessionals are used to supplant them. Less consciously, they may also fear that such supplantation would not affect the quality of the services rendered to the public, thus making redundant their professionalism (see Line & Robertson; "Users," above).

Adona Pearson comments with dignity, "I know firsthand that 'bad feelings can and almost certainly will evolve' if staff without degrees are not treated with respect by staff with degrees." One veteran staff member who went to work after her children were in school commented incredulously, "You come from an atmosphere [home] where people love and respect you into an atmosphere [work] where people routinely treat you like a stupid child" (Beverly Murray). "I am the librarian and you are the clerk, and even when I'm wrong, I'm right, and you'll just have to accept that without talking back," announced one professional public librarian to an indignant clerk who had just been accused of making an error that the librarian, in fact, had made. This librarian was unaware that "[a]n MLS does not automatically bestow infallibility on the recipient" (Miletich 42).

Professional librarians everywhere seem to perceive nonprofessional staff as "'people inadequate in some way—emotionally or socially—to be professionals" (Russell, quoting Davinson, "Professional" 301). Sarkodie-Mensah refers to librarians' "stereotypical perceptions of the paraprofessional as a second rate library worker" (8).

Ralph Munn chastised the field in 1949:

> Another destroyer of morale, one of the curses of our ... [profession], is the habit of condescension on the part of the professional staff toward the nonprofessional. I have seen it—so have you—this intolerable habit of certain individuals who think that a knowledge of what three dots on a catalog card mean places them on a level above the person who has not been initiated into those mysteries ["Morale" 518].

One *Library Journal* contributor was so impressed with the way one staff member helped him that he returned to the library the next day to commend the director on the choice of personnel. "Strange to relate," he has the temerity to record, "I learned that the particular person who had helped me was not professionally trained.... [I]n this library the administration had had much favorable comment on its people without training" (Kranick 60–61). Could this writer have possibly thought through what he was actually saying? In effect, he was surprised librarians did not have a corner on courtesy, efficiency, and helpfulness—a most unbearable form of condescension. One library clerk, hired to work in the Media Services contingent of her library, faced her first evaluation with her supervisor. She was very enthusiastic about her work, and excited about all the resources in her department. When her male supervisor asked her what sorts of things she'd like to be doing in his department, she enthusiastically mentioned bibliographies and user guides. His face settled into stiff repose, and he commented formally, "What I *would* like you to do, when you have any free time, is just dust off the cabinets and desks." The clerk was crushed. She was not uneducated; she was efficient and orderly and intelligent. In time, in fact, she happily went on to become part of the administration in the central public library, still without her MLS.

At its best, librarian condescension works very much the way Seavey describes it in his article about librarians' failure to have coped with the electronic onslaught:

> A documents colleague of mine saw the problem coming and managed to hire a library technical assistant (LTA) who really understood computers. They managed to get a pretty good, if limited, system up and going in the documents collection. Soon the computer LTA was getting borrowed by other departments, which eventually led to a split assignment between documents and everywhere else. At which point an assistant director decided that since the LTA was not a librarian, his decisions and suggestions weren't worth thinking about, and that he should devote himself to nonprofessional tasks like making sure the printers had ribbons and that there were enough disks around. The computer LTA, understandably, got frustrated and bailed out to private industry, where he is making a *lot* more money and gets to work to his capacity [944].

"If the attitude towards patrons must always be courteous, respectful, pleasant and considerate," wonders Miletich, "is it such a radical notion that staff people be treated the same?" (45). Unfortunately, this query, written in 1991, echoes one penned in 1905, to wit:

> If we have a great desire to make our library a power for good, to draw all people into it, to be kind, and sympathetic, and helpful to old and young who appeal to us, can we be quite sincere if we neglect this opportunity that lies nearest to us? Can we consistently spend hours of time in helping this young man or that young woman along the road to success, and not feel a similar duty to the assistant who is our coworker? Is our duty to her limited because she draws a paltry salary for her time? Surely the relation of librarian and assistant means something more than a strictly business arrangement, for a consideration of dollars and cents; it should mean more in commercial life, even though it seldom does, but in the library it should resemble the ideal relation we try to establish with our patrons [Julia Elliott, "Relation" 465].

Conversely, Frances Cox impatiently contended in 1960 that librarians irrationally believe that an MLS equips them to be the intellectual mentors of others and breed resentment in the public and the staff alike because of their elitism. "As long as caste systems prevail within a library," she argued, "librarians cannot be expected to take a different attitude to the public. It slops over on the public in ways that the librarian is completely unaware of" (1060). Cooper, in 1964, urged upon the field:

> There are many wonderful people who have joined their abilities to ours. They offer loyalty and respect to a profession we call our own. They perform diligent, often inspired works in a service we believe in. They are part of us, part of our work. They belong with us.
> If by word or deed, we make them feel shut out, or belittle their contributions, then we have lost the right to be called professional librarians, for we've lost the qualities, the intangible characteristics that make us librarians. We have left only the hard veneer of a library education.

Rosalind Hall, para turned pro, in 1975 begged for "a diminution of arrogance on the part of the professional *vis à vis* the para-professional." Clearly the field has not progressed as far as it might have in attaining percipience about the psychology and ethics of treating human beings democratically. Many, though fortunately not all, librarians have the same airs today as in the Victorian era. The same class snobberies inhere, the same cruelties of "ruling" class over working class, the same liberalism on paper, the same blindness to abuses committed at home. A very good argument for TQM (Total Quality Management) techniques in libraries, with TQM's emphasis upon teamwork to escalate service, and a resultant "flatter" organizational structure, is exactly that it moves away from these artificial snobberies and class distinctions which interfere with services to the masses. In TQM there is less emphasis upon people in general as underlings or unworthy entities. "Managements ... which retain a rigid 'them and us' management style are living in the past, and will not be able to supply the needs of present day and future users," asserts Jim Jackson.

In 1917, an anonymous "Traveler" told the tale of the civic-minded librarian "enthusiastic in her support of the cause of the girl in the factory." "BUT," says the Traveler,

> she will make her own assistants stand at a loan desk a whole afternoon when she might just as well provide a stool for them—she keeps her assistants at the loan desk for a stretch of hours that the average shop girl does not know ["Inconsistencies"].

Before today's very similar purblind librarians take on the human-rights issues of pornography, equality for homosexuals, nuclear disarmament, and the rights of South African blacks, they should look first to cleaning their own house (Baum 14, 28). The human-rights violation on their own home front is the plight of the majority of library employees today: the plight of support staff.

Deprecation in Library of Congress Subject Headings

Berman in 1971 authored a seminal work criticizing Library of Congress subject headings for reflecting "a host of untenable—indeed, obsolete and arrogant—assumptions with respect to young people and women" and all sorts of other cultural and racial groups (15). Certainly to his list of discriminatory (by omission) subject headings could be added the sole heading Library of Congress accords to library support staff: "Library technician (May Subd Geogr)." Under this subject heading one is to find, presumably, information on library clerks, library paraprofessionals, library assistants, and all of the host of other gradations that in fact exist among support staff in libraries, of which "Library technician" is probably one of the least descriptive choices, since much paraprofessional work is done with people, as well as with machines. Under the term "Librarian," however, one may find "see also's" for "Information scientists," "Library employees," "Acquisitions librarians," "Adult services librarians," "Afro-American librarians," "Catalogers," "Children's librarians," "Gay librarians," "Jewish librarians," "Minority librarians," "National librarians," "Part-time librarians," "Physically handicapped librarians," "Public librarians," "Reference librarians," "School librarians," "Special librarians," "Women librarians," and "Young Adult services librarians." All of these may also be subdivided geographically.

There are geographically oriented subject headings for librarians, as well, e.g., "Asian American librarians," "Cuban American librarians," "Hispanic American librarians," even, of all things, "Pacific Islander American librarians." Support staff, or "Library technicians," other than under the broader term "Library employees," cannot be found anywhere else; this term also is "used for" "Library assistants," "Library paraprofessionals," and "Paraprofessionals in libraries."

In addition, there are no subheadings, as there are for librarians, for "certification," "job descriptions," "professional ethics," "psychology," "recruiting," "United States," nor useful headings adapted for the paraprofessional, as there are for librarians, e.g., "[Librarians] in literature," "[Librarians'] unions." No support personnel, it would seem, are from the Pacific Islands; none of them are handicapped; no care is attributed to their training; no one is concerned with their psychology; they evidently have no unions; none of them are gay; they obviously have no place in literature; none of them are part-time; their job descriptions must be non-existent, though, as with librarians, parity is achieved in that evidently, as there are no male librarians (as in "Men librarians"), there are evidently no male library technicians, either (as in "Men library technicians")—it goes without saying that there are no "Women library technicians" (*Library of Congress* 2867, 2876).

As to the classes of employee in libraries, we have "Library administrators," "Librarians," "Library pages," "Library technicians," "Part-time library employees" (that should cover it), "School library supervisors," and "Student library assistants." There! That about wraps it up for the Library of Congress's concern for the dimensions of library employ. Did we leave anything out? No, we're into our seventeenth edition of these subject headings, aren't we, with lots of good brains at work, full-time and part-time both, no doubt, cogitating on this vast subject year after year. Does it seem that even the concerns of library literature are not adequately reflected in *Library of Congress Subject Headings*? Yes, it does. And if anything will lead to inaccessibility, it is the lack of subject headings in an authority file. It is a form of discrimination as great as a slammed door, or a sneer, or a slur.

"No one can fair-mindedly expect that LC compilers would be blessed with the gift of prophecy to a greater degree than anyone else. Hence, noting the list's failure to indicate the lately-expanded social concerns of the profession can hardly be interpreted as a criticism," temporizes Berman (128).

Deprecation in Library Literature

But even *Library Literature*, arguably the most important library-serial index in the English language, has been insensitive to support-staff issues. Paraprofessionals constitute a larger portion of the library community than librarians. They, or their functional counterparts of yore, have been covered in library literature, albeit not as extensively as other subjects. They have been identified as an increasingly expert and diverse group for over thirty years, but *Library Literature* for these last thirty or so years, up until 1992, cited literature on student assistants, clerks, paraprofessionals, and library assistants under a single heading: "Non-professional assistants." In addition, information about "Non-professional assistants" might be found under "Student assistants"; the equivalency implicit here is most discouraging. The idea of semi- or para-professionalism simply was not part of the Wilson Company's thinking, nor was any gradation among the various types of non–MLS help—perhaps because *Library Literature*'s inception was in 1921, when opinion was much more conservative, and habits then became entrenched. Early editions of *Library Literature* list all categories of library worker under "Personnel."

Both Kathleen Weibel, in a short but trenchant article, and Mary Kao, a library technology training program administrator, were instrumental in altering Wilson's approach (Weibel "I"). Weibel urged concerned library personnel to write to Wilson about the "non-professional" headings. Kao, taking her suggestion, wrote an open letter to Wilson, through *Library Mosaics* (a journal Wilson indexes), suggesting that it utilize the term "Library Technical Assistants" or a variant thereof as the main entry for the class of worker previously covered under "Non-professional assistants." Her letter seems to have fallen into receptive hands: searchers in *Library Literature* will now find relevant entries under the less demoralizing heading "Paraprofessionals."

It is ironic, considering even Wilson's change of emphasis, that an irate letter-writer, as recently as 1994, had to complain to *Library Journal* (home of John Berry) about the editors' use of terms in "Dean's List":

> The editors' use of "Nonprofessionals" as a heading in the article belies a not-so-subtle attitude found throughout the profession that a Master's Degree in Library Science magically bestows upon a graduate a deeper and more meaningful dedication toward and understanding of working with information and the people who need it [Selfe].

Class Warfare

It is not without irony, in light of this litany of slights, that British Pro-Librarian Norman Russell points out that "[i]n the Alexandrian Library, ... the hierarchy ranged downward from the King's Librarian to the assistants, copyists and archivists, then to the ordinary attendants—who were slaves" ("Professional" 293). Slaves, like clerks, were similarly "invisible," "disposable." Clerical and paraprofessional library workers are, in less congenial libraries, really often nothing but modern-day slaves, in the eyes of their librarian supervisors.

Wittingslow and Mitcheson surmise that "the initial reason for breaking jobs into small discrete units (scientific management) was the flood of illiterate migrant labor to the United States in the latter part of the nineteenth century.... [W]orkers had to be able to copy the designated task without clear verbal instructions" (67). This problem and its solution, appropriate for its time, may be the legacy that has left managers in general and librarians in particular with a permanent mindset that library "laborers" are somehow inherently senseless oafs, despite the extensive academic training many of them bring to their jobs.

"Librarians historically value the docile, tractable, meticulous employee who will work by rote, plug away until retirement and never question the status quo," claims Mary Bolin (Orahood 41). To ensure this valued docility, many libraries institutionalize rigid, though unwritten, rules guaranteeing this result (Grady). The practice of hiring non-challenging employees is the legacy of one school of thinking which arose in the 1950s and 1960s about the type of person who should be recruited for library clerical work, to wit: "[Q]uite frankly, I think we should look ... for persons below the highest levels of ability and intelligence ... [with] not a great deal of ambition for unlimited advancement.... We are not interested in qualities of imagination or leadership" (McDiarmid 244-6).

Libraries subscribing to this rationale deliberately hire clerical personnel whose unadvanced educational level and personal inertia ensure that they remain cow-like and placid in the library as Clerk I's forever—unchallenging, on the one hand, and needing never to be replaced, on the other. Moreover, even non-bovine clerks are thrust onto a clerical Procrustean bed. "Innovation and contribution beyond one's job description is blocked," fretted one boxed-in para (Kentfield 19). Such libraries enforce continuing vapidity among clerks by adamantly insisting that they refer all questions, including simple directional queries, to librarians for resolution. Clerks may not indicate where subject areas are, for example, or whether books are in the library or out; they are not supposed to place reserves; in some places they are prohibited from issuing software or making appointments for the use of the in-house public PC without invoking a librarian. Certainly such infantilized people are never allowed to do reader's advisories, nor story hours. And if they attempt these activities, they may actually be yelled at, like small, bad children. They are never trained in any way for anything besides the most routine jobs, which they perform day in and day out; they are treated like "scullery maids," and so become (Bellany). The authoritarian systems advocated by McDiarmid and others are the last to add the middle grade of library worker—the paraprofessional—to their employee categories. All these ploys, of course, are designed to prevent the clerk's getting above herself. In the end, however, they backfire, for, ironically, the public perceives these mentally battered, daft-seeming, and listless people as librarians, perpetuating the unflattering "image" over which so many librarians dash out their brains.

Clerks in suppressive systems are additionally insulted by writers who dislike their "casual" mode of dress, dictated by both poverty and a predictable defeatism: "[L]eave the blue jeans and baggy shirts at home.... It's up to managers to set the tone and enforce standards for nonprofessional staff who are viewed by the public as 'professionals'" (L. Wallace 25). What can one say to mitigate the disdain in the following? "[M]ost of the people you meet in libraries are *simply clerks* [emphasis added]," writes one pundit, who goes on to say, "The way librarians dress and conduct themselves gives the public the impression they are glorified clerks" ("Librarians' Image"). Excuse me? Did some slobby para force these librarians at gunpoint to dress like "glorified clerks"? Perhaps these librarians were simply dressing like *themselves.*

Nevertheless, in pockets of systems with rules enforcing limitations on their workers' spheres of activity, practice may run counter to policy because of the humaneness—or laziness—of the librarians in charge and because of accidental hirings. In such cases, clerks and certainly librarian assistants may in fact be found answering reference questions, putting together and proofreading portions of the librarians' monthly reports, choosing and ordering books, calculating their cost, doing bibliographies, planning and executing exhibits, being almost exclusively in charge of searching all sorts of book and patron information on the terminal, running interlibrary loan departments and AV services (Berry, "Other"; Mace, "Creighton" 15).

These "glorified clerks" also often train new librarians in the use of the simpler functions of the terminal, for many librarians seem not to be able to grasp the intricacies of the computerized systems in place in some libraries and hence are lost when they need to be able to place reserves, record fines, etc. (Appendix A). Miletich insists, "Some new graduates of library schools are ill-equipped with supervisory savvy or experience; it shows in the way they treat their seasoned but underrated staff people, who often have to teach them the details of the job" (40). Wittingslow confirmed this sense of things as early as 1984: "It is not unusual for the senior librarian to be less highly educationally qualified and know less about the actual working of the library system than staff two or three levels below" (67). Well-trained *pages*, in fact, in my experience, may know more about the workings of a discrete library area than a senior librarian.

Clerks complain, "[I]t seems that handling enquiries is 'professional' work when there are enough qualified staff available, and mysteriously becomes work anyone can do when there are not enough qualified staff to cope" (Taylor 14). "They treat us as professionals when it suits their purposes," states another (Billings & Kern 174). Not only Fatzer, but Billings and Kern, Evans (in "Evolution" 74), and Martinez, among many others, deplore the "caste system" extant in libraries (Martinez, "What's"). Clerks all over the world find "some professionals are consciously trying 'to keep them in their place'" (Billings & Kern 177). One MLS-bearing library assistant writes that at a state convention she attended, she "heard librarians scheming about how to keep clerks in the role and status of clerks" (Schwartz 1730). Surely there are better things to do with one's professionalism.

What can one make of the classist behavior evinced by library directors who are reported to have hidden copies of *Library Mosaics* from the staff, who have "chastised their staff" for their interest in the magazine, who have branded the publication "unacceptable" (Martinez, "Give")? Are support staff supposed to be too stupid to write? To read? While it is true that many librarians underwrite subscriptions to the magazine for the benefit of their staff, editor Martinez notes, "Unfortunately, it's those negative thoughts that you ... remember more often than the good words or the 'thank you's'" (*ibid.*).

In 1897, snobbery was manifest, and remarked upon, in the field of librarianship; it remains with us today as one of the least desirable customs of the field. "[T]hose of a higher grade look down on those of a lower, and as sometimes occurs, do not want to associate with or do the work of the other," recorded Hill, who did at least have the good sense to stipulate that "[i]f allowed to remain, such a spirit breeds continual dissension. Pluck it out at once," he exhorted, "even at the cost of hard feeling. When self is cast aside and all are working for the common good, the result is pleasing alike to the public, the trustees, and the staff" (381).

Why do so many librarians, ostensibly so democratic, genteel, and public-spirited, become so defensive, hence offensive, when they contemplate their clerks? Why, when almost a century has passed since the first portion of Hill's observation, might the same words just as well have been written yesterday? The history of the paraprofessional in the United States addresses this conundrum, at the base of which lies librarians' dread that they be found redundant. Since one-third to two-thirds of librarians' work has always been clerical in nature, and since not only the clerical, but many of the professional, aspects of their jobs have now been "off-loaded" onto support staff, what exactly are librarians supposed to be doing instead that makes them professionals? Kinzer's observation that a librarian needs time to just put his feet up and think is, alas, too often true (219). But then again, not all librarians are being freed of clerical tasks, notably the lower echelon of professional. One professional frets:

> Fellow librarians, is there something wrong with me? Am I the only librarian whose duties seem more clerical than professional? ... [W]hy is it that some libraries do not have a definite chain of command? Perhaps I am just not sociable, but it seems strange to me that some directors hire so called non-professionals in addition to a professional staff only to mix-up their respective duties to the point that the non-professionals are handling the telephone reference questions while I am dispatched to water the plants. (Is it too late to get a refund on my college education?) These indignities may sound foreign to those of you at large university libraries, but this misuse of professional staff is certainly evident at some libraries; I have experienced this problem over and over again since graduating from library school [Gale 13].

Gale lodged this complaint in 1987, but even back in 1941, the situation was the same. Library-school graduates complained that they were treated as clerks and janitors more than as professional librarians (Thornton 966-68). Librarians have always had to justify themselves as professionals; they have had to work hard to persuade both themselves and others that the work they do, or even that their nonprofessionals do, is not only manifestly useful—as indisputably it is—but that it has a respectable intellectual base as well, as befits a profession, rather than a vocation. Librarians debate their professionalism daily, monthly, yearly; they have always done so (e.g., Veaner "Continuity"). Their concern with their stereotype has been so pervasive that Pauline Wilson was actually able to write a book about the labyrinthine stretches of their anxiety. Starting with the first volume of *Library Literature* (1921), and running through April 1978, she gleaned a total of 499 citations pitched at concern about image (13). Many librarians keep their chins up as they face the dragon—smiling bravely through the tears, as it were (e.g., R. W. Lewis).

Others undoubtedly never think about the way they are seen at all. But some contemplate leaving the field because of woes attendant upon the unflattering stereotype: low respect from public and boards of directors, translating into low budgetary priority, resulting in subprofessional wages. In 1990, Hodges found in Great Britain that 60 percent of her respondents in a stress survey claimed they had contemplated leaving the profession within the past 12 months for reasons associated with these woes (754).

Now that library schools are closing their doors in embarrassing and distressing numbers, and tenured and skilled paraprofessionals are declaring their professional status, there is new energy in the debate, and new desperation ("Library Schools" 12, 14; Zipkowitz, "Fewer" 30). Both librarians and paraprofessionals need to reach consensus on what they really need to be doing that is "professional" and how it should be valued in dollars. And both need to become more unapologetically and crudely political. The whole history of the United States has been bent by special-interest groups notably ungenteel and raucous in the stating of their grievances. "Please" has not worked in the rough-hewn United States, nor has a simple statement of "It's not fair." As to deprecation of support staff by librarians, this statement—by a librarian—must be pondered: "Librarians are … highly critical people … in considerable doubt about themselves, their colleagues, and the standing or merit of their own profession" (Rothstein, "Why" 45, 46). The perceived reality, among many librarians contemplating their profession, is that librarians are whiners defending a bogus professionalism (Plaiss 589). Certainly, if librarians feel this way about themselves, how must they think of their underlings, the paras, and *their* claims of professionalism?

In any case, the result of restricting clerks' "realm of activity to protect … status" creates a monster: surly clerks with noticeable chips on their shoulders who, because forced to remain silent on subjects they may know as well as any librarian, are grudging and unforthcoming in every way (Billings & Kern 174). Unfortunately, it is clerks whom most people see first and thence most often in libraries. Most patrons think clerks are librarians. Even in academic libraries, "faculty often fail to distinguish between librarians and support staff" (Oberg et al., "Faculty" 217). To most library users, the "[paraprofessional *is*] the library" (Wakefield & Martin 9). Curran sums it up:

> [W]e say support staff are crucial, frontline ambassadors, but we:
> • pay them minimum wage, plus carfare;
> • exclude them from participation in decision-making;
> • contradict and embarrass them in the presence of clients;
> • and ridicule them with a lower-caste term: *nonprofessional* [999; Appendix A].

3. "Professional" versus "Nonprofessional": Getting the Picture Straight

A 1985 article entitled, prophetically, "Professional and Non-professional in Libraries: The Need for a New Relationship," states, in attempting to understand the present antipathetic dichotomy between librarians and other library workers, that historically "[i]t is ... difficult to discover the origins of the distinction between professional and non-professional library staff" (Russell, "Professional" 293). Certainly staff existed; titles among them existed, but what activity was more "professional" than any other?

The modern pro/non-pro antipathy is based, not only on professional abuse of support staff face to face and in print, but in the insulting connotations of the semantics involved in labeling them, with the great imputation of amateurism (in its pejorative sense) and inadequacy implicit in terms for support staff beginning with "non-" and "sub-." Refuting charges of insufficiency, one testy *American Libraries* reader claims, "Library staff [participate] fully in library affairs. We share common goals with librarians." "'Non-professional,'" she continues, "mean[s] 'not a member of or trained in a specific profession' [and] merely states what one is not.... No one appreciates being referred to as 'non' anything" (Abalos 524).

One of the first protestations over library worker terminology was lodged in 1914 in *Library Journal*'s letter column:

> [W]hy not eliminate that hateful term "subordinates" and substitute that of "assistants"? ... An assistant, regardless of her enthusiasm, zeal and professional spirit, if constantly referred to, and treated as a subordinate, naturally comes to the conclusion that she is a "flat failure." What incentive is there for her to put forth her best efforts in the work? Instead of the social, educational and business opportunities supposed to be open to a trained worker, the "subordinate" is made to feel that she is on a level with the lowest scrub-woman; with all her college education, she knows nothing... [South-Cliffe].

Another protest over terminology came in 1938 from Mixer, who urged the practice of giving library workers credit for the professional work they did by calling them not "assistants," but "librarians." The psychological truth broached by South-Cliffe that people called by demeaning names will lose their self-respect, and therefore their motivation to put forth their best efforts, was repeated in the early years by countless concerned library workers; yet it fell upon utterly deaf ears. "[T]reat your coworkers as equals, rather than inferiors," warned South-Cliffe; yet, unregenerate, the field referred to "subprofessionals," with its unsuitable connotation of "beneath," for another forty years. As recently as 1994 and 1995, in the *Virginia Librarian* ruckus, two "posturing" librarians were juxtaposing them with "security guards," much as Veaner has placed them on a level with "janitors," instead of regarding them as "natural allies," as does John Berry ("Professional").*

How far beneath librarians, however, are library staff? A survey made in 1990 by Timberlake and Boudreaux of special, public, and academic libraries in Louisiana noted the following:

> Half of the academic libraries reported one or more staff members with the title of librarian who did not have either an MLS or some other advanced degree in library or information science. The degrees listed for those librarians included several doctorates but were primarily master's degrees in education or liberal arts. An almost identical number reported paraprofessionals on their staff with advanced degrees in education or liberal arts and three others reported paraprofessionals holding master's degrees in library science.
>
> In 60% of these cases ... both librarians and paraprofessionals [bore] the same or similar non–MLS advanced degrees [165].

Grace Franklin observes that "Over half of the reference paraprofessionals [in Ohio public libraries] are college graduates; over 12% have post-college education" (6). Bénaud writes,

---

*In 1994, Veaner, in "Paradigm Lost...," commenting on "empowerment," teams, and flat organizations, concedes in earlier pages that support staff have become "knowledge workers," able to assume the tasks that for generations have characterized the "professional" librarian. Then for some reason, he sees fit, when governance becomes an issue, to see empowering support staff as a ludicrousness equal to empowering the janitor. So eager is he to see that support staff stay in their place that he undercuts his own argument—to wit, that not just anyone can step in to do the librarian's job, when he effectively has done just that, in allowing that support staff now do what librarians once did. His infelicitous coupling, not of librarians and support staff (the more obvious and correct alliance), but of support staff and emptiers of trash barrels, then becomes nothing more than a form of derision, since janitors are generally not hired for their intelligence, while support staff usually very specifically are (398). In 1995, the *Virginia Librarian*'s editors, faced with the suggestion that their publication become *Virginia Libraries*, offended support staff nationally by conceptually coupling them with security guards, secretaries, trustees, "friends," and student workers, implying a greater equivalence between members of these groups and paraprofessionals than between librarians and paraprofessionals (McCulley & Ream).

[I]n a university library, it is not uncommon for paraprofessional catalogers to also hold a subject master's degree (and sometimes an MLS). As with the professional cataloger, the paraprofessional cataloger is also required to have a reading knowledge of one or two modern foreign languages. In real life, the academic credentials for entry level positions for the professional and the high-level paraprofessional cataloger do not vary considerably. Even though the minimum formal requirements for paraprofessional staff are, on paper, not as "advanced," most paraprofessionals in academic libraries are equipped with the level of education needed to catalog. This brings up the sensitive issue of the value of the MLS degree ... [86-7].

Mort, in a 1992 dissertation, cited over half (56.9 percent) of her respondents as having attended college for "5 or more years." Over 70 percent had a bachelor or higher degree. In addition, almost 40 percent had taken or were taking "formal library science courses," and 16.4 percent already held their MLS (46, 93). Azad found 77.4 percent of the paras in his study to have had education beyond the second year of college (87).

Oberg and others, in their 1992 survey of support staff in 77 ARL libraries and 390 Carnegie institutions of higher learning, found, over and above the high-school diploma, "58% [of ARL libraries requiring] an associate degree, 76% a bachelor's degree, and 24% a graduate degree" and "62% [of Carnegie institutions requiring] an associate degree; 64%, a bachelor's degree; and 9%, a graduate degree" ("Role" 221). But 75 percent of their respondents (those with a large male paraprofessional contingent) "report that they employ some paraprofessionals who hold a degree higher than that required for the job" ("Role" 231). Fifty-nine percent of respondents in Dorothy Jones' survey had an undergraduate degree; 23 percent had or were working on a master's; a few even had Ph.D.s (441, 434).

In 1990, Kathman and Felix, describing St John's University's attempt to attain an accurate and equitable pay system for paras, commented that "[w]ork such as retrospective conversion, cataloging, bibliographic searching, and reference information services was routinely handled by paraprofessional staff, whose backgrounds usually included a college degree, previous library experience, work with computers, and coursework in foreign languages" (202).

In a reorganization typical of many occurring around the nation today, Georgia State University's Pullen Library took cognizance of the professional degree of functioning supplied by its support staff. Discussing implementation of an automated serials control module, as part of what in time would be a fully integrated library system, Presley and Robison speak with unqualified admiration of "the very high caliber of experience, intelligence and technical knowledge of" Pullen's "highly skilled support staff," many of whom were given higher salaries, along with increased responsibility (28, 25, 36). In this project, support staff took on many duties previously classed as "professional." One professional slot was eliminated, and in time a support staff member was promoted to the position of "Administrative Supervisor/Assistant Department

Head" (Presley & Robison 26, 28, 36). Even in 1966, called upon to speak on the subject of library education, Mutschler said simply, "I believe we have thousands of positions in libraries which can be filled quite adequately by persons who do not have an MLS but do possess a professional outlook" ("Library Education" 1772).

Library Mosaics, the pioneering magazine for support staff, features a column called "Supporting Cast," in which two capable and accomplished workers are featured per issue. One soon gleans the variety and complexity of what these "non"-librarians do. Many professional librarians do not do as much. For instance,

> I am the head of the Reserves, Current Periodicals and Microforms Department.... My job ... includes administrative and operational management of the department..., participation in the University Libraries' middle management ranks, and representation of the library at the local, regional and state levels.... I serve on a number of committees.... I also order books requested for reserve that the library doesn't own, deal with sales representatives for microform reader/printers..., orient new faculty members ... [Welker 20].

Another support staffer, Nora Symmers, supervises four catalogers. She "edit[s] and enhance[s] national cataloging records by adding headings, local notes, etc., ... [and] create[s] original MARC records, train[s] professional and paraprofessional staff in cataloging procedures and instruct[s] public services staff in the use of the bibliographic record[; she also] research[s] and write[s] local cataloging procedures for all new formats acquired by [her library, the DeKalb County Public Library]" (Symmers).

Lyle Mourer, working in Ferris State University's Timme Library, holds the title of Administrative Aide. However, he hires, trains, and supervises around twenty students and several clerical workers, schedules faculty's time on the reference desk, and serves there himself, often unaided. He also supplies BI classes, a function in many locales reserved for faculty and full-time professional librarians only.

Connie Ury, in addition to teaching freshman seminar students and acting as a faculty advisor, is also the Coordinator of Library Use Instruction and part of the "Information Focus (Reference) Team and Distribution (Circulation) Team." She serves on the information desk, teaches in the BI program she coordinates, and offers "one-on-one research paper consultations to students enrolled in upper level classes." She has both a BA and a master's in education (history specialization). Her curiosity had led her, years ago, to take an undergraduate class in cataloging and classification; her professor became the director of the library; Ury ended up as one of the administrative staff. Her library operates under a team-management protocol.

In a geography library, Kalnin, Eyler, and Ryan found one para—hired for his subject knowledge—hiring, training, and firing, deciding what should be ordered, writing procedure manuals, giving tours, and doing in-depth database searches and reference counseling (17-8). They cite another who runs a government documents library overseas "with full authority" when the librarian is away. Many paras are responsible for their libraries' computer systems (*ibid.* 18). Several respondents to my few queries on Libsup-1 perform original cataloging as a matter of routine, and are frequently left in charge. All of these are unarguably professional duties.

In 1990, Idaho State University granted its first professional leave to a non–MLS-bearing researcher, Phyllis Brown. She is classified as a Library Assistant III, but her title is "Head, Acquisitions Department." During her leave, she was expected to generate a computer database for indexing reproductions, critiques, and other portions of art books not accessible through standard indexing methods, utilizing artist, title of work, museum, location and owner of artwork, country and century of production, medium used, and critics involved ("Idaho"). Eventually she planned to network with other institutions, who would add their holdings to the database. This certainly sounds like work a professional librarian would do. In fact, this surpasses, in technical virtuosity alone, most of what most librarians would even begin to attempt. In addition, Brown is the Northwest Regional Director of COLT ("Idaho"). She notes that "[m]ore of us are being asked to manage and we must be ready to assume some of those duties which have been the traditional turf of the MLS degree holder" (P. Brown 20). She herself holds a BA and has done some graduate work. Her record calls into question the value of extensive formal education, as does the expertness of the interviewee in Appendix B. As one paraprofessional writes, "A piece of paper and 36 hours of theory [do] not make a person 'professional'" (Hilbert 20).

How many times have "subprofessionals" trained librarians on the job?: "[W]e have often had librarians fresh out of library school, with degrees, who don't know a thing about libraries and how to deal with the public. It was the staff present in the library who trained the new librarian," fumes an English library clerk (Russell, "Professional" 303). "If there are no real boundaries between positions, why is there differential pay or educational requirements?" query other commentators (Heim et al. 152). "Employees always should be classified on the basis of what they do, ... never merely according to the source of their training," chastised Evans ("Evolution" 75). "Arguments about the desirability or necessity of requiring a library school degree for reference work proliferate, but most miss the point," wrote Grace Franklin. "The fundamental concern ought to be the quality of reference service that is provided, regardless of the job title or the salary of the person providing the service" (9).

Miletich, with Bernstein, sees "professionalism as a function of how people behave on the job" (37). *Library Mosaics'* editor, Ed Martinez, suggests that the word "professional" be used "only in describing the style of work[, f]or by further segregating the library work force, we are inhibiting a unified work team" ("What's"). Their words echo those of an early, long-dead librarian who believed that professionalism had more to do with "the spirit in which the work is done" than with any other quality (Library Schools, New York State Library). Asheim states, "It is the commitment to the service, not to the tasks that are associated with it, that marks the professional in any field" ("Core" 157).

4. "Nonlibrarian" Professionals in Libraries

Nonlibrary professionals have worked in library organizations for many years. While the phenomenon is not new, it is a growing one. The library profession, a group often obsessed with issues of professionalism, curiously seems to have paid scant attention to the issues of treating nonlibrary professionals as partners rather than as second class citizens [Kaufman 216].

The so-called "nonlibrarian" professionals, as opposed to the "nonprofessional" librarians or paraprofessionals, are professionals who, because of their advanced training in any of a number of fields, are hired to work in libraries—usually research or "special" libraries, but often other kinds as well. Twenty years ago they might have had an MLS, but oftener possessed master's and other advanced degrees in subject fields, rather than the library degree, and were considerably better educated as a group than librarians (Trumpeter 464). They were also, across the board, even in 1968, a tad better paid: $550 more per year than the average librarian (Trumpeter 465).* But today, though they still often have advanced degrees, increasingly they are coming to libraries because of their degree of experience and expertise with some particular aspect of library work which librarians have not been adequately trained to cover.† The positions for which they are being hired

*Trumpeter adduces an instance of how pay scales change when one's label changes, the discrimination based, it would seem, on no more than one's title being "librarian." One respondent to research by Anita Schiller conducted at the University of Illinois noted on his questionnaire: "'Librarians are notoriously underpaid. For that reason I switched to being a systems analyst. I immediately received a boost of 25 per cent in salary with a promise of another 25 per cent in two years. This, by the way, was done at the same institution'" (465).
†Herbert White and Marion Paris in 1985 conducted a survey of library managers regarding their views of the way the MLS program could be improved. They decided to exclude libraries having fewer than four professional librarians. In eight cases, they felt impelled to note, large special libraries having professional staffs of over eight excluded themselves because most of their "professionals" were not librarians (6).

emphasize fewer and fewer professional characteristics as they rise higher and higher in the organization. They also seem to point a willingness on the part of library search committees and institutional chief executive officers to seek and hire candidates with specializations built upon experience rather than degrees, and with professional expertise based on education and credentials in nonlibrary fields and disciplines [Detlefsen 195].

"[F]ew library administrators will admit outright or go on record publicly to state that traditional M.L.S.-degreed professionals specifically *lack* these skills ... [and] the practice appears increasingly widespread" (Detlefsen 188).

Most of these nonlibrarian specialists are male. They are most often technical—computer and audiovisual—specialists and subject specialists, but may be teachers, archivists, accountants, lawyers, and various types of manager (Detlefsen; Kaufman; Trumpeter).

Indisputably better paid and generally better situated than the paraprofessional, probably because of their sex, this class of library worker nevertheless shares certain woes with paraprofessionals. They lack promotional opportunities and salary commensurate with what they might make outside the library field, but chiefly they feel estranged from librarians and are constrained by the "hierarchical nature of most library organizations" and the "many rules and rigid structures" libraries "seem to generate" (Kaufman 221 & 228).

In addition, like the paraprofessionals, they have come to be more numerous in the field, to the point where Detlefsen warned, in 1992, "New recruits to the field, newly admitted M.L.S. students who seek a career in research libraries, and those who would use the pursuit of additional academic work as a means to enhance their experience in order to change jobs, should be advised of the trend ..." (195-6).

The most striking similarity, however, is their self-perceived mistreatment by librarians, which exactly mirrors the deprecation that paraprofessionals suffer from degreed librarians:

> They are perceived to be involved only secondarily in the organization's central purpose, even when this is not the case.... [L]ibrary managers and professional librarians perceive nonlibrary professional colleagues to have inferior status.... [I]t is ironic that librarians, who are preoccupied with questions of professionalism, are often unwilling to grant similar recognition to those who have the appropriate degrees and knowledge required in their other professions.... Although non-library professionals may consider librarians to be intellectually compatible colleagues, it would appear that library professionals often do not consider nonlibrary professionals to be colleagues—intellectually compatible or not.... Common experiences [among librarians] and professional jargon often project elitism and sometimes arrogance ... [Kaufman 215-218].

As long ago as 1966, one nonlibrarian professional skewered this pretension:

Many people who cannot be called "true professional" librarians, like engineers, computer programmers, systems men, etc., are willingly taking over the responsibility of automating libraries—mainly because the "professional" librarians could not handle the job! Their "professional" library schools had not trained them in the latest information retrieval techniques (Pfeil).

Scanlon, involved in a project for the University of Georgia, lamented the "arcane" language of librarians and the "very different personalities" of computer programmers and librarians, and cited the propensity of librarians to regard programmers as mere "technicians," whose professionalism was in doubt because of the "difference in educational requirements" (320-1). Because there generally is "no formalized training for the computer staff," librarians evidently found it easy to transfer their scorn for their own paraprofessional LTAs to the computer programmers (321). Describing his difficulties with the two groups, Scanlon claimed,

> [T]here was a great deal of dissent between the library staff and the computer staff. Shouting matches were not uncommon and little respect was shared between the two organizations.... At the beginning of the project, the library staff perceived the computer staff as technicians, not as professionals. As technicians, the computer staff's opinions and needs carried a lower weight in the minds of the professional staff [321].

"[W]e need to acknowledge the non–M.L.S. professional as our equal as a provider of library service in the 1990s," insisted Kleiman, speaking of the army of special-program coordinators now recruited to oversee "social" (rather than "informational") functions of the library (Greiner, "Non-M.L.S." 212). And if "we" need to acknowledge these non–MLS holders as equals, we need also to acknowledge non–MLS "other 'librarians'" as equals (Berry, "Other").

Ironically, when called out, libraries will ultimately, at least as both Kaufman and Scanlon present it, take more time to compensate nonlibrarian professionals for gaffs of snobbery than they will paraprofessionals. Libraries will try to make the usually male professional non–MLS-holder feel less an outsider than the degreed, but usually female, para. They will grant him more autonomy and will work harder to make him content with his inability to rise very high in the library order than they will equally valuable non–MLS-holding support staff. To nonlibrarian professionals they will extend special projects, flexible time, cross-training, the power to participate in governing, verbal acknowledgment of "professionalism," and that valuable sense of "mission" and job satisfaction that always has been the library's earmark (and fiduciary undoing) all because, after all, of terminology: the male nonlibrary worker is termed "professional," while the equally experienced or educated *and female* paraprofessional is termed "nonprofessional." One Internet respondent commented, "[I]f someone who holds a BS (like my husband) is considered a professional how come someone with a BA isn't?"

PART II:
CYCLES IN
THE HISTORY
OF AMERICAN
LIBRARY WORKERS

5. The Shifting
Sands of Library Terminology

1919: There is, when it comes to essentials, no possibility of class distinction. The artificial divisions between ranks in the [library] profession are like the state line between Kentucky and Indiana, very easily crossed, once one has reached the place for crossing [Flexner, "Essential" 406].

The fates of librarian and paraprofessional have always been linked. The librarian's work has faded into the "clerk's" or into realms even more menial, and the clerk's has surged into the librarian's. At points, over the past hundred and fifty years, their functions and competencies have been indistinguishable to researchers studying them, and so their histories must be discussed together. "Fuzzy distinctions between professionals and support staff in ... early histories, if made at all, ... [were] probably due to the rudimentary development of library education and the still developing concept of professionalism in librarianship" (Kusack 10). The terminology—"library assistant" and "librarian"—was used extremely idiosyncratically in the early days. Indeed, as late as 1917, participants in an Illinois Library Association meeting concurred "that there was a general lack of definite opinion as to what constitutes library assistants, etc., in the library ranks" ("Illinois Library Association Notes").

Today, though the terminology may be more pointed, the qualifications behind the label are as chaotic as in the field's infancy. In 1962, Orange County Community College's president, William Dwyer, announced that a LTA project barely three years old would be discontinued. He announced, "At the core of this failure is the inability or unwillingness of librarians to define the difference between the professional and the nonprofessional in library management..." (1622). This refrain, alternating with the "them and us" cadenza, sounds constantly throughout modern American library history.

In the distant past, libraries, other than private, personal collections, were usually components of larger institutions, and library work was a part-time job for someone associated with the parent educational or religious body (Martinez, "In" 6), a "cleric," or "clerk," in fact. In addition to the more modern sense of clerk as a secretary or a drudge, or a cleric as a member of the clergy, one

58

of the older meanings for "clerk" was "a person who [could] read or read and write...[,] a learned person: scholar, man of letters" (*Webster's Third New International Dictionary* 421). Obviously, over time, and particularly in the twentieth century, the notion of clerk, like the notion of librarian, has undergone metamorphosis. As we will see, however, the expectation that a desk clerk should be above all things a learned person still existed into the infant twentieth century. This standard, though frequently unmet, was and is often still observed, though unfortunately more by chance than by choice. It is a standard which the field should never have stopped voicing and aspiring to.

It is easy to see the Victorians' notions of ideal library employees as touchingly quaint, and therefore ridiculous, but these stiff and unashamedly highminded people have much to teach our current undemocratic and ungenteel library hierarchies, if only by precept. Granted, there is also much to dispense with in their teachings. But the landmark document of the 1920s, the so-called Williamson Report, famous for stressing the necessity for dividing library work into two strait-jacketed divisions—clerical and professional—was massive and popular and the times were desperate, because recruits were not forthcoming, and salaries were abysmal. In the ensuing clean-sweep mentality of the twenties the baby, from shame, was thrown out with the bath water. The fluidity inherent in library work was stymied. Library assistants who had functioned as librarians and librarians who had functioned as clerks were to be no more. Williamson had made the field ashamed of its "clerical" chores, among which, evidently, was public service, that realm of the Ideal Desk Assistant, whom we shall soon meet, and really the *raison d'être* of libraries. Clerical situations and the title frequently, though not always, associated with clerical chores, "library assistant" (i.e., "clerical assistant"), became almost non-existent, because librarians did not want to deal with the stigma attached to the idea of "clerical" or "assistant." They wanted to distance themselves from that work which made the field seem vocational, rather than professional. If they thought about what they were doing at all, it was probably along the lines of burying the indignity of clericism beneath the imposing label of "librarian." Librarians, educated in all sorts of ways, for about thirty years served seamlessly as both clerk and professional. But they were still involved with what Williamson would have seen as routine dum-dum work, which was a fiber basic to the fabric of librarianship.

Then the field went back. It reversed direction in the 1950s. Implementing Williamson's bifurcation—the clerk/assistant (standing for indignity, hence her new title: "nonprofessional") and the librarian (standing for dignity, hence, "professional")—the field pushed into the 1960s and 1970s. We are living to see the circle close again, for now clerks—or "assistants"—are once more functioning as librarians. The reason for this persistent merging of function has to do with the type of person—pretty much the same profile, whether clerk or librarian—drawn to librarianship, as well as with the nature of the craft of librarianship. If the cultural standards of the vocal early practitioners were reinstated, without the sentimentality, and a concurrent commitment to adequate and appropriate levels of remuneration for all library workers who embodied these standards were made a first priority, we would have a clean and desirable model for library workers everywhere today and the carping would cease. For this idyll to occur, we must diligently hack away at the hierarchy encumbering Libraryland.

6. The Scene Is Set

Library workers as a class hardly existed at all until the second half of the nineteenth century. Then their numbers grew by leaps and bounds. For instance, the Library of Congress, founded in 1800, by 1876 had no more than a staff of 15 and a mere 293,507 volumes; now the staff numbers over 5,000 (Evans, "Evolution" 68). Private personal libraries were the rule in America throughout the seventeenth and eighteenth centuries. Benjamin Franklin founded the Philadelphia Library Company in 1731, accessible to those who could pay the required fee; this institution is often considered the first public library, though not the first "modern" public library, free to all. "Social" and rental libraries arose in the nineteenth century and continued into the twentieth century; their collections were "weak" (McMullen; Carrier 2). Obviously the staffing of these early libraries was minimal, and the intellectual equipment needed was not an issue.

In 1850, the impetus toward public libraries began; Boston Public Library was the first large "modern," i.e., tax-supported, public library. But the public library "movement" was really triggered by Andrew Carnegie's endowing, over a twenty-year period ending around 1920, 1,412 communities with 1,679 public libraries at a cost of over 41 million dollars (Ditzion 6, 13–19; Martinez, "In" 6; Ring, "Carnegie" 1). Superfluous women in the United States made for an abundant cheap source of labor for this and other blossoming "female" professions. Rosalee McReynolds notes:

> A generation earlier these women probably would have married, but demographic shifts that began in the eighteenth century had created significant dislocations in male and female populations by the eve of the Civil War. The first United States census, conducted in 1790, revealed that women already outnumbered men in the settled areas of the East Coast. By 1860 every coastal state from New Hampshire to North Carolina had a surplus of women. This was particularly true in the urban areas of the Northeast where public libraries flourished in the nineteenth century and where many women were forced to earn a living outside the home ["Sexual" 197-198].

Biggs points out another reason many women remained single at the same time an abundance of jobs opened up: because of the decimation of young men in the Civil War ("Librarians" 417). Wells observed that "[b]etween 1870 and 1920, the number of women gainfully employed increased by 6½ million" (71).

7. Portrait of a Lady

This burgeoning of the great American public library system set the stage for the rise of multitudes of library workers—but what kind were they? They are largely invisible to most historians writing either of white-collar workers, the new women's professions, or the labor-union movement, and are strangely absent from modern feminist indexes dealing with the same, but were probably most like the federal clerks painstakingly delineated by Cindy Aron.

These were women recently enfranchised at least to the point of completing their formal education through age sixteen (94 percent), and even into their twenties (13 percent) (Aron 838). They shed their bourgeois domestic trappings because of family illness; some were widowed, while others lost one or both parents and needed to feed, clothe, and educate younger siblings, or simply to shore up the sagging foundations of their basically middle-class households (Aron 840–42). A healthy number undoubtedly wanted to work just to be independent, for instance, married women saving for a divorce from recreant or otherwise undesirable spouses (Aron 847). This new class of worker flooded into the expanding federal government bureaucracy between 1862 and 1890, taking positions as clerical workers, where before the work force had been male; "[t]hese women created the first large-scale female clerical labor force in the United States," writes Aron (836). She continues:

> By the early 1890s, women held nearly 5,600 of the 17,600 positions in the executive departments in the nation's capital, and at the turn of the century 104,000 comprised 29 percent of the clerks in the United States. The women who worked in federal government offices from 1862 to 1900 opened the field of clerical work to other members of their sex. These pioneering female clerks came from native-born, white, middle-class families: they were the daughters, widows, and wives of doctors, lawyers, ministers, and other government clerks. At least 65 percent of their fathers worked as professionals, white-collar workers, small businessmen, or federal clerks. Less than 7 percent of female clerks' fathers earned their living through manual labor, and nearly all of these were skilled craftsmen such as carpenters, stonecutters, or engravers. Indeed some of these women came from old, established, and at one time very wealthy families [836–7].

Aron claims that about two-thirds of these workers were single women, but that an indeterminate number were also married women who concealed their status, because of societal norms that frowned upon married female workers: "[T]here is no way to know how many women lied, [thus] the data on married women are inexact: married female clerks represented at a minimum 6 percent and perhaps more than 13 percent of the women in federal clerical jobs during this period" (839, 843–4).

Federal library positions, up to 1898 (through Librarian of Congress Young's tenure), were still dominated by political appointees, though civil service had been in place to deflect such favoritism since 1883. Just prior to librarian Herbert Putnam's appointment, 70 appointments had been made with some effort to recruit those with either library experience or "aptitude," but most in fact were still political placements. Putnam in 1899 requested 96 new slots, and in fact eventually filled 110 with mostly female workers. For junior positions, women needed at least some high school. For the medium- and high-paying jobs they needed up to two years of college and often library-school training. By 1906, one-fourth of Putnam's appointees were library-school graduates—among librarians, library-school graduates outnumbered library workers with library experience only by more than two to one (Rosenberg 256–262).

In addition to these federal clerical and library workers, women office workers inundated the country's businesses in the late 1800s, increasing from 19,000 in 1870 to 503,000 in 1900. Like the federal clerical workers, these were mainly native-born single women, rarely even the children of immigrants (Wertheimer 233). Retail-store workers, increasing from 10,000 in 1870 to 100,000 in 1890, shared with library workers long hours for low pay in odious surroundings, often standing on their feet for hours and fainting from distress (Wertheimer 239). Like library workers, despite low wages, they were expected to dress genteelly; like library workers they worked unconscionably long hours, 60 to 80 hours per week (Wertheimer 238). Like teachers and nurses, both retail and library clerks were expected to maintain a nun-like celibacy.

The pressure to remain single has haunted the library workers of the twentieth century up until the present. Their salaries alone have militated against the support of even one person, much less many. Nevertheless, library workers have always been directly involved in the maintenance of families, despite the desires of library funding bodies. Since the library field was not willing to support even the single person it wanted the librarian to be, there was bound to be conflict. Many receiving the celibacy message, and more importantly, the hairshirt-grade salary message loud and clear vacated the field early on: the great librarian shortage really began in 1910, when Ahern worried, "There seems to be a greater demand at present for capable workers than can be supplied by available people" ("Demand" 426).

Like other female workers, library workers were leery of standard trade unions, and so hung back longer than blue-collar workers from unionization as a remedy for their economic and physical ills.

The nature of the early white-collar work to which these mostly young women subjected themselves, set tightly in the Victorian mold of "service" and self-abnegation, ineluctably changed the way women responded. Women had to bludgeon their way out of "niceness," to change the way people regarded them and the way they regarded themselves, in order to make a living wage. They had to change their jobs, always fleeing to work that paid a little more reasonably. They had to unionize. They had to speak up. The need to become hardened set the stage for the quest for self and money that has concerned working women throughout the twentieth century. Aron describes the problem:

> Female clerks realized that in becoming government employees they had crossed the boundary of what many considered to be acceptable behavior. Consequently, nearly every woman's job application contained repeated assurances that the candidate was "of good moral character" and from a "respectable and worthy" family. Besides emphasizing virtue and purity, applicants took great pains to demonstrate the requisite amounts of passivity, reserve, and helplessness demanded of well-bred, nineteenth-century ladies.... [However,] [t]he contradictions inherent in the domestic ideology became more apparent after women began to work in federal offices. Success as clerks required women to exhibit, not passivity and reserve, but assertiveness, competence, and skill in nontraditional areas [849–50].

Therefore, in time, "domineering" and "overbearing" were epithets frequently hurled at women who had learned to be better governmental clerical workers than "ladies" (Aron 852). In the other fields tender maidens soon grew into tough orators and obdurate negotiators (Wertheimer 233–248). It took library workers longer, perhaps because of the extreme pressure put on them to be embodiments of culture, gentility, and self-denial, or perhaps because there were so many of them at first that the market belonged to the employers, not the workers. Garrison states, "Not to surrender to the Victorian mystique was to run the terrible risk of being judged deviants in their society, of being judged abnormal because of a challenge to well-established norms" ("Tender" 142). She adds,

> Critical commentators who have studied the dominance of women in the conservative "moral uplift" efforts of the nineteenth century have generally failed to acknowledge the supreme courage that would have been required of any deviant group of women who sought emancipation from sexual role-playing and thereby suffered the loss of economic security and social isolation and ridicule [*Apostles* 185].

Thus, "domineering" and "overbearing" were cruel and frightening epithets in a time when "ladylike" was the crowning compliment a woman could receive. And library workers, for a variety of reasons associated with the presumed gentility of their work, worked harder at being meek than almost any group of emergent female white-collar worker, and were among the last, and the most briefly, to be unionized of any of the groups of workers who grew up with them in the early years of labor protest.

By cruel paradox—one of the many riddling the field—despite all the injunctions to be "ideal," in the library world even ladylikeness could be held against these pioneering white-collar workers. Bostwick skewers the library "with such an atmosphere of quiet good-taste and so lady-like a librarian, that the great public no more dared to enter therein than if a fierce lion had stood in the doorway" ("Three" [Pt. 1] 2). "To too many," bristles Ahern, "the public library does not supply cheerful encouragement" ("Duty" 227).

These ungenerous comments and a legion of like-minded cavils prompted Jessie McNiece, commenting on library assistants' coverage in the press of the late nineteenth and early twentieth centuries, to observe truly, "Such references as occur are singularly carping in spirit" (*The Library and...*, "Preface"). For instance, the librarian who penned "A Wail of Despair" mercilessly criticized new library-school graduates looking for positions with reasonable working hours for their "utter insubordination" and "deplorable lack of tone" (216). Perhaps these newly minted assistants were indeed as she said, but more likely it was that the unrealistic expectations the library field held of its "subordinates" was coming into conflict with the more realistic views of the new workers. Expecting to be treated like ladies in terms of their working conditions and properly paid for work professionally performed, these workers were finding out they would in fact be the profession's scullery maids, and they justly resented their apportionment.

8. Enter: "The Ideal Desk Assistant"

The same calibre of "ladylike" American women who became government clerks also constituted the ranks of library workers who poured into the burgeoning library systems of nineteenth-century America as both librarians and clerks, though these divisions were extremely fluid and had not yet ossified. "The first women library clerks were employed in the Boston Public Library when that institution was established in 1852, and the first woman librarian was hired by the Boston Athenaeum in 1857. Shortly before, women had not been welcome there even as library users" (Schiller, "Women" 237; Garrison, "Tender" 131). The notion and implementation of tax-supported libraries spread from the Northeast outward into the rest of the nation. This spread occupied the years from 1849 into the 1890s (Ditzion 30–37). Thus the field was very, very new when the new type of librarian entered it, and probably very precarious. Caution dictated that workers possess two of the characteristics that ruled the earliest days of library work, and which really then locked it into the defensive, low-status, poorly paid profession it has continued to be: an extreme orientation towards "service" and the exaggerated ladylikeness (approaching martyrdom) expected of women.

These clerical workers, both "desk attendants" or "assistant librarians" and "librarians"—terms applied so idiosyncratically through local whim as to become meaningless—like their sisters in government service, were, at their best, beyond intelligent or well-trained, expected to be "well-bred": "It would be hard to find a finer set of girls anywhere," enthused "[s]everal prominent club women" in St. Louis in 1916 of assistants in the public library. "They are not only girls of intelligence, but of breeding and refinement.... [T]hey go to any amount of trouble for you in the most cheerful way, and in addition to it all they are all such ladies" ("Speaking"; "Thank you" 174).

In the late 1800s, closest to what today we would call a "library clerk," a "library assistant," or a "paraprofessional" was the "desk attendant," the "desk assistant," or indeed the "library assistant." Sometimes she was referred to as an "assistant librarian." And she was sometimes, as she is today, also simply referred to as a "clerk" (Bowerman 645). In general, in the first sixty years of librarianship, the term "'[l]ibrary assistant' ... usually [included] nearly every member of the staff except the head librarian. But it sometimes [was] applied to an unclassified group of workers ranking below certain heads of departments" (Windsor 721). Josephson in 1900 terms "minor positions" those of the "order clerk," "shelf lister," and "junior cataloger" (226). In larger libraries, in the lowlier echelons, existed the delivery clerk, the gallery girl, and the obscure library "messenger," a ghostly presence glimpsed only rarely, because large libraries were fewer by far than tiny rural ones, which were staffed by a mere one, sometimes two, library workers. Delivery clerks were basically desk assistants; gallery girls were like pages; messengers appear to have been overdue-notice servers; at any rate they were paid extremely poorly, even more poorly than the lowest-paid assistant (Hewins 274; J. C. D. 9; Agg 356; "American Library Association. A Review" 410). "It is ... important to distinguish between the development of paraprofessionalism and the development of education and training for paraprofessionalism," instructed Nettlefold in 1989. "The latter is a recent phenomenon, but the former is a counterpart of the evolution of library professionalism since the late 19th century, with many librarians working as paraprofessionals in all but name" (526). Thus primarily, the functions of today's clerk or paraprofessional were performed by a series of "assistants": the reference assistant, the cataloging assistant, but primarily the desk assistant, or desk attendant.

Commentary from *The Library Journal* and *Public Libraries*, and other periodicals of the time, provides a fascinating and eerie pastiche of the plight of this seminal worker. On the one hand she was considered the hub of the library and the most important public representative of her workplace (much as she is, at least on paper, today); on the other, she was an employee so lowly that she did not rate a living wage, reasonable work hours and circumstances, or three square meals a day. In most ways, her life more closely resembled that of a female blue-collar worker than that of a lady. She was expected to be so ethereally idealistic that remuneration was ever her last consideration.

> [T]he library employee who does not experience the pleasure of wanting to do work for which she knows she will never be paid is very foolish to continue in the work,

wrote Mary Black in 1918 ("Concerning" 203).

Practically in unison, with few variations, librarians described the pivotal position of the desk attendant: "It is only within a few years that desk work has become of any importance, and that librarians have recognized that it is the chief point of contact with the public," claims the Librarian in the fictive dialogue between clerk and librarian in "The Desk Assistant..." (251). "What the library stands for in the community is determined largely by the atmosphere created at the delivery counter," continues Ahern ([Editorial] 12/1899,

449). "The usefulness of a library depends upon the efficiency of assistants and clerks employed, for upon them devolves the duty of meeting the public and its demands. The institution relies upon its assistants for its reputation at home and abroad," stated Hill (381). "[U]pon the assistant the efficiency of the library largely depends," observed Miss Adamson ("Library Meetings. Indiana" 22). "In a larger library there is no point so important as the issue desk. It is the point around which the whole library revolves. All the other work of the library is subservient to it, for at the point when books and people are finally brought together the purpose of the library existence is fulfilled," urged Countryman ("Contact" 397). "[I]n fact," wrote Bostwick,

> everything we have to do in a public library relates to the point of contact between the public and the library. The desk assistant is the point of personal contact, the point where the amount of pressure is greatest. ... The desk assistant, her training, education, and, above all, her bearing toward the public is, so far as the public is concerned, the *most important thing* [emphasis added] in library work" ["New York State..." 560].

Bowker dubbed this figure "the all-knowing 'information clerk'" ("Libraries" 6).

All the more peculiar, then, that almost a century has passed between the recording of these urgent sentiments and now, when writing about check-out desks and the women who pilot them is not notably different in gist or wording. All the talk about circulation clerks being the first and sometimes the only contact between the public and the library personnel; all the worry about clerks being mistaken for librarians; all the fussing about "image"; and still the library, now as then, is judged primarily by its public-service areas, chief of which, today as then, is the circulation area. Still the profession has not come to grips with the fact that because this figure is important—so important that the library's reputation frequently stands or falls by her performance—she must be paid in more than "fairy gold" ("Fairy"). It is still a "clerical" rather than a "professional" position, and people are still recruited for it practically from off the streets, from nothing more than stinginess and the aversion of librarians to exhausting work; "...newspaper ads [are] the most often used recruiting source by public libraries[,] ... the most effective source for recruiting support staff[,]..." wrote Pesek & Grunenwald in 1990 (52). And then, as now, eschewing the main desk clerk's practical importance, "the library school graduate looks down upon the work of the desk assistant and would rather do anything else" (1901: "New York State..." 561).

The ghostly and fascinating pastiche continues: "The ideal assistant should be willing to do whatever is asked of her," one commentator begins innocently.

> She should be always courteous and polite, good-natured and obedient, accurate, systematic and orderly, prompt and regular, attentive and faithful, enthusiastic and

forbearing, and above all things she should possess adaptability. It is better to be over-polite than overbearing, and the assistant must be impressed with the fact that she is a servant of the people, submitting many times to inconveniences and sometimes to insult, but never allowing the visitor to receive anything but the best attention [Hill 381].

Gratia Countryman, commenting on "Contact with the Public," gushes:

> Day in and day out you must stand at your desk; you must meet the rich and the poor, the dreadfully ignorant and the educated, the snobbish egotist and the well-bred gentleman. You listen to praise and blame, to thanks and to complaints, and it makes no difference whether you are tired or rested, or sick and well. And when you are ready to drop at night, and the circulation for the day comes up into the thousands, you almost forget the glory of the work; you are no longer soaring in the clouds, you are treading a thorny path.... The very first thing for an assistant to learn is, that she is a servant of the people.... No amount of knowledge will make up for an indifferent spirit, nor training for the least discourtesy of manner, even under the most trying circumstances.... Friction impedes progress, and friction should be avoided even if we often pocket our pride and swallow our vexation.... Next to willing and tireless service comes tact and cultivated manners[;] ... her manner must be an obliging one, without the least hint of bestowing a favor.... The ideal assistant or librarian who does the most good for the people ... will have these three characteristics. The ideal, I repeat:
> 1 A genuine, sincere character,
> 2 Kind and conciliatory manners,
> 3 A good education,
> and important in just that order.

Mary E. Ahern thunders:

> There is something wrong with the ideals of a library when day after day, year after year, those in charge of its efforts remain untouched by the spirit of kindliness, of helpfulness, toward its patrons. In recent conversation two or three attendants at the loan desk of a library were heard to lament that their position did not afford opportunity to get in touch with the real work of the library; that their duties brought them in contact with tiresome people who were a burden rather than a help. What to say to such people is a problem. All around them are great waves of that indefinable something called the library spirit, that in its sphere is tireless in doing all the good it can, in all the ways it can, to all the people it can. To the people at the loan desk, as has been pointed out over and over again, is given to do the greatest inspirational work of the library. ... If ... no enthusiasm over the opportunity of coming in contact with the great body of readers, and ministering in a courteous way, and with the spirit of helpfulness to one's fellow-man, refreshes and supports the workers' souls, surely the library field is not the place intended for the efforts of these people ... [12/1899, 449].

Two years later, she states tartly, "An attendant who is captious, indifferent to the duty required, and a hindrance to a full play of the true library spirit, has no place in a library.... A desk attendant should be well educated, have a kindly spirit free from fault finding, devoted to her work from love of it," and then adds, perfunctorily, "and then should receive due approbation in spirit and in advancement from the library" (11/1901, 538). Too many other authorities on this subject were to leave off Ahern's codicil.

At a 1901 meeting of the New York State Library Association, Arthur Bostwick griped:

> One assistant with a disagreeable manner, an imperfect training, who pronounces the title of the book wrong, or something of that sort, who leads people to think that she is a sample of what the library employs in its assistants, can do more harm to the library than poor cataloging or anything else [New York State ... (meeting) 561].

In "The Desk Assistant: An Imaginary Conversation," the Librarian agrees to converse candidly with her/his assistant upon the qualities of the ideal desk assistant:

> What I am about to say does not refer to a library school graduate.... I am talking now only to the average assistant in a public library who has had no previous training. We will assume, then, that you as applicant for a position as desk assistant are a woman with a high school education, or its equivalent. You must be neat in appearance, dress simply and always be prompt, as nothing is so demoralizing as an assistant scurrying in at the last minute.... At the desk you must be alert, approachable, good-tempered and patient.... [L]et the manner of the enforcement of the rules be as unobtrusive as possible. Be firm and decided, but pleasant.... Know the books in the library by reading the latest bulletins and catalogs, so that when certain books are asked for your face does not become a blank and you are compelled to refer the applicant to some one else. Read a newspaper, so that you may know what is going on in the world. Read some of the literary journals, thus keeping in touch with the new and interesting matters in the field of letters. Read a journal devoted to library economy, so that you may become familiar not only with the latest thoughts in your own field, but with the names of the leaders in the work. When not at the desk do with a vim whatever work may be assigned to you. Be anxious always to learn about everything that is going on in the library, even if not directly connected with your particular duties. Never grudge working overtime.... The assistant who cheerfully and without comment stays after hours to finish necessary work always scores a point. Learn to work without talking very much.... Above all, do not discuss your superiors or fellow-workers except in a friendly spirit. If you have a grievance go directly to the librarian without discussing it with the members of the staff. Accept *his* [emphasis added] decision in the matter, even if contrary to your own judgment.... Cultivate a spirit of loyalty, and keep from criticizing {251–2].

There was an absolute tidal wave of strictures directed at young workers struggling to advance in the field. Behold the tall order posited for this crucial figure, who in some locales was paid "$5 or less per month" (1914: "Salaries, Hours, and Vacations in Indiana Libraries" 196)! She must be:

"intelligent and faithful" ("Library Employment" 51)

able to avoid female "jealousies" (Hill 381)

"pleasing in appearance, neat and simple in dress[,] ... cordial and approach-
able, quickly responsive to the entrance of a patron" (Agg 355–56)

"right-minded" (Dana 250)

"well bred" ("Speaking")

possessed of "health, patience," and "a fair education, a fund of enthusiasm and
loyalty, and a constructive curiosity as to human reactions" (Flexner,
"Essential" 406, 405)

in possession of "some firsthand knowledge of books and real love for them ...
no reason for her being narrow, crude, ignorant...." (Rathbone, "Opportunity" 338)

"high-minded, conscientious" (Hadley, "Internal" 57)

"intelligent, rapid, and accurate" (Herself 877)

"[able] in all things to put herself in harmonious relations to persons and situations"; possessed of "maturity ... intuition ... courtesy, dignity and a
pleasant manner, ... cheerfulness ... enthusiasm ... unfailing good temper and self-control ... unlimited patience ... [a] sense of humor ... accuracy, punctuality and a good memory" (Hitchler, "Successful" 555–7, 559)

in "perfect health, [have] a quick, alert mind, ability to adapt herself to all kinds
of people, the power of analysis and comparison, a good memory, a knowledge of several languages—the more the better—familiarity with books
of reference, and habits of system and order" (Hewins 273)

possessed of "an open mind, alertness, adaptability, a love of people" (Van
Buren 372)

capable of "an unselfish, intelligent devotion to [her] work" (Pettee 586)

The amount of time apprentices spent learning front-desk procedures
punctuated the capital importance of the desk clerk's position: one young neo-
phyte recorded that of the 1,662 hours spent learning library work in her first
year, 463 of those hours were spent at the delivery desk. No other practice came
even remotely close to this number of hours; periodicals work came second,
with 181 hours ("Experience" 156).

Catalogers, whom many later commentators consider the bedrock of
library work and usually accord the status of librarians, originally were regarded
as clerical workers, though, like desk attendants, they were praised as central
to the library mission. Their status waffled to and fro on into the '20s, despite
their usually having attended library school or undergone some form of
advanced training (Schiller, "Women" 238). (An Iowa survey in 1917 showed
that out of 86 "librarians," 47 percent had attended college, 39 percent high
school, 19 percent library-school training, and 38 percent summer-school
training ["Reading" 270].) Actually, these two categories of library worker
were treated just as women have traditionally been treated—alternately set on

a pedestal because pivotal and indispensable, then regarded as unworthy of the least consideration and reviled.

Attendants or assistants never earned an adequate salary, not even when they were termed "librarians." And the attendant was almost always a "she." Only once or twice in these early tomes—any one of which, if it fell on your hand, would break it—did I find a single meaningful reference to a male desk attendant or cataloger, though there was frequent and pointed reference to the head librarian as a "he."

To me, the most curious result of sticking my nose into rusty old bound volumes of these journals, sneezing and itching, to ferret out the truth about my sister "clerks" was to see how perfectly history can repeat itself—in the high degree of erudition and culture, idealism, initial health, patience, proficiency, and ladylikeness required of women who were to be paid in absolute peanuts, and who were then forced to plod, unconsulted and unrespected, through long days of draining, soul-abrading work over cruel hours, confronted by rude or haughty patrons, and closeted in stuffy, unhealthful surroundings. Consequently, desk attendants became legendary in library literature for their high degree of disillusionment, and then of attrition.

Today, too, the lower level of library worker is noted for its high turnover. The unstated desideratum in hiring the present-day circulation clerk is that she shall be fairly well educated and ladylike, or seem so. Now as then, however, her salary will really only cover the needs of three-quarters of a person, not the whole person she is—so she had better be single, with no dependents and no appetites, at the very least. The reality of her job is that she had better be married to a well-paid man if she wants to do library work, and remain at all middle-class, much less a lady.

The above scenario was not that of absolutely every female library worker of the pre–World War I era. Some, though not many, occupied high-visibility, prestigious positions. It is, however, by far the truest for most of these early "missionary" workers. Evidently women found these conditions unacceptable, for when the First World War opened up more jobs to them, they abandoned their alleged idealism and took their leave of the library field, the lowest-paid of the new "women's professions," to find more lucrative employment elsewhere. "Before America entered the war there was ... no noticeable shortage of library workers," wrote Marjory Doud. "As a result there was discontent. There were a few vacancies in good positions, consequently small chance for promotion. For the thoro, conscientious, intelligent body of assistants there was almost no incentive in the way of advancement, in responsibility, or salary" (540). But in 1919 Clara Herbert, attempting to rustle up a new generation of library workers to replace the one which had absconded, lamented:

> It seemed as if the golden moment for recruiting a new training class had arrived ... Alas for our dreams! ... Four to five hundred young women, most of them

efficient and well educated, flocked to the library for further information.... 249 took away application blanks, 12 were filed, 8 took the examination and 1 qualified.... I was left with a vision of a vanishing procession of well educated, well trained, glowing youth, youth with "pep," and ability and enthusiasm. Ours, if we had but the price! [107].

An entire generation of diligent, dedicated, highly educated "library assistants" had been thrown away, much as they have been thrown away ever since the late '60s and into the present. By 1920, Mary Ahern was able to say with finality, "[T]he demand for trained people largely exceeds the supply" ("Mutual" 373). The library field had failed to establish itself as a desirable profession for the more talented of the upcoming generation, because the work called for people to work on the strength of sheer dedication for pitiful rewards.

From the point of view of men—another group much desired for recruitment, but standing in abeyance—Passet notes that "[w]hat [they] saw when they observed librarianship was an overcrowded, underpaid, and female-intensive field." "I hate the humility of the salaries that are in vogue in the library world," complained one ambitious male librarian. "In his opinion," Passet records, "these salaries would 'maintain their diminutive size' until enough librarians 'quit and [went] into other fields'" ("Men" 398).

The exodus of the field's "ladies" and the subsequent difficulty in recruiting workers of quality comparable to the earliest desk attendants or librarians accounted for the scramble for professionalism, and the stratagem of separating library workers into two rigid classes: "librarians" and "clerks," à la Williamson Report (Flexner, "Essential" 407). It readied the field for its first skirmish with trade unionism, and also accounted for the low grade of librarian described in articles and reports published through the '30s, '40s, and '50s: intellectually sluggish, complacent, small-minded, unambitious, and stubbornly devoted to clerical tasks, despite a dubiously appropriated "professionalism." Alvarez adjudged these librarian/clerk amalgams "loyal and contented"; perhaps they were just stupid (*Library* 55). "A sad spectacle," snapped William Henry in 1919, "that public library salaries appeal to only the most stupid, dull or unprepared" ("Living" 283).

Also undoubtedly this post–World War I, low grade of recruit helped give library education its bad name, which it certainly enjoyed even when I was young, and still does. I postponed getting my MLS because I always thought of librarians as second-rate intellects, based on what I had seen of librarians in my childhood, during my college years, and on into my working life. Writers commenting on the field have described the people who go into library work as "social misfits," "drifters," "discards"—what in this decade we would call "losers" ("What's Wrong" 1774; Edwards in Harris, *Librarianship* 63; Bryan 146; "Few Brickbats" 278). In 1913, a "Layman" in "A Few Brickbats..." took aim at young women who entered the library profession because they had "failed at some other work or because they desire a soft snap" (278). By 1917, calling library work a "grave," library director Hasse spat out her disgust at the great number of workers "engaged [in the work] as a refuge rather than as a career" (Wilcox 366). Criticism in 1966 was aimed directly at "the heterogeneous clutch of graduates in liberal arts, most of whom come to the field of librarianship as a last resort short of the dole" (Orne in "Library Education").

But it has been the men, in particular, from the earliest years of modern American librarianship, who have received the greatest number of blasts on this account. Too often they have been refugees from other fields—ex-educators, ex-teachers, ex-lawyers, ex-clergy, ex-journalists and publishers, ex-bookkeepers and clerks—even ex-doctors (Williamson, *Training ... Service* 37; Passet, "Men" 392–3; Borda). Hence arose the "stereotype of the early male librarian ... [as] a broken-down man who had failed in other lines of work" (Passet, "Men" 392). Reference to this phenomenon has continued throughout the library literature of the past 100 years. One library-school director commented, in 1918, of the male applicant, "I want to ask plainly if he has any physical defects that in a way have invited him into library service, or if he has tried other lines and failed" (Passet, "Men" 395).

Underpaid and underpromoted women working long hours, feeling their energy and enthusiasm for their work erode, were also undoubtedly able to see that these "lame duck[s]" were offered a better chance of advancement in the field than they (Alvarez, "Let's" 368). Why would intelligent female workers have wanted to stay on in a profession which rewarded such a large number of undeserving people solely on the basis of sex?

It was the "Gary library attendant" who finally epitomized for me not only the "ideal desk assistant," but one of the library field's greatest problems, both then and now. This young girl's heroic and probably well-meaning self-immolation in dealing with a dirty, rude, complaining, demanding, stupid, ignorant, and larcenous stranger looking for a room won her $50, a "politeness prize" doled out by the *Chicago Tribune* (*Chicago*). Her unflinchingly sweet behavior, despite the trials this surveillance imposed on her—her ability to stand up to the test of persistent discourtesy, the very notion that she would be deliberately baited without having any idea that she was being duped, that she would be *paid*, like a prostitute, for her self-abnegation and the abuse inflicted upon her, the very Christianness of it all, calling to mind the temptations of St. Anthony, the patience of Job, Christ's crucifixion, and all other manner of biblical masochism, all to prove an otherworldly saintliness—was worth all of a month's salary. Can a price be set on politeness in the face of abuse? Surely mutual politeness is a worthy social contract, insuring each party's dignity and good will. Surely this, and not meanness *vis-à-vis* martyrdom, is a more secure basis for society than the one played out in this ignoble Gary scenario. One can imagine the paranoia of perennially tense assistants all over the United States, as, already under unnatural constraints to exhibit a superhumanly perfect courtesy, an abjection total and absolute in their dealings with the public, they awaited the advent of the "white glove" at their respective libraries.

"Let us never," enjoined Charles Flagg in 1920, oblivious of the young women streaming away from library work to fields less demeaning,

> allow a reader to go away with the feeling that he or she has not had the very best service the library affords. This means constant attention and effort and sometimes sacrifice on the part of each one. No inconvenience on our part, or unreasonableness or incivility on that of the public lessens this duty.

This nonsensical standard is still upheld in today's libraries for their lower-level female clerks and librarians. Instead of insisting upon a standard of courtesy for *all* people—patrons and library workers alike—without which transactions would and should not go forward, libraries place the entire onus of good behavior upon their lowest-paid and least respected employees, leaving them in effect helpless, and, at severe inner cost, repressing well-deserved reproof. Tolerance of all license sends the message, "Beat me, beat me!" It makes the library a place which people do not need to respect. And, in fact, lack of respect was what commentators often bridled at throughout this century's infancy in contemplating the plight of underfunded and overlooked public-library facilities. They are still complaining today. And for the desk assistant, then as now, public disrespect makes of service servitude.

The disillusionment a generation of "ideal desk assistants" suffered, try as they might to please, by reading, studying, smiling, starving, scrimping, and serving, thus to get ahead, is captured by the astute Jennie Flexner, when she observes, with restrained, ladylike sarcasm, "The essential qualities of a good assistant in the public departments seem to me to be identical with the essential qualities of a good angel" ("Essential" 408). Rena Reese also refers slightingly to the "sprouting of angel's wings on the shoulders of young women" would-be library workers as a qualification "for librarianship on some celestial sphere" ("Training the" 391). Hitchler brings her five-page disquisition on the successful loan assistant to a quietly sardonic conclusion: "Finally I would thankfully express my relief that as cataloger it is not necessary for me to possess all of these qualifications—which is perhaps the reason I am still a cataloger" ("Successful" 559).

9. Promises, Promises...

> There is no goal in library work ... toward which any library assistant cannot legitimately aspire, and those lacking the formal, technical training of the library school may have compensations through an unusual endowment of native ability, the power to work and common sense [Hadley, "Internal" 58].

These tempting words flowed from Chalmers Hadley's quill in 1916, an echo of many other promises which had lured genteel young ladies looking for a suitable career into the field of library work. "As to assistants of lower grade," Hosmer had written in 1899, presenting an unclouded view of a field wide open to the ambitious novitiate, "the hope of reaching the highest place should never be lost sight of" (55). He then qualifies this grandiose statement with hesitant mention of "a certain discouragement that seems inevitable in the position of an employee in a large library" (55). His constant use of the masculine third person is a further deterrent, implying that men had hope of advancement, but not women. Bostwick, on the other hand, cheerily urges, "A library worker may properly look forward to the highest position for which *she* [emphasis added] is fitted by nature, training and experience" ("Internal" 57). He then sends a cloud over his prognostication by adding, Dewey-like, "Her natural limitations may hold her down."

"The assistants of today will probably be the librarians of tomorrow," hazarded library assistant Jennie Herrman in 1906. "Unflinching fidelity in a low estate is the discipline for larger duties in a larger life," counseled Lutie Stearns (69). The fictive Librarian (actually Beatrice Winser?) in the well-known "The Desk Assistant: An Imaginary Conversation" counters the assistant's query, "Suppose, however, that there is no opportunity for advancement, and that the salary schedule remains the same, what have I gained by my extra exertions?" with, "Of course there must be privates in the ranks, but there is always room at the top and ability never fails of recognition" (254). Very Horatio Alger. Aksel Josephson writes optimistically,

> It must be remembered that success in library work is in a measure the result of fitness, that the librarian, too, is born.... I would like to emphasize ... that our profession is not now, and never ought to be, so organized as to exclude from

promotion to the higher grades the assistants in minor positions who have shown ability and scholarship [226].

"An assistant should be an embryo librarian," begins another observer; "[T]he better their preparation and adaptation for library work, the shorter time they will serve in the capacity of assistant and the more value they will be to the library. Like good cream, they rise to the top" ("Reading" 272; R. Wallace 60). Hitchler, also, for all her understated cynicism, maintained, "The saying, 'there is always room at the top' is a very true one" ("Successful" 554).

More ominously, "A. D. L." assured underpaid assistants that if they wanted a raise, "[I]t's up to [them] to go to work and prove to the city fathers that the library is worth an increase and [they]'ll get it if [they go] at it in the right way" (308). Hard to know what the "right way" might be for lower-echelon workers under strictures never to go over their supervisor's head with work grievances. For Hadley is very clear on where workers' loyalties should lie:

> An assistant who is loyal to her chief and the library ... should guard against remarks outside which might reflect on the librarian's *professional standing* or *library habits*[;] ... no library trustee with any sense of justice will permit the reporting of library affairs to his ear except by the librarian.... If the working conditions in the library prove unbearable for assistants and this gets no recognition from the librarian, the assistants are entirely justified in selecting a committee from their number, notifying the librarian of their purpose (if they wish to be courteous) and then bring [sic] the difficulty directly to the library trustees ["Outside" 2, 4].

However, the prevailing view in the library field in the early days, when the supply of workers swamped demand, was the "rule of the three L's": "Like, Lump, or Leave" (Greer 891). There was very little question of standing and fighting. There was every expectation that if a worker disliked any of the circumstances of her work, she would simply need to "pack her trunk" and move on (A.D.L. 307). Of course, whenever she procured a better position, she was harshly criticized for her mercenary attitude. This tune was to change in the early twenties, when the very best of the lady assistants had, aided by the war, packed their trunks and vacated the field, and good slaves were no more to be had.

We have again reached the point where, if a war were to come about with attendant opportunities, or the bleakness of the economy were to dissipate, the field would be emptied of the assistants who for now are locked under protest into positions where their talents are virtually mocked. In the beginning, when the market was the employer's, no bones were made at all about obstreperousness. The Librarian in "The Desk Assistant...," challenged by his assistant, "Miss Gray," to remediate inadequate salary levels, says simply, "[Y]ou applied for the position knowing the conditions and accepted the salary without coercion. The alternative would be to find a better position elsewhere." She replies, "That is more easily said than done." "Exactly," he retorts, "and that is a point usually overlooked by the assistant" (253). Other librarians, in similar situations, riposte with comments like: "As soon as the assistant's interest ceases to be identical with the librarian's, it is time her connection with the library be severed" (1904: Pettee 587). Does this sound familiar?

No doubt the reason Hadley allowed that disgruntled assistants could band together and get a hearing was that he was writing in 1923 rather than 1904, and the earliest library unions had already been formed to deal with salary- and equity-related questions. In addition, few women wished to enter the shabby field of librarianship in 1923, whereas in 1904 there had still been a steady stream of middle-class women in exodus from domesticity, willing to put up with whatever was meted out to them. Hadley himself had written in a far softer note in earlier articles. He had decried "the gap ... between ... principles enunciated and their actual, definite accomplishment" and "the inability of ... [the A.L.A.] to transform its convictions into actualities" ("A.L.A." 357, 360). He had advocated a union function for the ALA, taking a very egalitarian view of the role of the assistant ("A.L.A."). Today we would call what he was describing participative management.

But in the early days "Like, Lump, or Leave" reigned triumphant. Or, as Carl Roden put it as late as 1923, "There is the job, there is the pay; take it or leave it" ("Mid-Winter" 80). Frank Hill, in 1897, wrote coolly, "Obedience is one of the chief foundation stones of the library organization.... One who is not satisfied to obey the rules as laid down should not make rules of her own, but should quietly take her departure" (382). Those words could have been penned in the present day. Librarians today say virtually the same thing whenever support staff complain, in the smug assurance that, in times of depression, departure is not easily taken.

It is not hard to see why library assistants, despite the high-sounding rhetoric, lay low in the early days. The sky was supposedly the limit, so any failure to advance was somehow their own fault. In short, it was "blame the victim," Victorian-style. "The library worker with a tale of woe must remain in a minor position," warned Frances Hawley darkly (361). She came down hard on "mental flabbiness" and advocated "more backbone" (361–62). Her vision of hope was bleak indeed:

> We are to learn to keep out of the way when people have not time to bother with us; to have our most brilliant ideas laughed at, or ignored, or overruled; to put our best efforts on work that we do under protest; to co-operate heartily with some other woman who we feel has the position we deserve; to quench with self-respect our thirst for appreciation; to accept the discomforts incident to our profession— even to irregular hours and cold luncheons ... instead of regarding them as personal grievances to be carried to trustees and reporters.... There are few people so prejudiced that we may not wring appreciation out of them if we deserve it

hard enough.... [W]e may come to be as useful and well-paid as if we were men; but at the very top there is no room for us [361–2].

Encouraging a desirable masochism, Greer puts the onus of blame for scatterbrained lack of progress in the workplace and upon the gossiping worker: "Seek the good points in the other fellow; the bad points in yourself" (891).

Assistants had no job security and usually no benefits, though in some places they had the right to go to library training classes, or even library school, at library expense. Some spots even offered paid vacation leaves, but, as with most things in the field, there were no hard and fast rules. There still aren't.

By and large, a democratic approach to library work was in practice nonexistent, regardless of claims of classlessness in libraries, or the isolated urgings of a few conscience-driven librarians who believed that assistants should be heard and that matters of policy should at least be made known to lower-echelon workers before the rest of the world was informed. The promises made but never kept—specifically the ones involving the possibilities of advancement—rebounded upon the library world when it could least afford to deal with them.

Speaker Putnam, addressing a 1914 audience at an ALA meeting, urged:

Our subordinates, as well as our other librarians are our professional colleagues; we depend upon them professionally in library work, upon their zeal and enthusiasm and professional spirit which is far above salary, and we depend upon their high sense of professional obligation. It is inconceivable that any librarian, asked by another librarian to lift one of his associates into a higher place, should put obstacles in the way of securing for the associate a better position elsewhere ["A.L.A. Meetings in Chicago" 79].

In his compassionate discussion of vacations and holidays, Harry Lyman Koopman urges,

So far as he controls the welfare of his employees, to that extent [the librarian] is a custodian of his profession as it will be in the next generation. The head of a library must see in his younger assistants the men and women who are to occupy the places of himself and his associates, the successors to whom, some day, his generation will make over its responsibilities [64].

"Some day? When?" an entire generation of young ladies could inquire. The pillorying lines of the anonymous poetaster respond:

...Librarians have waited long for me to show the trick;
Just let the menials do the work, and brandish a big stick.

Oh, I've the power, and I've the pull; no expert's needed here!
You do the work. I draw the pay; I hope I've made that clear.
Oh, the library director, he is blithe and full of glee;
But 'tis another tale to tell how fares the library.
[York State, 259]

Mary McMillan warned in 1903,

When a woman applies to be admitted into a library school, an apprentice class,
or a library, no effort should be spared to impress upon her the unpleasant features of the work, to bring home to her what it means to stay till nine o'clock
three evenings a week, to have only half a day in a week, perhaps not that, when
she may go to see her acquaintances or have them visit her, etc.; instead of which,
if the applicant is prepossessing, we strive to encourage her to enter, tell her how
enthusiastic we are, how we love our work, and all the rest of it. Not unnaturally,
she takes our praise liberally, thinks we are "so nice," and comes among us. Then
she finds many odd arrangements about hours, meals, time off, and distribution
of work, and often I have heard girls say, If I had known so and so, I would never
have come into the library, but now I can't afford to leave [McMillan, "Some" 412].

A starkly frank letter published in *Library Journal* in 1920 signed only "Under
Thirty" claimed,

[T]he salary question is not the only one that deters young people from entering
the schools: they come forward not so much because of the sage advice they have
received from their elders as from what they hear from those who are but a few
years in the service, and the talk and criticism among these is not wholly of
salaries, as anyone who has at all an ear to the ground can tell the chief of any
library or library school. The juniors hear talk of institutional politics; of promotions promised and deferred; of petty interference with clothing or personal
habits; of discountenancing unions without supplying any real chance for organizing for betterment; of libraries weighted down by sluggish institutional precedence, and of libraries embarrassed by autocratic control, which has wiped out
political systems in the world struggle but will presumably remain for generations
still in what we call "free institutions."

Confirming "Under Thirty's" accusations, Doud confessed,

With no organization to voice the sentiments of the staff, justified suggestions or
protests often looked very like personal complaints, and assistants hesitated to
make them. The very security of the position of the library under such even conditions, made insecure the position of the individual assistant. Some may have
been apparently inarticulate, but they expressed themselves to each other or they
seethed inwardly [540].

No wonder that four years prior to publication of these powerful condemna-
tions, Ahern, as editor of *Public Libraries*, dedicated an issue to assistant issues,
trying to defuse the power of the frequent "corridor conferences" so loathed

and correctly feared by the more insecurely despotic of librarians ("For"). "Under Thirty" in her missive urged "a new spirit" upon libraries, so prone to pontificating about Dewey's "Library Spirit" (Vann 23). This spirit has yet to evolve in Libraryland.

10. "I Serve"

The fascination the early desk attendant had for her detractors (the cat-aloger was less vilified than ignored and worked to death, or regarded as sim-ply dull) was that she failed to live up to librarians' image of the ideal desk attendant. She lacked that oft-cited "Library Spirit," and was seen to be fre-quently surly and deficient in culture and erudition. McNiece, prefacing her 1929 anthology of speeches and articles on library assistants, comments:

> The early files of library literature contain little mention of assistants, who were apparently regarded as necessary but irritating factors in the work.... The librar-ian's account of his staff seems at times all too like a feminine discussion of the servant problem. Assistants in turn appear to have cherished a sense of injury, and their infrequent appearances in print are devoted to the airing of real or fan-cied grievances [*The Library and...*, "Preface"].

In consulting indexes for information regarding my long-dead sisters, I soon learned to look under words signifying complaint, ill-health, or lamentation, since frequently a separate category for "assistant" simply could not be found, especially—tellingly—after 1920 (in 1923 the Williamson Report would hit the fan).* Perhaps this was because librarian and assistant were frequently the same person; perhaps it was because the "profession" simply averted its regard from the lowlier library workers, while simultaneously talking them up in grandiose terms on paper and urging them to greater efforts. Perhaps failure to index assistants' affairs distinctly was a ruse to put both their putative unsat-isfactory performance and their disgracefully poor rate of compensation and squalid working conditions out of sight, and therefore out of mind, much as underindexing does today.

Jennie Flexner writes earnestly,

*"A Wail of Despair," "Ill-Health Among Library Workers," "Meager Salaries," "Refined Cruelty," "Sick Librarians," "The Trials and Tribulations of an Assistant," "Distressed Librar-ian," "The Anonymous Assistant," "Some Grievances As Viewed from the Other Side," "A Few Brickbats...," "Antagonism Between the Public and Library Assistants," "Some Causes of Ill Health...," "A 'Real Chance' to Better Conditions," "Commitment Vs. Struggle"—all betokening stress, low pay, compromised health, abuse by patrons. It was not a pretty sight.

A library is great as its service to humanity is great, and it is insignificant as its service is feeble. I would like to give as a motto to every person entering the service that phrase which appears on the coat of arms of the Prince of Wales, "I serve" ["Essential" 406].

Lutie Stearns, quoting one Hugh Black, proclaimed, "At the end of life, we shall not be asked how much pleasure we had in it, but how much service we gave in it; not how full it was of success, but how full it was of sacrifice; not how happy we were, but how helpful we were..." (69).

The Riverside Public Library, describing a new program which purportedly combined characteristics of a training class with a library school program in 1915, continually refers to the library workers it proposes to turn out as "servants":

When these young people come to us from high school or college they have the academic mind and a certain amusing contempt for labor. No little part of our drill is to remove that habit and to substitute the idea of faithful service as a means of grace and the divining rod for treasure trove.... The "Riverside School of Library Service" is not an attempt to do something different, but its plan provides for emphasis upon those things that are necessary in a good servant ... ["Library Schools. Riverside" 142].

Did the publicists of this program think that the baldness of the notion of "servant" would be concealed if they refined the description of the goal of their schooling to producing the "personality and the genius of the servant"? Did they really believe that paying to attain the servant's "genius" would sit at all well with college-educated women increasingly exposed to literature propounding manumission and suffrage for women (141)? It is hard to say, although the great post-war assistant exodus advises the sentient peruser of library literature that probably it sat like a poisonous snake upon the loan desks of the nation's libraries. In the teens of this century, even my extremely ladylike grandmother was marching in women's-rights parades.

Charles Bolton effused, in "The Librarian's Duty as a Citizen,"

Is his life a life of service, like that of the clergyman? If he is not willing to make it so, he is not in the spirit of the coming profession of a librarian. The ministry will ever be held most in honor for the sacrifice of self which it requires. The calling of a librarian, to attract high-minded men and women, must be second only to the ministry in its aims and standards [219].

This craze for selfless prostration to public whim reached an apogee in 1918. Clerks and librarians alike had failed, despite their missionary zeal, to impress governing bodies with their professionalism or usefulness, at least as far as attaining decent salaries or working hours. Undoubtedly the continuing lure of what a '40s writer termed "spurious gentility," in addition to insuperable guilt over being at home while boys were being blown into grisly little pieces overseas, prompted Mary Black in 1918 to proclaim shrilly:

Service! What can we as librarians do to show that we too are serving? ... Service! ... It is truly only a backline trench we are keeping; a trivial, child's play task in comparison with that of many others, but still it is a legitimate part of the whole battlefield, and it is our bit. Surely we are going to rise to the occasion and do it, saying to ourselves, "Mistake, Fallacy, Disappointment! Thy name is even Friend, if by thy means we are able now to join the great civilian army of effective and sane workers: if by thy means we are able even now to say, 'We, too, do serve!'" [E. Williams 303; Black 199, 204].

In 1916, Chalmers Hadley oozed, "I know of no other workers today, *aside from those in religious orders* [emphasis added], where more cheerful, zealous, disinterested service is given than that furnished by the great body of library assistants in this country" ("Internal" 57).

But was this service really so disinterested? And in the 1920s, would it be seen as having been genuinely cheerful and selfless? Herbert's distress in 1919 at failing to attract quality recruits in requisite numbers to enter library schools belies this lofty view. Rather, perhaps all this desperately smiling service was but the sad denouement of a great restlessness that began in the nineteenth century, when women fled their domestic posts only to find that they were still expected to be perfect hostesses and servants, albeit clerical ones. Wells observes that

> In 1870, there were eighty times more women employed as servants than as clerical workers. In 1920, there were a half million more women employed in clerical occupations than as servants. The number of women professional workers increased about ten times between 1870 and 1920. The increase in women librarians was even greater, from forty-three in 1870 to 13,502 in 1920 [71].

But she notes that "[l]ibrarians were first counted in the census for 1870. They were not again counted until 1900, when they were grouped with librarians' assistants and attendants" (71, 75). Williamson guessed that of the 15,000 library employees active in 1923, 5,000 were trained in library schools, this course of study making them the "élite of the library workers" (*Training ... Service* 81–2). But still they were paid at clerical levels. And Williamson himself regarded them as no more than "assistants"; he does not even attribute the title of librarian to these new graduates, whom he moreover denigrates by claiming, "[Library schools] cannot pretend to turn out skilled workers" despite the number of courses these students had completed and their hours of field work (*ibid.* 91; 60). Clerical professionals, both the highly and the moderately educated, became—by the collusion of library literati as well as by external mandate—the new servant class. Even library workers who had trained extensively, had gone to library schools, had believed they were workers of a higher order, the world saw as mere servants in a minor service industry. Garrison observes, in her compendious *Apostles of Culture*:

Although the number of professional women increased 236 per cent between 1890 and 1920, most of these women merely left the home, not woman's sphere. They became segregated in the woman-dominated service professions, where femininity was newly defined on a vocational basis. Even if women of higher education and social class were drawn into professional life, they settled "like sediment in a wine bottle"—along with their unskilled, uneducated, and poor counterparts—to the bottom of the American working world.... [T]he only legitimate area for the operation of female intellect ... seemed to be through an extension of women's domestic service [184–5].

British ladies in the late 1890s remarked that they "[could not] understand how there is anything more ladylike in being a library attendant than in being a housemaid" (Webber 158).

The *Index to Occupations*, published in 1915, classed library catalogers, assistants, and clerks, as well as library errand boys, with circus employees, ushers, and stage mechanics under the heading "attendants and helpers" ("Library Work as an Occupation"). Thus, the giant step women had thought they were making out of the servant class and into the professional intelligentsia was but a step into another brand of servitude. In 1918, a librarian working under the Civil Service in Washington drew a salary "exactly the same as paid a typist, and the rating below that of a stenographer" ("Status" 430). The angry commentator notes that these workers were required to have no more than a high-school education, while the librarian typically possessed more extensive schooling.

An editorial in *Public Libraries* presents ads from a Philadelphia newspaper which show cleaning women being offered higher wages than librarians or library assistants (Ahern, "Day's"). The disrespect—and the implied vocational parallel—evinced by these salaries was adumbrated in the 1890s by a superintendent of schools serving on a local library board who objected to training for library assistants and to the need for them to be "highly cultured." As Mary Ahern warned in two different highly agitated and outraged editorials on the subject, this person of influence scoffed that "their duties really were on a par with janitor service," and that "the nature of their service was scarcely above that of the janitors of the building" (Ahern, "Editorial. [Training for Assistants]" [1897] 271 and "Editorial. [Library Assistants]" [1896] 270). In fact, the "nature of their service" may generally have been perceived as lower than that of the janitor. In 1914, South-Cliffe was to moan, "[E]ven the janitor, with no education, is receiving more salary than she."

Clara Herbert, candid in her distress over the multifold problems of the library field and their bearing on the giant recruitment problem that developed after World War I, wailed, "There was [among potential recruits] ... a general appreciation of the fact that to keep body and soul together costs money and that the initial salary at the completion of the training would not cover that cost and that the range of promotion did not justify the investment in the end" (107). She spoke of "a new note of distrust of the value of the work if it was so poorly compensated" (108).

The Salaries Committee of the ALA, also, minced no words in 1923: recruits to the field "have no natural aptitude for the work. They lack sufficient general education and adequate professional training" (A.L.A. Salaries Committee 68). The committee blamed low salaries for this disaster, and certainly low salaries have always been the biggest curse of the field, but other factors were at work as well, chief among them the curse of having to "serve" with unrealistic altruism, without adequate psychological compensations, and the often less-than-civil American public. Williamson observed that even library-school graduates were but "a very small group whose services ... [were] not likely to be valued as highly, on an average, as many kinds of unskilled manual labor" (*Training ... Service* 84).

What, then, was the earnest library assistant after all but the very merest of servants? In a field whose salaries were notorious for being among the very lowest in the country, the grandest consolation offered to disillusioned young ladies was that the service they rendered was "spiritual rather than material—where it is of the essence of life and not merely the machinery of living" (Henry, "Salary" 121). Exodus to other occupations was inevitable.

11. "Read, Read, Read, and Forever Read"

The qualifications not only for librarians but even delivery clerks at the end of the nineteenth century "would [have done] justice to a Renaissance man—including familiarity with the literature of three languages," remarked Mary Biggs incredulously ("Librarians" 412). Garrison set the number of languages with which librarians must be familiar as "half a dozen" (*Apostles* 182). Schiller, in her seminal essay, "Women in Librarianship," observed, "Oppenheimer's research on women's occupations in the United States led her to conclude that the demand for female labor in several female occupations is typically associated, not only with cheapness and availability, but also with educational requirements. Women's education is not a gratuitous accompaniment of the job but *characteristic of the demand itself*" (240). Librarians and library assistants with degrees from Vassar, Barnard, Wells, Wellesley, Mt. Holyoke, Oberlin, Radcliffe, and Smith were commonly employed for half the wages of men, and worked to the point of exhaustion (Wiegand 103; Wells 20).

H. L. Elmendorf wrote, "The position calling for the most intellectual equipment is at the loan desk" (289). Miss E. T. Canon, making a point of addressing her remarks not only to librarians, but to librarian assistants, directed, "[I]t is not enough that the librarian should read. He and his assistants are the only paid literary agents in the community and they should know books, old, new, good, bad and indifferent" (97). Flexner saw the best sort of desk attendant "loving books just after people" ("Essential" 408). Corinne Bacon, in accord, stated, "[T]he main thing is to know books, know them from A to Z, so that we can talk intelligently about them, and then ... be able to size up people quickly" ("Library" 54). Miss Donnelly called for "intellectual gifts" in library assistants, among many others ("Library Meeting: Massachusetts" 119). Josephine Rathbone proclaimed, "[Y]our acquaintance with books, all kinds of books, will be your greatest asset; ... one of your chiefest duties to yourself and to your work will be to enlarge your acquaintance in every possible way" ("Opportunity" 334). "Assistants must know the books themselves and know which one is the best if they are to get the best ones read," agreed Rachel Agg (357). "An assistant well-read in good novels is invaluable," enthused Hewins (274). In "Conditions and Requirements for Public Library Assistants," Marilla Freeman stated that assistants "must have at least a high school education, or its equivalent; a fair knowledge of books, good health, courteous manners, neatness in appearance and in work, accuracy, speed, reliability, general intelligence and good judgment" (80). Frank Whitmore saw the role of the assistant clearly as

> capable of guiding and helping a reader[,] ... add[ing] intelligent direction to the impulse to read. ... The work would call ... for knowledge. This would necessarily be a surface knowledge of many things and many books. It would call, however, for wide reading, an acquaintance with literature and a willingness to keep informed on the more important happenings in the world at large. The person so interpreting the library resources would at once be a teacher and a tireless student [16–17].

It went without saying that this paragon would also possess "discretion," "affability," and "patience." It would be amazing today to attend a staff meeting like those routinely held during the early years of modern librarianship, where young women sat and both offered and heard a plethora of book reviews; the emphasis was on literature, on the contents of books (e.g., R. Wallace 62, 63; "Indiana's" 621). They also often attended staff-association meetings on their own time to hone their intellectual skills.

"[L]et us each have a hobby," writes Kerr grandiosely, "and read and read ... till we are master of one field of ideas, ... [for i]f Library Worker takes no joy in reading, how can Busy Man be expected to rise above utility reading?" (427). "If you are a natural reader," cries Rathbone in rapture, "the sort who devours every printed page that has come your way, who would rather read directories than not read, you need no advice from me, all's grist that comes to your mill and you can be trusted to find your own without help" ("Opportunity" 338).

Hewins makes the following remarkable statement:

> If a girl of twelve or fourteen would rather live with books than anywhere else, if she has read or looked into every one within her reach, from Paley's "Natural Theology" to "Tristram Shandy;" [sic] if she can usually answer the outside questions in history or literature that are asked in school, and is never satisfied until she has found the author of every quotation or the meaning of every allusion in her reading; if Shakespeare and Scott, Dickens and Thackeray are her well-beloved friends, she should begin to train herself for library work, giving as much attention as possible to languages and history in school. After her school or college course let her go through the Library School if she can, or take one of the shorter courses. If not, let her make as plain and business-like an application as possible at the nearest library. She may have to begin as a "gallery girl," who waits until orders for books come up from below, and then takes the volumes from the shelves

to be put into a basket or truck for the delivery-desk. She may be told to sort old newspapers or overlook the cleaning of dusty shelves, or perhaps she can have only a substitute's place at first, but if she has the right stuff in her she will soon be promoted ["Library" 274].

What a creature so endowed should be training for, of course, is a full professorship in literature at a prestigious university, not the privilege of cleaning dusty shelves and hoping for a promotion to desk attendant. And the qualifications enumerated for her are, of course, ludicrous expectations, delivered with owlish solemnity by a woman who clearly had no idea what the word "subverted" could mean. She would probably be hurt and insulted that these measured words would be causing a similar sort of "girl" at the end of the twentieth century to roll about clutching her sides with laughter and shedding tears of merriment. Oh, the ironies of which humorless people are capable.

John Cotton Dana offered to a similar such wonder the "carrot" of one of the lowest-paying positions in the library. It is interesting to note his use of the conditional "might":

If you have always been a reader, and by reader I mean one who has seized the spare moments to devour books, papers and journals from the time she was six until she was, let us say, twenty-two; and if you remember what you read; if you have an agreeable presence and know how to say "no" as pleasantly as "yes," yet tend to be obliging rather than the opposite, then you might find a place as an assistant at the lending desk of a library [246].

Then he mandated,

[T]he librarian of the modest town and ... the humblest or the highest assistant in the large library ... must know her books. To know them she must read unceasingly; not much in a few books, but a little in all the books, all the journals, all the book catalogs, all the many pamphlets and all the newspapers which come to her library.... [S]he must read it all.... Any worker in any library who does not read, read, read, and forever read ... ought not to expect any notable success [250].

Expectations as daunting as these, set over against long working hours, skipped meals, an exhausting workload, and a prohibition against reading on the job, set up an insurmountable catch–22 for most of the rank and file, to wit: if one didn't read, read, read, and forever read, one could not get ahead, but one could never read because one was either at work or, when not at work, exhausted, or working at a second job to make ends meet. "The librarian of popular imagination is an omnivorous reader, but the actual American library worker is often so busy with routine duties that he seems to have no time at all for reading" (Chase 494). Moreover, from the beginning, most of the best library positions were held by men or pretty thoroughly subverted women. While it was obvious that being shabby, cantankerous, ill-bred, and lazy would never get a "girl" ahead, it was less obvious that being a near-genius never would, either.

In fact, "girls," even then, were in effect counseled not to appear too clever. One *Library Journal* contributor advocated "the tactful subordination of [the ideal loan-desk attendant's] too positive qualities" (Hitchler, "Successful" 559). She further noted that "the learned desk attendant is handicapped from the start.... Learned and scholarly men and women are ... apt to be obscure" (Hitchler, "Successful" 555). But, despite these cautions and disincentives, she soothed, "A knowledge of books and a liking for reading, a catholic taste, with the desire and the ability to reflect to some extent on what she reads will prove a support and consolation to the desk attendant in times of discouragement and weariness"—a fallacy Ethel McCollough skewers by complaining of having to read, in her precious scant free time *"things in books clothing,"* of having to read "under the lash" inferior books that were popular, "of which she professionally could not afford to remain in ignorance" (557; 5). Another carping article allowed that "[w]hen all is said and done a happy mediocrity seems a very desirable quality in a library assistant" ("Library Assistants: Shortcomings" 350). Caught amidst all these contradictory bits of advice, whatever was "the little desk girl" to do (Black 200)?

12. "The Cat Is Out of the Bag"

"A. K." writes drolly in 1916, about a magazine article fictionalizing a female librarian:

> [T]he genus librarian is usually reticent,—a deplorable quality in this publicity-mad age. The requirements of her calling foster this trait.... Her worth is measured by the quality of her altruism—which service leads not to the halls of fame, or Nobel prizes. She must be content to be known only as a hand-maid of Knowledge, an honorable position, in which one vaunteth not one's self, but one's master....
>
> But always ... one descriptive tag ... overshadows whatever other qualities the story-writer has seen fit to endow her with, and that,—the one she has always sought to conceal—her poverty.
>
> How did they discover that secret? She never told—she was partly too proud, partly too loyal, and partly too ashamed....
>
> Did she ever hold mass meetings of protest, or go on strikes, or form unions, or shout her grievances from the house-top?
>
> No, she grumbled occasionally, in the bosom of the library family, and wished she had entered some other field of work, but she stayed right on....
>
> But in spite of all subterfuges and precautions, the cat is out of the bag, the magazine writer has done it, and so, the "POOR" librarian has made her debut upon the stage of fiction. It is discouraging, yes, and humiliating, for her to have struggled so hard, ostrich like, to hide the ugly fact, and finally to have it dragged into the limelight as her distinguishing feature.

It is no mistake that the third-person pronoun is feminine. The nineteenth-century conceit was that women could afford to live on less than men, that women needed less to eat than men, and that, therefore, they did not need to be paid as much for equal work (Ahern, "Living" 143).* "In 1918," according to Lilore, "the U.S. Bureau of Labor Statistics said that the minimum needs of a single woman necessitated a salary of $1,140.42, but the beginning salary for a librarian grade one at the New York Public Library was $662.00," $478.42

---

*I have heard the very same argument soberly adduced in my lifetime as a justification for women needing and getting less of everything.

less than the female subsistence level (15). "Starving" is a word which occurs all too often to describe rank and file workers—overwhelmingly female—in the early days of library work. In the Boston Public Library of 1937, for instance, "[w]ages for many employees were at starvation levels," according to John J. Clopine, in his very enlightening exploration of library unionization (54). Starvation, then, was one of the premiere reasons library workers took to organizing with trade unions.

Ahern, always an opponent of inadequate and insulting wages for library workers, indignantly attacked a "large southern city" which paid assistants a disgraceful pittance: "[N]o other set of city employees were paid so low a wage, not even for manual labor," she raged, yet, though it was

> utterly impossible for ... library workers ... to live on the money they earn in that library ... there was no protest from anyone in regard to the matter, not even the librarian suggested that the laborer was worthy of his hire ["Demand" 427].

"I ... want to place upon [chief librarians] ... much of the blame for the meager salaries paid to many of their subordinates, and especially the younger ones who have good preparation and are doing successful work," accused William Henry, in his discussion of salaries appropriate to library service ("Living" 282). He was far from alone in placing the blame on the librarian: "Many of our working conditions are due to the librarian himself," accused "New England Parts." United States senator Thomas Sterling warned the field in 1923, after many workers had already departed, "[W]e must not place too great reliance upon intangible rewards to draw the right kind of people into those services that are to make us an efficient nation of trained, expert workers" (63). Miss Canon, a librarian, wrung her hands, saying, "I cannot imagine what would encourage some of us to keep on with it, with the long hours, short vacations and small salaries if it were not for this intellectual stimulation..." (97). But assistants were not as charitable about "intangible rewards," since their yearly salary was even smaller than librarians'.

> The librarian lays much stress upon "the spirit of the work" which he feels should be so ardent and so zealous as to rise above all considerations of salaries and hours, and make the assistant feel that sufficient for her work is the joy of doing it. Practically, this is absurd,

sneers the outspoken "Desk Assistant" in 1902 (Herself 877). Well she might sneer: in a presentation on working conditions in Colorado, where one librarian made $900 per annum, she was allowed but $100 for an assistant over a nine-month period ("Colorado" 26).

"The woman worker of to-day," explained Hitchler, "has a family to take care of or someone dependent on her for support almost as frequently as has [a] man." "There are too many temptations outside librarianship, too many calls to the business world for the capable worker for us to shut our eyes to this unwelcome fact," she warned (554). For instance, the staff of the Brooklyn Public Library petitioned its board of trustees in 1917 for increases in pay. Of its 287 women, "exclusive of cleaners and pages, 260 are dependent upon their own earnings; 120 are required to support themselves, and, in addition, are required to support, wholly or in part, other members of their families. Only 27 live at home, without the necessity of contributing to the family finances…" (Brooklyn 141). "[W]omen in this day carry quite as heavy financial burdens as men, and need quite as large salaries," confirmed McMillan; "if you see a worried look on an assistant's face that is not labeled 'library worry,' you may be sure it *is* labeled 'want of a larger salary'" (413–4). Ahern saw the library of her time, shamefully, as "willing to take from the family of its employees, the difference between what they would have to pay to one who did not live at home and one who did," a prerogative she did not believe was rightfully theirs ("Living" 143). William Henry maintained that "when we get what we can, but will not pay for, it is robbery. We cannot afford to rob a 'working girl' to give service to the well-to-do" ("Living" 282). Ahern rails at libraries willing to hold librarians captive in their jobs with salaries so inadequate they could not afford to move. She adds, "The families of these underpaid staff members are further unduly taxed for the support of the public libraries of their towns, no small share of which is often in the salary of the head librarian" ("Meager" 12). Mary Plummer fumed that tightwad libraries added insult to injury because they dared to rationalize that if the librarian would work for so little, she must like the work—"It is just what she likes to do"—and really didn't mind her minute wage, rather than seeing to it that she was remunerated for her good work at a suitable wage (41).

Cases like Plummer's prompted Hadley to suggest that "the meek professionally are more likely to inherit indifference at best" ("State" 38). Even when assistants were able to scramble away from low-paying jobs to marginally better ones, they were apt to be criticized. Hadley on the one hand castigates librarians for practicing this type of wide-spread emotional blackmail:

> Criticism has been passed on the library assistant who changes positions solely for an increase in salary. With few exceptions library workers in this country are given no protection against poverty-stricken old age, and no librarian should object to an assistant going elsewhere if he cannot compete with others in salaries paid. It is the right of every worker to protect himself in old age, and it is the privilege of every library assistant to secure the best obtainable financial returns.

Having said this, however, he criticizes assistants who change jobs just "for the sake of change," "to escape monotony" ("Internal" 58). (From this obtuse statement one deduces he had never worked as an assistant himself, never been bored into a coma from stupefyingly dull work, nor suffered "attitude" from supervisors, or he would have understood these putatively frivolous women a little better.)

Of course, the more spirited of the candidates for library work would not stand for shameful salaries. They resigned. In 1912 a librarian took her leave of the field because of inadequate salary and recorded the terms of her resignation in a letter to *Public Libraries*. Complaining that the library appropriation itself was but $1,000 a year since 1905, she demanded $40 per month, at least, for herself, or she "was willing for them to hire some one else." She touches on another disgraceful practice current at the time, namely, that if an assistant wished to have vacation time, she must pay a substitute out of her own pocket ("Significant").* This could amount to quite a sum if vacation was as long as six weeks, as one *Public Libraries* article claimed ("Positions"). Fortunately, vacations were frequently paid for by parent institutions, at least for library-school graduates (*Pratt*, "Salaries" 482). But in one-person libraries, run on a shoestring, the "librarian" may or may not have been a library-school graduate. She ran everything in the library herself. She was obliged to pay out of her own pocket for anyone who substituted for her during her absences. One such woman, in this case with "accredited college work," slaved

> eight hours a day in summer, five and a half hours a day in winter, two hours every Sunday, [had] no vacation but legal holidays, no sick leave, receive[d] a salary of $30 a month and also ... [acted] as janitor ["Colorado" 27].

The Colorado meeting found that generally "librarians" had no sick leave at all.

In 1918, four women entered an apprenticeship class, conducted as those classes generally were, with a tough entrance exam, five lectures a week, 10 hours a week practical experience, each course averaging 12 lecture hours. At the end of the class,

> almost immediately the salary question arose, with the result that one entered the Government service, one went back to teaching, the third entered the filing department of a business house, leaving only one out of the four remaining in library work ... [Muesser, "Interesting"].

At the time, this kind of dispersal was fairly typical. An assistant working in the Harvard library who left for a better-paying place in another library was sniffed at as she left and told "that people were glad to work at Harvard for nothing and she ought not to move for so small an increase" ("Few Gleams" 79).

In general, as Sawyer pointed out, "It has never been considered ethical

---

*It is worthy of note that as late as 1953, librarians were still paying substitutes to work unamenable hours for them (Bauer 37).

for librarians to express any great interest in their salaries. Askers have been snubbed and acquiescers belauded" (418). However, as we shall see, men were much more forward about their salary expectations than women, and expected to be so. Perhaps this bumptiousness was the reason they were paid so much more than women up to World War I. Young ladies in the teens of the twentieth century had had to evolve into a tougher sort of "lady" from the Ideal Desk Assistant of the end of the nineteenth century. Herbert notes in 1919, attempting in vain to assemble recruits for library school, girls' utter lack of "false delicacy" in discussions of money: "money considerations were frankly the determining ones, spoken of unblushingly and as a matter of justice" (107–8). Doud reports on the consequences of these young women's explicit interest in salary:

> When America entered the war, there was a general exodus of assistants from libraries all over the country. They went into war work at home, at Washington and abroad; they went into civil positions left vacant by men who had gone to war.... I firmly believe that consciously and unconsciously the much larger salary and the chance for adventure were contributing motives.... [T]he exodus did not stop with the armistice. It has gone on gradually but steadily.... [W]ith the lucrative as well as interesting positions open to librarians in other fields, even the meekest assistant has reached an alarming state of independence [541 & 543].

Yet librarians pleaded in vain with the powers-that-were to come up with the money (Eastman; Blackwelder; Elmendorf). Hadley called upon the ALA to "lead the way in establishing some proposed market value for library work" ("A.L.A." 359). To this day, the ALA has failed to perform this task, though it is fond of passing resolutions on the subject (e.g., Utley). In 1921, Lehlback, an official from New Jersey, introduced a reclassification bill for Library of Congress. It proposed a starting salary of $1,080 per year—deemed insufficient, yet Ahern urged its passing because it treated librarians "with greater fairness than any other measure which has been proposed" ("Reclassification" 68). Sad that it was a politician (who proposed the legislation) and trade unions (which helped pass it),* rather than library administrators, who saw the need for something practical, something that might alleviate the burden of starvation wages on many of the country's employees; pathetic that librarians would be grateful for a bill they considered inadequate. In 1923, this reclassification bill was passed (Hyde).

"[H]ow many young women go into library work as disinterested philanthropists?" challenged Pettee (or at least Pettee's alter-ego). "The average

---

*The National Federation of Federal Employees was instrumental in passing the Classification Act of 1923. At that time, 75 percent of the District of Columbia public library workers, both clerical and professional, belonged to this union, and passage of this act helped them achieve parity with other library workers elsewhere in the country (Bowerman 646).

young woman, either forced by circumstances to earn her own living, or seeking by preference to 'be independent' comes to the training school or apprentice class with a very definite idea of undergoing a preparation which will place her in the way of a fair salary" (585). Aron, writing of the period between 1862 and 1890, estimated "[t]he $900 average annual salary paid to [federally employed] female clerks, while still below what most male clerks earned, represented one of the highest salaries available to women in this period" (847). But non-federal library workers were not making even this salary ten and twenty years later. Moreover, by 1920, Doud was chagrined to write: "[T]he fact must be noted that within the last six years, the dollar has so depreciated, that the library assistant actually receives as little or less than she did six years ago…" (Doud 541; "Other").

"[I]t is not a fair proposition to ask library workers who have had four years college course, with one or two years special training, to be content to start with a salary that in most cases was exceeded by that paid, very often, to uneducated, untrained house servants," charged Mary Ahern, editor of *Public Libraries* ("Library" 271). Indeed, in 1916 a "Cub Librarian" fresh out of library school, in addition to finding that her schooling had not prepared her adequately for work in the field, started with a mere $30 per month ("Impressions"). Female library-school graduates were woefully recompensed even when they had a high number of skills other than those attested to by their degree. An expert cataloger with both French and German would be offered but $40 per month, or $480 per year (Bacon, "Relation" 398). A trained librarian—in some schools a reading knowledge of German, French, and Latin were required—might be offered $710.64 per year, while a bookbinder made $881.92, a baker, $932.88, and a stonecutter, $1,196 (Hadley, "State" 38). No wonder O. R. H. Thomson felt "humiliated" as he read the ALA salary figures for 1924: that "library assistants" in 14 of 32 surveyed libraries were making under $1,000 per annum—no better than the "clerks" of 30 to 50 years before whom Aron wrote about; that in 28 of 32 libraries, the maximum salary offered assistants was under average beginning salaries for library-school graduates. "[J]unior-library-assistants" made far less (295). In 1914 some of the libraries surveyed in the *Library Journal*'s "Salaries, Hours, and Vacations" survey of Indiana libraries were paying assistants as low as $5 or less per month; only one was paying the high sum of $102.50 per month (196). A *Public Libraries* notice for Illinois civil service exams in 1917 stated that the salary range for a library assistant was $50 to $100 per month; that of a library clerk was $40 to $60 per month ("Applicants"). In 1923, the ALA Salaries Committee found the salary range of assistants with six months of training to be $600 to $1,680 per annum, across all types of library; most paid under $1,200 per year (A.L.A. Salaries Committee 63).

"Our best basis for judgment for salaries in library service is the salaries of high school teachers, for the educational requirements are usually about the

same. In my own staff, ... below the Assistant Librarian there is not one getting a salary equal to the lowest paid high school teacher in the Seattle
Schools," admitted Henry ("Living" 283). Library salary ranges in his library,
in 1919, ran from $900 to $1,200; high school salaries ranged from $1,320 to
$1,950. Quoting Louise Hooper, of the Brookline Library in Massachusetts,
Ahern revealed a similar bias on the other side of the country, where "[t]he
general average of library salaries ... is still far below that of our schools."
Claiming that the teacher worked 35 weeks per year, and the library assistant
48; that the teacher worked 5 days a week, the library assistant 6; that the
teacher enjoyed weekends and evenings off, while the library assistant was
working; that the teacher could expect a pension, while the library assistant
could expect the poorhouse, Hooper set the salary range for assistants at $660
to $1,000, and the school teachers' at $900 to $1,100 (Ahern, "Library").

Yet head librarians, most of whom were, of course, men, were making from
$4,000 to $10,000 per year (Reese, "Facts" 311). Salome Fairchild ripped into
this practice in 1904:

> In the large library group the highest salary reported for men is $7000, the low-
> est $3000; the highest salary paid to a woman is $2100. The average highest
> salary paid to men holding responsible positions not administrative is $1208, to
> women $946. The average mean salary paid to men and boys in subordinate posi-
> tions is $532, to women and girls $530.

She gleaned these figures from a survey of 94 libraries of all sorts. Of the total
of 2,958 persons counted, 2,024 were women, yet subordinate positions were
held by 1,211 females and only 514 males. About one-third of the respondents
were male, two-thirds female, yet men occupied half of the superior, as opposed
to subordinate, positions. Fairchild was polite, but firm, as she stated,
"[Women] hold a creditable proportion of administrative positions but seldom
ones involving large administrative responsibility ... [and] they do not receive
equal remuneration for the same grade of work" (160).

"What are vacations and holidays?" queried Koopman. "Are they a compromise between the good nature of the employer and the aggressiveness of
the employed, or do they represent, on the other hand, an attempt to strike a
balance between overwork and underpay? (64). "Low salaries mean frequent
changes. It is cheaper to raise salaries and keep assistants who know their
work and their clientèle," advised Bacon ("Library" 50). "Work well paid for
is pretty sure to be work well done," confirms the "Desk Assistant" (Herself
877). Already in 1916, a surmise that was to shadow the library world for the
next 50 years was being breathed: "[Do] we have small salaries because we have
incompetent librarians or do we have incompetent librarians because we have
small salaries?" ("Few Gleams" 78). "The surprising thing," pondered Thomas
Sterling in the end, "is not that some libraries now fail to give the high type
of service which they ought to give but that under existing circumstances the
service is as good as it is" (63).

Miss Windsor snapped, "To sum the question up in a few words, give the desk assistant more salary" ("New York State Library Association..." 562). Reasonable salaries were not to be. In the Chicago Public Library in 1937, Clopine exposed "glaring inequities between [pay of library employees] ... and the pay of city workers doing comparable work" (93). In the Boston Public Library, a librarian received $10 per week, while the janitor received $35 (Clopine 54). Other workers were listed as "probationary," although they had been working in the system for five and six years, and under that rationalization received but $12 per week, while their director received $8,500 per year— just a bit of a gap, though clearly indicating that, if the library administration had been willing, the money was certainly at hand for institution of equitable salaries (*ibid.* 56). Almost thirty years later, the Equal Pay Act of 1963 was passed to curtail the more ludicrous wage gaps between workers doing comparable work. Nevertheless, in 1976, veteran clerks were still seeking, through litigation, wage equity with such unskilled workers as liquor-store clerks ("Md."). And in 1981, striking workers in San Jose, California, were trying to achieve wages at least equal to those of water-meter readers (Rush et al., "Long" 6).

To this day, library workers make less money than workers in other fields doing work requiring comparable skills. In addition, the lowest-paid positions in the library are those of circulation clerks and library assistants, and senior support staff who perform professional-level work have still not been given parity with librarians doing the same work. A typical library para, Virginian Debbie Wolcott, complained in 1991, "[M]any ... Support Staff, including myself, are performing tasks an MLS Librarian would be doing if hired and getting no compensation." Greiner underscored her pessimism: "[T]he value of the service provided to the public by the nonprofessional is not reflected in the reported remuneration. In many ... systems, the nonprofessional library employee is given management and service responsibilities equal to those of the professional librarian" (Greiner, "Role" 78). It is no wonder the world gives the laugh to paras as well. The moral of the story for support staff is clear: if in over 100 years, the field has not yet managed to award frontline employees a dignified, fair living wage, why stay in library work?

13. Nervous Breakdowns

The early library field was noted for the frequent breakdowns attendants and assistants suffered through overwork and starvation. "The chief trouble of women librarians is lack of health. Many of them appear to need medical help," commented one observer (Rocky 186). An "Old Librarian" excoriated library boards of trustees in 1922:

> I have been interested for some time in the editorials about librarians killing themselves by overwork—in plain English. Well, what else can you expect from the ordinary library board? ... There are cases all over the United States where the health and strength of librarians have been capitalized and eventually their lives taken by library boards who knew little, and cared less, what became of the librarian. They hindered her instead of helped her, opposed her in every way and treated her like a mill operative. I have served time on a library board—out of a few librarians who have done so, and I *know* of this attitude personally. Let's kill it! ["Library"].

"[T]here are many libraries doing good work on 65 to 75 cents per capita; but judging from our own experience, it is done at a severe cost of over work and loss of health in the staff itself in the effort to do 'satisfactory' work on an inadequate budget," charges assistant Jennings. Another librarian wrote that she could "never ... see why the library should be the vestibule to the sanitarium for women..." ("Ill-Health"). Although she believed she knew the secret to preserving health, still she was conceding that the problem of employee distress was a real problem for the field in general. An assistant librarian begged for "statistics [from large libraries] showing how many employees had left, through ill-health, in ... ten years," hinting that "it might be a revelation as to some of the things that go on in large libraries that are not always put in the printed report" ("Will").

McReynolds claims that there "are no reliable statistics about the number of librarians ... who actually fell prey to nerves at the turn of the century, because the library community never made a studied effort to determine the true severity of the problem" ("Sexual" 204). Librarians noted the problem in their writings, but the "lowest-paid desk assistants," she contends, offered "the most emotional testimony about feminine delicacy," sometimes in letters, sometimes in articles, "insist[ing] that breakdowns were precipitated by unpleasant working conditions" ("Sexual" 206). Mary Baker protested,

> In too many libraries she [the cataloger] finds herself seated for seven or eight hours a day, six days in the week, in a poorly lighted room, so crowded that she never ceases to be conscious of her neighbor's movements.... In other places, even where she reigns alone, the conditions are as bad [M. Baker 139].

The field always called for young girls "in good health," and then proceeded to destroy it. For instance, Hitchler named good health as one of the "main requisites" for a desk attendant, noting that, "the higher and more responsible the position she fills [and we have seen that the position of the desk attendant was seen as a responsible one indeed] the greater is the loss from ill-health and the lack of endurance" ("Successful" 555). McMillan (or Macmillan, depending upon the journal), in her treatise upon ill-health among library workers, criticized disingenuous job applicants for not being more candid about their physical frailties: "[T]hey probably do not consider their weak backs, delicate stomachs, headaches, heart trouble, and a dozen other ills that feminine flesh is heir to, as disabilities" (412). She queries, "[I]s it not better to make sure of a woman's good health before you engage her?" (413).

McReynolds seems to believe that "American nervousness," or "neurasthenia," as it was then called, in library workers may have been more the result of cultural conditioning than of workplace conditions, but I believe we must take the many concerned contemporaneous commentators at their word (McReynolds, "Sexual" 194–5). If we do so, noting the long hours, the lack of sufficient breaks and job rotation in most libraries, the ubiquitously low salaries, the monotony of the work, the number of libraries operating under the closed-stacks system, the degree of stuffiness or crowdedness of library buildings, the lack of prospects for most women library workers, the inevitable breakdown of idealism over time in very many of these library pioneers, and even the kind and amount of clothing then worn, I believe we will, first, accord these quite articulate and sentient people the respect due them, and second, arrive at a much more accurate picture of the health profile of women library workers of the early twentieth century. The testimony on the subject of library workers' health and the adverse conditions extant in their workplaces is enormous.

First, one must understand that most assistants were young women, to grasp that the abuses suffered by them at work must have been severe. Women over the age of thirty-five were discouraged from "the work": "They should be between 18 and 30 years of age" (Bailey 173; M. Freeman 80).* Problems

---

*Even Williamson, in 1923, was writing, "[A]pplicants must be at least twenty-one years of age and not over thirty-five," though he allowed that it was possible that some elderly over–35s could grasp the nuances of library work ([26]). A notice for a federal civil service examination in 1915 indicated that the acceptable age range for applicants was from 18 to 40 ("U. S. Civil" 364).

ranged from lethargy to chronic fatigue to death. One anonymous library functionary reported, "I know of one recent death which was caused, I have reason to believe, by requirements imposed by the librarian" ("Library Assistants: Shortcomings" 350). More than a death: a sacrifice to parsimony, and foolish and unrealistic ideals.

Library assistants and librarians need to be viewed in a larger context than the library field. In many places in nineteenth-century America, 60 hours was the legal work week. Some workers, in occupations other than library work, worked longer than 60 hours per week (Wright 50, 52; Wertheimer 239, 275). By 1906, in Massachusetts and New York, at least, laws had passed restricting the hours per week women could work (58 in Massachusetts; 60 in New York) (Wald 640/178). Women either lived at home, because of low wages, or lived in squalor independently. And very frequently, like library employees, their health diminished because of the nature of their work (Wright 63, 65–75). Library workers, while performing "spiritual," rather than "material," work, nonetheless in the most extreme instances were in fact living lives very like those of their sister blue-collar workers (Henry, "Salary" 121; Wright).

Seen in this general context, library workers were not working obscenely long hours—in most cases between 40 and 50 hours per week—but they were still working more hours than employees today would find comfortable, hours that unions became famous for reducing, and hours which promoted ill health regardless of the field in which they obtained. When that Everyman—or rather, Everywoman—of the library world, the "Desk Assistant," declares that workers like herself toil "on an average from 42 to 50 hours a week in service to the library" and make on average "$25 to $40 a month," she was certainly not exaggerating (Herself 876). She speaks of working an eight- or nine-hour day, of putting in one to three evenings a week, with frequent Sunday work. Figures reported in the *Pratt Institute Monthly* in 1899 gave hours per week for library-school graduates as 24 to 54, with 42½ the average ("Salaries" 482). Even longer hours than these are suggested in an indignant letter written to *Public Libraries* as late as 1920, when loss of workers had already become an epidemic:

> [C]ommon sense will forbid [the librarian] to work a twelve-hour day.... [I]n this matter of working conditions we owe it to our younger or less fortunate sisters to insist on reasonable hours and salaries.... It is not fair to the little girl starting in the work, to teach her that there is virtue in overtime routine, or labor that is physically too heavy. She is not in a position to protest, but we are [Rocky 186–7].

The ALA conducted a survey in 1910 among 137 libraries, and found library workers putting in a 40- to 50-hour week, "a reduction of between five and ten hours from 1900" (McReynolds, "Sexual" 209). Not for nothing did Julia Pettee refer to "the dim underworld of the assistant" (585).

An additional difficulty, found the "Desk Assistant," was the way time

was scheduled: "[The assistants'] time schedule varies on different days according to whether or not night work is required"; often they worked seven hours
in a row with no break for supper. She observed crisply, "[T]he assistant is 'not
supposed' to eat between morning and night" (Herself 876). She complained
that work hours often alternated a long day with a short, and that women working late one night might be asked to work all day the following day, thus

> great irregularity of hours is entailed. It is this constant irregularity, and partic-
> ularly the irregularity of meal periods, that is the desk assistant's most serious trial.
> The discomfort is not merely because she is obliged twice or three times a week
> to snatch a hurried and generally cold supper ... though every one who spends a
> day of tiring work knows that a hot and leisurely dinner at the end of it is an actual
> necessity; but it is because the hours of the meals are constantly changing. Eat-
> ing to-day at one time and to-morrow at another is a physical evil; let it but con-
> tinue long enough and health is seriously undermined. Many ... desk assistants
> in normal health have been reduced to a critical physical condition and years of
> ill health as a direct result of the hours imposed on them. It is pertinent here to
> quote ... a physician in the course of a conversation on "library hours"[:]"...There
> is nothing so conducive to a disarrangement of the entire organization as irreg-
> ularity both as regards hours and eating. When these two evils coexist the result
> is rapid, and the victim is soon forced to abandon the work or take a prolonged
> rest, with a foundation laid for lifelong invalidism" [Herself 877].

Stacks were usually "closed" in the early years of libraries, so, in addition to
long hours and little time to eat, the constant running back and forth ground
even the fittest worker to a nub of her former self and must be factored in as
a contributing cause of this "lifelong invalidism." And even when not required
to run back and forth, books in hand, many assistants were required to stand
for hours (Traveler; *Pratt*, "Some" 93). Testimony corroborating these accusations is sprinkled abundantly throughout the early literature. McMillan sums
up the catalog of factors contributing to women library workers' ill health:

> Last winter was a very trying one to most libraries; an unusual number of assis-
> tants were absent on account of illnesses, and, as a consequence, we began to ask
> ourselves if the pity often bestowed upon us by our friends outside the library field
> had not some foundation, whereas before this we had scorned their prophecies of
> an early grave. We questioned one another as to the various causes that might lead
> to illness. Some said long hours; others, night work, irregular meals, not enough
> people to share the work, Sunday work in addition to the rest of the week, great
> responsibility and not enough pay, the constant strain of being before an unap-
> preciative public; and all agreed that we do not get fresh air enough. Some thought
> too much study was required of us outside library hours; some reprehensibly
> light-hearted, or light-headed, ones thought we had not enough time for amuse-
> ment [412].

Great toil over long hours was certainly one of the biggest culprits. Dana
wrote of young women cutting "the pages of six or seven hundred volumes in
a week's time of 40 to 50 hours" (246). "J. F." complained, "[M]edical books

are very heavy and 40,000 shelved in a week very nearly killed me" (467). A poetaster notes the requirement of "catalog[ing] and classify[ing] at the top notch of speed, And rush[ing] thru tons of books an hour"; the short-sighted administrator "only want[s] the total done to mount up higher and higher" (York State 259). "For a salary varying from $300 to $900 annually," wrote Dee Garrison, "a library assistant had to write steadily six or seven hours a day, ... [and] be absolutely accurate in copying" (*Apostles* 182). One clerk in 1889 accessioned over 8,500 volumes in two months, working in a library where 50-plus hours a week was the norm ("Female").

J. F. cries,

> "Men have died and worms have eaten them—but not for love" and so have lady librarians—but not from overzealousness, not for love of the job, not from this overworked missionary spirit, but from mere enforced exhaustion.... All the excessive effort I have ever seen put forth in libraries, and I have been working in them since I was 14, was for the sole end and aim of making a living wage and later in a vain effort to save something.... Nearly all the women I have known were well educated, worked harder than any man and were paid like day laborers without the privilege of striking. And as for the system that compels me to work 12 hours a day, that too is selfishness ... [466].

A *Public Libraries* contributor, signing herself pointedly "Ex-Librarian," testifies, as late as 1917, that the Evanston, Ill., Public Library had increased hours of service for its workers from 41 to 45 hours a week. She included a little survey of 26 miscellaneous public and university libraries from all over the country and their hours of work, finding, from a range of 38 to 45 hours, an average of 41.5 hours per week required of workers in these places ("Hours"). Freeman set the average number of hours per week at 42 ("Conditions" 80). Rathbone, in 1914, reported a range of less than 40 hours per week to more than 42 hours, with an average of 40½ ("Salaries" 189). The New York Public Library up to 1916 required 40–42 hours per week from employees, but when a medical inspector reviewed working conditions, he recommended no more than 40 hours per week, year-round ("Reading" 273). More hours per week than 40 were those which impelled library workers to vociferate in letter columns, to wit:

> A 45 hours a week schedule, much of it being evening and Sunday work in outlying sections of the city (often necessarily a considerable distance from the homes of the workers), leaves very little time or strength for cultural reading, or lectures, or other pursuits really important and needed by persons engaged in library work. I know librarians are expected to keep informed on current events, and the best new things published on all subjects at first hand, but they are so occupied by the immediate demands of the public and the details of administration ... that they haven't time.... Persons employed all day, every day of the week, in the exhaustive mental work of the library..., need one-half day a week for purposes which cannot or should not be attended to on Sundays or evenings. Can't we be library

workers and human beings at the same time? ... I know I am stronger than the average library worker, and I get completely discouraged sometimes because I can find no time to read (if I eat and sleep), and I do almost nothing socially, for I haven't time or strength for anything outside of my work [Assistant, "Progressive"].

One librarian was found working 65 hours a week. She made a mere $45 a month and had been working at this pace for nine years. "This is outlandish," exclaimed the observer ("Reading" 272–3). Mary Ahern indignantly covered a specially convened meeting in Pennsylvania in her editorial column which was "called to grant a leave of absence for two weeks to a librarian who had continuously served for nearly nineteen years, and during that time had taken only four vacations of more than one day's duration. It is not to be wondered that the present leave of absence, the longest she has ever had, is asked on for account of ill-health" ("Refined" 106). Not surprisingly, she titled her piece "Refined Cruelty."

"Over-tired librarians cannot turn off work or meet people as they should," insisted Corinne Bacon in 1913. "After many years of experience in various lines of library work, on schedules varying from 38 to 48 hours, I believe that more work, and that of a better quality, will be done by a conscientious assistant in 40, or at the most 42 hours a week, than on a longer schedule" ("Library" 50). "[A] working day of too great length weakens the character of the work," asseverates the relentless Desk Assistant; "It is almost impossible for the assistant not to become narrow when her 'library time' is practically all her time" (Herself 877). "No institution should so use the energies of normal healthy people as to leave no margin of time and strength for legitimate growth and development outside the day's work," directed Rathbone ("Opportunity" 336). The Desk Assistant remarks slightingly upon "the general tendency to regard assistants' time schedules simply as problems in arithmetic, unrelated to the human constitution" and "the librarian's accepted hypothesis that the desk assistant has no requirements apart from her work in his library, to which she must gradually sacrifice strength and health and social life" (Herself 876, 878). "[P]rofessional common sense must draw the line at demands which drain ... the strength and vitality of the average worker," urged Pettee;

[a] devotion or supposed necessity which permits sacrifices which seriously impair the worker only tend [sic] to lower the standards of the profession.... [T]he librarian imposing such conditions on his staff that the death of an assistant could in the remotest way be attributable to these conditions is an impossible one [586, 585].

In 1914, a quite extensive survey of salaries, hours, and vacations was made in Indiana, the surveyor finding that hours per week "vary from 20 to 70 hours." With prim understatement the author pronounced, "70 hours per week is more than she [the library worker] should be required to serve"

("Salaries, ... Indiana Libraries" 197). McReynolds claimed that some libraries even exacted "in excess of seventy-five hours a week" ("Sexual" 207).

What then, of the hours remaining to the hapless library employee outside of work? Did the exhausted worker get to rest? Why, no. "[T]he physical strength of most women gives out under the double strain of work in the library and work at home," concluded one report ("Speaking"). McMillan agreed that "if [assistants] attempt to assist at home they are not fit to do a day's work at the library" (414). Nor was work in the library and at home all the work an assistant would undertake. Some commonly took on extra work, since salaries in libraries did not pay a living wage. One woman mentions typewriting and translating; other assistants cooked and sewed ("Other Compensations" 431; "Speaking"). Many male librarians responded to this grim necessity, of women working at a second job over and above a 45–70 hour week, with high-handed paternalism. One commented, apropos "free time": "[T]here undoubtedly is accruing to each of us ... today ... a great *unearned increment* [emphasis added] of time over and above that which is consumed in our necessary pursuits..." (Roden 493). Was free time somehow morally reprehensible, being "unearned"? Rathbone wrote a strong article advocating the pursuit of interests outside work which could all be brought to bear positively on the business of library work, pastimes which would forward each worker's "book knowledge" ("Some"). Another remarked that library workers "may not live irresponsible lives at any time, ... with ministers, doctors, teachers and welfare workers, they may not conscientiously close their minds to their work when they close their desks at night. Workers in educational and ethical fields are marked people in their communities and there are activities ... which may be taboo to them" (Hadley, "Outside" 1). "The outside world must not absorb her," stated Dana categorically of the desk assistant; he believed she must spend all her time after working hours reading (250).

More than one head librarian took it upon himself to curtail the careers of library workers who dared to work at second jobs, arguing that if he deemed that outside work was affecting the quality of work in the library, "[I]t is certainly within the library's province to demand that you give up either your outside work or your library work..." ("Desk" 252–3). In vain the overworked clerk would cry out, "This seems rather a hard doctrine, since I must live and you do not provide me with the proper means of support at a salary of $35 or $40 per month" ("Desk" 253). The delivery-clerk, mandated Caroline Hewins, "must be willing to work eight or ten hours a day, give up most or all of her evenings and know little or nothing of 'teas,' afternoon receptions, lectures, concerts, church sociables, or even week-day church services" (274). Cognizant of the burdens—both in and out of the regular library working day—upon assistants, "Head Librarian" sensibly urged, "[A] full day a week besides Sunday should belong to every library worker."

McReynolds concedes that in the early years of the twentieth century, a growing number of library administrators expressed alarm at the profusion of breakdowns among their staffs. Many librarians and assistants applied for long leaves of absence to recover their health. Even prominent members of the field were known to have lost their mental keenness, declining to the point of being "mere crank turners." Members of the Brooklyn Public Library Association were so concerned by the problem that in 1900 the organization proposed to build a seaside rest home for those who had broken down in library service.

The dilemma of nervous illness persisted and seemed to increase during the first decade of the twentieth century. In an address to the American Library Association's 1910 conference, Samuel Ranck ... declared that he could easily compile a list of fifty librarians who had disintegrated under the strain of their work. Many had never returned from their leaves of absence; others had died before their time. Ranck added that, although he could not prove it, he suspected that this state of affairs was worse among librarians than among other professional groups ["Sexual" 198].

She also notes that "Dewey's dream of the Lake Placid Club was built by weary librarians, since he not only encouraged them to vacation there, but to buy stock in the corporation as well" ("Sexual" 202).

Despite the fact that McReynolds' focus was more on the higher echelon of library worker—the many educators and female administrators who broke down under the strain of their workload—than on the rank-and-file worker, and despite her contention that "nervous" illness was to some degree expected of the female worker, the point is that, whatever the etiology of mental or physical breakdown among library workers, ill health was a real occupational hazard. People do not die from imaginary causes. People die because of very real "dis-ease." I think it is fair to suggest that the "neurasthenia" suffered by these early female working poor bears an uncanny resemblance to what today we call "Chronic Fatigue Syndrome," a form of total physical and psychological burnout, which is triggered, if not caused, by extreme stress or trauma. Perhaps lack of control over the circumstances of one's work was another irritant (McReynolds, "Sexual" 211).

To return to the requirement that the librarian be a "lady," it is worth suggesting that no *bona fide* lady was ever asked to slave; the essence of ladylikeness is leisure. How could the library field exact ladylike behavior from virtual lackeys? Perhaps the strain of the contrast between the pretense library workers were obliged to maintain about the gentility of their work and the actual factory-like reality of it caused collapse as well. And in point of fact, neurasthenia was found, in 1912, to be just as prevalent among industrial workers as among the more putatively "genteel" new women's professions ("Sexual" 210). Teachers suffered as much as librarians and library assistants.

McReynolds believes that "the victims of nerves probably never constituted more than a small minority of their professions since public schools and libraries would not have lasted long without a cadre of healthy women," but we have seen that the typical library recruit was a very young, healthy female, and that the field suffered from a surfeit of these extraneous women ("Sexual" 205). Even in 1886, one writer referred to "overcrowded clerkdom," noting that "the supply of this grade of help at low prices will always exceed the demand," a hubris in time to be smartly slapped down ("Library Employment" 51). Whenever there is this kind of over-abundance, management rejoices, because its laborers are "captive" (Oberg et al., "Role" 234) and can be worked to death from fear of losing their posts, and the workers who fall by the wayside are relatively unnoticed, since others quickly come to fill their shoes.

The library field was thus known not only for its low pay—then as today ranking in this respect palpably below teaching, to which it considered itself allied—but for the number of fallen workers it generated. To some extent, the two phenomena are related. Money buys a better quality of abode, better food, better ambiance, more privacy, more assurance that unexpected illness will not result in bankruptcy, reassurance that old age will not be a time of mendicancy and misery (most early library workers were totally without pension provisions)—in short, mental ease.* The many "sick," "hysterical," "nervous" women who worked in libraries at the turn of the century were in fact probably suffering from near-starvation, because their wages were insufficient to feed them properly (Biggs, "Librarians" 415). What of the news story Library of Congress archivist Knowlton unearthed in 1991, which headlined: "Library Workers Find Living Cost Exceeds Salaries"? *The Evening Star* reported that "Assistant College Graduate, Spends $47 More Than Her Pay for Year[.] Convention Will Hear Investigators' Report" (121).

Anyone who has ever lived close to the poverty line or stepped over it will comprehend that mental ease about money is no small thing. Try getting a good night's sleep when your bills exceed your income. The so-called "working poor" of today, among whom library assistants and clerks still number, can all eloquently testify as to their mental ease, or lack thereof, apropos of money worries.

"Low-grade help is often far from being economical," writes Bacon. "Tired assistants do not pay either" ("Library" 50). Frances Hawley describes burnout Victorian style:

> [T]here is a prolonged rush before which most of us falter, the long continued strain of too much to do. It comes upon us gradually. We can look back upon a

---

*Even by 1952, Bryan claimed more than half the libraries in her sample had no provisions for retirement or pensions, nor any health-care plans (113). She cited the case of an 87-year-old woman who "spends most of the working day in one of the Inquiry libraries sitting at a reading-room table, where very slowly, with hands crippled by arthritis, she cuts pictures from newspapers and magazines for the picture collection. The head librarian explains that because of her long years of service the Board permits this employee to go on working and continues to pay her tiny salary 'as a form of pension'" (100). How extraordinarily generous! Nor did this problem of no provision for old age abate until late in the century. Even today, it is bruited on Libsup–l that certain clerical workers lack pensions.

time when we handled our duties with ease, but they have grown faster than we, and we are at last forced to admit that they are getting the better of us. Little by little our work falls off in quality; where we once did fifty things well, we now do one hundred things poorly. Unable to keep up with our standards, we lose interest, we no longer drive our work but let it drive us. We plod on hopelessly, aimlessly, accomplishing less because of our state of mind than in the days when we had less need of accomplishment [361–2].

Concerned observers often couched the terms of their appeal to alleviate oppressive conditions of work in the argument that it simply didn't pay in the long run to work assistants to death: "Too many hours per day should not be allowed to work a hardship upon the employees. Too many consecutive hours depreciate the value of mental work, for with a constant strain one cannot always keep up to the standard that a library should try always to keep for its public" ("Reading" 272). By 1919, this issue was being discussed everywhere in the literature, because workers were streaming away from the field. Coverage of a conference in the Northwest included a segment on library assistants; as a sort of economic blackmail, Henry

mentioned as two of the sources of dissatisfaction with library work, the still inadequate salaries, and the working conditions of the assistants. He pointed out that night work, overtime and irregular schedules were unhealthy, discouraging and biologically wrong, and he maintained that library staffs will be limited in quality and quantity until better working and social conditions are devised. He broached the possibility of closing libraries at night as stores have been closed ["Pacific" 594].

In addition to hours of work, other working conditions contributing to ill-health were misplaced desire to please, lack of sick leave, and actual mode of dress. In an effort to measure up to the impossible standard of the "ideal desk assistant," workers often drove themselves beyond their limit, "go[ing] without ... breakfast rather than be late, and stay[ing] at [their] post until [they] faint[ed], rather than leave early" (Hawley, "Some" 360). Because of lack of sick pay, many workers kept themselves at their jobs because they simply could not afford to do without the salary. One writer, only known as "Anxious," recounts several instances of what became of workers unprovided for by an "emergency fund"; one of them gripes,

"I caught a fiendish cold, because of the insane method of heating the library. I am still barking, all because I would not give up and go to bed. I really couldn't afford such luxury and besides as a matter of principle, I would not forfeit one penny of my miserable wage to the library by remaining away when I was ill by reason of conditions which the management had created."

McReynolds notes that tight clothing was still being worn by girls enslaved by the old corseting custom ("Sexual" 195). Webber perceptively underscores the physical hardship even the expected weight of clothing caused library workers constrained by conventions of a more sedentary age. In Britain, the Rational Dress Society "campaigned for a radical reduction in the amount of clothing then considered decorous[, inviting] cries of libertinage by their proposal that the maximum weight of underclothing with shoes should not exceed seven pounds" (160). The field of library work and the cultural climate being so similar in both Britain and the United States, it is quite likely that the Rational Dress Society could have found much in the mode of women's dress in America to denounce. Salome Fairchild, herself hard-working but frail, wrote rather wistfully, obliquely condemning the oppressiveness of women's attire and societal expectations of female decorum, "It is quite probable that the physical handicap of women will be reduced as greater emphasis is placed on the importance of athletics and out-of-door life and sports for girls" (161).

To all the treacle and high-mindedness undertaken to direct the way for misguided desk assistants, Tessa Kelso snapped, in 1901:

> The fact is, you librarians do not mean what you say. You talk about the desk assistant being such an important part of the library, but do not treat her in that way. I have never yet seen, and in fact know of no library where the desk assistants are made to feel that they are the most important people. ... [T]he desk assistant [feels] she is but little better than an upper servant ["New York State Library Association..." 562]

An indignant commentator raged over the exhaustion callously generated by library work, "Some day industrial commissions are going to investigate these things. What gross violations of the labor laws—and of common humanity will the commission find in—what library?" (Traveler). In the end, it was the vaunted "library spirit" which came under attack:

> The words "library spirit" are used ofttimes glibly and thoughtlessly, and many claim it who have it not; but it is the "library" spirit that makes the underpaid and overworked librarian go and go and go, morning after morning, through storm, through headache and heartache to the appointed spot and do the appointed work and cheerfully stick to that work through eight or ten hours, long after rest would be so sweet [Stearns 71].

14. A Few Voices of Reason

Taking aim at the treacle were a number of clear voices. "I detect in myself some considerable impatience every time I hear the phrase 'missionary spirit' as applied to library work," insisted Matthew Dudgeon, who reasonably held that "[p]lacing the public's own books" before them was "no … more missionary" than "the act of the grocer clerk who sells the customer a package of breakfast food." He elaborated:

> Librarian and grocer alike are paid for doing these things. Both are in the feed business. He is feeding the body, the librarian is feeding the mind. He is not necessarily a generous minded, benevolent individual performing a virtuous but superfluous act when he is doing simply what he is hired to do. Neither is the librarian. I have also a mental antipathy toward the phrase "missionary spirit" for another reason. The phrase implies that one, ranking himself a superior, reaches down from some lofty position and serves in a self-complacent way some benighted individual below him in race or station. The librarian who takes that attitude is lost. When she feels that she has become an "uplifter" ready to "uplift" the lowly, ignorant persons around her, her usefulness is at an end. What we as librarians must do is to quit cultivating a sentimental spirit towards our duties [247–8].

Though the change in person gender mid-speech is intriguing and invites a tart comment, the point is well taken. Librarianship might have attained a more dignified, more worldly status had more practitioners heeded his words. Sentimentality masked—and was intended to mask—the raw hard work of library employment for most assistants. The aforementioned "spurious gentility" was constantly spread before these presumably "spiritual" laborers to gloss over rampant exploitation; it also contributed an unseemly snobbishness to library work. Dudgeon believed not in uplifting patrons, but in giving working folk what they wanted, since in time these gratified individuals would secure a better appropriation for the library. For Dudgeon, unsentimental service remitted to all members of the community—not just those in need of intellectual "salvation"—was simply a wise economic move, a case of enlightened self-interest (251).

The early emphasis on fanatic service still haunts us today, sabotaging the

111

public understanding of library workers as professionals worthy of respect. Instead the public often seems to view them as a species of punching bag. In the early days of the field, "missionary"—style service placed assistants in an awkward catch–22. "[T]he present tendency of our public libraries is to help people too much for their own good," stated Bacon, debunking the necessity of too-bumptious service at the horseshoe desk.

> We know her [the desk assistant]—as an ideal. Many of us have tried to realize her in the flesh. Lecturers chanted the catalog of her virtues (and it was a long one!) to us in our library school days. Speakers at library meetings have contin-ued to chant them…. Well, the mission of this omniscient creature with the tem-per of a saint who serves, or should serve, in our libraries is to please by helping the reader to whatever he or she may want, whether the knowledge be useful or useless, and in the way that calls for the least exertion on that reader's part. Her aim is to get between the book and the reader, to become a sort of private secre-tary or tutor, or a cross between the two. She seeks to do for the reader what some readers do wish and what more of them ought to wish to do for themselves…. [She] look[s] upon an inquirer as a kind of militant suffragette who must be forcibly fed whether or no ["Present" 241–2].

The earliest proponents of the public library were stern women and men who envisioned libraries as the "people's university," a far cry from a book-filled cathedral; its center was its books; people who entered the library were seen to be in quest of knowledge, not foot-washing, not intellectual proselytizing. This may seem like a fine distinction, and it is. Desk assistants *were* required to be preternaturally informed about every realm of book-knowledge (Mar-cum 96), but how zealous did they really need to be?

Bacon quotes Lee as he writhes before the Ideal Desk Assistants' "inde-fatigable unobtrusiveness, their kindly, faithful service I both dread and appre-ciate." She puts before her audience his consternation as he believes himself alone, browsing the collection, "only to find a librarian's assistant standing there wondering at him, looking down to the bottom of his soul." "One feels a kind of literary detective system going silently on in and out, all around one, a polite, absent-minded-looking watchfulness," he shudders ("Present" 246). She argues that such omnicompetence "irritates the readers who prefer to help themselves, while it dulls the minds and saps the energy of those who are will-ing to be helped" (*ibid.* 247).

One can imagine the kind of pressure this and its opposing view put upon the assistant, who must then, Hamlet-fashion, be constantly querying herself over and over whether to help or not to help. Administration's enforcement of a monastic model of service, complete with hair shirt and self-flogging device, in the interests of saving a penny, was really the imperative behind assistants' desperate hyper-helpfulness and a whole host of other unnecessarily introduced sources of worker insecurity and stress, and initiated the exodus of the field's most gifted workers. An early proponent of bibliographic instruction, the clear-eyed Bacon urged that librarians and assistants help patrons to become educated in use of the library. She scowled upon encouraging patrons "to lean entirely on us in the matter of references…" ("Present" 244). She believed library workers belittled adults' and stunted children's intelligence when they did everything for them, a view not widely enough held in her day, when closed stacks were much more a matter of course, and open stacks seen as an invitation to anarchy. "Great scholarship is a wonderful thing to possess, but it is really not essential, or altogether compatible with successful library work," pronounced Mary Black (surprisingly, for she otherwise swallowed the standard library line in toto); in fact, she sensibly points out, "[t]he librarian's duty is to know where to find information; it is not to carry it around in her own head" (201, 200). Further, "C. B. R." remonstrated, an acid counterpoint to Dana's "read, read, read, and forever read" dictum, that

> Miss Hazeltine's thoughtful plea to library assistants for more reading and a closer acquaintance with books for their own sake impels the observation that our good mentors do not always bear in mind that our daily task and common round is all with books, about books, of, by and through books and that it might be possible, in carrying books with us into our playtime, to carry them too far ["Papers" 420].

Sarah Askew, in "Library Heresies," questioned the requirement that librarians must smile all the time. In the interest of restoring perspective to the field, she broached the notion "If we find we have to change our personality to fit our work, don't let's do it. Let's change our work" (195). "Don't let's smile unless we feel like smiling, because while a genuine smile is very present help in the time of need, the forced smile is an abomination unto the public" (195). She, like Bacon, also skewered the field's exaggerated sense of mission; she propounded the

> arch heresy that librarians are the best fitted persons to undertake every job in the town, and that sometimes in doing so they even neglect the job they are hired to do, which is to furnish the people of their community with books and answer questions and do research work. Remember! Oh remember, that when you rush into playgrounds, civic work, women's clubs, teaching history to the schools, chair caning to the boys, sewing to the girls, manners to the tramps, politics to the politician, and civics to the town council, some day, the goblin of politics is going to "git you if you don't watch out," and prove you have forgotten that the man who butts in is cut down in his prime. Remember also that your successor may wonder why the books aren't in better order and … why that store room is in such a dreadful muss and why you didn't do some library work while you were resting from other more important tasks … [194].

Another issue early reasonable and fair-minded commentators stressed was according workers public acknowledgment of their efforts and accomplishments; they attacked the field's attempt to bilk library assistants of the credit due them for arranging conferences, writing reports, putting together bibliographies—in general, for being the powers behind the throne. They disliked the general effort to erase features, to keep lower-echelon workers anonymous, to deny assistants prominence under their own names and in the flesh. "Visitor" craved appreciation for the "assistant librarian" who, after doing as much of the work of preparing for annual meetings as her boss, is

> [u]sually standing round in some corner, a sort of outcast at the feast which she herself had helped to prepare. I should like to ask if this is quite fair...? ... Should she not by rights stand at her librarian's side where she stands so faithfully when there is work to be done? ... Are librarians selfish in this respect, or is it that they are only a little thoughtless of what is due their fellow worker?

One assistant librarian grieved that her library director gave her much responsibility but that whenever there was a gathering in honor of something, she was off-handedly told to "sit anywhere," rather than with other movers and shakers. She was very upset that "this institution will not give the office of librarian to a woman, and seldom gave official recognition to [her] predecessor, who most acceptably acted as librarian the last years of her service." In the end, unable to come to terms with anonymity, she indignantly frames a letter to the president of her college asking that "the person holding the position of assistant or acting librarian ... be assigned a seat in the body of the chapel, ... wear the academic gown ... and ... receive equal recognition at ... official gatherings," a request which was granted (Librarian, "Like").

Another critic boldly attacked the practice of withholding information on library workers' educational credentials from reports:

> Why do not library reports give credit of degrees, professional training, etc., to staff members, as do reports of other educational institutions? ... Will not this "honorable mention" react with credit on the general welfare of the library? Will it not help in solving the question of promotion on merit, be an incentive to assistants and those about to enter library work and at the same time show the public that the library as an educational institution has educated people on its staff? [Morse].

As we have seen, librarians often had assistants writing reports and compiling bibliographies, but usually, though impatient with their assistants for tiny errors, they took the credit for the finished work themselves. An anonymous assistant attacked this practice and this type of librarian obliquely: "Mr. Bookworm ... compiled a catalog.... The work was greatly praised, and though rumor spoke of an assistant and a stranger who haunted the library for two years before the volume's appearance, and who were said to be cataloging books—still only the librarian's name appears on the title page, so that rumor must be wrong again" (Anonymous, "A Librarian"). Another "anonymous assistant" attacked more directly:

The library assistant, through sheer force of tradition, hides her light under the librarian's bushel. Anonymity is the Immemorial usage in library economy, ... depriving an able assistant of the credit and position which is her due.... It is the silent subjugation of the assistant that restrains her from attaining her honest, appropriate level.... [T]here is a library which is especially noted for its bureau of information; and yet, although this work has been done by the same woman for the past 10 years, she remains anonymous both in and outside of her own city; her name is not found in any of the library's annual reports, nor is that of any of her associates.... Our best catalog of children's books bears upon its title-page, "Prepared by the State Superintendent"; while nowhere within its pages is found the name of the real author—the superintendent's *assistant*—who devoted months of thought to its preparation.... What possible harm could have come from placing the name of the painstaking cataloger, in modest type, on the title-page? The advantage of such an omission is surely for the man or men at the head of the institution or for the institution itself. When a woman tells us of the sleepless hours spent in worry while the sheets were going through the press, we can never believe the general supposition that a catalog is the "emanation of a corporation."

Contrast this with the experience of an assistant who prepared a reference list on an important topic, and who requested her superior officer to place her name on the title-page—little realizing that the fame of the pamphlet would extend to the executive circles of Russia and be the means, indirectly, of securing the compiler the offer of a position of distinguished honor.

Anonymous library literature ... such as catalogs, reference lists, etc., or work in some special direction, offers almost no hope to one who is ambitious for making a name for herself. The publication of the name would give to every assistant the same chance of personal distinction.

[T]he assistants who are *themselves* could be counted on the fingers of one hand. Library assistants are regarded as mere integrants of a library; "nameless shadows" [One, "The Anonymous..."].

This "anonymous assistant" is rebuked by yet another anonymous assistant, who sniped, "I haven't much opinion of the candle which doesn't burn the bushel" (One Who Has Been There, "The Assistant..."). Even Mary Ahern, so often co-opted by library establishment beliefs, on the issue of giving credit where credit was due, stated, "There is no good reason why the names of staff should not be included in the many reports from which they are omitted" (Ahern, "Where"). Yet today most bibliographies are still anonymous, and many libraries frown upon allowing librarians to take credit for brochures, publications, and reports they write.

Arthur Bostwick, who was in his later years to pen an iniquitous article equating library workers with bits of machinery, as a younger man criticized the library administrator who enforced anonymity on aspiring assistants, speculating, "Dull, routine administrators, who do not appreciate ideas, or are jealous of subordinates who advance them, linger still among librarians ... ("Internal" 57). "Invite the confidence of every member of the staff," urged Adam Strohm,

welcome suggestions, allow your assistants to voice the conclusions their experience and service bring home to them, listen with sympathy to suggestions
prompted by loyalty and daily pondering. There are times when we may well forget our official gradings, when it will prove profitable to learn from the members
of the crew how our theories stand the test ["Efficiency" 304].

In 1916, an anonymous assistant came up with the radical idea of forming a conference for assistants during which they could critique their bosses,
the librarians, and discuss flaws in the library system. "By all my hopes of
advancement," she exclaimed, "that would be a lively meeting!" She envisioned
assistants compiling lists of questions that pertained to the conduct of head
librarians, for example: "Does she know as much as you do about actual working conditions, by meeting the public at the desk, and does she welcome suggestions from assistants? ... Does she boss or do you all pull together, the
Librarian looking ahead, directing and guiding and inspiring the best in you?
... [Does she] draw an increasingly princely salary; while yours remains stationary...? ("From This Angle"). "Anonymous" may have been kidding about
this "conference of assistants," but she was prescient. Today assistants do hold
conferences, and discuss many of the items on her list.
      Hand in hand with the ideal of near-"religious" service to the patron—
which guided the harried assistant to overextend herself to patrons, believe she
must encompass all knowledge within her own head, and embrace anonymity
rather than recognition for her work—came masochism as the standard of
conduct to which young women in library work must aspire. This masochism
was criticized in its time, now and then, but seldom flouted, from assistants'
fear of being let go. An anonymous assistant pleaded with her superior:

> Bad temper is a luxury not permitted to the assistant. It has been justly held that
> he must endure the vagaries of readers and the peculiarly irritating remarks of
> self-constituted critics, as if he liked them and received them as a kind of
> perquisite.... Yet might I put up a plea that librarians would not forget that we
> juniors are human. They can remember, most of them, the many times when a
> harassing question, an idle lounger, or an impertinent critic has severely tried their
> good nature. They may remember that the end of a long day is not a favorable
> time for a test of courtesy. Above all, may they remember these things when they
> learn from an aggrieved reader that the assistant has turned and rent him ...
> [Anonymous, "A Librarian"].

Frank Hill, also, though in many ways a prototypical patriarch, postulated, "It
... goes without saying that [the librarian] should stand between his assistants
and unfounded complaints or unreasonable criticism from the public" (383).
      The more down-to-earth library founders did not see the library as a
"sanctuary" for every person with a derangement of character, nor as a charitable institution designed to solve a vast array of social problems, other than
to supply a civilizing influence in the form of books to an emerging American

culture. They thought the standard required of the desk assistant was both stringent and ridiculous. Dudgeon, Bacon, and Askew sought to apply a brake to the more exalted of Libraryland's flights. For them, the library's ultimate aspiration was simply to become an educational institution, the equal of the public school; to raise the sights of the American people, rich or poor; not to amuse, nor to perform psychiatric, religious, or theater functions. Even fiction, being presumably too frivolous, came under the hammer again and again as librarianship developed. Communities were urged to fund their libraries; learning was seen as a civic virtue and the presence of a library as a source of pride. Library staff members were supposed to be attending to the intellectual health of the country, pure and simple—not defending themselves, not worrying about starving and penniless old age, not pandering to sociopaths, not abasing themselves. Yet not so long ago, Clara Jones rebuked the field in no uncertain terms: "The word 'missionary' in the charge against public librarians implies self-imposed martyrdom, lack of sensible concern for worldly rewards and an aura of abject humility—the old image of the religious missionary" (18). The unattractive ideal of religious service in library work is chiefly to blame for many of the modern public library's besetting ills, from funding problems to patron violence; it was also the impetus for career change, in the early twentieth century, that drove the most clever workers from libraries into private industry.

We feel the curse of the library missionary spirit most in our interface with rude patrons who charge us with being their "servants" and with library abusers—like the homeless who use the library as a doss house and irresponsible parents who use it as a dumping ground for children—who debase the chief purpose the American public library was created to uphold, i.e., simple efficient provision of reading material and information to the public. We feel it whenever administrators tell us our job is to submit to any rudeness the public metes out to us.

Early library commentators pointed to tendencies which would in time hamstring the profession: the excessive missionary zeal combined with ridiculous passivity; the flamboyant insistence upon Godlike scholarship, coupled with ludicrous pay scales for same; the acquiescence to extreme hierarchy and a conditioning towards anonymity (the worker as "cog"). They also spoke up for the rights and creativities of the group that then was called assistants and today would be called support staff. They were harbingers of participatory management. They counseled a pragmatic view of library work, not the treacle which dominated the thinking of those library leaders who sought, more than to usher in fairness and decent salary scales, to focus the sights of the hapless desk assistant on humble and bogus expectations, in the interest of maintaining libraries "at the least cost."

Above all, there was no shortage of people who defended the experiential path to professionalism. Theresa Hitchler carefully listed the pro and con arguments in the library education debate, but she is very clear, at the beginning of her discussion, on one thing:

> [T]he disadvantages of lack of training may in due time, and by some individuals, be overcome and practically neutralized.... The deciding factor which enters into any discussion on the relative merits of training and experience is one which is not sufficiently considered. This is that *the individual* in either case and at all times must be taken into account.... [I]t must be borne in mind that the pioneers of the profession, among whom we number many of our greatest organizers and administrators, the men and women who have *made* the profession, had attained some degree of power with reputations well established, before library schools came into existence ["Library" 931].

These few voices of reason, had they been heeded, would have brought common sense and pragmatism to library work. Providing people with reading material, after all, is not so unlike the grocer supplying shoppers with food—neither occupation is more important than the other. One can be happy doing both, because one is doing something manifestly real and useful. But one does not need to be a fool over one's work, or be made a fool of. If these people had been heeded, the bombastic sentimentality would have fallen away; the field would have leveled its sights on attaining real wages for real intellectual accomplishments; and sexism, in its maudlin late nineteenth century form of "woman as mother and ministrator" (rather than as *ad*ministrator), would have been healthily shed.

The lack of attention to voices of reason and the huge salary problem brought the field to its knees for decades following the First World War. Libraries increasingly suffered from substandard help and a lack of ability to recruit that resulted in the 100,000-plus shortage of librarians in the 1960s, when the field struggled to rally. The pitifulness of library workers in the '20s, '30s, '40s, and '50s was limned in 1923 by Franklin Hopper and others, who wrote, unsparingly,

> If library work can be made so attractive that a sufficient number of persons of equal ability as those entering other vocations are ready to come into the library profession, well and good.... That we are doing this today, certainly no one will maintain.... No matter how delightful we may think our work, certainly it is not sufficiently attractive to gain for the profession at present salary standards a sufficient number of well qualified persons. At the present time there are being taken into the service:
> (1) Some, all too few, who are really fitted for library work.
> (2) Many who are young, without adequate preliminary education, and library training. Many of these, fortunately, drop out. Their work is never satisfactory, and the weakest of them are likely to hang on because they can get more in library work than they could elsewhere. They are the problem of every librarian. Often when a promotion is to be made for a higher position, there is no one to promote because we did not get the right material at the beginning.

(3) Many come into library work on a purely temporary basis because they want something to do and library work will do as well as anything else for the time being. Such assistants come and go. Every day there is a new one appointed for one resigning, whose length of service is numbered in days rather than months or years. The cost of labor turn-over in library service would make a report in itself. That it is tremendous cannot be gainsaid [A.L.A. Salaries Committee 67].

15. The "Dewey to Williamson" Period: Education for Librarianship in the Pioneering Years, 1887–1923

Sarah Vann calls "the era of library training prior to 1923 ... the 'Dewey to Williamson' period," which, though bowing to Western history's habit of breaking a continuum into discrete bites for easier digestion, is accurate enough in discussing early library training (190). Both Dewey and Williamson possessed considerable force and tenacity of character and made themselves omnipresent in the library world, and each published and promoted his ideas without stint. Each enjoyed, in short, influence. Though Dewey was a genuine dynamo of an innovator, the Williamson Report "was viewed, at the time of its publication," states Vann, "as a discussion of 'mostly matters of open record or common knowledge'" (1). It was simply Williamson's energy in bringing all this discussion into tight focus, and the fact that he worked under the aegis of the Carnegie Corporation, whose money had been spent and would continue to be spent on library-related matters—if only they were to become worthy of further financing—that gave his report its clout.

Melvil Dewey, who could not abide disorder in a grouping of any kind—from the goods in his father's store to a collection of books—burst onto the infant American library scene in 1873 with his scheme for organizing reading material at Amherst. He founded the first library schools at Columbia in New York and, after alienating the Board of Regents and the trustees of Columbia, in Albany, 1883–1887, at the New York State Library. The courses he drew up at Columbia were "pragmatic and based on the routine of a working librarian, involving typical activities both technical and clerical" (A. Elliott 668). The training he pioneered during the first two years of Columbia's library school experiment began as a twelve-week lecture circuit with intensive practice in cataloging and classification, accessioning, and card generation, conjoined with tours to libraries and printing presses in the vicinity. From this evolved an understanding that students might need up to three years of schooling to perform as administrators and jacks-of-all-trades in the libraries of the day. He advocated thorough knowledge of library materials and their costs, and routinized all library tasks so minutely that the steps involved were actually numbered. Librarians of the day were mere purveyors of male establishment, European-derived knowledge. Stacks in most libraries were closed (hence the need for all those highly qualified desk assistants who collapsed from exhaustion in the course of running back and forth), and effective card catalogs did not exist (Wiegand 102–5; Miksa 259–60). Consequently, prospective librarians—the frazzled assistants we have met—needed to memorize a mass of bibliographic data to purvey to library patrons the extent of the resources open to them in the library.

Miksa sums up Dewey's curriculum as follows: "In terms of the transcriptions available, about one-third of the library economy lectures over the two years were devoted to libraries as administrative units, just over one-half to library processes, and the remainder to buildings and equipment" (257). Already it was clear that librarians would be doing all manner of work, albeit not of the most exalted order, and that professionalism resided more in coordinating a vast number of tiny, draining tasks into a functioning whole than in impressing anyone with the intellectualism involved in performing each one. "Dewey emphasized that the aim of the training was practical[;] ... practicality was to be measured by one's ability to have a successful career in the library profession" (Vann 31). "Men full of the library spirit" would teach students of "sufficient natural fitness, ability and education" (Vann 23, 32).

The Columbia School of Library Economy opened with a class of twenty—three men and seventeen women (A. Elliott insists there were twenty-six, nineteen of whom were women [668]) (Vann 39). The Board of Regents opposed women entering the precincts of Columbia, but had they not registered, there would have been only three students to teach, and library education would have had an entirely different history, since the program would have died from insufficient enrollment. Vann asseverates:

> [T]he anomaly is that women, in their ready acceptance of formal training, were largely responsible for the continuation of the first formal training program and others which were to be developed afterward. Furthermore, had college graduation been made a prerequisite for admission, only five of the twenty could have been admitted and all five would have been women ... [39].

Dewey envisioned library work as a women's field (A. Elliott 668–9). His very first library classes, containing these fearless and ambitious women, whom he maneuvered into classrooms past the admissions boards of this hitherto male bastion to the horror of the school, ran a mere four months (Bohannon 216).

By the end of 1888 he was forced to leave Columbia because of the implementation of this vision, and moved thence to Albany, to start the school there. First, however, in conjunction with F. A. P. Barnard and others—among them, oddly enough in light of Dewey's anti–Semitism, one Annie Nathan Meyer—he left the legacy of the women's college, Barnard Annex, later Barnard College (Garrison, *Apostles* 134–5).

When C. C. Williamson studied American libraries and library workers in 1919, "he found the term 'librarian' was applied to everyone who worked in a library and that any distinction between different kinds of work was very vague"—a situation he would find intact today in many libraries (Bishop 1). But nonetheless he made a stab at separating the classes of library worker, and library work, into two: "professional" and "clerical." "Why?" one asks, since the vision of many of the field's most articulate writers was of a democratic force of uniformly educated and committed—and classless—workers. Even the overweening Bostwick was troubled by Williamson's view of the routine of library work as "in some way of low grade," to be handled by "low grade people" and gently suggested another view: "that routine is of all kinds, some high and some low grade, that it is so inextricably intertwined with the substance of the work that segregation is impossible and that the work must be taught as a whole" ("Carnegie" 497).

Williamson sought, through insistence on standardization of training, to raise librarianship to a "higher plane," but not in the manner of his professional forebears, many of whom were librarians "born not made" (*Training ... Service* 25). Like other concerned members of the field, he could see that librarianship, plagued as it was by innumerable clerical duties, underpaid, lumbered with unrealistic expectations, and widely seen as something that anyone could do, by the 1920s was simply not attracting a high calibre of student, and that extant library schools—not only in-service training programs, but university-affiliated programs as well—were allegedly not turning out the sort of graduate who could command a high salary. His avowed purpose in generating the landmark "Report" was to raise the standard of librarianship to a level where professional salaries could be garnered:

> The confusion of clerical and professional work tends inevitably to keep salaries down to the level of the clerical grade.... Until the distinction between clerical and professional workers is sharply made and adhered to the demand for adequate salaries for the professional group will prove ineffective because they will be economically impossible. A careful appraisal of the duties actually performed by many workers for whom professional salaries are demanded will show that they are often in large part clerical and *not worthy* [emphasis added] of higher remuneration [9].

"Much of the necessary work in a library is peculiar to libraries, yet it is distinctly of clerical grade," he declared. "Those who do this work, however, have not been called clerks but have been placed with all other library workers in one vocational group of 'librarians'" ([3]). He stipulated that "[g]raduation from an accredited college after four years of study leading to the bachelor's degree should now be recognized as the minimum of general education needed for successful *professional* [emphasis added] library work of any kind" (5). Despite his efforts, in the 1920s "'librarian' came to be the designation used for all members of the library profession" (Evans, "Evolution" 76). The ambiguity of library-worker titles is evident throughout the first three decades of the twentieth century. For example, Schiller, attempting to compile charts on the number of librarians by decade from 1870–1970, was forced to note that in 1900, the figures were "[b]ased on the classification 'Librarians and assistants"; in 1910, they "[excluded] catalogers, who were counted as 'Library Assistants"; in 1920, they "[included] catalogers, who were counted as 'Librarians" ("Women" 238). Discussing standardization in libraries—that perpetual pipe dream of Libraryland—Rathbone confessed, in 1922, that the "situation is considerably mixed" ("Standardization" 588). She reported that cities found it difficult to make "any very clear distinction between clerical and professional services," and that in grading plans there was "very great variation" and that requirements for these varying grades of work "differ[ed] to a bewildering degree" (*ibid.* 587).

Williamson was trying, much as librarians have done ever since, to raise the status and pay of one group of library worker by standing them on the heads of a lower class of worker. But he did not make provision for clerical workers to have viable careers in the field, in order that librarians could gain the status he foresaw for them, and scorned the work clerks were to do so heavily that no one could keep clerical positions filled. He high-handedly held that "[i]n many cases the law of supply and demand will make it possible to maintain efficient clerical staffs at salaries even lower than those offered by commercial and private employers" (*Training ... Service* 9). In so saying, he ensured that bright, nondegreed library workers of promise (the new generation of "born" librarian) entering the field unsuspectingly in search of pleasant bookish work would do as their foresisters had done. Lora Rich notes tactfully, in a kind 1920 article focused on providing better working conditions and opportunities for library workers to obviate the high turnover, "[T]he girl whose chief task is filing cards in a library might often as well be filing cards, usually, unfortunately, for a higher salary, in any business house" (366). As we have seen, all the library field's most talented double-crossed and disgusted Ideal Desk Assistants had made a beeline for more lucrative employment in precisely these "commercial and private" spots during World War I, none of them returning to librarianship for further abuse. They continued this pattern through the 1920s and for the next six decades, giving rise to a giant headache of a turnover problem. Clara Herbert's distress at her inability, despite an extensive campaign, to regain workers in the numbers and quality of those serving in the field before the war was replicated innumerable times in libraries all over America for more than forty years.

A certain number of young people did trickle into the field of librarianship, but because none but the most simple-minded would willingly work for salaries below the standard set by private businesses, they were not the very sharpest people. No one, except the veriest simpleton, would accept a clerk's position as a career move. One 1940s observer, noting the surplus of trained librarians available for clerical work, stated bluntly that "many of them are not good for much else anyway" (E. E. Williams 302). So libraries hired these people as "subprofessionals," a nebulous title which stopped just short of calling the possessor by the baneful term "nonprofessional." When they came with some undergraduate library work in college, they were termed "professionals." However, these terms were never meaningful, as Williamson had hoped they would be, because they were extremely idiosyncratically applied. The effect of Williamson's strictures was to shame libraries into hiring workers and calling them professional librarians, but as Bryan was to point out in the 1950s, few of them were educationally advanced enough to be the kind of powerfully intellectual worker Williamson envisioned, although they were innocuous and decidedly bookish. When later commentators beheld "professional" librarians at work in their field, they beheld an army of glorified clerks, and calls were made in abundance for scholarly, rather than merely adequate, or even merely library-school-approved, librarians (e.g., Montgomery). Rose Vormelker analyzed the chicken-and-egg problem in 1967, when technician training was raising its infant head:

> So long as library schools graduated an acceptable number of librarians for the professional opportunities which existed, and libraries could afford apprentice courses and/or in-service training for non-professional staff, and appropriations were kept at the proverbial low level, the "crisis" note was kept pretty much within the family. The situation was deplored, but the profession could only say we could do more if we had more and better librarians. We could get more and better librarians if they were better paid, if librarianship were a prestige profession, etc., etc. It was a little like, "If we had some ham we could have ham and eggs, if we had some eggs" [Nicholson et al. 14].

Librarians made no move for decades to make clerical positions careers. They settled for high turnover in the few positions the field sustained, and for the next forty years were to shoulder many of the tasks Williamson would have envisioned as "clerical," simply because of the persistent unpopularity of librarianship to all but the least ambitious and energetic college graduates, and, still, to high-school graduates. Accusations that the women working as professional librarians actually enjoyed or preferred clerical work over professional were to be discreetly voiced in the 1930s and 1940s; Louis Nourse called it a "fatal liking for routine" (Nourse 630; McDiarmid 233). Consequently, abundant openings—in 1942 Hostetter claimed 1,000 to 1,200—existed with no qualified staff other than these drones to fill them (384). This dearth of competent library-school-educated librarians escalated to a pinnacle in 1966, with a shortage of 100,000 professional librarians—some claimed the exact figure was 106,000—to fill a like number of spots ("Library Education" 1761; Reed 44). Hence, in the end, few clerical workers even existed in the field throughout the '30s, '40s, and '50s, save as student assistants and student wives, and their turnover rate was phenomenal. All the "clerical" workers were the "professional" librarians. So who was the paraprofessional in these times? Support staff in these decades consisted of every library worker in the field, despite the proclamations of Williamson.

By 1966, in addition to the shortage of professional librarians, there was thought to be a clerical deficit of 54,010 (Reed 44). Because of the unattractiveness of the field, which Williamson failed to grasp, "librarians" became clerks all over again in the decades following his effort, and some clerks librarians. In fact, librarians had never ceased being clerks. The were ever, in truth, "library workers." Thus the history of librarianship had by the 1960s (which is to say, for its first 100 years) arguably been the history of a variety of support staff, plus the history of male administrators making quite a bit of money while their staffs scrimped and made do. Williamson did succeed in mandating that true library education would be on a graduate level, after four solid years of undergraduate college work, but his sovereign aim failed, and was doomed to fail. Library workers post–Williamson were not abundant enough to be "librarians" and "clerks" as he envisioned. All kinds of compromises were made; the same old arguments for on-the-job training as a parallel mode of entry to professional echelons, and librarians being born, not made, and the same criticisms of the library-school curriculums and standards for admittance sprouted in the literature of the '30s, '40s, '50s, and '60s. And these were legitimate arguments.

In 1967, forty-four years later, as if no man called Williamson had ever lived, concerned administrators were still appealing, "It is recommended that the basic qualification for librarians be established as a bachelor's degree, from a recognized four-year college..." (Duchac 1798). Indeed, one could even argue that Williamson had a premonition of why his scheme would fail, when, noting the clerical emphasis in many of the time's college brochures, he scolded: "It is not surprising to find that able and ambitious college men and women hesitate to look to library work as a professional career when assured by the catalogues of the so-called professional training schools that 'a ready ability to use the typewriter is an important part of a modern librarian's equipment' and is 'necessary *in almost any library position*' [emphasis added]" (*Training ... Service* 33).

The field had already calcified in 1923 beyond the point where it could remediate its fatal flaw, namely that library work is in fact clerical in nature—even amateurish, in the best sense. This applies even to library work of a higher order, though it may not be the same kind of clerical work as other fields offer. There is little work in a library, other than book checkout, that is as mindless as Williamson believed it was. At the same time, libraries were simply not provisioned with the salary and the appeal they needed to attract a professional grade of recruit, namely, a deeply scholarly and extensively schooled and cultured individual. Training programs in libraries therefore continuously existed throughout the Depression and following World War II. In addition, training programs at the college level continued to cut corners on the requisite four years of undergraduate work needed to precede one year of graduate-level work in library training. These programs were issuing BLSs continuously throughout the '30s, '40s, and '50s, and calling their graduates "librarians." Today such people would be regarded as no more than support staff. In addition to these, there were legions of others, without even this minimal training, whom the field without compunction was terming "professional librarians" (Bryan 63–4 & 75–6).

16. Slim Pickings:
The 1920s to the 1960s

Already in 1919, Flexner was grieved to write,

[S]o scarce are trained people, so difficult to get, so hard to keep, and so expensive to maintain that we might as well face the thing squarely and try to say what we would make of the available material.... There are not enough library school graduates to go around. In the urge to get things done, these library school people are frequently given the necessary technical work to do ["Essential" 408].

In 1921, the *Boston Evening Transcript* lamented, "The small number of good applicants for library work in comparison to the demand is our present greatest hardship" ("Certification" 892).

Thus was the stage set for the next thirty years. Libraries were on their mettle because of the Williamson Report's insistence on the need to separate clerical from professional duties in order to gain professionalism, and because of a similar document, the "Telford Report" in 1927 (D. Weber 52). They were also still attempting to cope with the recruitment problem after World War I. As a result, the field recoiled from hiring, in any quantity, clerical or "subprofessional," i.e., non-library-school, employees. Nor did it need to hire them; there were enough recruits from extant library schools and training programs, albeit of distinctly low grade, to fill America's library positions. Nourse commented,

The crop of library school graduates turned out during the years of the late depression have had a hard row to hoe. Lower initial salaries, lack of salary increases, and even salary cuts have been the order of the day. Some administrators have frankly taken advantage of the times and have secured the cream of each year's class at the lowest figure ["Speaking" 633].

While the "cream" may have filled the field in 1937, we have seen that Williamson was not persuaded that even the cream was up to his standard. At any rate, though the cream was at first hired, the low enrollment of unvital people in library schools *vis-à-vis* an increasing number of professional library

127

positions ensured a lower grade of library-school graduate filling the field throughout the years from 1923 to 1970. Even more frequently, positions were filled by students with a four-year degree plus an undergraduate level of library training courses. This state of affairs transpired not only because of low salaries, but because of widely disseminated gossip regarding the quality of work in libraries before the war, exposing as fiction the notion that the field was wide open and democratic and charging failure to keep this "promise" in the form of ready advancement for assistants, especially for women. The long hours, the extreme hierarchization, the very "stuffiness" (E. Allen 518) of librarianship, also militated against recruiting any but the country's less gifted pupils, or those past their prime. These problems dogged the field until well into the 1950s. Hoage, studying staff turnover in libraries in 1950, pulled no punches: "[L]ow salaries and lack of chances for advancement have not been the only important reasons why employees have resigned from ... libraries" (32; also E. Allen 518–9). Alvarez lamented, "[O]ur work is ... seldom mentioned by vocational guidance experts, or by college advisors and counsellors in their talks with students. If suggested at all it is likely to be as a last resort to persons who do not seem to fit anywhere else" ("Let's" 368).

Despite Alvarez's contention that men were not entering librarianship (and his amusing conceit that "male" was somehow equated with "quality"), enough men remained from the prior era to dominate administrative positions way out of proportion to their numbers in the field and kept libraries unhealthily hierarchical, and they reached these positions in no time flat (Bryan 33). The librarians produced by library schools or schools offering library courses who poured into the great number of openings in the 1920s and stayed on in them were of little enough brain to content themselves with exceptionally low-paying positions combining much clerical work with a small bit of professional work. The clever ones scampered from the field. "What efforts the library profession has made to secure new workers appear to have been aimed more at securing a quantity rather than a quality of personnel," averred Alvarez in 1941. "These efforts were made largely before the last decade when the demand for librarians was considerably greater than the supply" ("Let's" 367). Librarianship was to evolve in a dispirited inertia for about forty years post-Williamson, from many failures, chief of which were recruitment, management, image, sexism, and funding problems. In 1957, an overview of placements from recent graduating classes could not resist the cutting aside, "[T]here simply are not enough librarians—not even enough in quantity, let alone quality—to go around" (Strout & Strout 1600).

The field was "not pressed to employ subprofessionals prior to the Second World War" (Evans, "Evolution" 79). Nor, by and large, could it sustain their employment for longer than the blink of an eye. Nevertheless, "subprofessionals" worked in substantial numbers in the field between the two wars. Clark in 1933 speaks of student and clerical assistants, the latter of whom would be paid $700 a year, a salary a mere fraction above the average salary earned by some of the lowest paid of all library employees in 1904: $546.66 to $666.33, excluding messengers and pages (265; in Washington D.C.'s Public Library, Bowerman 644). Just how low this salary was in 1933 can be seen by noting the average wage for library workers (including professionals) from 1931 to 1936, which was never under $1,200 (in public libraries, at least); in non-library occupations from 1929 to 1936 the average salary was never less than $1,000 per year except in two years when it fell just under that amount (Howard 219–20). "Pinch-penny clerical arrangements" like these prompted Brigham to write, "[S]alaries are too low to attract even good clerks" ("Point" 790; "Personnel" 602). Hence, turnover was considerable. Hostetter claimed in 1936,

> Turnover in staff in all libraries has to date affected the clerical and subprofessional services much more than the professional staff. The clerical and page services have suffered from constant turnover owing chiefly to prevalent opportunities for employment in industry at wages much higher than libraries can afford to pay. The subprofessional service in some libraries has also been seriously affected [384].

McNeal observed that staff reductions necessitated by the Depression "first affected certain clerical positions" (219). When World War II came, a commentator noted "an even greater shortage of clerical labor" than of librarians (E. E. Williams 307). Bowerman, speaking of the "considerable" degree of turnover in the ranks, stemming from expansion of government and other public-service jobs stimulated by the war, agreed that "resignations of late years have been predominantly from the lower grades" (648). Few people wanted to linger long in or could regard as a "career" a position paid at a turn-of-the-century rate. In 1949 Verna Melum conducted a survey amongst a variety of the nation's libraries. One hundred and one of them answered her queries regarding salaries and clerical workers. Pay for beginning positions ranged from $90 to $200 a month, averaging $132 per month. The trouble with these figures is that, as Melum confesses, only 65 percent of her respondents were willing to fill in this information regarding starting wage rates. Perhaps the other 35 percent were too ashamed; perhaps their beginning salaries were even lower than the ones reported. "Many will say," she wrote, "that the lower brackets included here are not living wages and will not attract workers. But many sub-professionals are now working in libraries at these wages" (693). Clerical workers were not the only ones paid abysmally: in one library, bindery operatives were paid more than assistant librarians, while in other libraries inclusion of building and maintenance personnel's earnings would have raised the average salary for all library workers (Mosher 852; Howard 220).

Resignations came about not only because of low wages, but because of the nature of clerical workers. Their enormous turnover rate was due not so much to stupidity or fecklessness as because these temporary workers were bright and ambitious, and went on to finer things. At the very minimum, the people who became the "subprofessional" grade of clerk were female college graduates who viewed their clerical duties as "nice" temporary work to be done for a brief time after college and before marriage (Ashwell 98). Some were housewives earning pennies while their husbands finished college (McLane). Some were working in libraries as they put themselves through library school. Many were highly educated, or about to become so; library work was even then, especially in urban areas, for clerks as much for librarians "a profession which presupposes and demands high educational requirements..." (Bowerman 645; Brigham, "Point" 790). Some were high-school students, or college students working towards degrees in non-library fields; some were WPA workers looking for a way up; others were war wives biding their time; still others were unpaid volunteers (Bluman 274–5). Melum points out the widespread use of "captive" (Oberg's felicitous adjective) workers—local people, unlikely to move from the spot, often married women taking a nearby opportunity to supplement the family income (693).

In the 1950s, because of a general desperation to staunch the flow of workers from the field and induce young people to enter it, another class of subprofessional library worker appeared, the "pre-professional." Described by several commentators, the preprofessional program was generally limited to pre-picked members of the community and was designed for people who wanted on-the-job experience concomitant with graduate-school training. They usually were not allowed to continue past two years in library employ without commencing their studies; in other places, they could hold their appointment for no more than three and a half years, during which time they were required to complete their fifth-year studies ("Pre-Professional" 2944; Heyneman 558). This ploy was often successful in recruiting permanent professional librarians. It worked partly because internships were made interesting to would-be librarians. "I did everything that professional librarians do," enthused Redmond Molz in 1957, of her experience in the Enoch Pratt Free Library. She was involved with all the types of library in her system (branch, main, bookmobile), and all kinds of jobs, though with an emphasis on children's work (story-telling, publicity). When asked what impressed her most, she replied:

> The library could have said, "She's not a professional. She can't go out of the building.", [sic] or they could have given me routines with no spice (that would have ended my library career), but they didn't. They gave me the best they had. I wasn't just an extra hand.... I was [also] free to attend all the library's in-service training classes, just as if I were a professional ["Pre-Professional" 2942].

Other programs, devised in the 1960s, did not pretend that inductees were MLS-bound. In Baltimore County Public Library, a library-aide on-site training program attracted up to 110 applicants, usually women between 32 and 47, for the 18 slots available in each class (Robinson, "Promise" 3757). These women were training for true paraprofessional positions, between clerical and professional, to fill positions previously graded for professional librarians but regraded to accommodate the great librarian shortage. Their work, though mostly with children, was adjudged to consist of tasks normally considered professional (*ibid.* 3758). Disadvantages to the program were "confusion about the differing levels of job responsibility, and therefore pay" and applicants' lack of undergraduate training (*ibid.* 3759).

Perhaps these perceived disadvantages led to a revamping of the ever-experimental Enoch Pratt Free Library's in-house training program. By 1968, Slocum was speaking of "bachelor" librarians, meaning librarians required to have an undergraduate degree and undergoing library training classes very similar to the old apprenticeship classes given pre–Williamson, and thought to have been stamped out. She claimed that these trainees and the earlier "pre-professional" ones

> have enabled these institutions [Brooklyn Public Library, Free Library of Philadelphia, as well as Enoch Pratt] to maintain their services during the past two decades of acute manpower shortages. That many fine librarians have come into the profession by this route is unquestioned, but ... [u]nless clear delineation can be made between the job of the Bachelor and Master librarian, the ... program is doomed to failure. Two staff members working side by side doing the same things are soon going to compare paychecks and question seriously the holding of a graduate degree in library science.... Library administrators will do themselves and their staff a disservice by providing training and work assignments for experienced Bachelor librarians to such an extent that the difference between the Bachelor and the Master becomes hopelessly blurred (3754–5).

Clearly, juggling the designations of clerical, quasi-professional, and professional but in fact allowing employees to do too-similar or the same work was like playing with fire in the end. Fire easily jumps artificial boundaries, being a force beyond petty considerations, and so, today, Oberg and other well-known commentators routinely speak of the "blurring" of paraprofessional and professional roles. "Blurring" had to enter library lingo, meaning exactly what Slocum hoped it would not.

At any rate, generally, pre–1960s straight "clerical" positions were not designed to be more than stopgap positions, any more than "pre-professional" were, though on the whole much less thought went into the designing of clerical posts. Like the later pre-professional posts, training took place on the job. And so with "subprofessional" positions, which were similarly unrewarding. Job qualifications for various library positions were murky indeed. "The number of libraries which have never undergone a job analysis survey, a job evaluation survey, or any other kind of survey, scientific or self-introspective, are legion," charged Nathaniel Stewart, in the first of his three articles on in-service training (17). In fact, at no time in modern library history have the lines between the classes of library worker been as crystal clear as pundits like Williamson would have had them be. "Not only were some employees uncertain about or unaware of their classification," exclaimed Bryan, summarizing results of her exhaustive late–1940s study, "but some library administrators reported that they experienced practical difficulties in differentiating between professional and subprofessional personnel, while several even showed us lists of 'problem' employees whom they were unable to place in either category" (28).

Clerks were often serving in positions putatively requiring professionals, and being paid clerical wages (Bryan 205). What Bryan was really describing were conditions that obtained in American libraries post–World War I to post–World War II. She recorded that "[i]n actual practice, only thirty of the fifty-eight responding libraries in the Inquiry sample use any type of personnel classification scheme. In the other twenty-eight libraries the staff, like Topsy, seems to have 'just growed' without benefit of any guiding framework" (206). She also found that "librarians, whether professional or subprofessional, men or women, administrators or assistants, are a remarkably homogeneous group with respect to their vocational interests and aspirations" (130). They also exhibited other types of homogeneity. For instance, "Recreational reading was by far the most popular pastime": 87 percent of librarians, both men and women, and 80 percent and 63 percent of the female and male subprofessionals, respectively, preferred reading to any other form of recreation (Bryan 46–7). "Listening to the radio was a fairly close second choice[;] … [f]ew engage in outdoor sports or games, in artistic activities, or in personal hobbies" (47).

Educationally, professional librarians were a big surprise, most of them having fewer scholastic qualifications than clerks and paraprofessionals today. Only 2 percent of professional librarians held the master's degree in librarianship; only *one* person from Bryan's sample of sixty libraries held a Ph.D. in library science (64). In addition,

> Graduation from an undergraduate college is universally recognized as a prerequisite for professional librarians; only 58 percent of the professionals in our sample have had this basic education. A fifth year of professional training is also generally recognized as necessary preparation for those seeking professional status; only 40 percent of the professional librarians have met this requirement [75–6].

However, Bryan did find that younger librarians were more likely than older to hold bachelor's degrees: "from five out of twenty in the older group … to seventeen out of twenty in the younger [group]" (76).

Nor were the teachers in America's accredited library schools likely to have molded a "professional" grade of librarian, either at the undergraduate or at the graduate level. Danton claimed:

Faculties in charge of M.S. courses and work are, almost without exception, the same as those concerned with the B.S. curriculum, yet few of these faculty members have their doctorates and a number [one-third] have not, themselves, even done graduate work at the Master's level [10, 20].

Few faculty members were full-time professors, and two-thirds of the ones who were full-time were directors, and typically, in those times, did little or no teaching. There were even faculties without *any* full-time teachers, and all this existed in the better grade of library school (Danton 12–13). In addition, these instructors had little of the "bookman" or "educated man" about them; salaries were never high enough to attract a top grade of faculty (Danton 14). But circumstances very like these early in the history of the field had prompted Josephson to write presciently in 1900, "If the standard of entrance requirements be ... continually raised without a corresponding progress in the instruction, the faculties of the schools may some day be confronted with the fact that the step from the college to the library school will not be regarded by the students as a step upward" (226). In the end, how "professional" was a student taught by a second-rate intellect apt to be?

Further, when we regard the type of work the great mass of library workers was engaged in, we find it mainly clerical, even paraprofessional, in our modern sense, rather than professional, in the sense of someone's needing to have graduate training to perform it. Danton points out that one of the New York City college libraries employed not one clerical worker; thus "professional" librarians were performing "all shelving, labeling, pasting, and typing." He remarked, "That such a situation can exist today is a serious indictment of the profession as a whole and, indirectly, of the schools" (22).

One can validly argue that paraprofessionals—if only we look at the sort of work library employees were actually performing—have been around longer, and in greater numbers, than was ever properly recorded: invisible in plain sight. What is a professional librarian trained at the undergraduate level in library basics by a "professor" without a master's degree in library science but a species of paraprofessional, in a species of training class? What is the qualitative difference between such a person and another person with a four-year degree trained on the job in library basics by librarians who may or may not have had the master's? What is a professional librarian who could be spending half her time doing the work of pages but a kind of para? But in any case, the conceit that there were "professional librarians" and "subprofessional librarians," and then clericals, persisted in the literature of the post–Williamson, pre–Presthus period. It is truly impossible to know on what nebulous basis these quasi-precise titles were ever assigned. In general, watching the library field "evolve" is much like watching clouds on a windy day: "There's a librarian—oh, no, now it's changed into a clerk—actually it looks more like a subprofessional ... What do you think?"

Bryan found the median length of full-time employment to be "17.4 years for the professional group and [only] 5.8 years for the subprofessional" (79). She also charged that "[b]y far the largest percentage of loss in all groups was through voluntary resignation of employees" (200). The disproportion between professional turnover and subprofessional turnover was striking; for instance, in one category, "[t]he mean loss by resignations ... was 10 percent of the professional staff" to "49 percent of the subprofessional" (200). The most frequent reasons for resignations were, unsurprisingly, "a job elsewhere offered better pay," and "dissatisfaction with job because of inadequate salary" (201).

The library field had not bothered to think through the implications of the Williamson Report, namely, that if librarians were to be members of a profession, and clerks were to be the other side of the coin, then clerks, too, if they were to be retained as serious permanent employees, would need to be members of a profession. Clerical library work had failed to be attractive enough to be a lifetime calling for most of its fleeting practitioners. "The problem of recruiting, training, and retaining *career* library clerks has seldom received adequate attention," charged the anonymous author of "A Personnel Formula" in 1955 (604). Librarians began to give this matter of a parallel profession consideration only in the 1940s and 1950s, but most especially in the latter decade, when Bryan declared, "Employee recruitment has long given librarians concern, but since the Second World War the difficulties encountered by libraries in securing an adequate supply of competent personnel have become so serious that it is now regarded as one of the profession's most urgent problems" (183–4).

Elizabeth Ashwell was one of the first to impress upon the field the importance of the career clerical worker. She insisted that "clerical assistants [be] recognized as an important group on the staff and as specialists in their own line of work" and hoped "that some day clerical work will be considered 'different' from professional work and not merely 'inferior' to it" (99). She advocated avenues of promotional opportunity for this "new" class of worker. Her argument was echoed by Dorothy Weber, who wrote,

> The clerical assistant must be accepted as an individual with a distinct, if different, contribution to make toward the realization of the library's goals. We cannot ignore the effect on clerical workers ... of a clearly defined status that carries its own opportunities for growth and advancement and its own place of dignity and usefulness.... We cannot hope to attract and hold the type of clerical worker we need if the only inducements are the pay envelope, convenient hours, and a comfortable place to work. Industry ... is learning that job satisfaction continues to be a strong force in productivity, regardless of the size of the pay envelope [54].

Dorothy Sargent advised,

> Consider the clerk's view of things. He or she may be treated as a dumping ground for all those unsavory tasks of which the professional wants to get rid. That is one of the best ways to waste not only money and time and materials, but personnel. It is an excellent way to make poor library management really bad [61].

Nor was the clerk the only class of worker dumped upon in the '30s. Attitudes like that of Elizabeth Clark, contemptuous and supercilious, were wreaked upon the lower-level professional "assistants," as well:

> There seems to be a firm and prevalent belief in our profession that "faithful services" alone are sufficient grounds to demand not only lifelong tenure of office but advancement in salary and in rank.... [An] assistant [should] be industrious, cheerful, and willing, even eager, to serve during the hours for which she contracted to work. Those things I take for granted as paid for in cash, and failure to give those things is grounds for dismissal.... [But she must make] a continued effort to improve herself along lines that will make her more valuable... "on her own".... There is, of course, no question that turnover is expensive and that an assistant who knows local procedures is worth more than one of the same ability who does not know those procedures. But it does not follow that the assistant becomes more useful every year ... unless she does more than learn the routine [264–5].

This high-handed administrator then gives examples of assistants who have improved themselves, but decides that each falls short of her criteria for promotion. Like many other librarians in the field, they were being treated as little more than clerks. Stewart speaks of "a 'failure' experience for the librarian in his or her initial library job" and wonders "[h]ow many individuals never recover from it and how many leave the profession" (17). Thus it is entirely suitable to discuss the problems of undervalued subprofessional library-school or training-course graduates in the same breath as those of clerical workers. One can see why all but the most unemployable would take umbrage at Clark's tone, which undoubtedly was as insuperable at work as in print, and flee from her company. Rather than searching for the most excellent workers available, Clark seemed more than anything to be fishing for a way to keep her assistants in a useful sub-category which could not otherwise be filled. No doubt she was typical of a certain percentage of supervisor, tight with a penny, low on loyalty to her employees, and unshakably hierarchical. She helped create and sustain the morale problems that produced the massive 100,000-plus personnel shortage that grew by leaps and bounds well into the 1960s.

In addition to this insufferable attitude, the root of so much dissatisfaction in the field, towards the underemployed low-level librarian, denoted by the condescending term "assistant," there were also undesirable class overtones to the term "clerical," which had come to refer to "a person who went into library work, who failed to achieve a satisfactory professional status and who remained to form a backwash of discontent, and so carries a certain stigma" (Rymer 393). In 1944, Bluman wrote,

> Now there is something unfortunate about the title "clerical assistant." It has become associated with low salaries, low qualifications, and sometimes a feeling that "professional" librarians look down upon "clericals." In offices "clerical work" is often thought of as a beginner's job, below that of typist, stenographer, and secretary. "Subprofessional," too, carries the wrong connotation... [275].

E. E. Williams was quick to concur: "[T]he term 'subprofessional' is unsatisfactory. If 'librarian' is to be included in the name of all professional positions, ... then 'assistant' might be proposed in place of 'subprofessional'" (306). Librarians came under increasing criticism for wasting the public's tax dollar on professional staff which spent most of its time doing clerical tasks. As they came under scrutiny, they struggled to come up with ways to diminish that high percentage and consolidate such tasks into clerical positions in which people would stay in order to free librarians from "the bonds of detail" (Pidduck 406). This effort was not to succeed until the late 1960s and 1970s.

In the Depression, "[r]eduction of library services ... ranged from the closing of branches and the shortening of hours to the discontinuance of acquisition work in the field of fiction" (Fetty 29). Library managers were "throttled" by lack of funding (Brigham, "Point" 790). Because there was also a shortage of willing long-term clerical workers, administrators may have thought it prudent to hire people bound to the profession because of their investment in schooling and thus obviate the numbing necessity of constantly training "ever-shifting" clerical help (Sargent 63). "[T]here is no reason," snorted E. E. Williams, "why unemployed professionals should not be hired for clerical positions—as long as it was not forgotten that the positions were clerical" (307). An additional use in hiring library-school graduates for low-grade work, he reasoned cagily, would be to "weed out" the "inferior" product, who would not stay in a low-grade job if he could find proper professional work, and if he could not find professional work would then rightly leave the field altogether to the better grade of practitioner. It is easy to see how this scheme might as easily weed out the best and the brightest. First, they could leave the field in disgust after their taste of being undervalued and bored as clerical workers. Or, once libraries saw they could save money by hiring library-school graduates to do clerical work, more would regrade professional jobs as clerical. If all libraries followed this policy, there would no professional jobs to move into, and the newest graduates would be stuck, then as today, in "assignments unworthy of their gifts" (Rymer 392). However, this latter notion was not to be widely implemented until the 1960s.

Throughout the '30s and '40s good "assistants" continued to vacate the field—miffed by attitudes like Clark's—leaving only the professional dross to fill clerical positions. *Bona fide* clerks in every line of library work were few and far between: in Rymer's small library, there was but one "untrained clerical" to four library-school trained librarians, and one business-school graduate (392). "Many large branches have ten or twelve trained assistants and only one or two clerks," offered Nourse ("Speaking" 630).

Nourse, purporting to speak for the "dissatisfied young assistant," refers in 1937 to "an increasing awareness of the deficiencies in staff management" ("Speaking" 629). He cites low salaries, lack of salary scales, monotony, resistance to new ideas, lack of promotional opportunities, recognition of ability rather than seniority as a basis for advancement, undemocratic management, and need for more salubrious working conditions, a shorter work week, better benefits, and, strangely, "a practical code of ethics" as the most pressing sources of discontent (629). Could this concern have been allied to the treatment assistants were getting from the Elizabeth Clarks of the library world? Probably, since a satisfactory, "living" code of ethics for Nourse would have included the "responsibilities of loyalty, obligations to the library and fellow-workers, ... and professional growth of the assistant," not merely the static codes— Bolton's and the ALA's—already extant ("Speaking" 633–4).

Nourse claimed the average "assistant" was emerging from library school to spend "50 to 90 per cent of [her/his] time at tasks which are purely routine and of a non-professional nature" ("Speaking" 630). In 1938, Ralph Munn also worried about the "discouragement" of recent young library-school graduates who sallied forth into the field "filled with enthusiasm and ideas [and found] ... policies and plans so fixed that no suggestions for change were welcome" ("Erasing"). In addition, the old habit of calling anybody not the actual head of a library an assistant, beyond being confusing, was also demeaning to people who had gone through either their fourth or a fifth year of schooling in order to be regarded as professional. "'Does not "assistant" bear the connotation of not being fully qualified?'" asked Charles Mixer in consternation:

> It seems to me that we are retarding the full recognition of our profession and unintentionally belittling the amount of preparation and experiences of our colleagues when we refer to them before the public as "assistants." ... Let us adopt the practice of speaking of our professional staff as "librarians," one and all....

Seven years later, in 1945, Mixer's suggestion had still not been implemented. Hazeltine, for example, was still calling newly graduated professional librarians "assistants," urging, with unconscious condescension, that they be kept "profitably busy" (943). "[W]ho is to be termed a librarian?" queried Jacobs. "Certainly we are all librarians by profession and now, by practice. Why not clarify this point by calling the head librarian the director of the library? This would immediately designate *his* [emphasis added] proper position and at the same time staff members could rightfully be called librarians" (336).

Evidently, many of the same medievalisms prevalent before the First World War were sustained until the Second, especially in the standards expected of women—*by* women, sadly. "Girl" was still used, gratingly, to describe young library-school-educated women, or indeed, any woman in the field, in some articles penned at the time (e.g., Thornton 967; Norris 392, 394; Ashwell 98). At no time, however, did I ever see a male library worker of similar stature referred to as a "boy." Women who were innovative were squelched; women who complained about lack of promotional opportunities were maligned as "disappointed and bitter"; it was made clear that their inadequacies, however, secured them their lowly lot, since they would not better themselves on their own time and suffered certain nameless "limitations" (Thornton 967; Clark 264). Longevity—or "faithful service"—was not held to be a basis for promotion (Clark). Tight, subverted women were still making prim lists of the busy cultural endeavors librarians should be engaged in on their own time (despite the fact that a forty- to forty-five-hour work week was still in effect), for example: "Museums visited," "Plays of distinction attended," "Theme on which purposeful reading has been done," "Libraries visited for observation," "Courses taken," "Health-building program," "Social life of a broad and inclusive type"—with the final arch query: "Are you a 'Bridge-builder'?" (Mosher 851; Phillips). This same forty- to forty-five-hour week was being belittled, viz., E. Clark, as being no excuse for lack of professional get-up-and-go (266). My goodness.

Add to these persnickety job disincentives in the 1930s the necessity for library-school-trained librarians to work at professional routines for, on average, no more than half of their time, since they were generally hired to comprise half the work force, and clerical tasks absorbed over two-thirds and in some cases almost three-quarters of all workers' time (Brewitt & Carter 774). In addition, they were paid wretchedly low salaries while doing 40 to 50 percent more work, as workers were let go in the Depression (Howard 220). It is easy to see why the advent of World War II emptied the field of workers of all sorts yet again.

Nor were overwork and low pay alone in driving library workers into other fields. The same dreary physical conditions in which many pre–World War I workers toiled prevailed in pre–World War II America. "Library service would stand below, rather than above, a median position with respect to the attitude toward and treatment of library employees," claimed William Mosher in 1937 (849). "[T]he library profession is the worst paid of all callings of a comparable professional character," he wrote, castigating library powers-that-were (849).

It is ... incomprehensible that those in policy-determining positions have so frequently failed to protect and advance the interests of public employees whose welfare depends upon their action.... Experience in all fields goes to show that the most prolific breeder of employee organization is unsatisfactory working conditions of one sort or another.... There is no more prolific breeder of discontent than inadequate salaries, particularly if inadequacy is accompanied by inequitability.... Although I have never seen a survey of ... working conditions in public libraries, I recollect more than one in which good standards are violated: Dingy and cheerless rooms, ill-lighted and ill-ventilated, are found in many a library. It would be an interesting experiment ... to request the local lighting company to make a report on the number of foot candles of light at the desks of staff members and compare their findings with accepted standards, both from the point of view of volume and the absence of glare.... [I]n surveys of public buildings, in which I have cooperated, it has been established ... that illumination, whether artificial or natural, has in nearly all instances been inadequate.... The question of fatigue is likewise a subject to which increasing attention is being given.... A fatigued and harassed librarian cannot be a good librarian.... I have many times observed expressions on the faces of library assistants which spelled in unmistakable letters the state of fatigue.... [A] group of librarians ... whose heads were asleep at the switch, both permitt[ed] and expect[ed] the library staff to meekly acquiesce in an exploitative salary scale, in an hour schedule and a volume of work that would become a sweatshop. These conditions led to the development of a well-knit organization whose spokesman approached one of the candidates for the mayoralty and ... bargained with him for the correction of almost intolerable conditions. This action was roundly condemned.... It was felt to be disloyalty, but it was the only available remedy.... [T]he librarian [had] urged his subordinates to put up with these conditions in the name of loyalty and public service ... and preached the gospel of meekness [849–852].

Evidently little had changed in the field by the late 1940s, when Evelyn Allen was moved to ask, "Are Librarians Good Employers?" and by implication, through examples, to answer negatively.

Librarianship evolved in such a way that by 1941, when Baldwin and Marcus, endowed by the Carnegie Foundation, studied thirty-seven public libraries, they found "professionals" spending "an average of 35 per cent of their time on routine clerical duties." In their study, there were 570 "professionals" to 311 "sub-professionals" and "clericals"; even when the 128 pages, messengers, and "others" were added in, there were fewer "nonprofessionals" than "professionals" (Bishop 4). Evans concludes that librarians were aware of the clerical nature of their work, but were "indifferent to it" ("Evolution" 80). "[L]ibrarians remained unready 'to sever clerical from other duties,'" averred Evans, quoting Reece ("Evolution" 79). Four years later, researcher E. E. Williams discovered in a Texas library—one of the few to keep such records—that while 41 percent of the staff was "professional," it spent "25 per cent of its time on clerical duties" (Bishop 4). In an ALA study conducted in the late 1930s of some fifty university libraries, he found that "at least half the time of the whole professional staff at some ... libraries ... must be devoted to clerical tasks" (306). He wrote, of the proportion of professional to clerical workers,

> In one group of libraries—which includes Harvard, California, Texas, Pennsylvania, Iowa State College, Oberlin, and Vassar—professional workers make up only from 30 to 40 per cent of the total staff; at the other extreme, with from 56 to 96 per cent professional, are Illinois, Michigan, U.C.L.A., Louisiana, Syracuse, Wellesley, Denver, Mount Holyoke, Smith, Arizona, Colorado State, Southern Methodist, and North Dakota. The average is very near 50 per cent ... [303].

Like a handful of other researchers, he advocated creation of a third classification to perform semi-professional tasks—"library assistants"—but was ignored (306).

In 1948 the ALA published guidelines for professional versus clerical duties. Of 283 activities, only 129 were viewed as nonprofessional (Bishop 5).

In 1952, Wight found the "ratio of professional to non-professional staff to be 5:3, while the percentage of professional to non-professional duties to be 32.3:67.7, indicating that the staff employed was in inverse ratio to the type of duties to be performed" (Bishop 6). McNeal in 1954 found the ratio in academic libraries to be 1:1, but recommended 1:2 (Bishop 6; McNeal, "Ratio" 223). In 1962 the Library Association of Great Britain published guidelines for professional versus nonprofessional duties; of 322 activities, it decided only 101 were nonprofessional (Bishop 10). Davison, that same year, found a ratio of 1:2 professional to nonprofessional staff in special libraries, but recommended 1:3, based on his perception of the sorts of work which needed to be completed (Bishop 11). The percentage of professional to clerical staff found in "A Personnel Formula" in 1955 was 3:4, but the percentage recommended was 1:3 (601, 605). In special libraries, in 1963, the estimated overall ratio of MLS-holding librarian to "nonprofessional" was 4:6 (Christianson 35). In 1965 Downs and Delzell recommended staff be one-third professional to two-thirds clerical (30). However, as late as 1966, librarians were still doing "whatever needs to be done"; professionals still outnumbered clerks in many libraries (Hamill 418, 420).

Today, however, an almost 1:3 proportion, and certainly no less than a 1:2 ratio is almost ubiquitous, except in one-person rural libraries, where, as Bement put it, in 1926, the "librarian" is the "most isolated worker in any profession" (Molyneux 293–94; Kopp; Wolcott; "Library Worker" 961).

Despite these and other studies (most of them not by library "scientists" at all, but by sociologists), "[b]y the end of the 1950s librarians still had not been able to either convert their defined professional duties into full-time professional positions in any type of library or to achieve recognition as a professional by the public" (Bishop 8, 7). In addition, though officially librarians paid lip service to the credo that only the MLS prepared aspirants for positions as librarians, "unofficially ... they [still] often utilized their more experienced or better educated clerks in roles that belonged—so the dogma said—exclusively to librarians," a cheap and hypocritical practice that has gone on until this very moment (Evans, "Evolution" 80). Despite having corrected, at least on paper, the extensive use of degreed librarians as clerks, the library field has still not addressed the issues that face paraprofessional workers today, a sort of mirror of previous personnel misuse, the increasing use of clerks as *de facto* librarians, despite their being maintained at a clerical level. The scale has tipped in the other direction; a perfect balance still remains to be struck.

But this problem, too, is not a new one. "[I]n one public system there are clerks paid a clerk's salary who have charge of a branch, and one case where a girl with library school training and a college degree is subordinate to a girl with two years of college plus the ____ public library training course," complained Thornton's "new assistants" in 1941 (967). "The Denver area constituted a genuine training problem in that within it is a large group of workers engaged in library activities that may range from specialized research to the mimeographing of a book list," worried Robert Luke in 1942 (201). In 1949 Melum, in a discussion of her library survey on the question of training for nonprofessionals, keened,

> The fact that such advanced positions as head of circulation department ... and professional assistant ... are listed [as suitable positions for sub-professionals] ... points to the danger of giving too much responsibility to those whose meager training is meant to qualify them only for routine work. But may not the fact that some advanced duties *are* listed indicate that sub-professionals without *any* library training are now being given such responsibilities? [693]

When Bryan conducted her massive research on public library personnel in 1952, she found that 1,837 of her respondents claimed they were "professional," 461 claimed to be "subprofessional," and 97 inexplicably "checked neither category" (28). Her assumption, in trying to explain this confusion, was that since the "official ratio" of professional to subprofessional was 3:1, that these 97 were really subprofessionals unready to admit to their true status. But what they may have been indicating in hesitating to choose one category or another was that they fell between the two, doing some distinctly professional and some distinctly nonprofessional work.

In addition, there were large numbers of "untrained librarians" running the nation's rural libraries, "women no longer young; women who want only part-time work, receive very little salary, live at home and are not at all likely to be lured from their present positions by ... opportunities elsewhere. One of their strongest assets is their intimate knowledge of their own community's people, problems and resources ... [and their] enthusiastic response to training programs wherever they have been advertised..." (L. Martin 134). As we have seen, this state of affairs is as true of rural libraries today as in the 1950s, or any earlier time.

These were early indications that the class of worker urged by Norris in 1951—the "third classification"—was in fact functioning in the field, but was improperly titled and uncleverly managed. The field's true paraprofessionals were already, in the immediate post–Williamson years, in their familiar limbo: on the one hand noted by the conscientious, and on the other, denied by the dichotomously oriented, Williamsonian purists. Surely they were immanent, albeit not as numerous as today (unless one takes the plausible view that most of the field's workers were really nothing but support staff, because of the mixed nature of their work and their degree of training).

The old "subprofessional" category adumbrated this class of worker, as Norris pointed out. "Subprofessionals," she insisted, were supposed to have a four-year college degree plus "six semester hours of library science or equivalent," according to the ALA's 1939 "Classification and Pay Plans" (392). She argued that the subprofessional in practice was often a person with a high-school diploma only; she could just as easily, however, be a college graduate, or a college student with any number of credits short of graduation. She sought to rescue the subprofessional grade from the gray area into which it had fallen and infuse it with new life. Older practitioners like Clark treated subprofessionals of her time as clerks only, though many of them were library-school trained. Norris wanted the "third classification" to be definitely library-school bound, and she wanted to call them "library assistants" (392). She believed that 20 percent of their work should be of professional grade, and 80 percent of it clerical (393). She did not want them to be so stultified by clerical work that they escaped from the field in an access of boredom. She sought to set the "library assistant" up as a recruiting category, to lessen the shortage of librarians (392). She saw that many clerks, although transient, were highly educated, and closer in their potential to what we would call "paraprofessional" today, but they were infelicitously called "clerks," and their classification was not seen as desirable or permanent. This is not a new dilemma, either. As noted in the ALA/SCOLE *World Book* study, people performing paraprofessional duties today are still widely, and erroneously, termed "clerks," and suffer the same dilemma as their sisters in the '30s, '40s, and '50s.

The same problem which existed in the "hey-day" (Clark 264) of the field stared library theorists in the face: that the field was dominated by clerical chores, yet every career library worker in the field yearned to be recognized as a true librarian, claiming to be so because of her degree of experience, degree of intelligence, degree of devotion, and degree of on-site or *bona fide* library-school training.

It is worth noting that although Howard claimed 1930–1936 was the period which saw "the abandonment of training classes and library schools connected with public libraries," *Library Literature*, even in the 1940s, utilized the subheading "In-service training" to describe one form of library training for library personnel (222). It is obvious that the concept of on-the-job training was at no point in library history ever totally discredited as a viable mode of entry into librarianship. What differs, from era to era, is the degree of candor with which its import is acknowledged. Early on, it was seen as a necessary concomitant to library-school training: "[J]ust as surely as school training is desirable for librarianship, practical experience is desirable for school training" (Van Buren 372).

At no point in library history, despite disclaimers, was entrance into a professional degree of *functioning* blocked to library workers. This train of thought was articulated publicly at the famous Portland Conference, and has been obstinately uttered ever since. Herbert Putnam insisted that "the cause of training is seriously injured by the examples we have among us of people who have gone into library work without training and made a success of it ... ("Portland" 174). Moreover, "Carnegie justified his refusal to contribute financially to Dewey's School of Library Economy by saying there was 'no difficulty in getting proper persons for libraries who were naturally adapted for that work" (Greiner, "Role" 76). "[W]hile we need the trained librarian much we need the born librarian more, non-graduate tho he or she may be," stated the *Boston Evening Transcript* in 1921, arguing against the certification of librarians. "[I]f the negligence of one's forbears [sic], or the occasionally honest absence of dollars and cents stands in the way of such degrees, the library and the born librarian will never meet, or will meet but to part. Certification will then have succeeded in excluding the fittest, for natural bent, since it may not be acquired, must remain our biggest single asset" ("Certification" 891).

Later writers in the literature were always to insist that degree of experience and intelligence should be a consideration in bestowing the accolade of "professional" on a worker, and they always argued for legitimation of other avenues into the field. They were possessed of exactly the optimistic and easygoing democratism that the field so sorely lacks. They were unfortunately no majority, and interestingly, many of them were male. Donald Powell suggested, "Perhaps what we need to do is break down the distinction between the 'professional librarian' who has graduated from a year of library school, and the nonprofessional who may be the professional's equal in almost everything but formal training..." ("Library Education" 1769). Robert Franklin proposed, for instance, "Let it not be overlooked that everyone chiefly learns by doing, on the job." He added,

> [P]romotion to [the higher grades of library work] could ... be by a combination of exams and academic credits and proved experience. If recruits want to become librarians by studying and reading and observing outside of formal classes, let them have that chance, and prove their progress by exam grades. ALA might well administer nationwide exams which would at least ... label candidates.... This has been proposed before, but ALA has been too busy proliferating divisions to do something as useful as this ["Library Education" 1762–3].

Agreeing with this notion were other writers of the time, like Pfeil. In 1975 director Martelle did in fact institute rigorous exams to allow the gifted, non–MLS-holding Sacramento library workers to move themselves into professional status without extra schooling ("Sacramento Proceeds"). An Orange County library also offered an on-the-job training program "designed to equal the M.L.S. study program" (Ratcliff). Cleveland Public Library Director Ervin Gaines, himself without an MLS, proposed, also in 1975, a reversion, in effect, to a nineteenth-century notion of equivalency: "[t]hree years of work on the job will be counted as one year of academic work: 12 years on the job could amount to an undergraduate degree, and an additional five years could equal a graduate degree in library science" ("Cleveland"). Commentators were not all averse to this idea: "The Cleveland Public Library plan to offer advancement to nonprofessionals via on-the-job experience ... sounds good. Alternative routes to professional positions should be available in all career fields" (Grundt).

"Library service has grown to the point that there must be an acknowledgement of the need for a career line in the professional section running upward parallel to the career development of persons with library degrees and advanced education. The increasing demand for manpower in all disciplines makes it imperative that we improve the use made of college graduates with subject backgrounds," maintained Shirley Brother in 1968 ("Commentary" on Asheim's "Education and Manpower for Librarianship" 1113). Archie McNeal, in arguing for the skilled, non-degreed paraprofessional, wrote:

> [T]here would seem to be a place in libraries ... for the well-educated library assistant who has developed certain proficiencies on the job.... Many libraries find on their staff persons of superior educational qualifications who for various reasons have not determined to secure a library degree. Many ... have particular abilities which ... enable them to function at a level above ... routine clerical tasks.... [Such individuals] may develop to such an extent that [they occupy] a major position without having experienced any formal library school training. Certainly some of our best-known and most effective librarians have entered the profession without benefit of the midwifery of the library school. This is not to say that such a procedure is advocated, nor is it ... intended to detract from the importance of formal training. Rather, it is a plea for those special cases where ability and application merit recognition.... [M]any libraries now have on their staff individuals who perform their duties with professional skill, and think and act in a professional manner. Such staff members may well be considered for equal compensation, as well as for equal consideration in matters of vacation, retirement, and similar matters ... [221–2].

Even the redoubtable Herbert White maintained,

> I have seen employees without library degrees and without even college degrees perform satisfactorily and even superbly in professional library positions. I have graded them and paid them as professionals.... I don't mean to imply that the library school degree is not important.... But it is ... possible to succeed without it, or to fail with it ["To"].

He recommended that "society (and librarianship) ... make allowance for the individual and his abilities" ("Differences").

"I cannot go along with the implication that all staff members must have college training," librarian Eleanor Phinney wrote emphatically in 1947, "there are many situations in the small and medium-sized libraries, as well as in branch systems, when an alert, well-trained subprofessional assistant will turn in a performance as good as or even better than a library school graduate." Evelyn Allen fired off, "People who have a love and a knowledge of literature and language and history and music and art and philosophy, people who are sure of themselves socially, people of integrity, resourcefulness, and imagination to my knowledge have often been barred from library schools without that college degree, ... [but] those ... who actually built the profession [possessed] few college degrees among them and we resent this requirement" (519). More lyrically, Constance Bement writes, along the same lines—those of needing to consider the individual worker before one:

> What are we going to say ... to one of our best workers, who, we shall say for the sake of argument, has not had as much formal education as the law requires, but has a background of European travel, knows more about birds and trees and flowers than I could ever hope to know ... and what is more has shared that knowledge with every child that comes to her library? ... [Y]et technically speaking that librarian would not be entitled to entrance to any of the training courses now being offered ... but she has an orderly mind, and would be grateful for help in the simplification of her routine [961–2].

John Dawson, whose academic library utilized nonprofessionals for original cataloging of "often ... quite difficult material," claimed he had

> encountered a good many with as much knowledge and ability—and sometimes more—than many library school graduates. We have all too often accepted the assumption that a degree from an accredited library school is a guarantee of successful librarianship. And yet all of us know some who have managed to pass through library school without its teachings having made any impression on them [38–9].

Franklin candidly agreed: [S]ome clericals are more valuable than some librarians, and smarter, too ... ("Personnel" 3548).

17. Things Heat Up:
The Late 1960s and 1970s

I predict that the debate on the relative roles of librarians and library technicians will never end. If there are too few librarians, we'll worry about technicians doing "librarians' work." If there are too few technicians, we'll worry about librarians wasting their training on "unprofessional activities." If there aren't enough of either, we'll worry about untrained clerical workers being called librarians [Weaver 149].

"Paraprofessional employees ... became a disturbing element in modern personnel management about twenty years ago," stated Evans in 1979 ("Evolution" 64). They were disturbing because, though they had been recruited to be "sub" librarians, and had been envisioned as smiling and unaspiring, but moderately intelligent, able to accomplish the more "menial" of the librarians' functions, ostensibly so the librarian could "plan" things, and "have the time to put his hand behind his head and his feet on his desk and just sit and think," they often turned out to be formidably overqualified—through the greed of hiring bodies/libraries—and thus threatened the very librarians they had been hired to help (Kinzer 218–9).

In the mid–1950s and then again in the mid–1960s, federal funding—from the Library Services Act of 1956 and the Elementary and Secondary Education Act of 1965—spurred library growth, and imposed on libraries a new pressure to acquire staff (Nicholson et al. 15).

In the 1960s, many young college graduates idealistically spurned wealth and refused to participate in power structures, hoping to usher in the Age of Aquarius. Bumper stickers of the time ordered the nation to "Question Authority"; among students riled by a multitude of problems which had lain unattended to "were some who were soon to enter librarianship" (Kaplan 317). Harrington, in 1982, discussing the development of participatory management, concurred: "A significant portion of today's workforce is people who were growing up in the 1960s. The demands of that turbulent period are now being felt in new ways..." (21). Some of these people were to enter the library field not only as librarians, but as support staff.

Thus by the late '60s, many Aquarian "bright nuts" had been employed and were working out very well for the libraries employing them. By the late 1960s these paraprofessionals started to become fierce, in accord with the times, and also because these so-called clerks were becoming tired of being exploited on the job for their intelligence, while being ranked on paper with dullards. They became a force to be reckoned with, often stormily vocal, often unionizing (Oberg, "Emergence" 102). Feelings ran high both for and against giving them due credit, from allowing them to be called "paraprofessionals" (a notion which to many was anathema: "horrified faces" greeted Steele's use of the term "library technician" in 1969), to paying them the salaries they deserved (45). This seething, vital group has been sparking and intermittently igniting, like any source of powerful energy ineptly channeled, from then until now. Many of these same people, young when researchers like Azad—half of whose sample, 54.8 percent, was under age thirty—were writing, are now "graying" (81). Kathleen Martin states that a recent Internet survey shows "over sixty percent of all support staff have worked in libraries for over ten years, and nearly one-third for over fifteen years." She herself comments, fairly typically, "I did not realize I was embarking on a career in 1971 when I took a job in the library at Gustavus Adolphus Colleges, and I suspect many paraprofessionals can say the same thing" (26). Today, seasoned in their jobs, under pressure from layoffs and job-freezes which burden them with extra work, these articulate, skilled people demand to know why years of experience spent performing professional duties do not entitle them to professional status.

In 1970 Robert Presthus, under the auspices of the U.S. Office of Education, U.S. Department of Health, Education, and Welfare, surveyed 1,110 library workers to ascertain the nature of library personnel and its readiness for the technological onslaught then anticipated. He observed:

> A large proportion (40 percent) of [the clerical workers] ... have college or university degrees ... and share ... to an unusual extent the occupational attitudes and aspirations of their librarian co-workers.... [P]eople in the field have an extraordinarily high achievement level [74% of clericals in fact had college training, ranging from "some" through "graduate"].... It is well known that the undergraduate major of most librarians is in either humanities, about 70 percent; history, about 25 percent; or social science, which accounts for about 16 percent [43, 45, 47].

Paras, sharing so many features of their librarian co-population, also had the same type, if not degree, of college training as librarians. Mugnier confirmed, in 1980, that all of her paraprofessional respondents had the bachelor's degree (*Paraprofessional* 28). Commenting on the "ready availability of a sizable pool of college graduates from which [the field drew] associates," Mugnier confirms that though the liberal arts degree "[lacked] utility in the job market, ... libraries have found that background of special value" (*Paraprofessional* 87).

Presthus posited that library workers tended to "drift" into the field—among librarians, he found the percentage of "drifters" at 32 percent, and the percentage of those who chose librarianship because they "always liked books" to be 28 percent (25, 68). With candor he continues, "Such a basis for career choice is not uncommon for young men and women with liberal arts degrees in humanities and social science who are not, in the popular phrase, 'trained for anything'" (68). Doubtless the many non–library-school-trained clerical workers Presthus found in the field then, and who exist in the field now, were viewed as very similar material, feckless and without firm focus—"bright nuts"—who could help libraries out of their major personnel shortage at minimal cost. Despite his assertion, above, that clericals shared a portion of the librarian profile, he also viewed them as "an anomalous presence in the library organization" (24). Plainly he was ambivalent—if not downright contradictory—about their status, for he states:

> The first great deviation from the older professions is seen in the field's crucial dependence upon a large number of clerical workers, who in almost every case outnumber trained librarians [by more than twice as many, according to Presthus' sample]. The role of these essential members of the apparatus violates several criteria of bureaucracy. They are rarely trained specifically for their library task; they are often transitory; they are largely uncommitted to literary work as a career; they do not always share the librarian's professional values or aspirations; they are generally much younger than career librarians, with lower educational achievement. Despite this, there is not always a sharp distinction between their functional roles and those of trained librarians [15, 24].

Two paragraphs later, he writes of librarians, "Commitment to their occupation is not very high, but at least is satisfactory, compared with clericals" (24). Then he writes, after presenting a table indicating that for both female clericals (12 percent) and female librarians (21 percent) career is a dim third choice, of five satisfying "activities" (the other four being family—by far the most important to both groups—leisure, social-political, and religion), "Here it seems, we have dramatic evidence that a rather marginal career commitment is characteristic of the library field, especially among female librarians and clericals" (67). Thus it seems that after all clerical workers were not so very different in degree of commitment from librarians (who always have been mostly female) in their degree of commitment to career.

Further, regarding education necessary for satisfactory performance of work duties, Presthus notes,

> It is a noteworthy commentary on the field's aspirations for professional status that 28 percent of ... respondents indicate that specialized training is either "not very important" or "unnecessary." This somewhat jaundiced view is reinforced by responses to a statement which suggested that library education has been too specialized, that, "too many skills are taught that could be better learned on the

job." Fifty-four percent (N=290) agreed; 16 percent were "undecided"; and the remainder "disagreed" [46].

He claimed that though an amazing 97 percent of librarians working at the time of his survey held a graduate degree in librarianship, "librarians are often assigned to do clerical types of work," a situation which concerned library administrators and commentators had battled for a good forty-five years, following the sobering Williamson Reports of 1921 and 1923 (53). In Hart and Griffith's 1959–60 study, librarians were still found to be devoting 17 to 34 percent of their day to nonprofessional duties (Hart & Griffith 2759). R. W. Lewis was quick to simply admit, "It's true that our professionals do the work of clerks, but their responsibilities are professional, nonetheless" (607). But, as we have seen, in the decades following the First World War, a less than stellar type of librarian had moved into the field, replacing the earlier, more vital workers. Mugnier, echoing others, condemned the field for having "permitted mediocre librarians to become permanent staff members and [for having] even advanced them to positions of greater responsibility" (*Paraprofessional* 101).

At the same time, clerks were taking on more and more professional duties, as librarians "off-loaded" them, and these same librarians began to fear for their jobs. Bona fide paraprofessionalism was raising its Medusa head in Libraryland, and librarians observed the realities of the matter before them: clerks were smart, and clerks worked cheaper than they. Already bureaucrats were hiring them to replace degreed librarians.

This was the state of affairs in 1960, just before the spate of unionization drives among paraprofessional library workers. Evans claims, at this point, that "libraries, in effect, returned to the system of in-service training through which all librarians had once learned their trade. But the clerks were not eligible for professional status even though they might work beside librarians, doing the same work they did—at reference desks or in cataloging—and often doing it as well as they did" ("Evolution" 80). Dougherty, too, writing of the 1960s and 1970s, asseverates, "Many tasks traditionally performed by professionally trained librarians were assigned to equally capable library assistants" ("Personnel" 109). Charlotte Mugnier's study of paraprofessional use in public libraries was to confirm that by 1980, "If assignment of a given task to a [first-level] professional and not to a nonprofessional can be used as an indicator of whether or not a task is 'professional,' not a single task tested was considered to be uniquely professional by even half of the supervisors" (*Paraprofessional* 50).

In 1969, Joseph Rosenthal published results of his scrutiny of five libraries—Chicago, Cornell, the University of California at Los Angeles, Yale, and the University of Utah—undertaken to study use of paraprofessionals in cataloging. He claimed:

At all ... five..., the use of paraprofessionals is ... well-established.... [A]t most of the institutions there was a clear feeling that the use of nonprofessionals should be expanded in the cataloging area.... Three of the libraries rated the degree of success for this program as "excellent" at all classification levels, and the remaining two applied the same rating to those in the highest grade—the nonprofessionals exercising the greatest degree of discretion and independence in creating bibliographic records.... [A]ll of the libraries were seeking to expand the number of nonprofessionals engaged in cataloging, and in some cases plan to fill vacant professional positions at the higher nonprofessional levels [324, 330].

Mugnier, in her 1976 doctoral dissertation, studied task overlap between high-level paraprofessionals and entry-level MLS-holders in ten libraries. She interviewed and surveyed "194 administrators and supervisors, 135 first-level librarians, and 264 library assistants." She conducted a pre-survey query of 136 public libraries and found that "[l]ibrary assistants are performing in virtually all large public libraries tasks that were once thought appropriate for assignment to graduate librarians only and that in the opinion of their supervisors they are performing the tasks satisfactorily" (*Library* [abstract 1, 2]).

In the book which grew from the dissertation, *The Paraprofessional and the Professional Job Structure*, she stated:

> 35 percent of the library directors would replace their associates with graduate librarians if they had unlimited personnel budgets and an attractive large pool of library school graduates to hire from; 36 percent said that regardless of their budgets or the availability of library school graduates, they would not replace their associates with librarians; 27 percent said they would retain the classification, but that they would reclassify some of the positions to require the library school degree [21].

Andrews and Kelley, tracing the development of the financially constrained Texas Tech's technical services staff, make no bones about the institution's reliance on paraprofessional help: "The Texas Tech Library has never met the ratios of professional vs. clerical staff indicated as desirable in library literature.... The limited manpower resources have forced departments to train and delegate to library assistants tasks that might be assigned to professionals in other libraries" (63). The advent of OCLC, in Texas Tech as in many other libraries, forced a change in personnel distribution and procedures. Using a team approach, in which librarians and, increasingly, paraprofessionals participated, monograph backlogs were reduced, and serials holdings placed online from 1970 through the writing of the article, 1988. Four paraprofessionals became "Library Unit Supervisors," on the basis of merit, and received salary increases accordingly. Unsurprisingly, this institution suffers low turnover, and Andrews and Kelley enjoy an amazing calmness in describing the cooperative spirit of participants. All staff members at Texas Tech participate in continuing education opportunities with the support of the institution. One support-staff member co-authored a paper with a professional librarian, and no one turned a hair. This kind of peaceable kingdom was *not* the rule throughout Libraryland during the 1960s and 1970s.

Despite Mugnier's finding "only a few" librarians who felt threatened by the paraprofessional influx, there was vicious controversy in professional library magazines in the late 1960s over support-staff encroachment on professional territory (*Paraprofessional* 86). Consider the hypothetical case of "Miranda," covered in *Special Libraries* in 1965. "What are the ethics involved," Louise Stoops wonders, "in recommending a non-professional for a professional position in a special library?" "Miranda" is without a college degree, but is interested in her work in a corporate library, and diligent in learning everything her boss, a professional librarian, has to teach her. In addition, she takes evening courses in cataloging and reference. She works for twelve years in this library, and then decides to apply for work elsewhere as a professional librarian, feeling she is as knowledgeable as her mentor, who receives a query in the mail from the library to which she has applied. "What kind of professional recommendation could or should he write about Miranda?"

"It's Miranda that has the problem," hisses one *Special Libraries* letter-writer.

> It is Miranda that needs a condemnation ... rather than a recommendation.... There are already too many Mirandas in the profession who lack insight into their own problems.... [S]he should take a cut in salary in addition to giving a portion of her salary to Mr. Samson as reward on-the-job-training tuition. Then perhaps with the right attitude she might earn her pay ... [Svorenick].

Fortunately such venom was not the only reaction to the hypothesis above, but it does characterize the fever into which many librarians worked themselves over the "nonpros" in their midst. The nastiness and condescension can be inferred, when not actually sizzling in printer's ink before one's wondering eyes, from indignant responses like the one from three impressively credentialed nonprofessionals who had obviously been driven beyond all patience by the condescension of librarians in the field, in particular one John Ayala, who did "not feel that nonprofessionals have the benefit of a broad liberal education" (842). After detailing educational backgrounds that rival or surpass the schooling of any number of professional librarians past and present, paras Gramer, Hintzman, and Parsil remark dryly, "[T]he profession would be making one step in the right direction if it would stop considering 'nonprofessional' as synonymous with 'uneducated,' and a second step if it began recognizing someone else's education" (Gramer et al., "Nonpro").

Of course, many directors were taking note of the educational level of their employees. Ralph McCoy states that a library should have a written set of guidelines for employing the three classes of library worker: "professional, clerical, and custodial," and then ingenuously writes:

What constitutes a competent librarian? He should be a professional, which means he should have a college baccalaureate degree plus at least a year of professional education in an accredited library school. A college educated person with some years of significant library experience but without the library degree may also qualify as a professional librarian, but evidence of his ability will be more difficult to appraise ["Personnel Policies" 492–3].

His statements appear to obviate each other. Nonetheless, as Mugnier found, "[a] substantial number of supervisors held that, from a personality standpoint, their associates were, as a group, superior to librarians" (*Paraprofessional* 59). She noted "the highly positive view of the associate's contribution to library services," especially those in children's work (*ibid.* 68, 86). "Poor service attitudes' frequently were claimed to be prevalent among recent graduates," she claims (*ibid.* 69). And, as earlier commentators found, her respondents criticized "[p]eople who happily submit themselves to the library school grind, or who become librarians because they think of the library as a shelter against the hard world, … the ones with the limited personalities" (*ibid.* 59).

Alfred Whitelock, throwing himself into the fray of epistles which was waged throughout the '60s and '70s in professional journals, waxed enthusiastic in defense of his paraprofessional staff:

> I have a staff of 37 in my library. Of these, only one has had formal library science training at a university, and another noble soul is taking correspondence courses. And yet this library has just won a John Cotton Dana award for publicity; it has 44 percent of the county population registered as card-holders (which I believe is one of the highest in the country), and is now embarking on cable television to televise regularly in-library programs as well as community projects.
>
> My punch line is this: All of us who work in libraries are librarians. That is our common denominator. After that we are either professionals or paraprofessionals or clericals or whatever. It is high time, professionals, that we got off our high horses and began to look outward to the people we serve rather than bickering about who is the most important among us. I wouldn't trade my staff for all the tea in China, and what are they? Paraprofessionals.

On the other hand, librarians and clerks, in more retrograde institutions, were not supposed to "fraternize" with each other, either on the job on breaks. We have seen how Larry Oberg and his wife flouted this convention back in the 1960s. His institution was far from alone in this practice. Clerks and pages in the public library I worked in told me similar tales of being rebuked throughout the 1970s and into the 1980s for "fraternizing" with *each other*—on the basis of *their* difference in status—and of course, it was the given that librarians were not to fraternize with either clerks or pages. (Fortunately, by the late 1980s, this "apartheid" was becoming a subject of mirth for ever-larger numbers of employees.)

Overwrought Eastern college librarians, at their annual conference in 1967, characterized the issue of nonprofessionals in academic libraries as "[a]n invitation to a hernia," and, at best, "a complex problem which will not go away until it is solved." One participant was sent to "the verge of hysteria" over the subject ("Academic Librarians").

Elsewhere, because of this hysteria, "nonpros" were held back from professional opportunities because of librarians' fright. For example, LTAs complained that they were being "kept away" from working with library technologies; in New York State, they were "barred" from certain librarians' associations ("Calif. Meet"; "NYLA"). Despite these stratagems, because of their perceived "competency (or over-competency)," they spread into all areas of library work ("ALA Seeks"). In 1968, participants in a University of San Francisco conference asserted that technicians would "debase the quality of librarianship" and "viewed with alarm the hiring of technicians in school, college, and public libraries—in place of librarians" ("Technicians Seen"). Out of this alarm grew CLOUT (Concerned Librarians Opposing Unprofessional Trends), composed of "middle-management" librarians, who blustered that "clerical workers and even unpaid volunteers ... [were] taking over many library tasks that require the [MLS], to the detriment of library service and the danger of the degreed librarian" ("Calif. Librarians").*

In the face of outcry at a proposal to allow qualified paraprofessionals to take examinations to acquire professional status in the Sacramento City-County Library System in 1974, Harold Martelle, SCCLS's director, nevertheless maintained that "degrees are no longer valid as the sole job criterion; it's a question of whether or not one can do the job." Insisting that "[o]ne year of graduate school ... doesn't make that much of a difference," he pointed out that "several LTAs at SCCLS have graduate degrees and yet are stuck at the paraprofessional level" ("New Career"). He defended his decision to acquire the best people for professional positions by pointing out that "only the extraordinarily gifted" would pass the exam—no more than three or four ("Sacramento Librarians" 2024; "New Career"). Of course, that is exactly the point—to allow the "extraordinary" individual to proceed unimpeded to her appropriate level, as Hitchler had urged fifty-seven years earlier. When confronted with angry professional librarians claiming that his was an "atavistic suggestion," and arrogating to themselves alone the power to exude a truly professional air and provide a superior grade of public service on the basis of that magic graduate year, Martelle impatiently charged that "to assume that ... paraprofessional[s]—some of whom have worked in libraries for a decade or more—have no sensitivity to the needs of the user or no sense of what the library is all about is utterly absurd, and indicates the worst sort of prejudice" (Robert; "Sacramento Librarians" 2025).

---

*Theodore Figura rebuked the field for formation of CLOUT, saying, "CLOUT and COLT should be pulling in the same direction.... Librarians and paraprofessionals must rise together."

Into all this internecine wrangling came the clear, sensible voice of John Berry in 1977, who claimed that one of the chief jobs of the librarian was to teach other people—"users"—to employ the tools in the library, so that they would in future be empowered, independent, capable of self-help. "The logical extrapolation of that notion was the idea that in the ideal world everyone could be his or her own librarian," he writes.

> We are not threatened when the user ... is able to grasp our lessons and learns to do ... searching independently. We don't interpret that success as a threat to our "professional" status. But when a paraprofessional comes along saying: "Listen, I can do those searches. You taught me," we are quick to respond: "You must not do that, nor should you tell patrons how to do that. That's professional work and we librarians are supposed to do that."

"We can't have it both ways," he concludes. "We can't say to the patron, 'Learn these techniques, then you won't have to ask us,' while we tell our own paraprofessionals, 'You can't do that, it's professional work'" ("Two 'Professions").

Alas, what goes around comes around. In their perpetual struggle to make the indubitably important work they do seem "professional," librarians have always tried to distance themselves from clerks and their clerical labors, however belatedly and unsubtly (Evans, "Evolution" 83). However, the nature of libraries is that, most of the time, they are and have been underfunded, taken for granted, and often treated with casual disrespect by both boards of directors and the public they serve (in this connection, see Peelle's sad story of a California library system's collapse). People who have gravitated towards library work have, at their best, generally been as the stereotype indicates: introspective, quiet, dry, "altruistic" people with interest in books ranging from the mild to the intense, caught up in learning and in bringing this enthusiasm to other people (Drake, "A"; L. Miller 6). Unless professionalism is made an issue, they have focused more on what needs to be done to keep their modest libraries running than on their image, other than to dress neatly, and this has meant, historically, that much of the time they are working as *de facto* clerks.

One elderly woman, *sans* MLS, ran her community's library in the 1970s from a small, musty building with a tiny staff of volunteers during limited hours. While she was not in this library, putting things away and making the place presentable, she was engaged in soliciting and receiving donations of every kind of reading material, which she would then store in her barn. To my husband and myself fell the honor or ordering these materials in her barn one weekend. This entire effort of hers, and the effort of each of her volunteers, was undertaken purely out of reverence for *the book*, with no thought whatsoever of professionalism. I think that, historically, some of the best library work has had this modest, bookish savor composed of equal parts dusty, down-and-dirty drudgery and the most ethereal idealism. Consider the librarians who took to the road with horse and wagon to constitute the first bookmobile service (Passet, "Reaching"), the plane delivery of materials to people in far-flung Alaskan regions, the backwoods community libraries run out of people's homes.

Commentators throughout library history have had no trouble identifying as "professional" librarians energetic, intelligent women who had some degree of formal education, but no library degree from a graduate school of library science, and who were largely self-taught and -driven—for example, Mary Lemist Titcomb and Anne Hadden (the former was educated, but initiated her career before the advent of library schools, the latter had only a certificate from a six-week summer course in library techniques at Berkeley, earned in 1900) (Marcum 94; Sallee 353–4). Or were they clerks? What's in a label? A lot, unfortunately. Even today, librarians in small community libraries take umbrage at being taken to task for performing "clerical" duties at the circulation desk, for performing tasks, presumably, beneath them (Woolson *vis-à-vis* White, "Small"). They do not consider their professional honor compromised when they are seen taking the time to know the folks in their area and to know their tastes. They are performing, as Roma Harris would probably agree, at a service level—that of interfacing directly with the people they exist to serve—appropriate for librarian professionals. Are these people clerks? Professionals? Paraprofessionals? Support staff? As noted, looking at librarianship is a lot like picking shapes out of moving clouds.

Bright people devoted to libraries are not always concerned with the MLS; they are concerned primarily with providing the citizenry access to books. They prove a quick study and learn the ways of libraries and librarians in the interest of running the library, i.e., getting and making books available to a voracious public, whatever that may involve. *Real* librarians—degreed or not—have always picked up the slack in tough times and performed dull clerical chores—largely though lack of money. Their professionalism has lain in their commitment and in their native ability.

Library curator Jean Longland exclaimed with irritation in 1968, perusing the snide letters sniping back and forth on the profession-nonprofessional issue in *Special Libraries*: "The uproar over sanctity of professional standards and all that only makes me impatient.... [A]ll we want is staff members who can do a good job, regardless of their degrees."

18. Persistent Overlap

In my situation the only place there is NOT overlap is where bill-paying occurs [MaryAnn Davison].

Librarians may not have cared whether good employees had the MLS or not, but good employees have always cared about their "good job" finding its just remuneration. Back in 1967, Karl Nyren made reference to the "rather muddled mess that has always characterized the library personnel picture" ("Libraries" 2115). In 1977, MacCampbell scolded,

> The line between professional activities and nonprofessional tasks has been very hazy and, in many cases, nonexistent except in terms of salary. In most libraries the nonprofessional group, particularly those members with the highest capabilities, has been seriously exploited in a number of ways. They have been carrying on professional work as well as, or better than, the professional members of the library staff. In hundreds of libraries they have been providing professional service simply because there were no professionals available to do it. In every case they were paid less, simply because they did not have the professional degree. This is exploitation of the worst kind [1718].

A Libref-l poster observed, as recently as February, 1995:

> This is the fourth or fifth library I have been privileged to work in. In each place I have come across the same unanswerable question: what is the difference between a "paraprofessional" and a "professional" library worker? Each library has split the duties differently (all my experience has been in reference services): in one ILL is solely a "Professional" function, in another it was "Clerical," for example. Some libraries care very much about labels: "She is NOT a 'librarian,' she [doesn't] have an MLS." Some don't care at all: "the public considers us all librarians, why confuse them?" I don't think definitions should matter much, but they do because in the end it comes down to money—and too often resentment: "what do you do that makes you worth twice as much as me?" when we both are responsible for full service reference, etc., etc. I know that some institutions have positions well codified and salary scales to match, but many of us don't, and anyway, that still doesn't address the deepest question of comparable worth expressed so often [Sherri Saines].

Happily, this librarian is, as she explains, "the type to root for the underdog." This query, juxtaposed with the historical path we have just followed, indicates that to this moment, the library field has still not addressed the continuing internal pressure built up by professional/paraprofessional job overlap, nor, more importantly, the question of remuneration for professional services rendered, regardless of status of professionalism on paper.

Kreitz and Ogden, in their large job-satisfaction survey of 889 library workers across California, conducted in 1983 and published in 1990, were perplexed by the "role ambiguity" they were finding in every facet of library work. They wrote:

> In developing ... the questionnaire, we faced the problem of how to describe the library tasks we included sufficiently so that they could be labelled "professional" or "paraprofessional." In fact, the difficulty we had in doing this parallels the problems faced by the profession in trying to define what it is that each class of library employee does that makes it unique and thus rewarded differently [301].

The largest area of dissatisfaction for the 563 library assistants they queried was far and away the question of money: more than 80 percent of them were utterly disgusted with the pay they received for doing professional-level work (*ibid.* 308). St. Lifer stated it simply in 1994: the "MLS means money": "having the degree ... translates into a higher salary by as much as 37%" ("Are" 47).

Overlap is a very old problem. The earliest "ideal desk assistants," like support staff today, experienced this sort of stealthy off-loading. "There is also the assistant who turns in an unfinished piece of work, the punctuation and construction, if it be a piece of writing, requiring to be gone over and revised, columns of figures requiring to be re-added, etc. .... I have known only one library assistant whose work it was safe to send to the printer without revision," snarled one librarian. Exactly what were these men expecting of barely trained assistants, often with no more than the high-school degree? Or even of college-educated women? An awful lot for a dismally low wage ("Library Assistants: Shortcomings" 356). Very likely, these women were the "anonymous" authors of the bibliographies and reports of the day, whose librarians took credit for their work, perhaps thinking this course proper because they had had to insert a few commas or re-add some figures.

In 1952, Edward Wight, while condemning the utilization of nonprofessional circulation staff to do "such professional tasks as advising readers about their selection of books, preparing reading lists and bibliographies, and answering reference questions," nevertheless saw "safely rated as 'clerical'" "[o]riginal cataloging of fiction, where no classification number is used and no subject headings are used" (31). This is the equivalent of an alcoholic on the wagon taking the first drink. "Off-loading" of professional tasks is amazingly easy to slide into. Since most clerical workers are hardly stupid, and library work is easy to learn, it is easy to go from letting them do the fiction to letting them do the biographies, to letting them do the whole thing. It is easy to go from letting them proofread your reports to writing them, easy to let them go from placing book orders and figuring costs to actually choosing the books, and thus taking the whole thing off your back. It is especially easy to do things like this when you are faced with budgetary constraints or a staff shortage.

And Wight, in describing "Relative Difficulty of Library Clerical Work," takes the easy way. He does not at any point in his listing of relatively easy or difficult clerical duties note that any of them are actually "professional" tasks:

> Simple clerical tasks may be illustrated by: charging materials, discharging materials, computing and collecting fines, counting and recording circulation, filing book slips, copying used-up book slips, returning books to the shelves, reading the shelves for accuracy, marking the spines of books, doing simple repairing of torn pages and spines, and answering directional questions....
>
> Work of somewhat greater, or average, difficulty may be illustrated by: adding duplicates to the shelflist, typing headings on catalog cards, searching in catalogs to determine holdings, marking off withdrawn books from the shelflist, sending overdue notices, maintaining central registration files, preparing statistical data for reports, and receiving applications from prospective borrowers....
>
> More difficult and responsible work is: assigning book numbers (as Cutter numbers), descriptive cataloging of fiction, filing cards in catalogs (without revision), and supervising routine work of clerical staff in lower classes of positions [54].

His third category is the paraprofessional one; clearly these are professional duties. In real life, these categories shifted and merged, the lines became a certain grayness at the edges of everyday work; yet those lines were etched in stone when payday rolled around. Williams examined in 1945 a 1939 Texas time study requested by the ALA, the only raw data surviving a larger study of fifty universities: "Over a two-week period, each staff member indicated exactly how much time he spent on each of 127 listed tasks. A number of these tasks, unfortunately, cannot be definitely classified as professional or nonprofessional...," he admitted (306).

In 1974 Ph.D. candidate Dana Gould conducted a study focused specifically on fifty-nine library administrators' perception of library paraprofessional roles in their respective libraries (28). The study was confined to directors of large public junior colleges, state universities, and metropolitan public libraries in five southern states—Alabama, Florida, Louisiana, Mississippi, and Texas (3). He found that of thirty-two borderline activities, only one could be agreed upon solely as a paraprofessional duty: the checking of order cards for duplicates (33, 35). The thirty-two realms of interest were:

1. Conducting tours
2. Explaining card catalog

3. Compiling reading lists
4. Giving book talks
5. Maintaining bulletin boards
6. Planning and designing displays
7. Supervising inventories
8. Running interlibrary loan
9. Supervising small branches
10. Replacing materials
11. Accepting small gift collections
12. Preparing bibliographies
13. Verifying entries
14. Maintaining circulation statistics
15. Cataloging simple materials
16. Cataloging materials using LC cards
17. Cataloging materials without LC cards
18. Dealing with patrons on lost materials
19. Answering simple reference questions
20. Organizing and maintaining vertical files
21. Revising filing
22. Checking order cards for duplicates
23. Ordering LC cards
24. Withdrawing materials lost or damaged
25. Indexing local materials
26. Selecting materials for purchase
27. Assigning cutter numbers
28. Collecting and recording fines
29. Assisting patrons in selecting books
30. Preparing abstracts
31. Inventorying and ordering supplies
32. Maintaining periodical checklists (33)

There was significant disagreement on items 2, 12, 23, 25, and 30. Gould concluded that "a paraprofessional task in one type of library might be classified as professional in another type" (44). Further, he indicated that "classification in some institutions may be based primarily on education, rather than on duty" and that "there was a concern over the hiring of paraprofessionals in place of professionals in order to save money" (58, 53).

Despite pundit Asheim's assurance that the characteristics of library clerks, LTAs, and library associates, respectively, were as clear as the morning sun, the field was in disarray (see his confident presentation in *LTA's* 5–13). Plus, Nicholson found the "core of information" set for LTAs "nebulous" (12). As to job differentiation, "[s]ome administrators classified all paraprofessionals as clerks, others technicians, and still others had either two or three different categories corresponding to clerks, technicians, and associates. Several library directors even reported that the technician or associate was classified as librarian I" (68).

Much detailed discussion and specifying of title and job description took place in the 1960s and 1970s, with the publication of the government's position-classification standards, the GS series #1410–1412, the ALA Library Education Division's "LED Statement of Policy," and the so-called *"LEPU"* (*Library Education and Personnel Utilization*) document; yet today there exists just as much confusion, if not more, as then.* For instance, Parmer and East found, in their 1993 article on job satisfaction, more than ninety job titles for support staff in a mere twelve libraries. They remarked with understatement that under these circumstances "categorizing workers was extremely difficult" (52).

Harrelson, also in 1974, reported that, in his study of information-desk staffing in 155 academic and public libraries, directors "varied considerably in their estimate of time spent on duties in each category. Some thought that none of the information desk duty was professional in nature, and some considered all the work professional" (24).

Donald Gould, in 1985, "found a definite, observable, measurable overlap between professional and nonprofessional library work" at what he called the "Stratum 2 level," basically the level which has come to be known as "paraprofessional" (244). Makinen and Speer's "evidence suggests ... that work assignment overlap is [still] prevalent" (139). Common sense tells us how situations prevalent today, and yesterday, evolved. Of course, librarians would promote the cleverer clerks to do what Wight called "more difficult and responsible work," some of which already is treading into "professional" turf: assigning cutter numbers (i.e., original cataloging), supervising (management), and catalog maintenance. And Wight's is a conservative list, from a bygone stage in library development. What would he have made of clerks with computer expertise? Where would he draw the line when "bibliographic instruction" was involved? "Clerks" today do much more than they did in his time. Libsup-l consists of library assistants doing work far beyond any of Wight's parameters. The very fact that these people are on the Internet, and that a paraprofessional designed their listserv, indicates the level of their skill. It is amusing to watch librarians over the last sixty or seventy years struggling with the concept of "a difference of degree amounts to a difference in kind"— whether they are observing librarians performing clerical tasks or whether they are watching clerks performing the work of librarians.

What use, then, were the efforts of Williamson, with his painstaking

---

*Though LEPU, in fact, according to the ALA/SCOLE study, "recommends some overlap between high level paraprofessional salaries and those of entry level librarians"; implied is a corresponding overlap in duties (*World* "Issue Paper #5").

1923 "Reports"; and of the government, with its 1966 civil service position-classification pamphlets GS 1410, GS 1411, and GS 1412; and of the ALA, with its 1970 and 1976 *LEPU* policy statements? Every effort to channel clerical work into staid, discrete conduits has proven vain, because the nature of library work is that any smart person can learn it. Bright paraprofessionals have been kept from professional status mostly through the efforts of librarians to misrepresent the sophistication of the jobs paras are asked to do, to repress them, or to restrict their sphere of activity. When paraprofessionals do function as professionals—often over decades—their efforts are almost never recognized in the form of title change or an increase in salary.

19. Paraprofessionals at the Reference Desk: A Trend of the 1980s, a Paradigm from the Nineteenth Century

The objective of a library is ... to help patrons find the information they desire....
[I]t is at the reference desk that the process of determining the patron's need, formulating a research strategy to fill that need, and providing accurate and complete information to the patron is finally tested [Christensen et al. 468].

One of the more hotly contested issues in the ongoing "off-loading" saga
is the steadily increasing use of paraprofessionals to staff "that once sacrosanct
preserve of the true professional, the reference desk" (Oberg, "Paraprofessionals: Shaping" 3). Trained support staff are more and more relied upon to
conduct reference interviews, that "most cherished ... [aspect] of reference
librarianship" (Hammond 98). In fact, Fatzer records that

> a survey of sixty-nine academic libraries in Illinois in 1983 found that sixty-one
> percent used paraprofessionals at the reference/information desks. A national
> sample of thirty-three academic libraries in 1988 also found sixty-one percent
> using paraprofessional staff to answer reference questions [159].

Grace Franklin maintained in 1991 that in Ohio, at least,

> 85% of the responding [public] libraries use paraprofessionals to provide direct
> reference service to patrons. This phenomenon is not of recent vintage. Over 70%
> of the libraries using paraprofessionals have done so for 20 years or more....
> Among the libraries using paraprofessionals, a majority (58%) report that para-
> professionals provide 50% or more of total reference desk service hours.... The
> vast majority of responding libraries (78%) said paraprofessionals work the ref-
> erence desk on their own. Just 24% schedule paraprofessionals only when a
> professional reference librarian is working at the desk or available on call [6].

But the history of using less than "professional" help at the "hallowed" (Schwartz 1730) horseshoe desk goes back to the inception of modern librarianship, when fresh young bookish high-school girls, quickly trained in on-site classes or summer institutes, were placed at the circulation desk, where they were expected to field any and all questions with skill and poise. "It is a happy day to discover a new assistant who reports an intelligent and exhaustive list of reference works that have been consulted without being told in advance," wrote one exacting director in 1904 ("Library Assistants: Shortcomings" 358).

Even after the Ideal Desk Assistant was perceived to have been a failure and a blow to librarianship's professionalism, she reared her bonny head again in the 1930s, summoned by a new group of senior librarians anxious to shed the stigma of clericism which was beginning to adhere uncomfortably to the field. The seeds for the proliferation of clerical, and later, paraprofessional, help at the reference desk were built into the earliest new training programs for library technicians designed in the '30s, notably the Clerical Library Aides course at the Los Angeles City College in 1937, where recruits with "more than the average amount of personality and intelligence" were admitted only after extreme vetting via tests and interviews. Like their early sisters, the desk attendants, these women were expected to have "acquaintance with authors and titles of important pieces of literature," ability to compile bibliographies, and familiarity with world events. Among the courses they were given was one on "the use of important reference tools and in the answering of simple reference questions" (Pidduck 408). Thus began the diminution of the professional librarian's sovereignty at the reference desk, despite what came to be the standard knee-jerk disclaimer: "A proposal to introduce such training in localities where clerical workers may successfully compete with professionally trained librarians," wrote Pidduck sternly, "is to be condemned" (409).

But in fact, over twenty years later, directors of library-technician programs were still trying to counter the prevalent, and valid, "fear that an encroachment was being planned on the professional status of the librarian and that technicians would be used to fill positions where graduate librarians might have been employed" (Dwyer 3620). "[T]he college should not represent this training as professional or even as pre-professional education," wrote Robert Meyer (455). Maddox assured the field that "[s]tudents are made aware that their training will not be such that they can be employed as substitutes for professional librarians" (294). Nevertheless, "We ... were dismayed to note," admits Dwyer, one community-college director, "the tendency of parsimonious or hard-pressed boards *and librarians* to employ our graduates in [professional] positions ... (3622).

Mugnier points out, however, that despite these displays of concern, the *LEPU* statement of 1970, which "officially" established the paraprofessional classification, merely "legitimatized a practice born of expediency and ...

blessed by success" (*Paraprofessional* 9). One of the administrators she interviewed commented simply, "We have a tendency to allow professional shortages to develop because we know we have the assistants to fall back upon" (*ibid.* 54). In 1978 LTAs were "still viewed as a job threat; concern was voiced 'that with tighter budgets everywhere the temptation to employ only LTAs is very real'" ("LTA's in"). And why should they not have hired these people as professionals? Rhua Heckart in 1968 was to report "[i]n answer to the suggestion that some library aide training courses are merely watered down graduate library courses": "in some instances they aren't even watered down: they may be pretty much duplicates" (*Progress* 11).

The utilization of information desks may have been a first step in the great reference-desk takeover that has been occurring for the past thirty years (K. Williams). Harrelson found that 47 percent of academic libraries and 64 percent of public libraries were utilizing them, and he believed, after studying his survey results, that the duties of staff at information desks were "basically subprofessional in nature" (22, 26). Though they were there nominally to answer merely directional queries or easy reference queries they certainly accustomed the field to seeing nondegreed library workers practicing the dissemination of information at reference-like desks. Bloomberg, the author of a popular textbook for technician training courses, stated that he held "a liberal view of the role of the LMTA [Library Media/Technical Assistant] in reference services" (86). He also envisioned them supplying an elementary form of BI (85). Since by 1977 his book was in its second edition (the first having appeared in 1972), it is clear that employing librarians shared his views of paraprofessionals in reference.

In 1975, Rosanna Miller casually noted: "[J]unior college paraprofessional[s] ... perform responsibly as ... general reference librarian[s]" (552). She further states with eloquence:

> No library is so rich in human resources or good will to be able to afford the wasted potential of a more than competent subject specialist shuttled aside for a less than tolerable librarian sailing under the false colors of a graduate library school degree. Establishing a rigid rule barring all but professionally trained librarians from the reference desk would simplify personnel decisions, but it is indefensible in any but the most ideal library. If it were possible to staff a reference service with only eminently qualified reference librarians, this would be ideal. Until that brave new world arrives, the door must be left open for the otherwise qualified person who, by choice or necessity, has not obtained the open sesame of an M.L.S. degree [553–4].

By 1990, Oberg found that "88 percent of the Association of Research Libraries (ARL) and 66 percent of the smaller college and universities libraries [sic] nationally regularly assign paraprofessionals to work at their reference desks" ("Response" 106). Three-quarters of Jahoda and Bonney's public library respondents, in the same year, admitted utilizing paras at their reference desks, 33 percent of them when no librarians were on duty (329).

Of course, in a pinch, when no librarian is present or available, clerks have always unofficially performed reference services. Hiebing in 1991 stated that "in certain parts of the United States, often in rural areas, all of the staff in the library are paraprofessional" (9). She goes on to imply, in reference to a paraprofessional reference training program in California—C.O.R.E.—that many of these workers also lack a bachelor's degree. In these many small, branch, or rural libraries, reference work is probably done as efficiently and expeditiously as any *bona fide* librarian could do with extant materials, because in such settings library workers process the books and often have time to peruse them as well. Also, the reference works to which they have access are few. They may enjoy the wisdom that comes of job longevity, and, there is usually a family or team atmosphere and a lack of rigid hierarchy that permits them to carry out their duties eagerly without self-consciousness or threat.

In the past, all librarians were trained on the job, either as apprentices or as students in on-site training programs in large libraries. That was their road to professionalism—hardly surprising that, unofficially, it still is. And officially, graduate library programs increasingly acknowledge the truth behind the older apprenticeship venues to professionalism in "generic' education" requirements, in which some MLS aspirants must "learn the specifics of a type of library on the job" (Hiebing 6). The large number of clerks and paraprofessionals who start out in libraries and then proceed through library school for their MLS are vastly better trained than people who enter and complete library school from other routes. They are better trained because most of their training has already taken place on the job. I believe that any prowess or intelligence shown by any MLS-holding library worker was firmly in place and functioning before she ever sat down in her first library "science" course. The MLS arose because there finally were not enough large libraries to train the growing numbers of library workers to staff the growing numbers of libraries being built in the infancy of this century. In addition, pundits believed setting library schools, *which would mimic on-the-job training*, in universities would enhance their prestige, hence the growth of both undergraduate and graduate library programs.

In larger public and especially in academic libraries, there has been doubt that experienced nonprofessionals could perform at the level of experienced librarians. Hence, in the 1970s, studies of paras performing professional-level work commenced. These studies were largely inspired by two factors: the "perceived" librarian shortage (Dougherty, "Personnel" 108), and the notion that librarians' precious professional time could be more profitably spent in collection development (Halldorsson & Murfin 386), faculty liaising, computer database searching (Oberg et al., "Faculty" 215), research, publishing, teaching, attending conferences, sitting on committees (Emmick 151), and general administration (Veaner, "Continuity" 14).

St. Clair and Aluri, in a speculative study dealing with the kinds of reference problems typically presented in academic libraries, thought paraprofessionals could probably deal with most of these questions. They categorized and counted the types of queries fielded at a reference desk over a 44-day period. Utilizing 31 categories to assess the content of 5,588 questions, they determined that 44.1 percent were directional, 18 percent instructional, 32 percent reference, and 5.9 percent "extended reference." They postulated that "nonprofessionals *with adequately planned training and an orientation program* [emphasis added] could [handle] ... 80 percent of all reference questions," 60 percent of these being instructional or directional, and 20 percent ready reference. The other 20 percent, the more difficult reference questions, could be referred to librarians (152–3). Their 80/20 percent finding still underlies paraprofessional/professional staffing patterns both proposed and actual in libraries today.

A Canadian librarian, Margaret Beckman, claimed in 1973 that the percentage of questions which could be competently handled by paraprofessionals could be even higher—85 percent (Boyer & Theimer 193). Courtois and Goetsch note that research undertaken even as long ago as the '60s showed that

> the relationship between library education and reference efficiency demonstrated no significant difference between nonprofessional and professional performance in answering questions accurately, although professionals took significantly less time to answer queries [383].

In the 1980s a number of studies were made, not upholding this early sense of buoyancy concerning the capacity of paraprofessionals, but appearing to impugn it. Emmick charges the "nonprofessional" with the "tendency to become over-zealous in his/her desire to be useful" (153). She pronounces, "When nonprofessionals make initial contacts, they must do so as employees who are well trained, not in the reference skills but rather in recognizing the types of questions that may indicate the need for a full reference interview" (153). She sees nonprofessionals at the reference desk as useful low-cost creatures, albeit a mite too enthusiastic, like large, immature dogs apt to prance up to people and place muddy paws on shoulders, licking faces without restraint. She believes they could be muzzled, however, if trained to answer "safe" questions, and if made "clearly distinguishable by the patron by the use of badges, signs, physical separation, and any other useful means" (maybe whips, fetters, pens?) (155). On the positive side, she sees "nonprofessionals" answering "safe" questions as a means to effect "significant improvement in the morale of the librarians," since librarians "have been educated and trained to respond to reference questions; doing so stimulates their creative abilities and raises their estimation of themselves as professionals *when they are successful* [emphasis added]" (154). She advises the use of "nonprofessionals" to "reduce the sense of harassment and anxiety that is prevalent in some libraries at peak times" (154). One wonders how five to ten reference questions per hour, which is what Emmick discovered reference librarians answering on her 1981 survey of 367 academic libraries, could "harass" a librarian to the point of low morale, especially since she concedes only 41 to 60 percent of these questions require "searching or instruction" (155). Obviously reference librarians are a sensitive lot.

Gloomy statistics are also adduced—those, for instance, of Halldorsson and Murfin, albeit in 1977, who whale away at the reader with statements like "Professionals personally arrived at the correct solution in the reference interview on 52 percent of questions, while nonprofessionals did so on 20 percent" and, concerning "wrong type of source" questions, "On 50 percent of these questions nonprofessionals probed further, while on 90 percent professionals did so" (388, 390).

By the mid–'70s, Boyer and Theimer had found that in approximately 69 percent of typical academic libraries, reference desks were staffed by nonprofessionals (paraprofessionals and students) approximately 33 percent of the time (195, 198). Unfortunately, *"more than 80 percent [of these libraries] indicated that formal in-service training was not provided* [emphasis added]," nor were informal orientations, and only five of the 141 surveyed had written manuals for their new reference-desk personnel (195, 197). These statistics clarify the reasons behind Halldorsson and Murfin's grim findings.

Here it must be noted that studies of the competence of librarians in answering reference questions during the 1970s and 1980s, when questions about paraprofessional competency in and suitability for reference work were being debated, give us an important perspective on the studies of paraprofessional reference competency that burgeoned in the 1980s. In "Half-Right Reference: Is It True?" Crowley in 1985 prefaced his overview of research on reference testing conducted throughout the '70s and early '80s with the flat statement that "half-right" was "an accurate [statistical] reflection of the reported state of reference quality in academic as well as public libraries" (59). His table showing results of studies held in nine different public library surveys indicated the accuracy percentages running from 40 to 80 percent, with most occupying a more moderate middle ground: 56.4 percent (60). Moreover, he claimed the questions used in these and other studies of reference adequacy had been adjudged "easy" or "easier than average" by commentators (66).

A study by Hernon and McClure in 1986 claimed that librarians answered factual and bibliographic questions correctly only 55 percent of the time. Needless to say, these findings cast a pall over librarians' claim to superior authority in the reference interview.

Christensen et al. published a comparison, in 1989, of professional and student assistant reference-desk successes. True, student assistants are not quite paraprofessionals in the usual sense, but some of the problems raised here cross over into the paraprofessional studies. The undergraduate student assistants generally were working in the same subject area of the library that they were majoring in; the graduate assistants were often MLS candidates, but often were not working in departments where they had any subject expertise. The article claims that students were not adept in negotiating "implicit" questions, though they fared well in answering "explicit" ones (470). "Only 36 percent of the seventy-five questions asked by proxy patrons resulted in completely correct answers. Another 25 percent received partially correct or incomplete results from their query[, hence] ... only [a] 61 percent ... degree of correctness," proclaim the authors (472).

Still, does this figure not compare favorably with the 55 percent record of professional librarians? Well, no, according to the authors: "[S]tudent reference assistants do not perform at a desirable or acceptable level" (472). The authors claim that "over a third of the time they do not seek more informed help for patrons." There are subtle problems with these findings, and the tendency to judge assistants as inept must be questioned.

First, the assistants had been working for only one semester under this experimental arrangement (469), whereas the librarians must have been doing reference work for considerably longer. Second, no evaluation of professional abilities was done before the study. Third, though students felt "comfortable" with their workload, at the same time they felt "more complete service could have been provided had there been sufficient time or additional desk personnel" (474–5). Fourth, re: the "emotional climate" in the library, "the lowest ranked relationship [was] that between the student reference assistants and the subject specialists..." (475–6). Fifth, "[b]ecause the specialists [were] often not available, the department assistants felt the students should be trained in the complex strategies themselves, or at least have an opportunity to review the strategies used by the professional to solve a problem..." (476–7). Sixth, no written manual existed to aid these workers in the absence of thorough person-to-person training.

These flaws in presentational emphasis appear in studies of paraprofessionals at the reference desk, as well as of student assistants. Lack of on-the-job training and experience are the greatest and most inexplicable lacunae in the whole phenomenon of nonprofessional reference-desk performance, with some exceptions—for example, Woodard and Van Der Laan's experience setting up training programs and instructional materials for Illinois reference paraprofessionals, and an earlier, quite extensive (c. thirty-hour) effort in San Diego, described by Coleman and Margutti (218). Thus, lack of real experiential or educational comparability between paraprofessional and professional—lack of fairness, in short—distorts practically every research result.

A study comparing library technical assistants with graduate students holding library assistantships and student assistants majoring in library science claims, in discussing proper referrals of reference questions, that

[r]eferrals made by graduate assistants were 83.3% correct, those made by student assistants were 74.3% correct, and those made by library technical assistants were 54.4% correct [Woodard 461].

How to account for the seeming doltishness of the paraprofessionals, since "the assumption had always been that the library technical assistants, as long-term, full-time employees, would know the library better than the other groups" (461)? The analysis continues, obliviously, and then notes casually:

> Probably the most important factor, though, is that library technical assistants staff the information desk during weekly meetings, so that student assistants and graduate assistants may all attend. This exclusion from weekly meetings *may* [emphasis added] be a significant factor in the quality of referrals, because there is not as much formal opportunity to ask questions, to receive feedback, to hear about other units, or to receive instruction in new procedures [461].

It is this discriminatory nonchalance about inequities in training opportunities, fortunately at least alluded to here, that often skews statistical study results.

In a study by Courtois and Goetsch, a grievous lacuna in training emerges as the article proceeds. About 61 percent, or over half, of academic libraries in their purview used nonprofessional help at the reference desk. Seventy-three percent of these said nonprofessional assistants worked alone for certain "non-peak" blocks of time. Most devoted only a small percentage of their working time to reference desk work (so just how good could they get at it?), generally only from five to ten hours per week. Eighty-five percent of these participated in departmental meetings every week (what of the other 15 percent?) (388). While most libraries had some plan for referral of hard questions or call-backs on the part of absent reference librarians, in none of the responding libraries did a "team approach" exist for screening or referral of questions appropriate to professionals or nonprofessionals. The astounding result was

> that it is almost always the nonprofessional who must judge when a question is beyond his or her capabilities[;] ... the non-professional must make this decision in the absence of detailed guidelines and without a chance to consult a professional [389].

In this situation, as in that described by Christensen et al., paraprofessionals expressed a wish "to develop a closer and more precise working relationship between nonprofessionals and librarians" (389). Thus (although fortunately this is changing) the surveyed institutions utilizing nonprofessional help offered clearly insufficient training programs. Lack of appropriate training programs in libraries utilizing temporary student help or paraprofessionals calls into question librarians' capacity to be the "managers" Veaner wishes them to be. Further, though some libraries "recommended" library science courses, there was no formal training by professional librarians of nonprofessional staff in the use of reference tools, although in some settings, professional help worked side by side with nonprofessional help.

Courtois and Goetsch rightly recommended "[expanding] training of nonprofessionals," given this signal lack of instruction on the part of "professional" librarians (390). And if proper training is implemented, at what point do these trained nonprofessionals become professional? Professional training is professional training, whether it is taught in a library school (albeit usually by non-practicing librarians) or by practicing librarians on the job.

Was it spite, a desire to see the non-degreed practitioner fail at a new kind of work, that caused librarians to overlook, in such a widespread way, an essential thing like an extensive training program prior to assumption of reference-desk duties? Were professionals trying to keep paraprofessionals "in their place," as Billings and Kern's interviewee suggested (177)?

One study, by Murfin and Bunge, is filled with gaps. This study found, naturally, that "professional reference librarians scored significantly higher, both in information provided and quality of service given, than did paraprofessionals … in 80 percent of … [surveyed] libraries," but there is no indication, for instance, of the educational background of the paraprofessionals studied (10). Were these the paraprofessionals required to have no more than a high-school diploma (Timberlake & Boudreaux 164)? In addition, there is no mention of the respective length of paraprofessional experience on the reference desk relative to the professional, nor any mention of the relative length of training these paraprofessionals received prior to assuming these reference posts.

Four out of twenty libraries studied showed higher-than-average rates of success among their paraprofessionals (higher, even, than among the professionals). These exceptions give the reader pause: somewhere in these four libraries, somebody was doing something right, but what? Hiring the right personnel? Training them extensively? And by what means?

The Halldorsson and Murfin study likewise omits any exploration of the background and years of experience of the studied paraprofessionals, though training programs were definitely recommended here.

Indicated, either implicitly or explicitly, in all of these 1980s studies was a vast need for much more training of paraprofessionals for reference work than was at that time given. A study can hardly be fair to the latent reference talents of paraprofessionals unless their parent institution has a proper training course in place. Babies do not run until they can walk, but libraries seem, from these studies, like places with no common sense whatsoever in this regard: one cannot refer unless one is trained in basic reference tools. Even professional librarians were neophytes at one point. How would they have fared had their competence been surveyed one semester into their working lives?

It is doubtful if the native intelligence of paraprofessionals—many of whom, as we have seen, have advanced degrees, if not in library science, then in other fields—differs palpably from that of librarians. Training, conjoined with experience, is all. Nahl et al. recently measured by means of pre- and post-tests the advances novice library-science students (with fewer than two LIS courses, on average) make in the space of a mere *one semester* in approaching librarians' competence in answering reference questions. The pre-test, in the three groups studied, showed these neophytes scoring only half as high as librarians. As the semester progressed, the students were apprenticed to librarians and exposed to a course on reference work. Voilà! Post-test scores showed the groups scoring, respectively, 85 to the librarians' 91; 87:89; and 74:89 (292–3). A similar approach, with any intelligent para, would yield a similar result.

There are many statistics involved in library "science," and they can be made to prove many things. They also cloak a great deal of subjectivity and slovenly percipience. Oberg remarks,

> This particular literature [evaluating paraprofessional performance at professional tasks] betrays a remarkable degree of apprehension on the part of librarians about the advisability of assigning to paraprofessionals tasks that were previously performed by professionals. At the state and regional levels, the literature has been anecdotal, often condescending, and has added little to our understanding of the problems that beset paraprofessionals ["Emergence" 102].

In addition, "[s]cores of studies have shown that traditional reference service is not very effective, and that there is no reason to cling to it so piously," writes Massey-Burzio (Oberg et al., "Rethinking Ring" 147).

Libraries planning to rely on paraprofessionals to staff their reference desks must implement comprehensive training programs, in a return to yesteryear, when all professional training was given on the job and there were no library schools. These programs would benefit not only paras, but newly graduated MLS students, who frequently require almost as much orientation as their nonprofessional cohorts. "[L]ibraries must become more directly involved in the training and continuing development of both new and experienced staff ... [and] libraries ... should provide the hands-on training," recommends Richard Dougherty, editor of *American Libraries* ("Are").

20. Technology and the Paraprofessional

Technology, and the assignation for its mastery to support staff, is one of the major conduits through which intelligent support staff have migrated away from their "station" in the "caste" system—traditional library hierarchies—and into competition with librarians (D. P. Gould 236).

"Paraprofessional and clerical employees comprise the bulk of library staffs and ... spend more time working directly with computers than do most librarians," avowed Dorothy Jones (432). Many supervisors do not know how to use PCs and have only a rudimentary grasp of CD-ROM programs, giving the clerks who deal with them daily an incredible leg-up in proficiency at searching, manipulating systems, turning up and churning out information. Veaner worries, "[T]here probably remains a significant number of librarians—sandwiched in between the expert database searchers and the expert clerical staff—who do not have daily contact with terminals or microcomputers and have little or no hands-on experience" (Veaner, "1985 [II]" 300). "If subordinate staff develop skills greater than our own," he mulls, "what does that imply for the future?" (Veaner, "1985 [II]" 299).

Moreover, it is frequently nonprofessional library technicians who set up these systems in the first place, and keep them running. In addition, Bénaud maintains that "it is often the case that paraprofessional catalogers train and revise professional catalogers' work" (86). Speaking of a similar situation, in which the unit head "acts as a resource to cataloging assistants," Fehlman and Verma inquire, "[W]ho supports whom?" (21). Such situations lead Weaver to suggest that "Information technology seems a natural alternative environment for librarians. I believe, however, that it offers more promise to library technicians than to librarians" (149). Library directors discussing library education recently were also able to see that for library technicians, machines were "home"; Toni Bearman said, "What are support staff going to be doing in the future? They'll be building networks, and they'll be helping to run the National Information Infrastructure (NII). They're not just going to be doing things that librarians don't want to do" ("Dean's" 61). "Already," announced Dyckman, "libraries are losing a steady stream of technically trained employees to higher paying jobs outside the library" (81).

"The growing availability of bibliographic information in computerized data bases will stimulate gradual changes in the way services are offered by reference staffs," predicted Dougherty in 1977 ("Personnel" 114). In a monograph evaluating reference services, Riechel asserts that nonprofessionals must evince, among other qualities, the ability to "search effectively using manual or computerized end-user systems" (95). In 1993, Sarkodie-Mensah, chief reference librarian at Boston College's library, described her reference department's "electronic information sources [as including] 11 databases, on 10 work stations, on the Multiplatter Network, 3 Infotrac work stations, and over a dozen other databases on various work stations ... [e.g.,] Dun's Million Dollar Disc, Lexis/Nexis, Dow Jones, GeoRef, (Geoscience) [sic] Cetedoc (Christian Latin Text) and the Boston Library Consortium Gateway" (9). Further, "the public access catalog contains the holdings of the University Libraries, and of the St. John's Seminary; several Wilson databases, Boston College faculty publications, and the Legal Periodicals Index." She proclaims that the "person sitting at the reference desk"—whether professional or paraprofessional—"should be able to instruct and assist users as they navigate through this ocean of information in various formats" (9).

In the Health Sciences Library at Creighton University, paraprofessionals must do "computer searches of ... MEDLINE, UNIX, and PALS" and must know the following protocols: SAVEIT, OCLC, ILL MICRO ENHANCER, WordPerfect, JAYNET. They must also be able to negotiate the Internet (Mace, "Creighton" 16).

At the George Washington University National Law Center, support staff operate in-house catalog JACOB (a Unix system), OCLC (for interlibrary loan and cataloging), LEXIS, WESTLAW, DIALOG, VU TEXT, and NEXUS (Laurence 8 & 10).

At UCLA's medical library, RDAs (reference desk assistants) are obliged to be expert in online systems *Index Medicus* and MELVYL MEDLINE, online local catalogs ORION and MELVYL, and MeSH (Deeney 191–2).

In a survey of ninety-four medical-library directors in 1993, Makinen and Speer found 27 percent of "technicians" utilized to do professional reference duties in answering "in-depth reference questions" and 38 percent performing "ready reference online searches" (137–8).

There is no doubt, therefore, that increasing computer technology has contributed to the migration upward of savvy support staff, following the transference of "very complex functions" "downward in the work hierarchy" which makes Veaner so very nervous ("Continuity" 16). In fact, even a very conservative and inconclusive survey like Estabrook et al.'s concedes that "[s]taff who use computers at a moderate level [allowing time for experimentation] report significantly greater discretion in applying procedures to tasks than do their counterparts who report low or high computer usage [associated, respectively, with unfamiliarity, on the one hand, or with rote input, on the other]" and feel they are rewarded for "[a]mount of initiative [and] originality" they demonstrate, which presumably has been able to blossom because of the optimum time they are required to use their computers (240–41).

Riechel maintains that, in addition to these skills with computer programs and online services, a "nonprofessional" should be able to "troubleshoot equipment problems" (99). Despite her *idée fixe* that "intermediary searching, professionally conducted by the librarian, is in no danger of being phased out...[; o]nly an expert can handle complex requests, complicated search protocols, and intricate database systems," Riechel nevertheless in her case studies cites several crafty student assistants and library interns who are clearly managing to do these very things. One, in fact, on his own initiative, created an index to hardware and software review articles to supplement higher "complicated search protocols" at the reference desk (55 & 89). Rubin predicted in 1992 that library service would require "new *skills*, rather than the mastery of a body of knowledge":

> Additional technical skills such as knowledge of desk-top publishing, word processing, and data-base management may in some cases be skills possessed *only* by support staff. In any case, possession of such skills will exacerbate the already ambiguous lines between many public service support staff and degreed librarians.... As technical skills blend with professional skills, the function of support staff and degreed librarians will also blend.... The consequence will be increasing reliance [by boards and administration] on support staff rather than degreed librarians [26 & 24].

In the 1990s, a model of training, monitoring, and perpetual feedback between paraprofessionals and librarians staffing the reference desk is Carol Hammond's Arizona State University West, a new campus (est. 1984) associated with ASU. ASU West's library treats the main library on the main campus at Tempe, thirty-five miles away, as a base collection to which it will refer patrons, or more frequently, from which it will request materials, thus necessitating sprightly interlibrary loan negotiations. It supplements this collection with materials that support ASU West's curriculum—current publications not duplicating ASU's collection, much reliance on microforms, no arcane material, electronic search media, and a strong reference collection.

Paraprofessionals assist substantially at ASU West, devoting "75% of their time" to reference work (102), but before they perform these duties, they are thoroughly vetted:

> The librarians train library assistants in interviewing, information gathering, verification, and referral skills.... It is an ongoing and continual effort that includes formal classroom instruction for staff as well as informal and individual mentoring [Hammond 98].

In addition, "[p]eriodic tests [are] given to the staff by the librarians on CD-ROM search strategy and use of system commands..." (96). Hammond claims,

> The instruction is on-going, with intensive training in reference sources provided for the paraprofessionals at the time they are hired. The training is coordinated by the Information Delivery Specialist, who supervises the staff, with instruction and follow-up exercises provided by all of the research support services librarians. Interviewing techniques are also covered. Training in subject areas and reference tools is considered to be an ever present need, and classes are given for the paraprofessionals on a regular basis [99].

Teamwork—or "partnership"—is emphasized at ASU West (102). Hammond asserts that these methods "have produced highly positive results" over the four-year period they have been in effect (96). "Until more expert systems and gateways are developed," she maintains, "the demand for assistance with electronic tools will most likely continue.... A model that uses paraprofessionals as information providers, mediators, and instructional assistants has been a large part of the solution to these circumstances at Arizona State University West" (103).

In most libraries plagued by increasing budgetary constraints, paraprofessionals—whether career support-staff members, student assistants, or library-student interns—after adequate training are trusted to staff reference desks not only during peak-use times, when they generally work side by side with librarians, but also late at night, on large portions of weekend days, and early in the morning, when they are usually totally alone (Sarkodie-Mensah 9; Riechel 99; Mace, "Creighton" 16; Deeney 192; Imm 78; Freides 468). To this I, too, can testify abundantly. I wandered through several large libraries on weekend and evening hours and saw not only no librarians, but no paraprofessionals. *Undergraduate* student help had been left to do it all, obviously with the most minimal training. In one library attached to a prestigious school, only one copier was in working condition for the whole library, and the first (and last) two microfilm machines I tried were inoperative, though not so designated. Thus students were left not only to answer reference questions, or whatever else was requested of them, but had no time (or inclination) to see to the minimal operation of common library machinery. In another library, an extremely competent woman I took to be a librarian in fact was a support-staff member, covering the empty weekend hours.

The literature indicates that, following thorough in-house training, support staff are to be found operating as satisfactorily as MLS recipients in institutions all over the United States, and in England as well, where, as Jones and Jordan claim, because "most libraries spend more than half their budgets on staff salaries...[,] changes in staffing structures" have led to "professional staff [spending] less time on routine operations which para-professionals are perfectly capable of doing" (1 & 5). "Thus," they continue, "senior para-professionals may supervise the daily running of public library service points, where previously this was done by a professionally qualified branch librarian" (5). They claim that the situation is identical in academic libraries.

Hiebing in 1990 reported on some of the more promising training programs for reference trainees: the above-mentioned heavily used C.O.R.E. (California Opportunities for Reference Excellence); Western Maryland's Public Library distance-education option, the Basic Skills Self-Study Course; the University of Wisconsin-Madison's ETN (Educational Telephone Network) correspondence course; and the RLTP (Rural Library Training Project) developed by the Washington State Library and the Southern Alberta Institute of Technology.

PART III:
SEXISM: BLUEPRINT FOR INEQUITY, THEN AS NOW

1938: [T]he public and the private worlds are inseparably connected; ... the tyrannies and servilities of the one are the tyrannies and servilities of the other (Woolf, *Three Guineas* 142).

1983: It is inconceivable that a [liberating] history of librarianship ... could be written without considering the gender system (Hildenbrand 389).

1989: Women's work both at home and in the work force is undervalued (National Commission on Working Women/Kenady 86).

1989: Salaries are political. The historic wage gap between female jobs and male jobs is well documented (H. Lewis 20).

1994: [W]omen make up to close to two thirds of the adults living in poverty in the U. S. (Napoli 60).

*   *   *

21. Women's Clubs: "Founding Mothers," the Earliest Paraprofessionals?

Ring claims, studying the genesis of Montana's libraries,

> At least 50 percent of the pre–Carnegie Montana libraries owed their founding to ... civic-minded women. [Their] petitions were usually ignored [by Carnegie's secretary, James Bertram]; but once the city officials took up the Carnegie proposal, the library was no longer a woman's issue. It became a civic virtue, and men embraced it with a passion ["Carnegie" 15].

In fact, after 1850, women were behind most early moves to found libraries: "The early history of most of the public libraries of the country shows that in the majority of cases the initiative in establishing the first collections of books was taken by the women of the community" (Bagley 355). Watson claimed this movement started after the Civil War (233). Early observers in *Public Libraries* wrangled over which women's groups were the "first" to be founded: Winifred Cook maintained the Minerva Club of New Harmony, Indiana, was the first, founded in 1859 as a literary club (153). Watson notes that Michigan was an early leader as well, in 1863 already having formed associations for the express purpose of establishing free public libraries, open to everyone "'without regard to color, sex, or race'" (248–9). Both Ring and Valentine, in their studies of the growth of public libraries in the early history of struggling towns, credit women's clubs with having been the impetus behind the founding of the first town libraries (Ring, "Origins" 432–3; Valentine 292–3). "Lerner [too] has drawn attention to the role of women as institution builders," records Barbara Brand:

> Nineteenth-century women organized to establish such institutions as schools, hospitals, orphanages, and libraries. Many of these later became incorporated and licensed and were taken over by the community. She suggests that at this point such institutions acquired predominantly male boards of directors. Meanwhile, the women who had done the initial work remained visible only as members of a

178

ladies' auxiliary or as unpaid volunteers.... Musmann's recent study of early California social libraries indicates that almost half were founded by women's organizations.... In studying women's influence on professions it is important to note that many institutions in which women were employed as professionals might not have existed at all without women's initiative [Brand 401].

Watson notes that by 1904, Mrs. Charles Perkins was able proudly to proclaim that women's clubs had established as many as 474 public libraries. In 1914, Utley credited women's clubs with having been behind the formation of "'fully one half'" of the nation's libraries. In 1933, Sophonisba Breckenridge claimed women's clubs crucial in "'initiating seventy-five percent of the public libraries now in existence in the United States'" (Watson 235). After they founded these free libraries they often also served as "librarians" in them. They were responsible for a tremendous number of books being shunted around America's countrysides in the form of traveling libraries. They formed the equivalent of powerful PACs (political action committees) before this acronym was ever coined (Watson 236–245). By 1889, in fact, women's clubs all over the United States, triggered by the active Sorosis club in New York, had incorporated themselves into a national federation, the General Federation of Women's Clubs (GFWC), active in all sorts of civic and environmental issues. "Libraries," claims researcher Watson, "were an early and prominent item on this agenda" (234–5).

Bixby and Howell delineate how a women's "Christian Association" undertook to fight evil in Union City, Michigan: ultimately, in lieu of being able to vote, and in the absence of the efficacy of prayer, they put on some plays and squirreled away a small amount of money, determined that cultivation of the mind through the venue of a public library was their best shot at doing good. The local Young Men's Christian Association then agreed to contribute more money, but only if they could control book selection; they stipulated that there were to be no dime novels. On the surface, this looks, although bossy and autocratic, fairly innocent, as if quality control were the agenda. But from the feminist point of view, dime novels were significant because they usually portrayed women doing some very unvictorian things: asserting dominance, reducing men to subservience, indulging sensuality, exposing the ignominy of marriage, bemoaning their second-rate status in society, and in general posing "a challenge to patriarchal authority" (Garrison, *Apostles* 87).* Though the women were unenthusiastic about the men's proviso, Union City's library was thus started; it later became incorporated, and a board was added (the sex of whose members is not specified). It is easy to see how buying power corrupts integrity of purpose, and how money corrals influence.

Thus, in examining the foundation of America's public libraries, we need

*Dee Garrison offers a fine discussion of "immoral" fiction in the Victorian era in *Apostles of Culture*, pp. 67–87.

to speak of "founding mothers" as well as of "founding fathers" (Watson). These women were not trained librarians, any more than were the men. They were amateurs with a bent towards the literary, fanatically committed to books as the way out of ignorance for the nation's Everyman. In effect, most of America's libraries could be said to have been founded by a hoard of nonprofessionals—women and men both.

Outside of large Eastern cities, women's clubs were the instrument through which "born" librarians civilized many a community. This fact is not as frequently voiced as it might be, perhaps because (as Ring noted), while community women were capable of sounding the need for libraries, men, once these libraries were funded and founded (interesting word similarity), were not disposed to credit the women with initiative—in short, with the qualities of leadership and foresight which they in fact possessed. Watson has urged that more research be devoted to our "founding mothers" (257–66). I believe we should also understand that these zealous early advocates of libraries were also the first in the mass of enthusiastic nonprofessional women who have formed the mainstay of libraries in the United States.

22. Shooting Ourselves in the Foot

All kinds of young women soon were employees in the institutions the founding mothers had been so energetic in seeding. Kenady found:

> In the 25 years between 1876 and 1900, library work became a predominantly female occupation. An 1876 study found 1,612 librarians in the United States, of whom 306 (19 percent) were women. By 1900, 74.7 percent of the 4,184 librarians were women. The proportion of female librarians continued to grow until 1930, when it reached 91.4 percent [3].

In addition, the impressive Dee Garrison records, "In 1890 almost one out of every fifty women broke the bonds of conventional femininity and attended college. By 1900 almost 40 per cent of all undergraduates were women. Female college enrollment tripled between 1890 and 1910" (*Apostles* 175).

However, all this daring and erudition was to come up against a wall. "During the nineteenth century, employers had the legal right (and were expected) to pay women less than men for the same work," Kenady writes, in her 1989 monograph on pay equity sponsored by the ALA (3). "[T]he fairest employers, in simple justice, usually pay men more for what seems to be at first sight the same work," expounded "ladies' man" Melvil Dewey (Dewey 89; A. Elliott 668). The ALA's credo ran, "The Best Reading for the Greatest Number and the Least Cost." Certainly women were the workers who would be got at "the Least Cost," so it was expedient to hire them (Wiegand 105). The men who hired them had no intention of giving libraries over to their charge, however. Women were always seen primarily as cheap labor, except by the most exalted idealists, who were usually active only on paper.

Melvil Dewey, in "Women in Libraries: How They Are Handicapped," declaimed, "Women ... are ... crippled by physical weakness[,] ... lack business and executive training[,] ... [suffer l]ack of permanence in [their] plans..." (Dewey 89–90). On the one hand, he saw librarianship as a budding new women's field, and is commonly thought of as women's champion; yet on the

181

other, because of their failings (which he allowed might be overcome), he believed they should be paid less than men.

In so saying, he cursed the field of librarianship, like a wicked but smiling stepfather, for all time. We have seen how little librarianship, over the years, has been valued by its constituencies, as demonstrated by how extensively they are funded. Dewey set the stage for the double inequity under which librarians have long labored: in a men's world, women are paid less and, being under men in an underpaid women's profession, they will be paid less than the relatively inadequately paid men. But he laid upon "support staff" a triple inequity: 1) being mostly women, they are ill paid; 2) being beneath librarians, both male and female, they are more ill paid than librarians; 3) being beneath professionals in a women's field, they are more ill paid than their female counterparts in other professions.

Why would and why *do* women settle into fields in which the pay was, and is, so low, and in which such condescension is bestowed upon them? First, women flocked to this new field, as to nursing and teaching, because they were struggling for independence on all fronts in the late nineteenth and early twentieth centuries: personal, economic, religious, legal; indeed, they still are, as the history of women in librarianship alone will attest.* Therefore women had to take whatever jobs would have them, and librarianship was attractive because it was viewed as "one of the 'proper' fields open to women" (Kenady 3; Garrison, *Apostles* 177). From approximately 1940 on, libraries seemed a modest haven for women raising or finished raising children and looking for something compatible with their non-predatory dispositions which they could quickly learn how to do. Many, many women brought their children to the library for books and story hours from the earliest days of librarianship, or were brought there themselves as children. Of course libraries would draw them as employees later in their lives, especially if they had been trained for nothing else and held, perhaps, a relatively useless BA in liberal arts.

Second, libraries, then as now, were "symbols of knowledge, intellect, reason [and] logic[:] ... they stand for gentility in an often hostile world"; they were "hallmarks of decent and respectable communities and societies," and thus particularly attractive to the more bookish of these women (Miletich 46; Martinez, "Say"). Virginia Woolf, the groundbreaking verbalizer of women's fears, hopes, and angers in the twentieth century's infancy, writes, upon attempting to gain admission to "Oxbridge's" library and failing, "I was a woman.... Only the Fellows and scholars are allowed here..." (*Room* 6).

Being in a library, much less working in one, had the cachet of breaking

---

*"A check of *Library Literature* from 1921 to date shows, for example, that in the past fifty years only one published monograph has appeared on women in librarianship, and this was done recently in Great Britain," observed Anita Schiller, in her influential 1970 article, "The Disadvantaged Majority" (345).

into a hitherto taboo, but highly desirable, inner sanctum. Attending a university had a similar cachet. Woolf goes on, "Some of the most profound thoughts in literature fall from [woman's] lips, [yet] in real life she could hardly read, could hardly spell, and was the property of her husband" (*Room* 45–6). Woolf, though a trenchant landmark essayist and feminist thinker, always bewailed her own lack of comprehensive classical training, her "amateur"-ishness, and it is fair to say that anything thought proper for a woman to do in the wider world of commerce would also be thought to be amateurish, no matter how much education or sensitivity or hard work was brought to bear on the job. And unfortunately, this cast of thought really overlies thinking about women's work in general, "proper" or not.

Women have historically served and nurtured, perhaps through nature, but certainly because of nurture. "Male librarians ... touted women for their domestic and social attributes. They viewed them as homemakers in the library" (Kenady 3). "'[T]hey soften our atmosphere,'" cooed Justin Winsor to a British assembly ("Proceedings" 280). The struggles of women's private world were thus dragged into the library with them, baggage they have yet to shed. Garrison has been accused of coming down hard on these foresisters. Though I don't believe this to be the truest view of her work, in a qualified, general sense, seeing women as colluding in their oppression is a correct emphasis, as valid as blaming the powers that be.

On the one hand, Anita Schiller, discussing women in librarianship with a panel and an audience in a "Melvil's Rib" Symposium, writes, quite correctly, "The problem is that the burden of discrimination has not been placed where it belongs, on the institutional factors which create it. Instead, the burden continues to be placed on women themselves, or else discrimination is seen as an individual matter which arises only in isolated instances" (*Women* 64).

On the other hand, when a women's section was proposed in 1892 for the ALA, it was a woman, Tessa Kelso, who shot down the notion (Garrison, "Tender" 140). Again, in 1893, during the Chicago World's Columbian Exposition, when 188 feminists convened in the Woman's Building and presented powerful speeches in favor of women's rights, equal pay, and suffrage, not one librarian was among the presenters, though nearby a group of them were running a booth promoting libraries (Biggs, "Librarians" 409–10). "[T]he few women library leaders," charged Biggs, "declined to criticize discriminatory norms in their profession. When they took any note of unequal treatment, they tended to agree with their male colleagues, who found its cause in the faults of its victims" ("Librarians" 414). Further, Garrison notes, "[I]n the library literature before 1900 there is hardly a hint that the hundreds of women librarians across the country were seriously disturbed at the inequality that was freely admitted to be their lot" (*Apostles* 180).

And what can we make of the tale Milden tells in his must-read article, "Women, Public Libraries, and Library Unions: The Formative Years"? Maude

Malone, of the New York Public Library's Library Employees' Union (LEU), largely dominated by women, made a wonderfully vitriolic and right-on performance before the ALA's Catalog and Trustees Joint Session (ALA Annual Conference, 1919), cutting through the sanctimoniousness and doublethink that characterized most library literature of the time. Accusing the library establishment of "perpetuating discriminatory hiring and promotional practices," this "firebrand of early library unionists" launched into a diatribe denouncing the "'undemocratic idea'" of "professionalism" in librarianship, and pointing out the intrinsic elitism of people who purported to "'educate the great outside body of people ... not as good' as they...'" (154–5).

The denial which has fed the library field from the first prevailed during this conference; the ALA Committee on Resolutions, constituted not only of men but of women, *rejected* the LEU's resolution regarding sex discrimination in the library field. This resolution stated, among other juicy truths, that "'discrimination [in assignation of high administrative posts] is based on sex, and not on any superiority of intelligence, ability, or knowledge on the part of the men appointed....'" It charged that men were given the plum positions, and that women formed "'the rank and file'"; it proposed to "'[throw] open all positions in library work, from Librarian of Congress down to ... page, to men and women equally, and for equal pay'" (155–6). This resolution was resoundingly defeated "121 to 1 by voters who were four-fifths women" (156). But what is new? In 1990, the "membership" (mostly female) of ALA was again "divided" over whether it should have flown, as it did, an ALA banner in a NOW (National Organization for Women) march for women's equality (G. Flagg et al., "Issues" 261). Never let it be said that women do not collaborate in according themselves second-rate status. That we acquiesce so foolishly in our own second-rateness is the shameful other side of inequity's blueprint, and a side each woman now alive needs to examine very psychoanalytically.

On the front lines, many women were inexplicably shying away from trying for the top. Corwin examined the state and local organizations in the field's early days, concluding,

> [I]n prestigious organizations, women were more likely to be in subordinate than in superordinate positions.... [W]omen were very active in associations at the local, state, and regional levels [but] it is apparent that even so, their participation is never in proportion to their numbers in the profession. When the offices were governmental positions, women were even less likely to be involved [143].

Thus, despite the fact that women were by no means inactive in providing leadership, they practically always held second-rate positions. Mary Ahern criticizes a Miss Browning of Indianapolis for leaving a job she had ably filled for twenty-five years because it had "'grown into a man's job.'" Ahern crossly held women "to blame" for their lowly lot: "[T]he public regards library workers no higher than the library workers regard themselves" ("Man"). "We need principles applied which will remove from women employées [sic], from kitchen to reference room, the mildew that blights them everywhere," agreed another concerned party:

> the assurance that ... no effort or excellence of their own ... can procure for them the reward of such advance as shall give them *free time* for free development.... [Y]ouths show more ambition than girls. They earn and demand advancement. If you refuse it, they leave you.... But girls give you faithful unaspiring service.... When I try prodding [them], they say, "What's the use?" [Connolly].

Whence this acedia? We have seen many of its possible sources covered in the history of the ideal desk attendant. McReynolds offers another. She speaks of the

> paradox that faced women with aspirations for a career in librarianship. They were told that they would not advance if they exhibited emotional or typically feminine behavior, but at the same time they were led to believe that commitment and intelligence could make them sick. Undoubtedly, many talented women were cautious about fully applying themselves or seeking higher positions [McReynolds, "Sexual" 205–6].

Helen Marot, in her important early book *American Labor Unions*, discussing the "apathy of labor" and particularly the apathy of women, spells the problem out most simply and truly:

> Women are discouraged from taking an active part in the executive affairs of organization. There are no women among the national officers or the national executive of the American Federation [1914]. In the 111 national unions there is but one woman president.... [*vii*, 67].

She explains,

> Labor union men are like other men: they are not eager to trust office-holding to women. Labor union women are like other women; they lack the courage and determination to overcome the prevailing attitude that women are unfit to assume executive responsibility.... The real problem of the organization of women in labor unions is not discrimination, but the position of women in their domestic relations and industry. This is complicated by a special attitude assumed toward women, of which their attitude toward themselves is a part [68].

"Library work, like the other women's professions, such as nursing, social work, and ... teaching, rates, not surprisingly, as woman herself rates," intoned Joyce in 1961 (4247). Thirty years later, Roma Harris was to echo him in an entire book (*Librarianship*) devoted to the same fields and the same thesis. "Societal attitudes, overt discrimination and hiring barriers in 'male' fields," combined with the deeply ingrained "middle-class [woman's] own internalized rules of acceptable behavior" have militated to keep female librarians sheep-like and genteel to the point of paralysis, hence the meek acceptance of disparate pay scales and promotion opportunities for men and women in the field persisting to this very moment, which it is thought uncouth to be loud and nasty—or "'assertive'"—about (Kenady 3 & 7). A library clerk of long standing remarked of her workplace, dominated by male librarians who all enjoy very relaxed sinecures (instances of Alvarez's complainants' "'deadwood at the top'"), "the men up here sure have their 'little women' in line" (*Library* 127; anon.).

I believe, with many others, that Melvil Dewey, being as prominent as he was, so much the spokesman for the field and the direction it should take, was primarily spokesman for a severely patriarchal society, not a voice for liberation or freedom for women. He was responsible for playing on Marot's self-deprecatory "attitude of women toward themselves." He saw to it, with his seeming good nature, his appearance of being a "liker" of women, and his air of stating unassailable truths, that women usually placed themselves out in quests for the highest library positions, and indeed, even in fulfillment of their reproductive rights. He built timorousness into the structure of the field he was so influential in constructing for women, because his act of construction was, of course, far less about the good of women than about the good of Dewey's ego. Women for Dewey existed to orbit around him, provide him with ears, and afford the field cheap labor.

Nevertheless, "[w]omen have held the presidential power in the ALA two times per decade between 1911 and 1939 and three times per decade since 1940" (Garrison, *Apostles* 181). The first female ALA president was Theresa Hubbell West Elmendorf in 1911 ("Year"; "New President"). But no woman served as ALA's executive director until 1989, upon the election of Linda Crismond, who did not last long in this position (Kniffel, "First" 622).

23. Reproductive Curtailment

Dewey was one of the first to belabor the issue of women's weakness and unsuitability for manly pursuits, and to call for reproductive curtailment on the part of "serious" library workers. In "Women in Libraries" he called for nothing less than giving up the having of a husband or a child in order for female library workers to convince the world that they were truly dedicated to their calling: "...with women the probability ... that her [sic] position is only temporary and that she will soon leave it for home life does more than anything to keep her value down.... If woman wishes to be as valuable as man she must contrive to feel that she has chosen a profession for life and work accordingly" (Dewey 90). So we find early female librarians, mindful of Dewey's prohibitions, unmarried or childless. By 1920, for instance, only 7.4 percent (1,000) of the nation's 13,502 female librarians were married (Wells 92). They were really quite nun-like, the more prominent among them by example, if not by precept, holding their sisters at arm's length from normalcy by making success seem contingent upon sexual abstinence. Without making too much of a point of men's never having been asked to give up the prospect of reproduction in order to be paid a living wage, I wish to note that Dewey is asking women to give up "normal" lives to work for a substandard wage until such time as the world would adjudge them to be dedicated enough to be paid adult male wages for their work. When will this be, since over one hundred years has evidently not been time enough?

How much did sentiments like Dewey's influence early career librarians to become spinsters, so much a part of the librarian stereotype in the popular mind—the wispy, somewhat prudish, bookish lady peering earnestly through glasses and wishing to be of service? And in fact, to this day, the stereotype of the if-not-single, then at least childless woman continues to prevail, at least in academic libraries. Cravey wrote in 1991, after researching the nature of women academic librarians, that

[a] thumbnail sketch of the "average" academic librarian revealed a white, protestant, married, middle-aged woman with no children[,] ... the progeny of professional parents[, who began] ... her career at age twenty-three after receiving an M.L.S. in 1971 from a library school in the east—probably Simmons College,

Columbia University, or Rutgers. She has practiced academic librarianship for eleven years [154].

Only two of Fennell's eleven women-director respondents had borne children, one before she had gone for her library degree (84). Dewey's circumscriptions were formidable indeed, to have been effective into the 1970s.

Bryan noted in 1952 that library workers, in general, had few if any children: "Married librarians, as a group, have few children. The average number of children born to the married professional librarians is 1.4 for the men and less than 1 for the women; for the subprofessional group, less than 1 for both men and women" (38). Though it is true that library work does not pay enough for its workers to afford children at all, much less 1.4 or less than 1, that is hardly the complete explanation. In the 1930s, women who had had the temerity even to be *married* were among the first to be terminated when cutbacks were enacted (Howard 221). Thus there was always an active disapprobation—nay, a punitiveness—toward marriage and reproduction working upon the field's female employees. Greed is the simplest explanation, really. People who have children to feed are more likely to do militant things, in the age-old instinct to protect offspring, in order to procure adequate sustenance—things like unionizing and striking.* How else than by placing severe psychological restraints on reproduction could giving the nation's readers the best reading "at the least cost" be effected? Clericals as well as librarians suffered this reproductive insult.

And in a cruel catch–22, critical of the field's bizarre attraction for and insistence on single female workers, Ervin Gaines in 1966 charged, "[S]ince the women who ... remain active and who fill most of the supervisory posts are not married, we may find by and large that the library profession is peopled by a group whose familial patterns are not consonant with those of the society at large" ("Library Education" 1771). Speak of blaming the victim...

---

*And "women," stated Marot, "make the best strikers" (74).

24. The "Weak" Woman

Dewey, again in "Women in Libraries," offhandedly deems women unable to lift heavy things (90). In my workplace, women—chiefly clerical workers—probably carry a good ton more per year more than their male supervisors, who are commonly bound up with sitting and paper work, because to women falls the work of trundling books, magazines, and media materials back and forth all day long (Periodicals, Media, and Reserves are all areas closed to the public and are staffed exclusively by women). Over time, these articles add up to lifting a lot of weight, but Dewey was only able to see a man more capable of lifting the occasional heavy case than his female counterpart.*

Even today, though "at the support service level" workers are "entirely women," "lifting and moving heavy objects" is male librarians' "most frequent complaint," and blind oblivion about the draining, exhausting, quotidian, hour-by-hour and minute-by-minute bending and lifting, carrying and shelving suffered by female support-staff colleagues is the rule (Carmichael 227).

Add to Dewey's (and therefore, other men's) perception that women were limited creatures of dubious value as workers, thinkers, and executives the perception that libraries—public libraries, in particular—served a degraded function, namely, supplying America with that work of the devil known as FICTION, and it is easy to see that for *any* library worker to command a respectable wage would forever be an uphill battle in a country dedicated, as ours is, to a Protestant credo. "The Puritan condemnation of fiction reading influenced American society for many years," maintains Carrier in her discussion of "the fiction problem" (2, 8). Since the late 1800s, fiction has constituted anywhere

---

*It is amusing to read of the reluctant acceptance in wartime America (1942) of girls as pages. "The 'boy tradition'" quivered Karl Brown, "will be hard to circumvent." He admitted that "the common argument of heavy work (handling cumbersome volumes, wheeling unwieldy trucks...) curiously does not seem to appear in the considerations of the girls themselves" (723). Kirkpatrick was surprised to find that "[g]irls ... state that carrying books is no harder work than waiting on tables.... Farm girls, likewise, report paging is easier than farming" (919). It was true that female pages could not "carry as many books in an armload as can men, and consequently ... [were] slower," but girls were found to have "practical approaches" to their work, and librarians, after initial misgivings, were happy to have them (Kirkpatrick 718; Brown 723).

189

from 50 to 80 percent of public library circulation (Carrier 20, 33, 73). It is the *raison d'etre* of public libraries. Over the years, the most avid users of the public library have been thought to be women ("that most elusive [female?] figure in library history, the library user") (Hildenbrand 387). Public library workers are mainly female. How much has the old Puritan association of fiction and frivolity affected the ability of library workers—librarians and clerks alike—to command wages that are not actually substandard?

25. Inequity in Wages

The National Commission on Working Women found that "[i]n 1985, full-time women workers [in all professions] earned only 64¢ compared to every $1.00 earned by men...," a differential that had risen less than one percent since the '50s, despite women's countless political battles. By 1993, *Ms.* was able to report women "earning about 77 percent of what men made each week, up from 62 percent in 1970," still short of economic equity with men (Judd and Morales Pope 88). *Working Women Count!* suggests, however, that a 77 percent figure is still too high: 71 cents to every man's dollar is its proportion (21). And Diane Harris set the figure as 72 cents to the man's dollar (26). Female librarians average about ten percent less wages than male librarians (St. Lifer, "Are" 46). The "Placements & Salaries Studies" appearing annually in *Library Journal* bears out the National Commission's contention that, generally, "[t]he predominance of women in any job results in lower pay compared to what the job would be paid if it were done by men" (Kenady 86). The Fair Pay Act, passed in 1994, is the most recent instrument through which women hope to see pay equity enforced. It is expected to help raise the salaries of 62 percent of the women working in women-dominated fields (Hermelin).

Paraprofessional library employees' status mirrors professional status in a field in which "[i]n 1990, the average (mean) beginning salary for women was $25,204, a 2.7 percent increase over 1989; for men, $25,724, a 4.3 percent increase. The median salary was "$24,000 [for women]; for men, $24,700" (Zipkowitz, "Losing" 46). In 1993, Zipkowitz found, "[T]he median men's salary for this year's placements is $300 higher than the women's salary, and the average for men is $263, higher than the average for women" ("Fewer" 35). In 1994, however, the average male salary was $323 higher than the female. The median salary in 1994 (for 1993 graduates) was $2,000 more for men than for women, up $1,700 from 1993 (Zipkowitz, "1993" 30). Zipkowitz remarks, in a severe understatement, "[T]his figure bears watching."

The average beginning salary range, for both men and women librarians, in the 1993 report was from $24,652 (*beginning* public librarians) to $28,793 ("other libraries") (Zipkowitz, "Fewer" 36). In the 1993 report, the average

191

beginning salary was $26,666; in 1994, the average beginning salary had risen to $27,116 (Zipkowitz, "1993" 32).

These are the figures for MLS-holders. Among non–MLS-holding librarians, salary inequities are even more glaring. In 1994 St. Lifer found that among *Library Journal* readers, at least, more MLS-less women than men were hired as "librarians" (25 percent vs. 10 percent), but that "women lose more than twice as much as men for not having an MLS." "Women without an MLS averaged $23,590 in annual pay, while those with it earned $37,980, a difference of 38%" ("Are" 45, 47).

For support staff, *Library Mosaics'* 1990 Salary Survey found average salaries for "clerks" in highly populated urban areas at all degrees of longevity ranging from an average low of $15,099 (academic two-year colleges) to an average high of $22,982 (public libraries); for assistants an average low of $17,026 (two-year colleges) to an average high of $23,869 (public); for technicians a range of the low $15,500 in special libraries to the high $26,882 in four-year academic libraries; and for "other," the highest paraprofessional catch-all class, $23,500 at the lowest end of the spectrum (special libraries) to $29,574 at the highest (four-year universities), with highest salaries showing in the West (Martinez & Roney, "Library" 11).

In 1993, Martinez and Roney conducted another survey. Results were based on 203 questionnaires (out of 400), and all responses were from workers in the nation's 100 "top-ranked" cities, i.e., highly populated metropolitan areas ("1993" 6). It is not clear whether questionnaires were sent to workers individually or whether this was one of those surveys depending on the whim of the library director for its success. At any rate, it is based solely on earnings of volunteer respondents in large cities, so it does not purport to cover the earnings of workers in smaller cities or rural areas. Martinez and Roney claim this 1993 survey showed highest earnings in the West in four-year academic libraries and public libraries, with many paras making over $24,000 per annum, and "large clusters" in the $20,000 to $21,999 and $22,000 to $23,999 ranges. The lowest salary range they found was in the $10,000 to $11,999 range for clerks, and the very highest salary they do not list, other than to mention that it exceeds $24,000. The East and South had large clusters in the $18,000 to $19,999 and $16,000 to $17,799 ranges, respectively. Two-year academic-library support staff made between $18,000 and $21,999 ("1993" 7–8). A report from the Net shows many grade-one employees, where many support staff languish, as low as $12,600 (Michigan Technology University) and top-level paras as high as $51,800 (at Cornell) (survey posted by Jean Flak, May 1, 1995). At Texas Tech University, which recently *upgraded* its support-staff positions to reflect current reality, $14,664 was the entry-level salary, over $10,000 below what starting librarians make (Kemp 37). Unfortunately, none of these sources of information give us any idea of gender difference as it relates to salary.

Some of these figures at first glance are impressive, showing, at least, that paraprofessionals do indeed overlap MLS holders—often massively—in pay as well as in job responsibilities. But in fact they point up a sadder truth: the lack of a career or promotional ladder that adequately rewards them for doing, in many more cases than show up in salary reports, the work of professional librarians and bearing impressive academic credentials (including the MLS), for which they are not recompensed, but upon which the hiring body draws in the utilization of para as pro. "Assistants" in most libraries overlap with librarians significantly in duties, but Martinez and Roney in 1993 show figures for them as low as $11,934 (in special libraries) ("1993" 10). This is not equity.

"Divide and conquer" has a special meaning when we view librarian/non-librarian salaries. Perhaps management's intent in setting such unequal wages, while knowing full well that some paras are performing the work of librarians, is to induce us to be so absorbed in hating each other for salary differentials that we don't notice managers making decisions about our wages above us, counting their savings and smiling upon our perpetually tempestuous teapot.

When we see the higher of the paraprofessional salaries, it *looks* as if the "specious line we draw between the 'professionals' and the others on a library staff" has been crossed (Berry, "Other"). It *looks* as if paraprofessionals are being paid like librarians and should be grateful. And some are. But the higher figures above cover only a few paras at the very top of the paraprofessional ladder, probably in these jobs for virtual millennia. They hardly amount to equity for the mass of support staff. Equal pay for equal work—not only for support staff *vis-à-vis* librarians, but for female paras *vis-à-vis* male—is a notion that has not yet come to Libraryland.

Support staff have "roughly the same percentage of women ... as librarian[s]": 85 percent (Kenady 1). There is little current research indicating that discriminatory pay scales along sex lines exist among paraprofessionals, though it is probably safe to assume that they do, given the monotonously parallel nature of male/female discrimination across the board. For example, "[a]t Yale University, a union-sponsored study of clerical salaries in 1987 found that female clerical and technical employees, including those in the library, were underpaid by approximately $1,280 per year relative to men ... performing work with the same characteristics" (Kenady 1). Bryan, scrutinizing the field in the late 1940s, stated that the salaries of the male subprofessionals averaged "$170 more [per year] than those paid to the women" (82). Most subprofessional women at this time—89 percent—made under $2,000 a year; 42 percent of male subprofessionals made over $2,000 a year (81). Yet Schiller, in 1975, speaking before an audience concerned with the status of women in librarianship, claimed that in her library, at least, a survey of paras revealed that female library assistants were bringing to their jobs higher educational levels than males, which were reflected neither in their job classifications nor in their rate of pay (*Women* 77).*

And even after paraprofessionals join trade unions, as those at Yale did, seeking to redress wage inequities, discrimination continues: "[W]orking under a collective bargaining agreement raise[s] male wages somewhat more than female wages," Kusack explains. "[A]nalysis indicates ... that the effect of unions on wages should be significantly lower for highly educated, female-dominated service employees such as library support staff employees than for workers in other [male-dominated] occupations and industries" (36). In fact, women working in service jobs suffered a 4.2 percent hourly pay decrease in 1994–95, according to *The State of Working America, 1994–95* (cited by D. Harris 26).

Nor is this gender discrimination remedied in higher library positions where, according to R. Harris (1993), "[w]omen are consistently paid a lower wage than men" ("Mentoring" 38). In 1970, Schiller pointed out that there was a $1,500 disparity between academic men's and women's median salaries. "Men were twice as likely as women to be chief librarians, and ... men who were *not* chief librarians tended to earn more than women who *were*" ("Disadvantaged" 345). In public libraries, in 1985, Greiner points out, "males predominated in the salary category of $30,001 and higher. More than twice the percentage of the female directors than of the male directors reported salaries of $30,000 or less; 35.60 percent of the females and 16.03 percent of the males. Salaries of more than $50,000 were reported by thirty-five males compared to fourteen females" ("Comparative" 269).

The exception to this rule of lower wages for women than for men in higher library positions, at least in 1991, is the increasing number of women who serve as library directors in libraries belonging to the ARL (Association of Research Libraries). In 1991, Myers and Kaufman were able to report that, according to the *ARL Annual Salary Survey*, "for the past three years, female directors earned an average salary higher than the annual salary of male directors" ("ARL" 252).

---

*To be fair, though I do not believe these findings are at all typical of most libraries at the time (or at any time), a 1978 survey revealed that women LTAs in medical libraries were more highly educated *and* also received more pay than their male colleagues ("LTAs in Medical Libraries").

26. How Others Shoot Us

In 1981, "70 percent of ... men and 54 percent of ... women in the labor force [were] concentrated in occupations dominated by their own sex," Treiman and Hartmann found (Kenady 2). The NCWW found that "[o]f all employed women in 1985, 77% were in non-professional occupations: clerical, sales, services, factory, or plant jobs," with the highest percentage falling under the heading "Administrative support, including clerical" (29.4 percent) (Kenady 85).

It seems sensible to assume that, in general, this ghettoization probably will continue, not only in America, but worldwide. Characteristics associated with the sexes are given arbitrary value. Kenady notes that in pay-equity debates, men's physicality is more highly valued in the work world than women's capacity to care for and nurture—really nothing more than an arbitrary, culture-dictated judgment (2). These primitive notions about what is "valuable" divide men and women everywhere, promoting ubiquitous disharmony. The war of the sexes is as rampant in the 1990s as it has ever been, though women have made some strides forward: men, though they may feel women do not belong in any number of places, do not feel as free to voice these bald-faced opinions as they were 100 years ago—a chivalry preferable to holding open a door. Their repressed feeling, however, still smolders, and the inevitable venting may take a more insidious route. This is no doubt why the general patterns of inequity are as solidly in place as they ever were, and why Faludi could apprehensively entitle a book on the subject *Backlash*.

How ironic it is that though women and men tend to cluster in discrete fields of work, men have always occupied the dominant positions and the most princely salaries in Libraryland, where women greatly outnumber men. We do not, however, find in fields where men greatly outnumber women that women occupy the throne or draw the most lavish remuneration.

Despite Selth's contention that women are more "ambitious" than men (as why should they not be in a woman-dominated profession?), women in library work do not, as we have seen, occupy positions of power in proportion to their numbers in the field (Selth 3–4). Ambition is therefore hardly a predictor of or precursor to success. Perhaps men do not manifest ambition because they don't need to: they have merely to want something, and it will be given them. However, when one is a member of an underclass, one must devise ways to seize power in that effortless way one of the ruling class has merely to "want" it. We have covered the ways in which women are their own enemies when it comes to getting ahead. Now we need to examine how power has been bestowed and taken despite women's best "devisive" efforts.

In 1929, the seemingly thoughtful director of the New York State Library mused,

> Undeniably for a generation men have been displacing women as librarians of college libraries, and this has been so noticeable within the last five years as to fully warrant misgiving and uncertainty among women who are ambitious and competent to fill such posts.... [M]en have replaced women as librarians at Northwestern, Chicago, Kansas, Nebraska, Illinois, Iowa, New Hampshire, ... Syracuse, Ohio, Delaware, Pomona.... I can recall instantly four college libraries where women under professorial librarians have carried the technical and internal administration of the library with such competence as to suggest their ability to run it outright but have been denied this opportunity in favor of men.... [W]hile women are holding their own in the women's colleges, in colleges for men or coeducational institutions they are represented, with very few exceptions, only in small, relatively unimportant institutions.
> ...Those doing most library placement work in this country can cite numbers of cases where men not only of limited library experience but of no library experience or training have been chosen before women of unquestioned ability, professional training and pertinent experience.... I am ... a bit curious as to the reasons for such consistent male preference. I have never heard one given [Wyer 227].

These words have a marvelous ring. Alas, they are mere hypocrisy. Wyer knowingly and willingly came to work, almost thirty years before shedding these crocodile tears, for the same intransigent man who, as new chancellor of the University of Nebraska, fired the hardworking and innovative Mary Jones as library director. This George MacLean announced he would "'secure a man for librarian as soon as the University could pay a fitting salary.'" He cut Jones' authority, budget, and staff, and thus forced her out, when she did not leave forthwith (McCaslin 188). Wyer showed no compunction at benefiting from Jones' mistreatment, nor presumably at collecting that heftier salary; nor did his brother in 1899, when MacLean, now the president of the University of Iowa, supplanted another able female library director with the younger Wyer. "In protest, Iowa's entire library staff resigned," notes McCaslin (189).

Wyer's rather well-known and truthful sentiments conceal a deep invidiousness, from which I believe all women, and certainly library women, have suffered often and deeply. The sound of compassion serves to conceal that the utterer is in fact no nicer than the unregenerate men he is condemning, and will never hesitate to take advantage of the many perks the library world likes to offer him. To some extent, Wyer is like Dewey, giving with one hand and taking away with the other. And what he takes away, in fact, in both the short and long runs, is the ability of women to earn a dignified sum of money for the very hard work they do.

Passet, as noted above, reviled the field for accepting—and guiding to prominence—"broken-down men." She confirmed that some schools (e.g., the University of Wisconsin) established a sort of "fast track" for men, in which they could skip the clerical and technical courses the women were made to take and focus solely on administrative techniques ("Men" 395; Wells 68). "[W]omen, as a rule, have more patience and enjoyment than men in work requiring sustained attention to details," adjudged Chalmers Hadley in 1912 (see also Wells 64).

> Do not library school courses ... appeal largely to the housewifely instincts, and cannot courses be devised for men who never intend to fill library positions where exercise of these instincts will ever play so important a part in their work as will problems of administration and questions of library policy? ... I fail to see why a man destined for administrative work should necessarily have to do expert cataloging in order to appreciate it ... ["Library" 403].

Men's

> belief that this ... field would enable them to ascend through the bureaucracy was affirmed by library school directors who assumed from the start that most men would rise rapidly and command the highest salaries. Thus, the experiences of these men set the context for salary structures and gender stereotypes that have persisted for decades ["Men" 399].

"The commonly shared perception was that most men were destined to hold administrative posts," Passet claims. "Even after describing men who were lacking in 'initiative and executive work,' needful of 'friendly criticism,' 'self-distrustful,' and 'more or less nervous,' directors would conclude: 'He ought to be at the head of his own library'" ("Men" 397). We have only to think back on the treatment accorded women with no such character flaws as these, who were shunted directly to the bottom of the heap, not to the top. We have seen that women whom phrases like these described were hounded from the field. Certainly beauty, in the library field, has been solely in the eyes of the beholder.

In 1920, Tilloah Squires, uncompromising president of Library Employees' Union 15590, took aim at R. R. Bowker, who had recently maintained that "no woman has at this time sufficient standing and experience in the profession to be thought of for that foremost of professional posts [Librarian of Congress]." She blasted away:

> ...[I]t does appear as something of a joke that among all our splendidly qualified American women there are none of sufficient standing for this high post.... How

are all these men equipped to fill the high positions in library work? A glance in "Who's Who" would convince an "outsider" that a dash into law, engineering, newspaper work, business, school teaching or zinc or lead mining gives just the proper experience needed to manage or organize a large library. We find very few of these "leaders" in the profession are graduates of the library schools, which appear so necessary for the young women in order that they may advance to even a modest position in the service.

There is no reason why ex-newspaper men, ex-principals, mediocre lawyers, tired business men and etc., should be appointed to the "chiefships" while the women remain—faithful, tireless, efficient, and indispensable adjuncts—drawing their rewards from those "many other than salary compensations" which have for so long been the chief solace of the "weaker sex." There is no reason for this condition except sex discrimination in the library profession which we have pointed to before.

We recall that President Wilson has lately appointed a woman to the position of assistant–U.S. attorney general ... Is it really so "unlikely" that some day the President may appoint a woman to direct and manage the Library of Congress? And if that time were now would it be necessary to go outside the "profession"? ["Masculine" 436]

Has any woman yet been appointed to Librarianship of Congress?

Stearns, ambivalent early defender of the status quo that she was, nevertheless indignantly denounced the hiring of a male head librarian "who had not an hour's experience" in library work, but who "had reviewed books" and "bore the endorsement of the local labor union" (68). Bryan, too, corroborated the prevailing view that the men entering librarianship were, for the most part, deficient in some way: "more men, proportionately, than women said they turned away from other careers because of [among other things] lack of ability" (128).

Circa 1930, "men were actively recruited in order to raise [professional] status and pay," despite the perception that the men recruited were an "inferior type" (Kenady 3; Heathcote 518). Ralph Munn, ALA director from 1939 to 1940, in an 1949 article with the pull-no-punches title "It Is a Mistake to Recruit Men," stated,

> Women have had to become reconciled to the preference of library boards for men as top administrators.... [M]en now direct the public libraries in 71 of the country's 92 cities of more than 100,000 inhabitants. Men are now appearing in much larger numbers as administrators in smaller cities. The universities and major colleges display a strong preference for men, not only as chief librarians but as department heads.

But, he reflects, many of the men being recruited are "run-of-mine," with "no cultural background ... [who] would never have gone to college had not the G.I. Bill made that the easiest path to take." He exhorts the profession to be "certain [that the men recruited] give every promise of raising the standard and prestige of the profession ... and not [consist] ... merely [of those] seeking a shabby security in positions to which able women should advance."

Unfortunately, Munn's plea must have fallen on deaf ears. In 1994, Suzanne Hildenbrand queried indignantly, "What about the dreadful men directors who maintained their positions for years in the 'good old days'?" (Carmichael 228). I, too, remember these "good old days," when one embarrassingly self-important bubble-brained male director or supervisor followed another in the university library system in which I worked.

Now, as then, women "are underrepresented in the senior positions in the field[: ... as of] 1990 ... only 45 percent of the faculty in North American library schools were women[; o]f the 43 deans and directors of library schools, 70 percent were men[; o]f the 98 directors of American university libraries, approximately 70 percent were men..." (Harris, "Mentoring" 38). Parsons in 1976 noted that in 1958, and up to 1973, there were *no bona fide* women directors at all, and in 1973, only four, plus one *acting* director (613). This inequity is partially remediated today. In 1989, Myers and Kaufman claimed, "31.7% [32] of the 101 permanent [ARL] directors" were women ("ARL" 244). Still, "[m]ale directors generally control larger resources than their female counterparts" and remain in office longer (Myers & Kaufman, "ARL" 251; 245). And more female directors leave the field entirely—for reasons other than retirement—than do men: 28.6% of female and 4% of male directors (Myers & Kaufman, "ARL" 246). Inadequate pay, suggests Cravey, may be one reason (154). In addition, women stand a better chance of succeeding male directors than female directors, though "[m]ale applicants continue to have an equal chance of replacing a male or a female director" (Myers & Kaufman, "ARL" 245 "; *ibid.*, "Letter"). Greiner confirms that among public library directors, also, men predominate in high administrative posts in numbers out of proportion to their numbers in the field: "61 percent of the 420 directors identified [in her 1985 survey] ... were male and 39 percent were female" ("Comparative" 268–269). These logistics show a continuing Blakean "fearful symmetry" with a pattern which had already clearly emerged in the century's infancy.

The final irony in all this litany is that despite overwhelming evidence to the contrary, "...[f]orty-five percent [of male librarians surveyed in 1991] denied that men have an advantage in advancement (although over 53% of the sampled male librarians were in administration)..." (Carmichael 229). Even Wyer, who benefited so greatly from a woman's deposition, never made such a preposterous claim.

On the other hand, it is precisely this favoring of men, even "unaccredited" men, which can be turned about and used now as an argument in favor of "unaccredited" paraprofessional women. The scorn heaped upon workers untrained for librarianship exists side by side with the librarians-are-born-not-made argument, although the former is reserved for women and the latter for men who advanced the field through their enthusiasm and single-mindedness, through their organizational capacities or their intellection. For instance, "There once was a librarian who had worked in a coke and coal industry, had been a surveyor, a civil engineer, and a lawyer. He has a little over a page in the *Dictionary of American Biography* which says of him, 'He had no specific training for librarianship and needed none.' ... John Cotton Dana's place in our special hall of fame can never be questioned," insisted Evelyn Allen (519). Dana, in addition to his prominence as a practicing librarian, founded the Special Libraries Association in 1909 (Varlejs 4).

Henry Black, director of Commonwealth College's library in the 1930s, "had no formal library school training" (M. Sandler 52). However, he had an obsessive interest in librarianship, reading far and wide on the subject, and contributed, while building Commonwealth's collection into an impressive body of labor literature—now, sadly, dissipated—a small body of seminal publications on labor librarianship. He was a "'librarian's librarian,'" responding to all queries for the specialized information at hand in his library. Like the many male librarians criticized for being inferior physical specimens, he was physically handicapped, a victim of cerebral palsy.

Like many support-staff members today operating at a calibre of work similar to Black's, he cited "lack of money" as a reason for not attending library school. He did not consider library school a "prerequisite to library work" (53). But he was superior—"professional"—in his work. Thus no one questions his lack of credentials. Why has not this grace been accorded similar female library workers who are demeaningly termed "support" or "nonprofessional" personnel?

*   *   *

McCook claims that "[t]he demographics of occupational entry indicate that the mix of students entering the profession has changed little over the past 20 years. Overall, women account for 75% and men 25% of new entrants. Given these figures, administrative posts of high visibility (i.e., ARL libraries, large public libraries) ought to reflect the same ratio," but do not (Carmichael 228). In addition, women who do ascend to high-level jobs "spend significantly more years in professional service prior to their appointments as chief librarians than do their male counterparts" (Harris, "Mentoring", 38). McNair notes that in tenure considerations for librarians, as for faculty members in other departments, "sexual bias was revealed in a study by Fidell where male names were 10 percent more likely to be recommended ... than were female names" (21). In this study, conducted in 1970, when women in academia had dropped from "28% in the 1930s to 20% in the 1960s," Fidell discovered, when he disseminated fictive vitas identical in all ways except gender to various academic institutions, that the "men" "received more 'on line' (academic positions leading to tenure) responses than women," that "[o]nly men were offered full professorships," and that "higher levels of employment were indicated for males on all of the experimental paragraphs [but one]" (Fidell 1094, 1097, 1096). This situation may slowly be ameliorating, however. In 1991, Daniel reported:

The male-female balance of the faculty has improved with a gradual rise in the percentage of female faculty each year since 1978. Over the past 10 years there has also been a substantial increase in the number of female deans and directors, from 20 percent to 39 percent [100].

However, Zipkowitz's 1994 report on salaries on new library-school graduates reports men "creeping up" in academic libraries ("1993" 30).

Carmichael's gender survey, conducted in 1991, yielded a strong sense that "[v]irtually every assistant librarian I've known is female. The male librarians I know are directors," and, "More men [are] in administration," even though, as one respondent noted, "I have seen men and women exchange responsibilities without affecting efficiency" (Carmichael 227).

Women and women are also exchanging responsibilities without efficiency being affected, as we have seen—women MLS holders and women paraprofessionals. There is, in academic libraries, at least, "a distinct shift in overall staffing ratios to fewer librarians with MLS degrees and more paraprofessional and clerical staff" (Euster [3]). Given, as shown in previous sections, that support staff are performing work hitherto considered the work of the professional librarians, and in greater numbers than ever before at any time, it is no wonder that the field of librarianship is in a parlous state both financially and professionally, and no wonder paraprofessionals place the blame squarely on librarians' perfidy ("women don't trust one another") when they fret about being underpaid: librarians let staff perform their work, but avert their eyes on payday from paraprofessionals' pathetically meager checks (Flexman 34). Therefore, "support staff resent the M.L.S. degree barrier" (Parmer & East 48).

The professional/nonprofessional dichotomy really is a reenactment of an older drama. Human beings are always caught in patterns, the geneses of which are shrouded by the past, and which result in unexamined insult or injury in the present. The librarians of today, boosted to professional status following major reports like the Williamson Report of 1923, clambering up and away from the clericism that is the hallmark of all library work, nattering on about their professionalism, are the "men" of yesterday, saying in no uncertain terms to the "nonprofessionals," the "non-men," the "women": "the best woman [read: non-professional] [is] intellectually the inferior of the worst man [read: librarian]" (Woolf, *Room* 55). We do to others what has been done to us. This is really no stretch, since, as a parallel, the whole hierarchical structure of today's work world has been described as an unwitting reenactment of the manner in which factory owner dominated illiterate immigrant worker and, in academia, the way faculty postured before librarian, as well as of classical male dominance.

In addition, when library schools close, one of the reasons they are targeted is because their student body is mainly female (Paris, "Dilemma" 25; White, "Why" 52). Women's pursuits are seen as trivial; triviality can and should be dispensed with. The closing of library schools is not wholly a slam at women, however, since women rarely get to administer the very programs that most concern them. At a recent ALISE conference, Kathleen Heim noted wryly, "Of the 17 [library] programs that were closed, … only one was managed by a woman at the time of its closing" (Berry, "Old" 54).

ALA representative Leber, in a recent article in *Wilson Library Bulletin* on the promising Fair Pay Act, noted, "Throughout the world, with the exception of Japan, the United States has the largest wage gap between men's and women's salaries" ("Fair Pay Act Endorsed"). "Morale," admitted ALA's SCOLE, "is … influenced by low compensation. Not only is earning enough to live on a problem but in a society that equates value and money, those who earn less may tend to question their contributions to society" (ALA/SCOLE, *World* "Issue Paper #10"). No wonder, then, that the USA has "(unsurprisingly) the most highly developed Women's Studies network…" (Doughan II).

From pay equity struggles—between paraprofessional and librarian and between women and men—to worship of the "goddess,"* women at the end of the twentieth century are really dealing with the same realities limned by Woolf at its beginning.

---

*Indeed, a precursor of the goddess movement arose in the early twentieth century. Positing equality between men and women, theosophy throve from one side of the country to the other, and is still practiced world-wide today. Anne Hadden, a stellar early "nonprofessional" librarian, a member of this sect, whose friend bore the name of "Airmid," for an Irish goddess of witchcraft, was arguably involved in a goddess movement, too (Sallee 368).

The involvement of the powerful women's clubs with environmental and social reform issues is an earlier form of the "Green" movement and a precursor of "Eco-feminism."

PART IV:
CHANGING MANAGEMENT

27. The "Bugaboo of Disloyalty"

"Put yourself in his place" is a good motto for both librarians and assistants.... Part of a librarian's business is the care and conservation of his staff.... Leaving them to look out for themselves tends to make them selfish and disloyal to the chief [Assistant, "How"].

Writers discussing the many problems of the library field have more than once touched on the issue of loyalty, usually supposed to move from the lower echelons upwards to rest at the feet of upper management in a prayerful kowtow. Talk of loyalty began early and was soon debunked, at least on paper, as a proper job requirement. Ethel Sawyer, quoting "Mr. Reede," dissects the unfairness of loyalty as a job requirement (the focus on females is revealing):

> ...[F]rom earliest childhood the girl is taught "to please," to seek approval as the goal of her labors... "...[S]o much more valuable is approval to a woman than her pay check that when she gains approval it handicaps. The possession of approval generates the grateful feeling known as loyalty. Loyalty is a motive for further work. The loyalty of a woman to her employer places her in the position of unconsciously expending energy which is unpaid for.... This loyalty-motive lays the woman-worker open to easy exploitation. Every form of energy in pursuit of a goal should be convertible into tangible symbols of the goal. If loyalty is valuable, it should be paid for" [417].

Very shortly, Sawyer speaks in her own words on the subject, with much less restraint:

> Esprit de corps ... costs the administration no little amount in time and in patience. It can be maintained only at the expense of personal contacts between the administration and the working force. Frequent consultations with subordinates are good investments of time and ... careful explanations of policy ... [are not] necessarily a lowering of executive dignity. After all, library assistants are not "hands"—they are co-workers. The coöperative spirit is the imponderable that every enterprise is anxious to get from its workers—but it costs something in coöperation in exchange....
> I have left loyalty to the last because it is one of the imponderables most talked

about and ... least understood. There is probably more Pollyanna sentimentality uttered in the name of loyalty than in that of any other imponderable except perhaps "optimism." Loyalty is not an outward thing which we can be exhorted to don as a garment. It is a matter of the inner self—a flower of our personality and an expression of our whole intellectual, spiritual and social attitudes of mind.... [Loyalty is] called forth by great or appealing qualities in the ... person toward which loyalty is felt. Therefore it is ... futile to exhort a person to be loyal.... [L]oyalty ... must be an outward expression of an inner state of pride or trust or sympathy.... If loyalty is absent in the members of any profession, there are ... only two explanations. Either the profession or institution is incapable of appealing to the pride or trust or respect of its members, or the personnel is made up of individuals incapable of finely adult intellectual, spiritual or social attitudes of mind. We must, both as executives and as general workers, cultivate "loyalty" in the interests of our own development as well as that of our profession [418–20].

The continuing shortage of library workers, which had started as early as 1910 and continued for fifty plus years—or about half the field's entire history—argues more forcibly than words that her persuasions on communication, trust, and respect were not heeded by more than a handful of sentient administrators.

"Disloyalty" was a useful tool in subduing genteel library workers, however. It was always quick to be charged whenever workers seethed with discontent, as we have seen above in the history of the Ideal Desk Assistant. A charge of disloyalty puts such people immediately on the defensive and keeps them from remembering that they are fighting for just causes. It is so unpleasant to think of oneself as disloyal that all one thinks about is dispersing the stigma, instead of the accuser's questionable motive in adducing it. A charge of disloyalty is a form of emotional blackmail. So when the Chicago Public Library unionized, circa 1937, union president Korman reported, pulling no punches,

> Disloyalty was another bugaboo dangled before the eyes of the Staff by some of our older staff members who ought to have known better. "Who is disloyal?" Mr Korman inquired, "and disloyal to whom? Since when has it become disloyalty to take an interest in Staff welfare and in the welfare of the library?" [Clopine 86].

In ALA's "Code of Ethics for Librarians," loyalty "to fellow workers" is enjoined, also "a spirit of courteous cooperation, whether between individuals or between departments" (Bloomberg 258). Loyalty and courteous cooperation are termed "essential" in this document. Alas, that such qualities need to be codified to be heeded, and that though they have been codified, they have still been ignored.

"Being sensitive to staff needs" was, likewise, another of the qualities deemed "essential" for library administrators by 99 to 100 percent of Winstead's university library population (19). But Lawson and Dorrell's disturbing study on staff loyalty and library directors, conducted in 1990 in seven Missouri state academic libraries, does not indicate any administrative sensitivity to staff whatsoever. Predicating that "[the best] method for developing loyalty is for the supervisor to be loyal to those whom they supervise," they found that

> [w]ith regard to directors' loyalty to their staff, over 50 percent of the respondents perceive it to be average or below. Staff loyalty to the director appears to be worse, as over 80 percent of the respondents see staff loyalty to the director as average or below [188, 191].

They conclude, "[L]ibrarians in the sample libraries do not see their directors practicing the management style they profess to practice" (191). Likewise, Margaret Schneider's perceptive article on stress and job satisfaction uncovered a great deal of disgruntlement among surveyed staff. Her study was commissioned by the union in place at her library; it surveyed eighteen librarians and eighty-two paras, mostly female. It is interesting to see that people are less enthusiastic about library service when they are surveyed away from work than when they are surveyed through supervisors or through obscurely or over-tactfully worded survey "instruments." Raw dissatisfaction with "organizational climate" was rampant; for example, "only 16% of respondents agreed with the statement, 'Management is concerned with the happiness and well-being of employees,'" and even fewer workers thought management appreciated how hard they worked after having suffered drastic staffing cuts (394). Certainly, if loyalty is in short supply in library leadership, sensitivity is not in the cards at all. And if loyalty and sensitivity do not proceed downwards in a generous shower from those who "lead," it certainly will not be found below that level, either, in people generally thought of as "followers." People put in solely reactive positions will take their cue from those they are hired to react to. Only 10 percent of Schneider's respondents, for example, believed they had appropriate input into decisions which concerned them (395). Moreover, people who questioned procedures felt "blacklisted for not going along blindly with ... ideas and policies." Furthermore, deprecation of staff by administration was undissimulated: "Well-educated individuals are treated like children," was one remark. Another concerned management's making workers feel like "peasants." One person said, "'Divide and conquer' seems to be management's motto" (394–5).

The field historically has evinced little care for the way its lower-level workers are treated or how they feel, as high turnover and frequent inability to recruit intelligent people have demonstrated. Thus, disloyalty repaying disloyalty really does look like payback. To hire bright, qualified people, or even ordinary, well-intentioned, and alert people, and then treat them offhandedly, or fail to go to the wall for them, or decline to open lines of communication with them or heed their suggestions brought straight from the front line of work, is folly for the director looking for true cooperation from his staff. A director so behaving and meanwhile drawing down a terrific salary to do his staff knows not what (other than brush them off like so many ants) is inviting such survey results.

Branch librarian Martha Brown, in the early days, hit upon the pith of the loyalty nerve when, after urging directors to respectfully heed suggestions from the assistant, she wrote, "The plans suggested may not be feasible, but an explanation of why ... not ... will ... do much to destroy any germs of iconoclastic criticism that may be lurking in the southeast corner of her brain, just waiting for a chance to develop into a grievance" (77). But, lest the administrator think that humoring employees by simply taking their proposals under advisement would suffice or that merely an appearance of participation in governance would settle the fretting worker, Sharon Baker cautioned, in 1989, "Token participation for employees is not enough. Participative management will only ease resistance to innovation when employees truly believe they can influence the change" (58). Sager agrees: "The degree to which management is required to adhere to recommended changes directly relates to the extent of democracy in that organization.... If the manager ignores the group decision, then participatory management is only an illusion" (*Participatory* 21–2, 27). Touching on the managerial fear that allowing worker participation in governance "will create a Frankenstein's monster," Sager pens succinctly: "It is the usual response by employees that management has been creating Frankensteins for years..." (*Participatory* 155).

It is wondrous that any of this would ever need to be written in a field in which so many bright people work. Unquestioning adherence to the hierarchical model in librarianship has blinded ordinary people to common sense. In life outside the library, in dealings with friends, relatives, peers, or even "inferiors," would an attitude of knowing it all best serve anybody? Is autocracy a workable tool in "real" life? The fervid and undissimulated "boss," unless he carries a gun or walks with a gang, in free social intercourse would most likely suffer a swift uppercut for trotting his hubris out into the open. It is good to remember that whatever won't wash with the man on the street, won't wash at work, either. If loyalty is a priority, it is smart to grasp that people are very sensitive to "cheapness"—monetary or psychological.

28. Democratization of Management: "'Tis a consummation devoutly to be wished"

[T]o the extent that you abdicate [the] right to self-representation, eventually something bad happens [Kris Rondeau in McClure].

A sizeable amount of writing in Libraryland has harped on the theme of giving workers a voice in governance.

> The only real remedy for bureaucracy which I know is organization and proper recognition of the representatives of the organization as having a partnership share in its administration. There is probably no single remedy or device which does so much toward uplifting the spirit and morale of a group of employees as official recognition of the fact that they have a stake in the enterprise and a voice in its conduct,

wrote Mosher with perfect common sense in 1937 (851).

In 1994, researchers Freeman and Rogers interviewed 2,048 workers in their *Worker Representation and Participation Survey*. They claimed "82 percent want their workplace 'jointly run.'" Eighty-seven percent believed that if workplaces were democratized, "employee well-being would be improved" (Hardesty). It is fair, given the intelligence of most library paraprofessionals, to assume that similar percentages of them share and have shared this desire with their fellow working Americans. In fact, Dorothy Jones, in her survey, found that 71 percent of the workers she approached felt support staff should be involved in decisions affecting their work (449). "Having a part in the decision-making will often induce a sense of responsibility in employees thereby promoting productivity," Brenda Turner persuades us ("Nonprofessional" 63).

"Esprit de corps" was a great buzzword in the early days of librarianship. Along with Dewey's "library spirit," it was used to exhort workers to ever-greater self-denial and ever-higher standards of service. But, admonished

208

Theresa Hitchler, "*Esprit de corps* does not begin at the foot, among the assistants, but rather at the top, with the librarian, whose example, good or bad, is instinctively followed" ("Successful" 558). "[T]hose at the top must remember the days when they themselves were at the bottom, either in libraries or in other business, and how dearly they loved to feel themselves 'one of the firm,'" advised McMillan (413). In 1913 Weissenborn pleaded:

> Inspirational leadership cannot exist without loyalty on the part of the librarian, not only to the library and to the Board, but to assistants as well.... We ask ... that we ... not be left standing as some deluded audience to wonder what is going on behind the scenes. Keeping assistants in the dark does not aid in the cultivation of ... loyalty to the institution which ... [brings] about ... enthusiastic service which the stranger feels the moment he enters the building [74].

"Another Librarian" offered, "Assistants are not machines! But they will become so if they are required to give their time and energy at the whim of their librarian. And above all, if they find that their 'chief' receives all the favors of holidays, while they have the arduous and uncongenial tasks, they will be inclined to rebel" (262).

Bunge, almost 100 years later, writing of stress in library workplaces, believes that among the "serious" stressors in library workplaces are "[f]eelings of helplessness and lack of control or power" (98). Heading the list of the six leading stressors in American jobs, according to Miletich citing Brief, is "lack of participation" (45). Bunge, tellingly, cites "the vulnerability of working women to distress and burnout" (97). Undoubtedly their general holding of the lower rank of job is linked to this finding. He held that "[l]ibrary managers should provide staff members with the maximum feasible autonomy and control over their work including participation in collective decision-making" (98).

Nevertheless, despite these common-sense observations, lack of empathy, lack of imagination, indifference, love of power, or just plain laziness has caused most library directors to overlook incentives which might have induced the brighter among the field's workers to remain. Repeated cries for task rotation, cross-training, even transfers from one library to another—management moves which would have made work more, rather than less, congenial and workers more flexible and knowledgeable—were largely unheeded (e.g., Flexner, "Essential" 407; "Meeting ... Louisville. Lending" 321; "Indiana's" 621; "American Library Association. Counsel Meeting" 76; Strohm, "Efficiency" 305–6; Agg 356; E. Henry, "Staff Rotation and Exchange").

Goulding wrote, "Remembering the maxim 'a change is as good as a rest', cross training in other parts of the library can help better morale by allowing individuals to function in alternative capacities.... [T]he possibility of moving should certainly always exist" (98). Jacobs suggested, "Too many staff members know the workings of only their own library or department and have no conception of the system as a whole…. In-service training and rotation might be combined and called an acquaintance program…" (337).

But there is a reason why libraries may have preferred to keep workers compartmentalized. Kaufman has suggested in her discussion of nonlibrary professionals that though "[m]oving [them] … across disciplines allows the library to expand the knowledge base of key personnel[, i]t may also weaken the links of traditional hierarchical organizations. Job rotation also allows people to work together in different roles and reduces reliance on hierarchical decision makers" (226). In addition, allowing workers to move from department to department reduces management's ability to "divide and conquer," alluded to above. Secluded workers make resentful, bored, self-protective workers fond of nesting in one area and perceiving slights or lazinesses proceeding from workers in other areas. One Net poster has a wonderfully apropos aphorism in her signature, along the lines of "Dogs bark at that which they do not understand."

In addition, sexual inequity, as we have seen, has been an incongruous monster dwelling in a field in which women had hoped to find a profitable outlet for their creativity and ambition. Libraryland, had it heeded the strong minority voice of reason, need never have developed along the rigidly hierarchical lines for which it has come to be known.

In general, I believe, with Roma Harris, that women, unless they have been very keenly subverted by the temptation to be like men, or to conform to the way men think women are, tend to work in a spirit of cooperation and "partnership," with authority laterally diffused, rather than to form pecking orders military in their design and spirit ("Gender" 875–6). Perhaps the male compulsion to win has to do with this need to order things from top to bottom, as in, "What is your favorite color, movie star, book?" "Who is your best friend?" etc, etc., rather than across a continuum of more or less equal entities. If men had not so strongly been thrust in positions of authority, there to perpetuate Victorian patterns of subjugation, the whole look and feel of libraries would be different, as would society.

"[A]utocratic library management and rigid, hierarchical structures have generally inhibited thoughts of change," remarked Rader in 1989. In 1916, already pondering the librarian/assistant "chasm" born of reliance on hierarchy, Martha Brown mused:

> How often the well formulated plans that have been thought out by the librarian for the development of his library are never communicated in any way to *his* [emphasis added] staff, who are left groping in the deepest ignorance of what they are supposed to be working toward, and yet intelligent service is expected of those assistants…. [A]ssistants should have the confidence of their librarian…. [In addition], [t]o welcome suggestions in regard to the work, probably does more than any other one thing to help an assistant to see something in the daily routine beside monotony. It gives *her* [emphasis added] a larger view of the work [76–7].

Complaints from respondents in Bryan's survey included, first and foremost, in a tie with salary and status woes, "poor relations between administrators and staff," e.g., "staff has no voice in policy, they are regarded as automatons." "Poor personnel administration" came next, e.g., "lack of leadership, and discrimination; assignments made in spirit of military discipline; administrators too far removed from actual situations they supervise; inequalities in staff placement" and, of course, "preference for men over women" (145).

The bane of the field's existence has been the idea of employee as cog in a machine (see Wittingslow and Mitcheson, and "Another Librarian") and the related idea that the monotony, belittlement, and attrition of soul suffered in consequence is irrelevant. The metaphor of machinery enjoyed quite a vogue in the earlier part of the century, and remained as an influence so deep in the fabric of the field that it is practically impossible to conceive of librarianship without it. Bowker in 1901, after a discussion of the history of libraries in America, the number of volumes they contained, and the types of services and personnel proffering them, lumped the whole business under "the machinery of the profession," which was to be "subordinated to ... large uses" ("Libraries" 7). Surely there were other, more felicitous terms in which the founding fathers of the field could have spoken of the group effort that constituted library service in that time. Bowker's choice of words—"machinery" and "subordinated"—conjures images of galley slaves and miners descending to the bowels of the earth, there daily to risk their inconsequential little cog-like lives in service of a more magnificent reality. And in fact, as we have seen, employment, not only in the library, but in all manifestations of American work, was not unlike that of the galley slave or miner. Upton Sinclair's *The Jungle* no doubt seems an extravagant exaggeration to most current-day readers, but its success in its time was in fact predicated on its accuracy in depicting the details of work in Chicago's stockyard industry, on its revelation of the inhumanity of treating human beings as well as animals as mechanical trivia.

In library literature, one of the least inhibited expressions of lust for hierarchy and inconsideration of the worker lay in Arthur Bostwick's view of the library as machine, the librarian (male) at the helm and library worker (female) as cog—unfortunately a part of many a director's thinking from then (1909) until today. This influential man had absolutely no shame in condemning the "increasing tendency among all workers to put self first and work second," despite abundant evidence that if the worker did not put self first, she would be eradicated by overwork and penury ("System" 477). This was "teamwork" Victorian-style:

As our libraries are growing larger, our organizations more complex, it is, I know, growing harder to take a live personal interest in the work, so much of it is specialized routine; one feels like a mere cog-wheel in a great machine. The assistant who pastes labels or addresses postal cards in a big library, finds it [hard] to realize that *she* [emphasis added] is doing something interesting and useful.... Yet the rapid, accurate and efficient performance of the lesser task is as important as that of the greater. A label pasted awry may ruin the library's reputation in the eye of a casual user.... Dullness is in the worker, not in the work.... Now, it should not be forgotten that there is in a machine something akin to personality.... Every locomotive has tricks and characteristics that its engineer knows and sometimes loves. *He pats its back affectionately and speaks of it as "she"* [emphasis added].* The idea that to be part of a machine excludes personality and individual work is all wrong. ... [W]ithin the limits of motion and action assigned to a person as his part in the larger motion and action of the machine, there is still room for moving well or ill, for helping on the greater work or ... throwing it out of order. If a cog-wheel thinks that it is manifesting its originality in some meritorious way by making the whole machine creak and wobble, and turn out an inferior product, that cog-wheel has the power to do just this; but it should not complain if the machinist throws it into the scrap heap.

Now, in our library, the parts of our machines are workers of all kinds; their connection and relationship are conditioned and limited by customs, rules and orders. To test the desirability of these or of any change in them there is just one question to be asked: first, last and all the time, namely—is this for ourselves or for our work? ... And as one broken cog will throw a whole machine out of gear, so one assistant who does not realize his or her responsibilities in this matter may mar a library's reputation, otherwise well-earned.... A librarian whose bad judgment—or whose kindness of heart, perhaps—has misled him into admitting into his machine one false cog may find to his sorrow that this will slip at the critical time, betraying both him and the whole engine that he had hoped to wield for good.... Let no one, then, deride or decry the formation or the operation of a library machine; we live in an age of machinery—of machines formed by effective human co-operation, as well as by interlocking gears and interacting parts ["System" 477–8 and 481–2].

To this prevalent view, Julia Elliott, an early democratizer, offered a codicil and an objection: "[L]et us make our assistants feel they are part of a great work, not merely cogs in a wheel; that they can help by thinking as well as by doing; that upon them depends much of the success we are striving for, and that in the end, they shall receive their full measure of honor" (465). "The individual is, of course, just a cog but under this 'coggishness' we are all different," temporized Flexner ("Choosing" 431). Julia Pettee, otherwise so very stern, also pleaded, on this count,

> Unless the librarian believes in substituting for a fine professional spirit a military régime of cast-iron discipline, which practically reduces his library organization to a book distributing machine ... *he* [emphasis added] will test ... candidates for appointment not only as to their ability, but as to their ideal of their work. ... If the librarian or department head looks upon the assistant as merely a mechanical cog in the wheel, with no personal interest in the work *she* performs, *he* [emphasis added] will probably be at no pains to give the assistant the opportunity to cultivate a knowledge and interest in the workings of the library as a

*Alvarez, speaking of complimenting support staff, says, "Even an animal needs to be patted and made to understand that he is an appreciated member of the family..." (*Library* 106). The tone is very similar: condescension is its overriding quality.

whole. The natural result will be work performed mechanically and indifferently. Efficiency will be maintained solely by the feeling of competition and the desire to retain the position for its money value. In so far as this is true the assistant becomes dead to the profession.... [I]t is necessary that assistants should in large measure have the confidence of their librarian, that they should learn through *him* [emphasis added] the policies and plans of the library and share his own personal interest in their realization. With nothing less than this will the maintenance of a high professional spirit among assistants be possible [586–7].

The *Boston Evening Transcript* added its voice to this chorus, fearing anything (in this case, certification) that "would make the operation of libraries more a process of machinery than an expression of ideals and personality..." ("Certification" 891). Dee Garrison noted that "the expanded maternal role was to result in [women librarians'] early definition as the *mechanic* [emphasis added] in the library" (*Apostles* 185).

Librarians arguing for the humanization, rather than the mechanization, of the library ended up a minority. In 1920, a pithy anonymous letter-writer, "Under Thirty," on the eve of the era of the great library-worker shortage, sniped, "The young people to-day will not make good timber in any organization that employs the same governmental machinery that was common a generation ago, and institutions, as well as industries, must be touched by the new idea." Her scorn for "governmental *machinery*" is palpable, and her inference that it was the reason for the scarcity of young, bright workers is unmistakable. But in 1950, observers were still comparing typical "clerk" work to work on a "production line" (Sargent 63).

Nauratil, in her discussion of burnout among librarians (and if librarians get burned out, how much more do support staff?), perceptively allies job burnout to Marx's ideas about alienation:

Marx believes that the roots of alienation lie in work and particularly in the division of labor.... Bureaucracies tend to replicate ... factory-like conditions, including fixed jurisdictions, hierarchical chains of command, internal mobility based upon performance of uniform tasks, and extensive division of labor.... [The resultant] narrow specialization both increases the risk of one's skills becoming routinized ... and reduces the opportunity for broadening one's professional expertise.... Another tendency of bureaucratic employers, again with obvious parallels to the factory assembly line, is the intensification of the labor process. In government agencies, this speeding up is often the result of or, at any rate, is ascribed to increasing public demands for accountability.... Professional workers have come to resemble industrial workers in their dependent status, in their surrender of control over the pace and technical aspects of their work, and, perhaps most significantly, in their subordination to organizational goals.... When an individual, whether carpenter or psychiatrist, must sell his or her labor in order to make a living, alienation is inherent in the transaction.... Almost 150 years ago Marx described the subjective experience of alienated labor as "external to the worker ... he does not fulfill himself in his work but denies himself, has a feeling of misery rather than well-being, does not develop freely his mental and physical energies but is physically exhausted and mentally debased. The worker, therefore, feels himself at home only during his leisure time, whereas at work he feels homeless. His work is not voluntary but imposed... It is ... only a *means* for satisfying other needs" [15, 23–25, 30].

She further claims that "across all job settings, 'workers' [comprise] the highest proportion of the high-stress category (62.6 percent), followed by administrators (22.6 percent) and supervisors (14.6 percent)" (31). This is because "[o]f all the stresses identified, ... low employee participation in decisions affecting their work had the greatest harmful effect" (31).

Chalmers Hadley in 1920 wrote,

> It is not easy to forget official gradings in our libraries since they have an important place in library organization, but if such gradings impose silence on any group of employees to the point of suppression and inarticulation, such organization is defective.
>
> I entirely agree with a library assistant who recently wrote to me, "If Democracy is not an empty word, it certainly must mean that our workers should be taken into the councils, where decisions governing their everyday existence are made and executed, and that no longer shall they be considered as a commodity, but as separate entities whose intelligence should and must be recognized" ["A.L.A." 358].

In 1940, Herbert Goldhor exhorted the American library to come into line with the expanding emphasis on democracy that was demanded by the ethos standing behind America's participation in the Second World War. "Staff participation in determining library policy is in tune with the general trend in this country in the last twenty years.... It is fit that librarians, both administrators and assistants, ... purposefully plan the adoption and use of practices that will result in increased democratization of library administration," he stated (31 & 33). He anticipated, by a few years, the devolution of the "Human Relations" philosophy of workplace management which was first implemented in the 1920s and 1930s, but which surfaced into the larger polity after World War II (Kaplan 314; Harrington 18). A. H. Maslow submitted that there was a link between "self-actualization" and productivity (Harrington 18). Unfortunately, research examining this hypothesis, which mainly covered librarians but also stole a look at support staff, did not prove him to be entirely correct (viz., job satisfaction is not necessarily linked to productivity).

In the 1950s, the concept of participative management in vogue was called the "Circle" style of management (Kaplan 316). In the 1960s and on into the 1980s, the term became "participatory management"—basically rebellion of "[e]mployees ... no longer satisfied to be considered 'merely extensions of machines'" (Harrington 20). Recently the TQM (Total Quality Management) movement, with its emphasis on quasi-autonomous "teamwork" enlisted in support of higher qualities of "service," seems to have picked up where other buzzwords have left off.

Jacobs, in 1945, sorting out the supervisor/assistant relationship, recognized that there must be a "definite system of reporting opinion from the librarian to the staff and in turn from the staff to the librarian": "[T]he young girl at the desk ... represents the library to the public. She is their first contact with the library, while too often the administrator is out of touch with the public" (336). She faulted the field for allowing the younger employees to "feel they are not part of the organization[,] ... that they have little or no part in the formation of ... administrative policies" (336).

Discussing "in-service training," Stewart insisted that it "bear the mark of democratic effort": "Representation from all levels should be invited in the planning" (18). Doud offered, "There should be more responsibility for each assistant, with the privilege of developing her own ideas.... Too much supervision is a bad thing" (542). "The day of the autocrat in American civilization is waning," hazarded Sidney Smith in 1954; "[s]o it is in libraries" (2043). He continues,

> [T]he greatest responsibility on the part of both the librarian and the staff is communication[;...] the central problem of all group activity is to let the other fellow know what is going on. This participation, this interchange is crucial and must be done sincerely and continuously by everyone in a group situation.... [P]articipation, consultation, and information should be encouraged, even demanded... [2043–4].

But Miller and others wondered, "Is our profession so inherently hierarchical that the structure and nature of the profession itself tends to perpetuate traditional values?" (L. Miller et al. 2).

The few earnest advocates of participative management have been plugging this idea for the last half-century in hopes of getting it to work in libraries. But in 1982, Donald Sager noted

> considerable disparity between those library administrators who state that they practice participatory management and those who actually implement it. In large measure this is due to a general lack of understanding regarding what the techniques are, and either inability or reluctance to implement them. There are many administrators who more correctly indicate they practice a participatory style in their leadership, ... [meaning] that they allow some input into the decision-making process and may actually delegate some decision making [37].

But there has been at least one big drawback in all merely quasi participatory practices:

> Fundamental to those theorists who have shaped job reform as a major management trend during the 1970's is a hierarchy of factors influencing job satisfaction among workers. The first of these is achievement. Without this sense of accomplishment, most theorists agree that employees cannot be motivated, or can be motivated only at great cost to the organization. In a library application, it [is]

possible to identify those positions which offer the greatest sense of accomplishment and those which offer little. In that context, *the clerical, page, and technical processes positions usually present the greatest management challenge, but are often the most ignored* [emphasis added]. That is where turnover and absenteeism is greatest [D. Sager 10].

It is not too much of a surprise when he adds the coda to this observation:

> Historically, the professional librarian has not been a militant employee. While the stereotype has changed substantially in recent years, there are still many librarians who believe they are "professionals" and above labor and management issues such as greater democratization in the workplace. Some library administrators report much greater militancy in their clerical and paraprofessional staff than among professionals. Curiously, when many library administrators review the steps they have taken to democratize their institution, they refer only to what has been done in concert with the professional staff. Groups such as clerical, paraprofessional, and maintenance personnel, who have greater cause for grievance, are often ignored in the process [43].

Paraprofessional associations and unions arose when management failed to accommodate intelligent people's universal need for "self-control." For instance, the Paraprofessional Forum of the Virginia Library Association (VLA) came into being because of desire to implement "job training and career development and increased involvement in staff decisions affecting them" (Mayo 17).* Behind formation of these groups, in many instances, lay the liberal-arts background of the many "aquarians" who entered library work in their salad days. They resented extraneities like social background, number of capital letters after name, rank, and so on. They acknowledged only the authority of intellectual peers, among whom they did not number librarians.

The stultifying hierarchy of the library field, outliving generations of similar disgusted malcontents flouncing from Libraryland into other lines of work, exists as a now-covert ideal, the last refuge for all those professional "drifters" who sought library work as a bastion from the real world (Rothstein, "Why" 47). These insecure people welcome the handy recourse of the almost punitive institution of hierarchy, in which the "haves," namely those with MLSs, control the "have-nots" with impunity, attempting on a daily basis to belittle and break their putatively too-proud spirits—spirits which cry for a voice in policy and governance, for the recognition of ideas originating with them, for cross-training, for continuing education, for variety in work assigned,

---

*Ironic, then, and ever so Victorian, the fuss recently made over the title change proposed for the *Virginia Librarian*, namely, to *Virginia Libraries*, to accommodate the contribution made by dedicated paras, in the course of which paraprofessional involvement in the association was likened to "the tail wagging the dog" and other niceties. This incident brought to national attention a common problem with paraprofessional involvement in "professional" organizations: namely, as one commentator in the ALA/SCOLE *World Book* project put it, "'ALA [but here read any professional organization] takes my money, my time, but doesn't care who I am, what I do'" ("Issue Paper #4").

for the right to move upwards and be paid according to demonstrated intellectual capacity, for the right to be treated as equals instead of as a species of serf. A recent posting on the Net demonstrates that this form of artificial oppression is still alive and well: "I was very gun[g]-ho when I first started working here, but after seeing 10 out of 12 workers with MLS's delegate all day (because shelving a book would be beneath them and directing patrons is not what they worked so hard for...), I find it very difficult to stay motivated" (anonymous Libsup-l poster).

Though writers encouraging, specifically, support-staff involvement in management have not been numerous, they have sounded a steady note on behalf of the latent abilities of this segment of the library population. Garten, in 1981, wrote,

> Often, what we initially perceive as morale problems, can be directly traced to power/authority issues. ... [S]upport staff in the automation-laden work environment have the need *to identify with the entire operation.* The contemporary experience with support staff suggests that we are now dealing with a worker who has a higher educational level, who explicitly expects a certain level of growth and challenge in the work environment, and who desires to have a clear ... understanding of the interrelationships present in any contemporary technical services operation. ... [They] have the need ... for task significance. Technical workers have a high need, as do all workers, for a sense that what they are doing is of significance. We have not come far from the ever underlying 'cog in the wheel' notion. We only have surfaced its destructive consequences to a higher level. Significance in the grand scheme of things still remains critical in any human resource development model ... [as well as] a high degree of autonomy [2, 4–5].

Gisela Webb, who believes the democratization of the workplace to be "inevitable," in 1988 deemed the administration of libraries "to be especially well suited to participative management. The work force is highly educated; even support staff members often have college degrees." She warns, however, "Some professional librarians will be unwilling to accept that the input of support staff can be considered as valuable as their own on certain issues" ("Preparing" 51). Allen Veaner, for example, though a perceptive observer of the librarian/paraprofessional jousting match, condemns the use of "total quality-management, team work, statistical-quality control, flat organizations, and empowerment" out of hand as forces which would "marginalize" the profession ("ACRL Personnel" 3).

Few libraries have implemented any sort of true participative management.* Generally, where it has been formally attempted, it may include only

---

*Eleanor Lewis in 1907 described an experiment in self-government among Northwestern University's staff in an article so entitled. The eight women scheduled themselves and held monthly staff meetings presided over each time by a different worker, during which they discussed books and "mooted questions of library policy," and heard presentations. Lewis praised the "delightful spirit of coöperation" which ensued.

the librarians; it may involve only the recommendation of committees; it may involve only the passage of information to and from governors and governees. Something resembling it, in the occasional use of a suggestion from the lower depths of the library hierarchy, sometimes transpires, but real participation—institutionalized participation, as it were—especially from the support-staff level, is rare.

But sometimes it occurs unself-consciously, as a result of harmonious, unclassed relations between workers, as in Bryan's example, circa 1947:

> In one library, ... where four women are employed, the head librarian, when interviewed regarding personnel organization, replied that there was no difference at all between the work that she did and that performed by the other three members of the staff. "We all do everything," she said. "It relieves the monotony to do different kinds of work." Who allotted the work to be done—did she? "Oh, no. We just do whatever has to be done. If a borrower comes in, the one that happens to be nearest and freest waits on him. When we get tired of doing one thing, we do something else. That way, the work gets done and everyone is satisfied." Did she supervise the work of the others? "Oh, no. They've all been here a long time. There's no need to supervise." When asked whether the library made any distinction between professional and subprofessional work, she replied, "No, we don't. There's no need to. We're all subprofessional—none of us had any professional library training" [205].

While it would undoubtedly be naive to argue that all libraries could function like this, we don't really know, because library administrators have never tried setting a library up from scratch to function like this. This, however, to me is the true library "machine," functioning easily, naturally, effortlessly, democratically, a model Roma Harris could approve of as a uniquely feminine sort of work arrangement ("Gender"). Gisela Webb has touched upon the gender component of this kind of cooperation, as well: "Women, predominant in the profession, are ... conditioned by society towards cooperation and consensus..." ("Preparing" 51).

Although there are not many documented instances of democratic and compassionate workplaces in the library world, some examples do exist. One instance of a library freeing workers to work communally (although librarians covered the initial stages of planning) was in the Denver Public Library's Booktech 2000 project, in 1993, in which support-staff volunteers undertook to "self-manage" readying 40,000 volumes for two branch libraries under a brand-new system. "We're supervised by our work," remarked Nan Mullens, "...we've learned to do it all.... Anyone who primarily does one thing all day long could benefit from the variety of tasks" (McCune 35). While the Denver library system is, obviously, still very much a hierarchy (some people planned, others ordered), still, the spirit in which the three women have gone about their work is cooperative. It is the truest kind of teamwork—teamwork which comes from the willingness of the worker, and a sense of human equivalency.

But workers turn stubborn when treated like lesser beings. Stephens set out to prove that "successful implementation of new policies and strategies would be 'strongly affected' by the 'degree of staff involvement throughout planning...'" (175). She followed the course of two libraries in their planning of data-collecting projects. Library "A" apprised its staff only cursorily about what would be happening; Library "B"'s director expended considerable time and energy towards including staff—meaning here, largely librarians—in the planning process. Library "A"'s staff failed to muster enthusiasm for their director's project. Only 12.5 percent of its employees were content with the outcome. Library "B," unsurprisingly, showed that a "majority of the staff members indicated acceptance of the goals and objectives chosen by the planners and satisfaction with their library's overall planning experience" (178). However, dissenters from the satisfied majority claimed "certain levels ... of staff were given attention while others were not." Their advice? "Paraprofessionals' input should be considered"; "Paraprofessional and clerical staff [should be involved] as a subcommittee to support or counter the professional staff committees"; "Make the Process mean something to even the lowliest clerk" (178–80).

"How often are paraprofessionals, particularly those working in service areas, tapped when a new policy needs developing or when an old policy needs updating?" queried Kathryn Deiss in 1994 (730). Citing the successful updating of a policies-and-procedures manual utilizing support staff at Northwestern University, she stated, "I am certain that, more often than not, more policies can and should include the expertise and opinion of paraprofessional staff members" since in this instance they were the people who "actually [did] most of the work [in question and] will understand, interpret, and apply the policy" (733; 730). What is more, staff want a voice in governance. In the backhanded way peculiar to statistically grounded surveys, one researcher studying staff reactions to automation in three university libraries found that although employees rejected the hypothesis "that most library staff members do not favor participatory management styles in the implementation of automation," 62 percent believed that automation "would not cause a diffusion in decision making," an increase of 9 percent over the 53 percent who felt this way in 1987 (Winstead 19). Staff wish to help govern, but realize they have a snowball's chance in hell of doing so. They feel the reins have tightened, rather than loosened, in recent years.

One writer confessed, "[T]here is still no consensus as to what is meant by participative management [in librarianship]" (Kaplan 320). I believe we need to really work to discover what it is, however, and how it can best be implemented. New recruits to the field will only stay, history teaches us, if they are treated like intelligent human beings—regardless of title. Bryan's women and Denver's Lopez, Mullens, and Nelson provide a model for how things should be in libraries. Moreover, if it is possible for these diverse "subprofessional"

women to accomplish democratization, why is it that their presumably more
evolved superiors have not understood before now that this sort of work mode
is not only possible, but extremely desirable? Turnover would diminish to a
trickle if people regarded their coworkers as friends, rather than as manifestations of position titles. But librarians, characteristically condescending, worried, apropos the Denver volunteers, "'Can paraprofessionals be expected to
summarize bibliographic material independently?'" (34).
   Consider this early rumination by Crunden:

> [T]here is a great deal of drudgery in library work, just as there is in the work of
> the world in general; somebody has got to do it.... "We have only the alternative
> of breaking in girls of very little education and no social culture at all and hav-
> ing a social cleavage right down the line in the library service.... Or you can do
> it and learn as you are doing it, so that in time you can direct others, and gradu-
> ally you can learn all the details of library work." ... I think that this would be a
> good system for the whole world to be conducted on—for all of us to take our
> turn at digging ditches, and washing dishes, and doing drudgery while we are
> young, and not have one class of people set apart distinctly for the lower work
> and the others doing the higher work and not cultivating their hands or learning
> the details of the work that they are afterwards to direct ["Portland" 175].

Contrast with this the remarks of a paraprofessional about to move on to "professional" library work in 1975: "[I]t is ... necessary to take into consideration
the stultifying effects of routine tasks upon the professionalism of the librarian" (Miller, "Paraprofessional" 552).* Why, we want to ask, are these routine
tasks any less stultifying when done by a paraprofessional?
   "'Boring'" was the one word Sherrer heard most often in her 1985 job-
satisfaction survey to describe "clerical tasks," probably accounting, in large
part, for over 60 percent of her respondents reporting undue stress "sometimes" to "frequently." Employees with the least seniority (working for the
least pay at the most humdrum jobs) expressed the most job dissatisfaction (18,
20). Aston and Lavery claim, "[W]hen women are in positions of high demand
and low power in their place of employment they are likely to be depressed,
particularly so because they are in this same situation in other roles" (21). It is
hard to see why the library world, composed, presumably, of educated policy-
makers, let itself get so sucked into status and hierarchical lunacies. No one—
especially someone intelligent—is willingly or cheerfully, or for long, going to
do the scum work while others "'put their feet up,'" unless somehow coerced.
Why did a Victorian man intuit and articulate this as plain as day, while most
current administrations, presumably more "modern" and hip to the abuses of
democracy, are still in the dark ages?

*I heard that Japanese executives empty their own trash, clean up their own offices, that there
are not "janitors" in Japan. If the Japanese can do their own dirty work, why can't we? If this
bit of hearsay is true, cleaning obviously does not diminish executive honor; these people
are still "executives" when they have finished tidying up.

We need more directors like Charles Robinson, director emeritus of the Baltimore County Public Library, long concerned with the support-staff issue, who recently wrote, in a letter to *Library Journal*, expanding on Herbert White's claim that BCPL has been "innovative and nontraditional" for thirty years, "First of all, the innovation comes from all over the place, clerical and professional." Another director, Pat La Violette, director of the Brown County Library in Wisconsin, recently lionized by *Library Journal* as the third recipient of its Library of the Year Award, pronounced, "I don't like hierarchic management.... I feel that everyone on our staff is an equal partner" (Berry, "Brown" 30). Claiming that everyone on the staff regards Brown as "their library," she said, "Our staff ... truly feel empowered. They feel free to start projects, to suggest projects to community groups. It works real well" (Berry, "Brown" 31). Further, "[m]uch notice has been taken of the library's willingness to be the first agency of government to adopt TQM. Staff at all levels have been trained in TQM principles, and TQM process teams have studied and improved several library processes" (Berry, "Brown" 32). *Library Journal* concludes that the Brown County Library "offers useful lessons for every community and public library in America" (Berry, "Brown" 33).

William Beard recently offered a model of democratic, participatory government devised by the Hennepin County Library (HCL), in which both professional and paraprofessional library workers—numbering over 600—serve, on a rotating basis, on the Staff Development and Training Committee to elicit input on new systems, dispersal of continuing-education monies, and development of in-house training videos. HCL's goal? To become "one of the nation's premier public libraries" (36).

Both the University of Arizona and Samford University have utilized participatory management to effect satisfactory reorganization of their respective libraries. Encouraged by Carla Stoffle, new dean of libraries, Arizona utilized all levels of staff to implement a more team-based, user-oriented, and considerably flatter reorganization in 1994 (Giesecke). Samford University's professional librarians initially began brainstorming towards reorganization along TQM lines without paraprofessional input ("Frankly, it did not occur to us to include them"). Eventually, support-staff members, in the interests of "empowerment," contributed cooperation and suggestions exactly like everyone else, even serving, in two instances, as unit coordinators. The resulting organization was far less hierarchical and more "circular" than before (Fitch et al.). Gisela Webb, discussing the future of technical services staff, asserted that "paraprofessionals should be included in all deliberations and decisions concerning their departmental affairs" ("Educating" 117). Library administrator Jill Fatzer, concluding her overview of paraprofessionals in the academic environment, writes, "Libraries ... wise enough to bring paraprofessionals, with their unique viewpoint and expertise, into the mainstream of managerial decision-making are the better for it" (162).

Arolana Meissner in 1995 became the first winner of *Library Mosaics'* "Supporter of Support Staff of the Year" award. A former paraprofessional herself, she has invited staff to serve on committees, attend paraprofessional conferences in unheard-of numbers, and hired a consultant to give on-site Internet instruction to interested employees. She organizes a staff retreat each year, and has allowed her library to serve as a "Soaring to Excellence" tele-conference site. She states,

> Libraries have always had what business is now calling a "service recovery" atti-tude[;] in fact we have sometimes been accused of going too far in helping patrons. Unfortunately we have not always maintained this attitude towards library staff. They have been expected to serve without being served and adequately supported by their institutions.... [W]e need to back up and bestow some of our concern upon those who are on the front line ["Arolana"].

Kemp, in an article on reevaluating support-staff positions at Texas Tech, presents "a rationale for the library of the future as a posthierarchical work-place, where the skills base is more homogeneous," the library hierarchy "flatter," and relationships are "governed by the necessities of learning and performance rather than by the rules of an older faith—rules that sort, rank, and separate" (citing Zuboff, pp. 37, 39). He accurately insists that "learning has become more or less constant in most library support staff jobs. Learning can no longer be concentrated into initial training periods or limited to class-room settings apart from productive activity" (38). He believes that "[a] strictly hierarchical, authoritarian philosophy of management is not responsive or flexible enough to serve in this environment" (39). In several departments, because of desire to conserve funds in a shrinking budget, management saw that supervisory responsibility migrated "from the purview of a librarian to ... a support staff person" (39).

However, because base salaries underwent such an extremely small upward adjustment, failing even to reach $15,000 per year, I feel confident that the wages of staff given librarians' supervisory responsibilities also failed to reach any respectable professional level. Kemp does not reassure us on this score, other than to applaud the "willingness of the library administration to commit the financial resources necessary to fund the upgrades" (43). "Equiv-alency," in the course of Texas Tech's reorganization, came back into vogue: substitution of work for college education, and vice versa, college education for lack of work experience. To allow more fluidity in task assignment, job descriptions became "generic"—in other words, extremely general, describing broad capabilities and responsibilities rather than defining individual tasks, e.g., "Development and maintenance of skills needed for high levels of interaction with library computer systems"; "Routine maintenance of computer and non-computer equipment and programs"; and "Involvement in the development and review of work unit policies and procedures" (41). It is easy to see how support staff, while they seem to have been elevated by these procedures, have at the same time been put at risk in the long run. Administration eliminates professionally paid positions to put equally proficient but lesser-paid employees in them—the old story from the 1960s—and generic job descriptions open staff to exploitation, since the expectation is simply that they will acquire higher and higher levels of expertise to work at jobs which may offer the same low salary year after year, and not rise commensurately with job-holders' enhanced capabilities.

Thus support-staff democratization of the workplace, though devoutly wished for at one time or another, may result in "ambivalence." Walton and Botero, in the results of a survey made of a paraprofessional/professional librarian team-cataloging effort at the University of Florida, received the following reply: "I can see a point where an LTA and a librarian's cataloging may not vary as much as their paychecks might" (68). So why "ambivalence"? Well, why should a library worker exert effort to perform at the level of higher paid employees without getting paid the same amount of money for her work?

"Librarians have long assumed that support staff members lack the knowledge necessary to perform at a level approaching theirs, and that assumption remains unquestioned and libraries remain organized around it," wrote Rush Miller ("Support" 358). He claims to have been "amazed over the years at the multitude of talents going to waste in libraries among the support staffs" (*ibid.* 363). In a 1992 survey of 137 academic institutions undertaken by support staff of the Association of Classified Library Personnel (ACLP) at the University of Nebraska-Lincoln Libraries, 97 claimed support staff had a voice in the governance of their respective libraries. Only 19 denied paraprofessionals participation in library governance (Winkler 13). However, Kozsely found in 1991 that of 124 ARL libraries solicited for information about their paraprofessionals, only 69 responded, and fewer than half of these had even advisory councils proffering suggestions about library governance (18, 20). Anecdotal evidence on the Net indicates similar spotty participation in governance, some paras extremely pleased with their lot in all regards, but, in my opinion, a larger number seeing room for improvement not only in the realm of governance, but in every aspect of employment, especially in pay rates.

The ultimate argument, from the field's point of view, for increased democratization in library governance lies around Jurow's concern for the development of future leadership in libraries. From what pool could new leaders be recruited? The sad fact is that libraries, in remaining rigidly hierarchical, fail to allow the scope and opportunity for fledgling administrators to flex their managerial wings. They cancel innovation; they curdle new blood. Thus hierarchical libraries stunt growth of potential leaders, and then they bemoan the fact that outsiders, the dreaded non-librarian professionals—the subject specialists, the scholars, the techies, and the MBAs—have entered the highest levels of their domain, stolen away still more of their turf, and confirmed yet again librarians' already weak image.

But in the end we must ask ourselves an unwelcome question. If support staff and student workers constitute the greatest source of recruitment for the nation's librarians, as John Berry and others have maintained, are these ex-paras to blame for the persistence of the library hierarchy, the lack of democratization, the peremptory derogation of their former co-workers?

29. Job Dissatisfaction

The desire to want, to think and then implement things is not reserved for higher level staff, as is often popularly imagined [Thapisa, "Burden" 148].

Wittingslow, basing his 1984 comments on the *Work in America* report, claimed, "Satisfaction surveys in America show falling satisfaction and this is of concern ... as productivity has also fallen as claimed satisfaction has fallen" (61).

Job satisfaction surveys, where they have included support staff, indicate that high among perceived needs, aside from the obvious one of adequate salary, are variety in workload, autonomy, compatible co-workers, ability to advance in the field, and, above all, a real voice in management. Burgin and Hansel claim that generally, studies on support-staff job satisfaction have shown paras to be less content than librarians (68). And in the larger work world, Aston and Lavery, in their study of women, work, health, and cynicism, found clerks' level of cynicism "significantly higher" than managers' (17). They claimed, "Depression was negatively related to intrinsic rewards for the clerical group suggesting a link between a lack of intrinsic rewards on the job and depressed mood" (12). Why is this no surprise?

Though generally job satisfaction has been associated with the degree of closeness to the top of the hierarchy, across all fields, and the assumption traditionally has been that job satisfaction is tied to quality of performance, researchers in the library field have not always seen these truths borne out. One of the earliest job satisfaction surveys to include library clerical workers, Lawrence Prybil's in 1973, found clerical workers the "most satisfied" of the three classes of worker studied: professional librarians, clerical staff, and maintenance workers. His survey also included supervisors' assessments of their subordinates' job performance. Thus he found to his surprise that among unsatisfied clerical workers, performance was rated "actually ... 'better' than the satisfied subgroup" (97). In attempting to explain the disparity between his findings and other researchers' results, he merely remarked,

[I]t seems evident that library science is not a *fully* developed profession as yet. And … clerical workers … represented an educationally heterogeneous group, with several individuals possessing baccalaureate and even advanced degrees in disciplines other than library science. Thus, in certain important respects, … [these workers] differed considerably from the 'professional' and 'clerical' employees examined in previous studies [99].

He believed the heterogeneity of his clerical group constituted an "important [limitation]" of his study's findings (100). In addition, his sample was exceedingly small.

A more substantial study, Lynch and Verdin's, conducted in 1971–72 but inexplicably not published until eleven years later, found job satisfaction among support staff to be frighteningly low: 73 percent of these workers expected to be elsewhere than where they presently were in five years (444). Vaughn and Dunn's study of six academic libraries' staff also showed that despite the occasional high degree of satisfaction in one library or one library department, still, depending on the issue, anywhere from 30 to 50 percent of most workers reported little job satisfaction. Professional librarians in this study reported far greater satisfaction than "nonprofessionals"; only 17 percent planned to leave their current place of employment in five years (443). Staff overall was 82 percent female (though neither sex expressed more satisfaction than the other) and more likely to be satisfied if older (441–2, 445). Workers in non-supervisory posts always reported less satisfaction than supervisors; nonprofessionals in circulation were miserable (442, 445). In a marvel of understatement, the authors wrote, "That different occupational groups within the same functional unit may have differing degrees of satisfaction toward their work has been underestimated by some library managers and theorists writing about library organization" (445). "[M]anagerial performance," concluded Vaughn and Dunn, "has a causal influence upon employee satisfaction and employee productivity[; nevertheless,] … [i]n the short run, employees can be dissatisfied and still be highly productive. In the long run, however, dissatisfied employees tend to adopt either 'fight' or 'flight' patterns of behavior" (175).

This observation was borne out in Lynch and Verdin's 1986 replication of their 1971–72 study. Professional librarians were still happier than support staff, and supervisors happier than non-supervisors. Still, despite the field's consistent bias against females, no greater satisfaction was discernible among the study's men than among the women. But in this study, 50 percent of professionals and 46 percent of support staff planned to be in the same institution in five years, reflecting, most probably, the drying up of outside library-job opportunities (200). Both professional and support staff were "graying" (195). Few respondents were under the age of twenty-five (only 18 in 1986, over against 119 in 1971–72); the total number of respondents was smaller by almost 100, and every department had diminished staff overall, especially cataloging, reflecting budget cuts and automation (193, 195). Overall job satisfaction was greater, perhaps because automation had reduced repetitive manual tasks (198). Lynch and Verdin almost covertly suggest that management (did being surveyed unsteady them?) had somehow varied the assignment of tasks, as well, so that work overall was less monotonous in 1986 than in 1971–72: "[W]hen work design is undertaken with the objective of making jobs less routine, some change in employee satisfaction is likely to occur" (199). Perhaps this is only wishful thinking, but Vaughn and Dunn share their delusion: "[T]he managerial climate will elicit positive change strategies from those who have participated in the 'data feedback' process of organizational development" (177). Early support-staff researchers thus urge worker "participation," if only through the vehicle of statistical studies like these, upon library management.

Voelck's study, conducted in 1994 in thirteen Michigan academic libraries among support staff, is categorical in its insistence that the dissatisfaction she found among paraprofessionals with more than five years' experience stems from an "unfulfilled expectation ... that they will be included in policy, procedure, and decision-making activities as they gain experience and become more proficient in their work" (164). Moreover,

> [w]hile respondents in all education categories show dissatisfaction with the opportunity for promotion, those with the highest education levels show the most dissatisfaction. These findings suggest that there is a conflict among staff with higher levels of education between the expectation for participation in organizational communications and for promotional opportunities and the actual level of participation and opportunity for promotion in the organization [167].

Perhaps, as I suggested above, we need above all things to regard colleagues as friends. Perhaps a feeling of friendliness, rather than attention to vita, should be first. Friends would never dream of treating each other as a human sub-genus, or a cog, or a "robot" (Schneider 394), existing to do grunt work and to be treated offhandedly. Bringing people at work into focus, treating them as peers, would do a great deal towards alleviating the ghastly lack of civility which has come to dominate this country, emanating as surely from hierarchical workplaces as from any other readily identifiable source. "Hire a friend today," should be the library motto. Perhaps we could be credited with starting a revolution. Friendliness, rather than reification, is a more reliable solvent in creation of a melting pot than anything else I can think of.

PART V:
BURNOUT: THE NEED
FOR PROTECTION

30. Repression of Criticism

Nonetheless, hiring a "friend" is possibly the farthest thing from the minds of most management freaks, not only in Libraryland, but in the wider American employment scene. The Clinton administration's *Working Women Count*, which draws on the feedback of over 251,200 working women, maintains that stress rates as the number one concern of the country's females (29). Stress, as we have seen, historically has also ruled the rank and file in the nation's libraries. Today, the many books covering burnout among library workers, though focused upon librarians, advise us that not much has changed.

In libraries, high turnover among the lower echelons has been legendary. It would be hard, if not impossible, to ascertain how many support staff leave their positions each year, each decade, and why they may be leaving not just for a different library job, but permanently. Utterly demoralized paras do not normally testify on the Net, where support staff is largely tenured and long in the tooth, committed, despite all the inequities, to continuing with library employment, by and large accepting the status quo, and doggedly improving their private lot whenever possible. In addition, the very worst-off of support staff are not given free e-mail accounts, as are many academic paras, viz., most public library clerical staff. To track down people whose degree of burnout most certainly puts them beyond reach of library literature, which might solicit information from them, is near to impossible. Library administration, through whose hands the "instruments" of surveys usually pass and in whose hands the contents of exit interviews rests, would also be of no help in gathering information on the topic of paraprofessional disaffection, because it actively strives to muffle any clamor or complaint arising from embittered staff. The public ear is a carefully guarded thing.

And administrations do, as a matter of policy, systematically stifle unseemly, un-"ladylike" rage on the part of employees as much as possible. One has only to read Clopine's incredulity and hurt astonishment at the suppression and destruction of early records of employee unionizing activities, which had been handily accomplished in a number of libraries by the early 1950s, to grasp this. Libraries, on paper so enamored of freedom of speech and so devoted to lack of censorship, disgracefully saw to the eradication of rare early labor serials, and, when approached by Clopine, evinced a convenient memory lapse over issues of labor unrest, even for events occurring not a decade earlier (Clopine 35–38, 81–82, 108, 126, 135). Even the library presses, in the teens of the century, came under suspicion of hiding pertinent activities on the part of angry, desperate rank-and-file library workers fighting for fair compensation and benefits, equity in hiring and promotion, equal rights for women, and less punishing work schedules (15–18, 23, 71).

In this connection, Marjory Doud, in 1920, with humorous encouragement, dreamt of the day when some library luminary would pen a paper called "Articulate Assistants: ... How Can They Be Suppressed?" (543). She was a tad more ingenuous than the library administrators above who quietly did away—no questions asked, no quarter given—with great chunks of library labor history. Despite the wholesale destruction of valuable staff history, certain singular librarians encouraged support staff to be heard;

> I hope that everyone that takes home a paycheck from a library reads "Education and Manpower for Librarianship." I hope they think about it, that they talk about it in the staff room, at the district meeting, at the state convention, and that they speak up, put it on paper—make their feelings known.... Will it really help the nonprofessionals get the recognition so long denied them? ... I hope all kinds [whom he designates] will speak up. They needn't be afraid. They will be heard. Ears always perk up when a new horn enters the chorus,

encouraged Gerald Shields, editor of *Special Libraries* in 1968 ("Editor's Choice").

Recently, support staff were pleased to see an issue of the *Journal of Education for Library and Information Science* (*JELIS*) devoting most of its space to the more articulate among them, as did the *LLA Bulletin* in 1990. But evidently paraprofessional writers grate on librarians' sensitive nerves. Any expression of aggrievement not directly under their control seems to make many of them seethe. In the main they are able simply to ignore paraprofessional quibbles and queries,* but when the blind-eye approach fails, they often become rabid. As we have seen, Ed Martinez, editor of *Library Mosaics*, tells us that his offices

> receive countless notes and comments from librarians who question the value of this publication, and state that there is no need for this type of forum. The magazine is accused of serving no purpose, except to raise expectations and create problems for librarians and support staff. Their concern may stem from their fear of the power of the press to empower those who put their thoughts in writing to be shared with others, particularly ideas that question the status quo in libraries.

*Denise Green suggested, in a 1990 letter to *College & Research Libraries*, that the editor solicit a manuscript written by an academic support-staff member to ascertain the paraprofessional view of their role, specifically in regard to serving on reference desks, in academic libraries today. As far as I know, no such solicitation has ever been made.

To read of support staff being introduced to new staffing arrangements that enable them to successfully perform "professional" tasks, like assisting with reference services or cataloging, may be unsettling to some. The last thing some librarians may want is to have their staff read of such arrangements, because "it will never happen in my library" ["Writing" 39].

Sentiments like these lie behind the "book-burning" previously enacted by libraries, and govern the archaic administrative behavior which makes front-line library workers want to bite and claw. Manley has said it so well, too, writing of the initial effervescence and eventual sullen decline of nouveaux circ clerks' idealism (*Manley* 47–9). These people, when they leave library work, are burned out, fed up, in flight. One can only make educated guesses, based on one's reading and experience, why this is so.

As long ago as 1950, researcher Annette Hoage stated with concern that "little has been published concerning attempts to control turnover in libraries" (29). She claimed, "Library literature and approximately 200 annual reports of individual libraries were searched for statements of rates of turnover. Very few reports contained such data" (29). Nauratil, also, insists that "a burned-out individual may not have the time or desire to return [a] questionnaire" (7). But certainly the experience of the Library Clerk I interviewed in Appendix A, caught before she fled the field, adumbrates some possibilities: lack of a salary adequate to live independently on, lack of respect or consideration from administration and patron alike, only the remotest chance of promotion, failure of administration to address the issue of job monotony with proven tactics to make clerical and even paraprofessional positions less tiresome, like job rotation, cross-training, participation in decision-making, continuing-education opportunities, or chances to attend meetings and conferences—all advocated by sensible early library workers, librarian and assistant alike.

31. Problem Patrons
in Public Service

[H]aven't we some grounds of complaint against the people? Oh, yes; they
do make heavy drafts on our best tempers and our best manners ...
[Countryman 399].

"A rarely documented source of concern for public library staff appears
to be confrontations with users," concludes Hodges from research she conducted on stress in the library (753). One of the largest factors in "line-worker"
burnout occurs in their unprotected interface with the public. Bunge saw
"[r]elationships with library patrons" as "an obvious source of stress for public-services staff members" (95). Voelck in 1995 advised the field that, in her
survey, at least, "support staff who spend the greatest percentage of time working directly with library patrons are significantly less satisfied overall..." (167).
Vincent's clerical respondents "resented what they saw as public exploitation
of the library" (406). Sherrer noted in her 1985 job-satisfaction survey that
"[m]ost stress in public services ... was indicated by circulation staff members
who felt victimized by the public" (20).*
    Nor is this a new development. Since the inception of public libraries, the
library worker-patron relationship has been stormy.† It has not always been
as formidable as it is today. Usually the interface, when not amicable, is at worst
irritating and wearisome. But sometimes the interface is dangerous, or incip-
iently dangerous. Sometimes it is lethal. "Librarians rarely note that many

---

*There are studies which indicate that public service creates the greatest satisfaction among
frontline workers, e.g., Azad, whose study of eight institution's "self-selected" paras indicated that public-services employees garnered higher job satisfaction than technical-services
workers (61, 63, 110, 125), Parmer and East (49), and Palmini (125). Disgruntled from my
own extensive interactions with the public in two out of three public-service positions in
three different libraries, I can only imagine an ideal patron population in these cases. Workers in these situations can only be counted lucky.
    †Viz., Library Assistant in "Antagonism Between the Public and Library Assistants" and
Librarian in "The Antagonized Public Again."

service jobs have inherently high risk and stressful conditions," accuses Neville (243).

One of the most sobering and common sorts of risk emanating from patrons involves sexual misbehaviors. "Libraries are a magnet for sexual deviants," states O'Connell (17). Even Will Manley, normally cheerfully irreverent, sobers at the response he received from his controversial sex survey, which "revealed a shockingly high rate of harassment by library patrons: 78 percent of the women who sent back the questionnaire indicated that they had been victimized by sexual harassment by patrons." "Unfortunately," he adds, "this is in many ways a hidden problem because many employees are too embarrassed to report these activities and many supervisors simply don't want them reported" (*Manley* 138–9). And, sad to report, while "[m]ost ... associations ... have up-to-date policies ... [concerning] sexual harassment[,] [t]he same cannot be said for ALA," comment Watstein and Wilcots in their series on sexual harassment in libraries (29). This prim averting of the eyes has no place in the modern library work scene.

Herbert White, discussing the helplessness of employees in general, puts the case against pusillanimous library administrators strongly:

> [E]mployees have no access to ... outside decision-makers except through their own bosses. If they refuse to decide or act, to take risks or to fight, nothing good ever happens.
> The same can occur when bosses refuse to protect their subordinates in dealing with clients. The library customer is not always right. Sometimes customers are wrong, unreasonable, and abusive, and managers are expected to do more than shrug their shoulders and counsel patience and forbearance. It doesn't "come with the job," as some have suggested. It doesn't come with any job worth having ["Tough" 134].

Once again, the old library albatross, "I serve," hangs conspicuously around the necks of library administrators, inhibiting their capacity to see clearly ways to ease the drain on the energy of frontline library workers by insuring that they deal with a public appropriate to the library. By and large, libraries believe they would fail in their "mission" to the public if they were any less a social-welfare agency than they have ended up being.

The most obvious change, in the past twenty or so years, in the composition of library clientele, has come about not only because of an increasingly depressed economy, but because of the huge number of mentally impaired "enfranchised," i.e., released from institutions, in the late 1960s and early 1970s (Cart 11). Quigley, in 1992, claimed the number of homeless "range[s] from 200,000 to 3 million" (668). Further, she claims, "[S]ome studies seem to indicate the number is rising" (669). Many, but not all, of these are the deinstitutionalized disturbed. While most people view these people as they wander, mumbling, through downtown urban areas, or settle into cardboard boxes, or push grocery carts laden with garments and miscellany, or lie in a state of heedless collapse on streets and benches, the library worker—especially the public library worker—is exquisitely situated to have to deal with them on a daily basis, but not specially trained, rewarded, or necessarily suited to manage the myriad problems they present.

In addition to the deranged homeless, there are the latchkey children, the alcoholics of all classes, the sexually perverted, the unwashed from every socioeconomic group, the vastly ignorant, the idle and directionless elderly (A. J. Anderson; Kamm; Leek), the unemployed in all their bitterness, the psychopaths, the sociopaths, the murderers, the library thieves, and the everyday, run-of-the-mill nasty, spiteful, devious, arrogant, aggressive, pretentious "normal" people. ULC/*Library Journal*'s survey of urban libraries revealed

> an average of 54 incidents of "willful mutilation" of materials; 156 patrons ... asked to leave the library; six indecent exposure incidents; four patrons barred from the library; 1.5 patron incidents involving a weapon; and 40 calls to police regarding safety threats [St. Lifer & Rogers, "Urban"].

The hapless "circ clerks," as Will Manley terms them, in the course of their day will deal with every kind of "attitude," every kind of pretense, every kind of bullying, including identical behaviors, often, from their superiors at work ("Facing" [1988] 82). They are useful scapegoats.

Farther up, at the college level, public-service paras will deal with all manner of students with "single-digit ACT scores" and with the state-funded perpetual students: those who enter, on federal tuition grants and loans, institutions with "lenient admissions policies," usually state community colleges (Salter & Salter *xiii*; Mulcahy). These people cost the taxpayer "$6 billion in college-tuition grants and $15 billion in guaranteed loans." Mulcahy claims that "[f]rom 1988 to 1993, $14 billion was lost to student-loan defaults. The default rate of students without a high-school diploma [without a high school diploma?!] has been more than 50 percent." People of this sort may cost the taxpayer a bundle, but they also tax the patience of line-working staff in the schools they attend with their truly punishing stupidity and incredible ignorance, not only of academic matters, but of issues pertaining to the living of life itself.

In my own experience, one student was astounded to discover that there were no more than thirty-one days in a month; another had no idea that library materials were arranged in any kind of order; another was surprised to learn that Bolivia was a country; another believed that the mythical Diana was a character in a movie; and one was unaware that "ask" was a word. I once found a student who had sat before a glowing, empty microfilm machine for twenty minutes before asking for help; she said she'd been looking for the *New York Times* and couldn't find it. When told she needed to have film for the machine to work, she was amazed. In addition, college library paraprofessionals or clerks are exposed, like their public library counterparts, to unwashed and unhygienic students (recently one lifted up the front of his T-shirt in front of me and a whole roomful of people and blew his nose in it not once, but three times), spoiled students (who have no notion, for instance, that a waste basket—not the library carrel or study table—is for disposal of waste), and a smaller but still meaningful percentage of all of the library animals detailed above.

All of these patrons believe that they "pay [the clerk's] salary" and therefore are entitled to abuse them endlessly (Salter and Salter *xiii*). I suggest, however, that in public and college libraries clerks not only pay—usually in exorbitant taxes—their own salaries, but often subsidize the very institutions these insults are being bandied about in. In addition, as Mulcahy has detailed, they are footing the bill for innumerable of their problem patrons' continuing education.

Furthermore, all problem patrons know they can torture clerks in all sorts of little ways which no one will stand in the way of, because if circ clerks respond to them even remotely in the way they deserve to be responded to, human being to human being, an outraged patron can report them and know that his word will unfailingly be taken as gospel by library administration, which consistently fails to stand behind its employees. Administration will back down on anything from enforcement of fines policies to loyalty to its own workers in the face of outrageous patron misbehavior, a practice library director Alvarez deplores: "[I]f one of your workers is falsely accused of an error, be sure to come to that worker's defense. You expect your subordinates to work for you; be aware that they also expect your loyalty and support" (*Library* 110).

In addition, "[a] whole list of 'thou shalt not' statements normally govern and restrict the options of library personnel, in effect protecting the problem patron from being hassled, and leaving them effectively free to hassle others with comparative impunity," charges Shuman (9–10). On top of this, administration will also be endlessly reiterating a truly unrealistic expectation that underpaid, tormented, and humiliated frontline workers field abuse, accusations, and psychosis with unadulterated niceness seven hours or more a day, just as they did in the early years of librarianship. Paraprofessionals are still expected to be "ideal desk assistants." No wonder they suffer high turnover. They are "under pressure to answer questions quickly, to appear pleasant and courteous irrespective of how they personally [feel]" (Hodges 751).

This unnatural and extremely wearing stance of sweet patience is a standard to which administrators themselves are less capable of adhering than their clerks, in my experience. Even a small percentage of the daily madness and staggering stupidity which the circ clerk endures will usually send the administrator into sputtering rage, and ensue in an impoliteness which, if the clerk were to have unleashed it, would result in disciplinary action. But the world will not often see administrators on the front line. They prefer the quiet hidey-hole of the front office; others may deal with the riff-raff—and they'd better do a bang-up job of it, too. "I feel like a front line soldier in the First World War being given orders by high ranking generals sitting safely, miles behind the trenches in large chateaux," offers one of Thapisa's British library-assistant survey respondents ("Burden" 141). It needs to be said of administrators *vis-à-vis* the formidability of the public, as Herbert White noted in the context of procuring funding, that "of all of the attributes of a successful manager, the most important is courage" ("Our" 54).

Salter and Salter believe that there are some forms of madness library staff will not see. "People with certain kinds of mental problems would most likely never find their way into a library or cause trouble there," they opine (117). But I believe only the hopelessly immobile, the most radically immobile retarded, and the dead and buried are the only members of the public that support-staff members will not encounter at some point and suffer from. While library workers are not the only employees in America to suffer abuse from the public, few other white-collar workers will ever confront, unmediated, the multivariate panoply of human nature which the library clerk confronts. This is because other institutions—except hospitals, where depredations are high (Rosier, "Assaults")—have developed ways of limiting their scope; the public's access to vulnerable employees is not allowed to pass beyond certain tolerable limits, and incidents are quickly curtailed when they do occur. They have policies that do not broach the sorts of uncouth behaviors that library workers face every day. They see "problem patrons," but are nowhere near as helpless in the face of them as their library sisters. Banks do not allow bums to loiter or harass; libraries do. Other institutions with problem clients also at least warrant coverage from the general press. Libraryland itself, in popular magazines, is as invisible as support staff are within it. Recently, on Libsup-1, paras were incredulous that the persisting popular image of the library worker—as evinced by both family and the folks they know—is of one who reads all day in quiet, congenial surroundings. Surprised to find that "libraries have no model for formulating patron behavior rules," judges ruling in the Kreimer case in New Jersey confided, a tad condescendingly, "Maybe we'll write them one" (Flagg, "Insurer").

Libraries seem to have adopted a Mother Theresa–like role in society. The people who pay the bill for this pose are not the taxpayers, but the front-desk workers: the clerks, the library assistants, and the lower echelon of librarians, all usually female. In the beginning a maternal/servile/religious role was exactly the one women were expected to play, the smile on the face despite martyrdom of all sorts. But society is not so homogeneous today. Many women now alive have not been raised to believe that martyrdom is a desirable or acceptable venue for them, and many of these people are support staff. Also, gentility is hardly the aspiration of the public these days, perhaps less than ever. Rosier states:

Nearly 1 million workers each year are injured by violence on the job, according to the Justice Department.... [C]ontrary to popular perception, workplace violence is not likely to be committed by fellow workers. Violence by co-workers, former employees and management caused only 6 percent of the total 1,063 fatal assaults in 1993 [funny coincidence: 6 percent of librarian respondents to Manley's "Librarians and Death" survey believed they would be killed "by a circulation clerk suffering a psychotic episode"—no matter that he was probably kidding].... Retail workers suffered the highest number of occupational homicides—totaling more than 2,700 between 1980 and 1989. The service industry had the second highest with 1,275.... [S]uch public employees as teachers, social workers and nurses [and, of course, frontline library workers, both clerk and librarian] are subject to workplace violence but have no recourse because they are not covered by health and safety laws in 27 states and the District of Columbia [Rosier, "Assaults"; Manley, "Why"].

Most libraries do not protect their employees from a vast range of evil and inappropriate behaviors. They put their lower-level employees at risk by their placatory, non-interventionist stance, and despite a concern, on paper, for the high turnover rate of support staff, they make it clear that individual howling departures are of no moment whatsoever. Like any beast—in the absence of internal restraint—anywhere on the planet, the public will get away with whatever it can, and administrations avert their eyes whenever they possibly can. Whether it is a patron so filthy and fetid that he or she has stunk up the entire library within minutes of arriving, who decides just to sit all day in his seat opposite a circulation desk and stare bizarrely at his favorite clerk, or a madman wielding a gun (yes, clerks and librarians do die in the course of their work with the public), libraries generally have nothing in place to draw the line. One has only to regard the headlines:

"GEORGIA LIBRARIAN MURDERED WHILE WORKING ALONE" (Gaughan)
"TWO LIBRARIANS SLAIN BY GUNMAN AT SACRAMENTO PL" (Kniffel)
"LIBRARIAN RAPED, MURDERED IN ARIZONA PUBLIC LIBRARY" (Gaughan)
"GUNMAN OPENS FIRE AT CLEVELAND PUBLIC LIBRARY" (G. Flagg)
"PRISON LIBRARIAN FREED UNHARMED AFTER BEING HELD HOSTAGE" (Gaughan)
"BOMBER HOLDS LIBRARIAN AND PATRONS HOSTAGE AT UTAH PL" (St. Lifer & Rogers)
"LIBRARIAN STABBED AT DESK" (Kulp & McCormick)
"KNIFE-WIELDING YOUTH SLAYS PUBLIC LIBRARY STAFF MEMBER"
"BOMB BLAST JOLTS LIBRARY AT MICHIGAN'S OAKLAND U." (Kniffel)

Most have no set of procedures for dealing with "incidents." Seven out of ten urban libraries "have no staff guidelines for handling violent or threatening incidents," claims a 1995 article in *Library Journal*. ULC president Rodger explains:

It's important for people to understand that historically, libraries have been more concerned with systems that protect collections.... But in cities we need to be increasingly concerned about systematic approaches to protecting staff and patrons [St. Lifer and Rogers, "Urban"].

Twenty-five percent of librarians surveyed by ULC and *Library Journal* admitted that their libraries were "not very safe" (St. Lifer and Rogers, "Urban"). Rural library workers insist they're not so safe, either (Cole, "Killed"). In many places, support staff are not waiting for their libraries to protect them, but are taking steps of their own. The Fall 1994 newsletter from NYSLAA covers a workshop/self-defense class recently offered at LeMoyne College. Unfortunately, although paraprofessionals were learning effective ways of dealing with dangerous patrons, the reviewer laments, "Each of us felt that if we used any of the techniques taught in the library we would probably be fired" (Butcher 2). Manley warns,

> As a profession we have dangerously put the rights of the patron ahead of the rights of the library staff. The sad truth is that many of our most professional spokespeople simply do not want something mundane like employee safety to interfere with their heroic advocacy of the patron's intellectual freedom [*Manley* 139].

Latchkey Children

A smaller version of the adult library-going sociopath, the so-called "latchkey child" is often a little more sinister than this euphemistic term implies. One pictures a winsome, slightly worried-looking, earnest, brave, sweet child with a briefcase and a key on a string around his neck, the offspring of professional parents who both are working when he gets out of school. The reality is far different. Long surmised that "20 percent of all American youth" were latchkey children, and Dowd, among others, claimed that a large percentage of these, unsupervised for at least as long as two and a half hours every afternoon, make for the public libraries after school (Dowd 8). She claimed there was no documentation as to their numbers, but a survey conducted in Los Angeles in 1984 "revealed that in 50 out of ... 92 facilities ... more than one thousand children were using the library for day care purposes" (Dowd, citing Markey 9). Cart insists the number is larger: "[I]n an average week more than 5,000 latchkey kids 'hang out' in L. A. area public libraries" (18).

We live in a country that is relatively heavily armed (considering we are not at war—save with each other), a country in which everyone now can expect to be shot either on purpose or by accident and in which "an American child is ... arrested for a violent crime every five minutes" (Davis and Meddis 1; Briscoe 26). British public servants, like us in so many other ways, mirror our lot with the unruly child as well, lamenting:

[S]taff had verbal and physical confrontations with potentially violent members of the public. In particular, "youths" were considered to be the most disruptive, especially those "not interested in the books" preferring to shout, swear, throw things about, and misuse the facilities. They are "prepared to assault you if you ask them to leave, or even to keep the noise down" [Hodges 753–4].

The "latchkey child" is more often than not a neglected, unclean, often abused, and utterly unsupervised wolf-child, who makes the hair of everyone around him stand on end. At his best, he is a subdued child who doesn't know what to do with himself, who gets bored and requires repeated stimulations, whose mother has surreptitiously dropped him off at the library to be baby-sat all day while she does what she must.

And there is the disaffected teenager, directionless and randomly hateful and violent in consequence. Attitudes of participants in a recent "workshop … dealing with 'raucous' behavior" in New York City ranged from sympathy— a view of teens as frightened children in adult bodies fighting "invisibility" and deserving a "place where they can be safe and protected"—to "fear of violence," resulting in a quest "to keep certain teens out of a library" (Mark).

Dowd put it well:

Latchkey children present awkward choices, challenging dilemmas, and unique opportunities for libraries, primarily because service to this group seems to both coincide *and* to conflict with the very mission of these institutions…. Yet most public librarians … agree they are neither staffed nor trained, nor are their facilities equipped (or licensed!) to function as day care centers. Librarians also generally agree that their role should not be that of disciplinarian or babysitter [12].

Guards

For all of the reasons suggested above many systems have had to hire guards for the afternoon and evening onslaughts of danger and creepiness (in some places they're in place all day), but all too frequently they are superannuated policemen, the retired, or the down-and-out in uniform, hired at cut-rate. They doze on the job; they are unarmed; they have no training in mob control, if you will; they may be actively cowardly; they sometimes smell; they may stare; they are frequently annoying to clerks; they often are themselves, in short, a species of "problem patron."

Thieves

Larcenous behavior is another of the great treats of public service in libraries. It is also, of course, a monumental problem for administrations. The

Library of Congress recently closed its stacks, amidst outcry, because it was losing so much of its collection ("Librarian Explains"). Clerks must daily deter theft on an immediate level, often responding to and occasionally watching patrons speed through ringing security gates and calling out to patrons to check out books. They weekly replace pages torn from books and magazines, straining interlibrary loan services. They are the staff who most frequently must explain that desired books are missing and why gaps exist on index shelves. I will never forget the expression of incredulity and exasperation that flooded the face of the long-time clerk who trained me when first I entered public library service and asked her, all aglow with the idealism of a lifetime, whether people ever abused the library by stealing books (something which had never crossed my middle-class mind). With total disgust she brushed me off with, "Of *course* they do." The rest of her response was lost in mutterings, head shakings, and dismissive motions.

32. The Library Circus and the Library Mission

A tour of the literature will show all of the above politely touched upon, usually from the librarian's perspective and in far more depth than I will attempt. Implicit in the number of convoluted problems covered is the plain fact that libraries lag behind other institutions in deciding what it is they really are. All too many librarians seem incapable of deciding that a child roller-skating through the library laughing and jeering does not, in fact, have an equal right to be there with the peaceable patron who is determining his or her weekly reading.

Criminologist Alan Jay Lincoln admits that in libraries "[p]rotection of the staff and patrons is still a soft area" (St. Lifer, "How" 36). Belatedly, state governments and the ALA are awakening to the magnitude of the problems of larceny, vandalism, and hooliganism in libraries, probably the last place on earth which should have to be host (or, more accurately, hostess) to them. In the past ten years, "35 to 40 states [have] enacted measures" on security issues and library crime. "Hidden dangers," according to the nation's courts, have come to include "violent behavior on the part of third parties," as well as building pitfalls. The ALA is still in the discussion mode concerning library security but is at least aware that the problem requires its scrutiny (St. Lifer, "How" 38–39). Spurred by the Kreimer incident, the ALA by 1993 had at least proposed some "guidelines" on controlling patron behavior (Turner, *It Comes*, 138–40).

Libraries in the vanguard of internal reform, like the San Francisco Public Library, have brought in security guards actually trained in law enforcement, "Prior to that," SFPL's director admits, "there were people coming into the library that the staff were literally terrified of, and nothing was ever done" (St. Lifer, "How" 39). Las Vegas public libraries have barred, through decree, the troublesome homeless from their libraries, and the Ann Arbor Public Library, similarly, bans patrons who sleep or reek (Quigley 679; "Local").

Unions also are moving towards a stance of protectiveness toward their membership, realizing that little else is in place to shield it from society's sociopaths. The AFL-CIO and fifteen affiliated unions have formed the Inter-

Union Workplace Assault Coalition, which tries to interface productively with OSHA and other sluggish federal agencies "charged with addressing workplace violence" and workplace safety (Rosier, "Assaults"). If they succeed in erecting a perceptibly effective barrier against the public, this perceived protection may cause even more library workers to vote in labor unions at their workplaces, aware that management, left to its own devices, would never do more than twiddle its thumbs in the safe confines of its inner offices.

The library is host to literacy volunteers, tutoring programs for those who have been barred from school; it tries to serve the linguistically handicapped, the physically handicapped. It does outreach to schools. It is still like a religious order, even in the 1990s, in the number of folks it feels it must serve, and still "ladylike" in the number of insults it feels it must bear with sedate forbearance in "service"—more like "servitude"—to the public.

While several of the services just ticked off are in fact valid and valuable, legitimately warranting whole departments or space in the library's meeting room, why is it that in today's public libraries, one can hear rock-and-roll bands, be served ice cream, or behold a man with a crystal ball telling people about their Indian spirit selves? In this Haight-Ashbury, this hurdy-gurdy carnival atmosphere, the desk worker, never made party to hosting decisions, is an incredulous captive, bound by her need to put food on the table, to co-pay the rent (few can live alone on base-rate library salaries, which constitute the salaries of most library workers at the support-staff level), to raise children, or to pay for a car. They often wonder if librarians have gone mad in their religious commitment to offering sanctuary to—nay, seeking out, even, on any silly pretext—the masses—anything to raise "circ."

It is true, this foolishness has its precedence. Early libraries, seeking to make themselves the social centers of their communities, were driven to such stratagems, in one case even offering baths to the public. One proud librarian in Pennsylvania boasted, "During the year 1913 our bath circulation was 68,113, being 1,310 for each week or 218 for each day..." (Lamb). At the end of the twentieth century, we have come full circle; people are once again using the library to take baths, in an ironic grotesquerie, only their numbers are not statistics of which we can be proud. This time the bath-taking has not been planned: this time the bathers are the militant homeless. Allowed such astonishing license, they have had no trouble persuading themselves they could also litigate against public libraries and thus move in. After all, libraries have for so long been fostering the notion that libraries are all things to all people, with such a guilty desire to "serve," to earn their keep, that they have lost sight of something they should have been believing in and promulgating without stint: the power of the book. Instead of unabashedly proclaiming its strength, regardless of scoffing philistines, they have acted as if the potency of the book is insignificant. Nobody, including librarians, now seems to believe books have a drawing power of their own, that the contents of books constitute a fully

Burnout: The Need for Protection

legitimate *raison d'être* for libraries. People in search of books and information are libraries' appropriate clientele—not miscreants, not people needing social services, not children on the loose with nowhere else to go.

In spite of audience-drawing tactics, the public library has never served much more than 10 percent of the country's citizens appropriately, as some cynics hold (Hyman). Or, as Carl Roden put it in 1923, "The Gospel of Books is not a tale of crowds" (493). Though Curley maintains the percentage served today is "more than 50%," and Berry puts it at "some 60 percent of the people," one wonders if these higher percentages are not due to the "bath" phenomenon: the ubiquity of media materials, the sense of the library as a play area (Curley; Berry, "Maybe"). Linda Wallace maintained in 1989, citing a Gallup poll, that "three-quarters of adults rarely visit libraries" (24). But exactly what is the problem with serving only one-fourth of the population?

David Ring, describing the growth of Carnegie libraries in Montana, wrote:

> Fort Benton boldly proclaimed in planning the building that "it would be more or less a social center for the country people." These pleas fell on deaf ears— Bertram [Carnegie's administrative secretary] was adamantly opposed to Carnegie libraries being used as anything but a library, in Montana or anyplace else ["Carnegie" 14].

In philosophical alignment with Carnegie and Bertram, clerical workers are a pragmatic lot, as Ida Vincent's research in 1984 revealed, to wit: "Most regarded printed materials and print-based activities as especially appropriate to the library's purpose[;] ... provision of nonbook materials and the arrangement of activities programs in the library ranked fairly low" (Vincent 402). Noting that "[a]mong the various stakeholder groups which have an interest in public library goals, library staff have been comparatively little studied" and that "[t]his lack of research into staff's perceptions of public library goals is rather surprising, since staff can be both a limiting factor and a potent resource in attaining or modifying goals," she stated:

> Staff who are uncommitted or hostile to a goal can undermine the library's success in achieving it.... Bankstown staff's perceptions of goals were very much influenced by pragmatic considerations, and many judgments were apparently made on the basis of practical rather than philosophical considerations[, e.g.,] ... [r]anking of goals was ... affected by the belief that the budget was inadequate.... While nonprofessional staff's perception of goals seemed sometimes to be based on a somewhat narrow and pragmatic conception of the philosophical basis of public library service, there were other instances in which their attitudes could be seen as more dynamic, and less bound by tradition, than those of the professionals.... It seemed too that many respondents held social and political values which induced sympathy with the underdog, and a measure of hostility toward wealth, privilege, and formal institutions [397, 405, 407–8].

Other Australian researchers "noted a similar mixture of idealism, naiveté, and conservatism in nonprofessionals' perceptions of goals" (409).

People come into the profession at the clerical and paraprofessional level, perhaps naively, with love of books, idealism, and promise, prepared to work themselves to the bone as part of a team working towards the betterment of the nation's intellect. They leave in loathing and incredulity, in part because of libraries' diffuse focus and librarians' inordinate concern for every class of underdog on earth except their very own staff, with whom they share no decision-making and over whose plummeting morale they waste not a moment's thought. So much for teamwork.

I have always loved libraries. (Though more recently, through burnout, I have had to modify my focus; now I have to say, "I have always loved books.") As one paraprofessional on the Net proclaimed, despite shabby treatment from the library employing her: "Libraries are my life" (Sue Greenhagen, Libsup-l poster). "There are people who gravitate toward librarianship, at one level or another, as naturally as others turn to the soil or feel their fingertips tingle at the sight of shiny new tools," wrote Rosanna Miller in 1975. "The initial impetus toward a particular field of endeavor is often an essentially sensual reaction" (554). In common with most librarians and paraprofessionals, love of books and libraries was the reason I entered the field. As one distinguished manuscripts and archives specialist put it, "Books, you might say, are in my blood.... Sometimes there's no escaping destiny" (Ravdin). But even as a child, I found librarians and their attitudes—disdainful and unencouraging, with only one exception I can think of, almost positively unwilling to see books go out, especially books deemed to be "above" the child's reading level—to be unequal to the greatness of the Library *qua* Institution. I hope that libraries will continue to flourish. I hope I can occupy a useful place in one or more of them. But working in them, suffering patron abuse in them, and observing the often extreme petty-mindedness and lack of intellectualism of the librarians in whose care these valuable institutions lie has been a lifelong source of disillusionment for me.

The field's disaffected support-staff emigrants, unsurveyed, uncounted, and unexamined, have vital and valid perceptions. They are a resource as valuable as any patron group. Indeed, they *are* a patron group, a tax-paying patron group. And they are being treated by libraries in a way not even a coprolaliac bum would be treated. They are being "wasted," in all senses of the word. In fact, there are indubitably clerks who would be treated better if they entered the library as bag ladies, rather than as employees. The lack of any writing on this unfortunate lost worker is a big lacuna in library literature. The acid comments of "Para" in a 1989 *Colorado Libraries* article, intending to leave but not yet having the means, give us some insight into paraprofessionals who exit. This book and the first interview (Appendix A) give even more. (One ex-library clerk, unemployed and desperate, was offered her old job back; she simply sat down and sobbed at the prospect of returning to library work.) But to accommodate the valid perceptions of those who leave, the entire library world would have to turn around and reorganize, putting itself behind *all* educated people of bright promise rather than myopically hiring for cherry positions people who have the three magic letters—MLS—after their name and disregarding any other intellectual assets. It would have to adopt participative management techniques *in toto* and accept radical new salary schemes which rewarded accomplishment, ability, and experience, regardless of number and type of degree, or lack thereof.

Perhaps I, clerk to the bone in this matter of the circus function of libraries, take an exceedingly dim view of patron license and library foolishness because when I was a child, libraries were stringent places in which nobody talked, much less screamed, cursed, or flashed. I was never served ice cream, nor did I expect to be. I went to the library for reading material, nothing more, and it sufficed. When I received my first library card, I had to sit down and memorize ten rules and then be quizzed by the librarian before I was allowed to receive and use the card. I was so well indoctrinated, in fact, that in the many decades of my life, I have never lost a library book—other things, but never a library book. I believe that a well-behaved and book-and-information-focused library clientele is an attainable ideal, but not unless limits are set. The clerical common sense Vincent described has much to offer hare-brained librarians who believe rock bands should constitute library programming.

It is in fact possible to serve The Public, a public appropriate to the library, by eliminating unthinkable kinds of behavior from the library's venue entirely. Entirely. How is the public served when a madman, habituated to lounging without any meaningful restriction upon library premises, suddenly decides to accost a patron? Or kill a clerk or librarian? How are people who are reading or studying served in having to listen to a person who cannot stop talking to him/herself, and who is usually cross and odiferous to boot? How is the discreet patron benefiting when a man lies down on the floor in the next stacks over in order to look up her skirt? Why should a muttering woman be tolerated when she pulls all the books off the shelf and shoves them back in at random? Why should a foreign-born clerk have to sponge xenophobic sentiments off her carrels, or a periodicals attendant try to obliterate penises drawn with indelible ink on chairs set out for public use in her area, or a page emptying the book drop recoil in alarm from books and videotapes covered with excrement? Who does the library administration think will be responsible for cleaning up these items, or disposing of them? Clerks deal with these problems because most library administrations, with security and aesthetics as with innumerable other subjects, will not define the boundaries of the library's mission.

And why does a library have to run a virtual fair to promulgate its usefulness? Wouldn't a strong congressional lobby serve libraries much better? The "Library" will not define its mission because librarians cannot define theirs. Just as they allow professionals from other fields as well as each other to decry their professionalism (Bishop 8–12), they allow people quite literally to shit all over their libraries and their staffs, and encourage an unserious view of their mission because they too often play ring-master, rather than book-master. When the homeless are allowed to enter the library in order to take a bath in the men's or ladies' room, have not the libraries gone a full negative circle, back to Pennsylvania in 1913 when in fact most librarians were fairly horrified that a patron should expect to come into the library expecting to bathe (Kartman, "Demonstrators" 709; Distressed)?

In 1990, in response to public outcry, the hapless Joint Free Library of Morristown and Morris Township sensibly imposed a hygiene, dress, and behavior policy upon library users. This policy fell most heavily upon the homeless, who were making the library less a haven for book-lovers than a doss house. Richard Kreimer, aided by the ACLU, managed to convince the U.S. District Court that his civil rights were being violated. However, library director Barbara Rice stated correctly and succinctly, "Morristown does have a homeless problem, but we're not social workers" (Gaughan, "Long"). And one of the defendants in the Kreimer case, Morristown's Mayor Norman Bloch, also observed with great justness that "society absolutely has a right to have reasonable rules with which to maintain itself in a civil way" ("Homeless").

In 1991, homeless advocates filed a suit against the aforementioned sensible Las Vegas-Clark Library for instituting policies, again to protect *bona fide* library users from odoriferous library abusers. According to decree,

> librarians must now telephone any one of three homeless representatives who will have final say over whether the patron will be ejected. The library is subject to a $250 fine if the procedure is not followed. Unfortunately, library director Charles Hunsberger feels that the new policy may prove to be unworkable. The policy states that the homeless representative is supposed to arrive within a half-hour; however, ... it has taken [representatives] an hour and a half to arrive, and ... even then they have failed to find a single patron objectionable enough to eject.... Hunsberger feels that homeless advocates are using the library as a rallying point following Richard Kreimer's nationally publicized lawsuit against the Morristown, N.J., public library.... He said that anywhere from 25 to 250 homeless individuals use the facility as a shelter daily, but when a homeless-rights action is being staged, they fill up all 125 available seats. The situation, concluded Hunsberger, "makes it impossible for us to work as a library" [G. Flagg, "Las"].

When has there been written a story regarding libraries *vis-à-vis* the law more flagrantly outrageous and absurd? Whatever became of common sense—the courts' and the ALA's? The ALA, it seems to me, needs once and for all to become a militant organization, which can flood any court, and any congress, with as many crazed, unifocal zealots lobbying on libraries' behalf as can the homeless, or any other group which threatens libraries' existence as libraries. I leave aside the obvious question of whether the "I-pay-your-salary" argument can even come into play here, since, as homeless persons, the unhoused are hardly in a position to be billed, or, being unemployed, in a position to pay into any fund for the common good. Yet they seem to have a lot of energy for destruction—in this case, destruction of an institution which can arguably be said to stand for civilization.

And what of the nation's libraries who stand by foolishly applauding their own downfall, in effect, so caught up in discussions of civil and constitutional rights that they seem to have lost sight of both their own self-interest and that of their legitimate constituents: tax-paying citizens with habits of nonobstruction and common courtesy, using the library as book-borrowers and researchers? Are the rights of such people, meek as they may be, less important than those of the vociferous, problematic homeless? Are disruptive, smelly, rude people using the library as a convenient protection from the elements really the citizens "The Library Bill of Rights" was written to serve? After suing the Morristown, N.J., library for $80,000, Richard Kreimer, self-appointed discipliner of the ALA and public libraries objecting to reeking people, actually received offers to speak from "libraries throughout the country" ("Kreimer"). I find this ridiculous. I see no reason to applaud the noxious, no matter what the excuse. I have watched people like Richard Kreimer, aggressively unclean, empty libraries of their less bumptious patrons. We have had to open doors to air the library out. Library staff members on duty have not been as fortunate as the patrons who could choose to leave, and have had to stand in place bearing this starkest of air pollutions.

As a tax-paying, burned-out (played out in exactly the way Manley delineates) clerk and public library user, I insist that the library deserves better, and that people working in my capacity deserve better. Librarians' problems with self-definition, like many of their other problems, ultimately become the legacy of support staff on the most elemental level—that of opening doors to admit breathable air, discarding library materials contaminated with feces and urine, and being the staff most frequently withstanding untoward verbal abuse. "Library is not a social service agency, has right to adopt conduct rules," read headlines in the Ann Arbor *News*, supporting library director Hernandez in his effort to salvage his library from Rescue Mission status ("Local"). With Ann Turner, I believe we "need to say loudly that we are in the information business, not the shelter business, and that if shelter is the need, the community is going to have to find a way to meet it" (*It* 42). I hail Herbert White, who urges librarians to revise the scope of their perceived expertise, to understand what their "unique" skills are:

> [W]e have missed the opportunity to spell out our profession.... [T]he missed opportunity may have come from the insistence, from both inside and outside our profession, that we need to make filling the needs for "doing good" our first

priority. If we were to define our unique capabilities in both the areas of education and information intermediation, it would give us plenty to do. I haven't mentioned a role in the areas that seem to fascinate us so much—work with adult illiterates, with latchkey children, with the homeless, and with an ever-growing list of societal problems to which crime and drugs must certainly be added; while we can "do good," we have only our frail bodies and not any unique expertise to throw into this fray…. If such programs are worth having, then they are worth municipal and federal support … ["Lead"].

33. Sick Buildings, Sick Workers

> There is hardly a citizen of the United States who has not at some time or other made use of a Carnegie library building.... All of them have one fault which dims their many virtues.... They are full of stale, foul air, disease-breeding, headache-creating.... Why people who are presumably desirous of being intellectually stimulated will put up with the mind-dulling, sickening closeness is a mystery. But they do [Liverpool 59].

This condemnation, penned in 1917, indicates that complaints about "sick buildings" are hardly unique to the 1990s, and suggests another reason why library workers in the late nineteenth and early twentieth centuries suffered from ill health. However, at least the Carnegie and the WPA libraries built in the '30s had windows which opened. "[W]ith the increased emphasis on energy conservation that began in the 1970s, such as using more energy-efficient building materials and reducing the air exchange rates of ventilation systems" has come a new rash of complaints about building air quality ("Indoor"). Modern-day complaints point to something a little more sinister than stuffiness:

> I work [in] a new, big, beautiful edifice with no windows that can be opened, literally no fresh air, and a multitude of fluorescent lights.... When the heat is turned on I leave work at the end of the day with a blinding headache.... Why? Why are buildings like this being erected? They may be considered energy-efficient but they are anti-human. Why aren't the people responsible for building new libraries cognizant of the fact that in such structures indoor pollution is usually higher than outdoor pollution? Are these people blind to the costs in terms of the ruined and wrecked health of the employees? [Karpin, *anno* 1991].

Our libraries, built with materials containing formaldehyde and "volatile organic compounds," are perhaps a little more dangerous than buildings built with wood and marble. The substances we use to clean floors and machinery and exterminate insects with in these edifices are dangerous, too. Dirty air conditioners; lack of fresh, oxygenated air in hermetically sealed buildings; noxious fumes seeping from new carpets; dust mites, fungi, and the filth of the ages rising from old; the chemical effluvia of modern office furniture and paraphernalia

250

all contribute to what a number of government agencies see as "the 'growing problem' of indoor air pollution" ("Indoor"). Brenda Turner, commenting in 1992 on the mismanagement of "nonprofessional" staff, wrote,

> We hear much regarding the environment for our collections and justifiably show concern for temperature, dust, humidity for books, computers, etc. Yet, many times we expect our staff to work in drafty rooms, surrounded by dust, with poor ventilation and temperature control. Do we bother to improve conditions or listen to legitimate complaints? [60-61].

The General Accounting Office (GAO), the Environmental Protection Agency (EPA), the Occupational Safety and Health Administration (OSHA) are all charged with protecting air quality for American workers, but only the former two are actively concerned about the mounting effects of noisome air upon the inhabitants of modern sealed office workplaces. In 1987, in fact, "the EPA ranked indoor air pollution fourth among 31 environmental issues" ("Indoor").

OSHA "concentrates on industrial and manufacturing workplaces because it doesn't consider indoor air pollution risks in an office to be significant" ("Indoor"). Libraries, like other white-collar businesses, are among the most insidiously unhealthful places to work, and most library administrations, with a few notable exceptions, are as impervious to concern over indoor air pollutants, excluding cigarette smoke, as they are to the mounting horrors of problem patrons. *Library Mosaics* puts it bluntly: "No OSHA regulations exist for libraries" (Bianco 11). And because no one imposing is telling library administrators what they need to do to meet health standards in libraries, they feel no obligation to heed the large number of complaints they hear from workers annually about the state of their buildings, or the poisons that enter these substandard workplaces in pesticides, solvents, and cleaning solutions.

Carmel Bush, a library supervisor recently involved in a troubling series of worker illnesses ultimately attributed to biocides and anti-corrosive chemicals steeping in standing water, coupled with a malfunctioning air-pressure system, advised

> administrators of 25-30-year-old facilities to be especially "alert to what staff are saying" about building temperature fluctuations and minor sensory and upper respiratory irritations, and provide extra ventilation in chemical-laden areas such as preservation labs [Goldberg, "Colo." 826].

She and other administrators were "immediately supportive" of their workers. Unfortunately, all too many library workers reading such a story can muster only the greenest envy.

Three out of the last four libraries I have worked in, for instance, have been sick buildings. People exposed to particles from walls and ceilings being improperly demolished and reconstructed in these buildings with inadequate air exchange and windows which were never made to open have developed chronic respiratory conditions—asthma and decreased lung capacity, for example.

Pesticides and fungi cause eyes and lungs to burn; the unperceived, long-term damage may be even more dramatic. Yet administrators of these buildings have routinely countenanced spraying of cockroaches or other insects not only while library workers are present, but while patrons—including the susceptible populations of children and the elderly—are browsing.

Roofers are bidden, by thoughtless officials who can afford to take the time off while work is being performed, to come and work while people are inside library buildings. Tar boilers are placed anywhere expedient, often near intake vents. Recently, roofers worked on our library for two months—unchecked, even though we filed a complaint with OSHA—day after day filling the building with vapors which induced headache; burning eyes, throats, and lungs; bloody noses; extreme faintness; and impaired cognition, to enumerate only the most egregious symptoms. One worker developed a cough which persisted long after the work was through, and was told by an examining physician that she had oil in her lungs. While the cough was later subsumed under a diagnosis of lupus, suspicion lingered that exposure to roofing fumes might have triggered the disorder. Other people suffered increased sensitivity to pollen during hay-fever season that year. Any time off which we took to avoid pollutants had to be taken out of sick or vacation time, as per the personnel director.

There was not the least consideration extended to us, and quite a bit of skepticism. Most of the workers exposed were full-time support staff; librarians were scheduled to come in only sporadically because of reduced library use during summer, and thus could not be brought to comprehend how insuperable it was to live with these fumes day after day. None of us could imagine what subtle forms of damage had been wrought which years down the line we would be paying for. One office—housed in the library building, but not a library department—removed itself in protest to another building on campus, its director more attuned to reality than the library or campus administration. The report from OSHA, arriving months after the work had been completed (in deference to the administration's perceived wishes?) was dismissive and curt, in effect accusing complainants of suffering mass hysteria, to wit: though

> [t]here is no OSHA Permissible Exposure Limit (PEL) specifically for asphalt fume [and the outside sample] was analyzed for ... pyrene, phenanthrene, chrysene, anthranene and benzo-a-pyrene [and n]o detectable levels of any of these chemicals was found ... [therefore n]o overexposure was documented. No PESH violations were identified. The odor noticeable in the library probably results from low concentrations of sulfur compounds. The complaint is not sustained ["investigation narrative" from T. W. Shiel, written by R. Jankowitz, NY State Department of Labor, Sept. 19, 1994].

No OSHA inspector responded to our initial written complaint until weeks of work had been done on site. Thus, even if by some miracle OSHA had found for us in the end, they would have been too late to protect us from the fumes that even students complained about. We did not need Selma Benjamin to tell us that OSHA has "never [been] a good tool for public employees" (5).

In another library, carpeting was laid and workers expected to take vacation time if they wanted to avoid the resultant formaldehyde fumes. There was some sniffing on the part of administrators in this case, who always seem to feel complainers about environmental poisons are somehow more wimpy than they, and that their complaints are without substance. However, Benjamin points out that formaldehyde, a common office-place pollutant, "even in minute quantities," causes nasal cancer (5). Experiences like this, in which common sense is flouted and complainants ignored or ridiculed, make one justly cynical about the beneficent paternalism of governing bodies in general. One becomes particularly cynical of library administrators who stand quietly by on the few days they work during an unhappy farce like the one we suffered, making no effort—not even a verbal one—to protect either themselves or their longer-suffering library workers. This sort of behavior exemplifies Bunge's criticism of managers "who will not risk advocating strongly for their staffs" (96).

I have seen brown and then yellow water running from taps at work, oily to the touch even days after the color had gone, and emitting a nasty odor, another unremediated problem. This water at the best of times tastes industrial, for want of a better word. Authorities called in subsequent to complaint have white-washed the situation, testing for one element of pollution only; upon finding none of that, they assumed that everything else about the water supply was okay, when one taste of it would call into question its provenance. (I now bring my own filtered water.)

I once listened to a library director threaten us with loss of our jobs if we called in the health department to investigate the general deterioration of our facility—in particular a cockroach infestation. He further accused us of trying to inflame patrons by telling them about these beasties. We pointed out to him that patrons could see for themselves roaches making their way across the covers of the best sellers on display. He was not amused. But, of course, neither were we. We were incredulous at his tasteless truculence. We were also cowed, because we knew he would make the life of our branch director, of whom we were very fond, a misery if we proceeded as we should have.

Clerical workers at Brown University, a locus for many strikes, tried to make an issue of air quality in their 1979 negotiations, the union attempting to mandate that workers be allowed to go home when the temperature and humidity were too high. This was one among many issues termed "emotional" by a commentator (Lynden and Fark 97, 93).

"Emotional," however, is precisely what complaints about sick buildings are not. Kreiss offered that "[t]he findings of different rates of building-related symptoms among workers in buildings with different types of ventilation makes a psychogenic explanation for the symptoms unlikely" (878). Indignant Molly Karpin frothed, "Should anyone reading this believe that this is all in my head, be aware that this problem has a name: sick building syndrome. You'll find it on InfoTrac" (843). Conceding that researchers are not yet close to understanding the cause of sick-building syndrome, she mourned that "the science to support prevention, correction, and the setting of standards is woefully undeveloped and unsupported in the United States" (878).

As a glimmer of hope for library workers and other types of employee suffering from sick-building syndrome all over the land—in 1993 estimated to be "at any one time 10 to 25 million workers in 800,000 to 1.2 million commercial buildings in the United States"—I draw attention to Glenn Hartwell, of the Kelso Public Library, who closed his building after "'sick building syndrome' ... felled all four clerical workers in the facility" (Menzies et al. 821; Kartman, "Sick" 979). These people were plagued with "headaches, respiratory problems, throat irritation, fatigue, and other ailments." The library spent $30,000 trying to ascertain the reason for these disorders, which in the end were suspected to be caused by dust in the building's filthy vents, and a certain amount of fiberglass. Would that all library directors were as responsive as he.

"Terminally" Ill?

We have seen that increased involvement with technology has touched all library workers, but particularly paraprofessionals and clerks. Overwhelmingly the involvement has been with computers and computer terminals, video display terminals (VDTs), whose safety has been called into question ever since their inception. In addition to exposing workers to trying screen glare, VDTs emit both ionizing and nonionizing radiation. Ionizing radiation "can break down chemical bonds in cells, which causes them to change in ways that can be damaging to the larger organism" (Fernberg 36). VDTs set up very-low-frequency (VLF) and extremely-low-frequency (ELF) electromagnetic fields, both forms of non-ionizing radiation, associated with blurred vision, cancer, miscarriages, and birth defects. ELF is the more feared of the low-frequency electromagnetic fields, causing anomalies in the growth and well-being of cells and their chemical composition. They are thought to be involved in tumor formation, hormonal variation, and compromised immune systems (A. C. Greiner). There is a whole body of speculation associated with these forms of radiation, dominated specifically by Paul Brodeur and Karel Marha. The relevance to support staff (or any VDT worker) is obvious and needs to be mentioned in connection with workplace hazards encountered on an everyday basis.

Along with the general threat to the body posed by radiation, VDTs cause specific and ascertainable damage to both eyes and wrists. Betts reported in 1993 that 1,307 optometrists across the country reported "that 14% of their patients had symptoms such as eye strain, headaches and blurred vision from the use of VDTs." Thus, he suggests, approximately 10 million people per year consult specialists for VDT-related eye problems.

Wrists and fingers are also under assault in the library workplace, as in other occupations, when workers use VDT setups. Repetitive-stress injuries (RSIs) form the basis for one of the largest classes of litigations in the country, costing employers $20 billion a year (Galen 142). One supervisor, writing on Libsup-1, confirms that until her library invested in ergonomically correct devices for wrist support, all three of her clerical input operators had their wrists in braces.* In places which fail to accommodate such a warning sign, carpal-tunnel surgery, paid for by the library or library system, may be the next inevitable step.

In addition, furniture used with intensive VDT operation needs to be specially designed and chosen. Exercises must be taught and practiced to keep at bay a host of skeletal and muscular disorders associated with the tense stationary position typically maintained at work stations.

The long and the short of the introduction of VDTs, the existence of sick buildings, the panic of unprotected workers in the face of mounting cultural dissolution, the perennial shame of poor salaries is that unions, poor as they often are, in default of administrators shouldering responsibility for safe and equitable workplaces, seem to be a required presence in every library.

---

*VDTs are not wholly to blame for RSIs, however. Many long-term clerical workers have developed wrist injuries—spurs, carpal tunnel syndrome—from excessive filing, lifting books off shelves, little motions that by themselves seem like nothing, but which cumulatively, in older workers, cause pain and hand dysfunction which require surgery.

34. Unionism and Support Staff

The history of abuses in libraries, as in many other workplaces, gave rise to the history of unions in libraries. In 1899, graduates of the Drexel library school attempted a drive, unfortunately "short-lived," to standardize wages and hours (McReynolds, "Sexual" 212). Federal library workers were the first to actually unionize, in 1914 (Clopine 4). On May 15, 1917, the New York Public Library was granted a charter for its local, the Library Employees' Union (LEU), which included both librarians and clerks (15) It was followed by public libraries in Boston, the District of Columbia, and Butte (Flexman 27; Kusack 10; Clopine 7). Attempts were made to unionize Philadelphia and Louisville libraries, but these attempts were abortive (Clopine 6, 7). Library of Congress employees organized in 1917 (Berelson, "Library" 492).

By 1919 five AFL-affiliated library units existed, though all but the Library of Congress ceased union activity in the early '20s, perhaps because their interests were not strongly enough served by this form of representation, perhaps because of "poor leadership," perhaps because of "the strength of the opposition" (Berelson, "Library" 496; Kusack 10; Flexman 27).

Milden charges that "[l]ibrary historians have substantially neglected the role and development of library unions" (156). He delineates a convincing picture of why unions have had a tough time succeeding in libraries, dominated by the "lady" library worker devoted to a servile ethic. Marot also analyzed the problem of galvanizing women similar to library workers in 1914. As was the case with the early Ideal Desk Assistant, other

> wage-earning women are in trades which yield the lowest scale of wages, ... and where a worker can be quickly replaced by other workers.... [I]t is extremely difficult to persuade workers who are not receiving a living wage ... to join an organization which will require time, money, energy, and many serious sacrifices for a reward in the future which for them is certain only in its uncertainties.... This is the problem of unionizing the unskilled worker, and, as the mass of women are unskilled, it is in part the problem of the organization of women.... [In addition] women, unlike men, are not relieved from home duties.... They perform their day's work ... in addition to their obligation at home.... They have very little

conception of their place in industry...but they have a very present realization of how they can help out at home. With this attitude toward their work they readily accept a wage which is an auxiliary wage, that is, a wage which supplements the wages of others; a wage which does not pay, but helps to pay, the rent ... [68–70, 71–72].

Despite these general truths, fields other than librarianship (where workers were abundant, if not unskilled, and eminently replaceable) in the early twentieth century had given rise to fulminating female activists constantly developing and forwarding unions—largest among them the National Women's Trade Union League (WTUL), which was active for forty-eight years from 1903 to 1952—run by women and composed of women, well in advance of the rather belated beginning of the New York Public Library's famous LEU (Wertheimer 265–92).

Coverage of unionization in the reigning periodic library literature of the day—*Library Journal* and *Public Libraries*—was predominantly derogatory. "[I]t was [the] image of librarianship as a genteel occupation that anti-unionists exalted," Milden claims (153). Mary Ahern, editor of *Public Libraries*, in fact, made no secret of the fact that she deplored unionization of librarians (e.g., "Trade," "Library's," "Trade," most probably an unsigned piece, "Labor..."). Refusing to give the issue broad and fair treatment, she was typical of most vocal librarians of her day. *Library Journal*, for example, accords small space to the whole issue of the dismissal of the radical Adelaide Hasse from directorship of the unionized NYPL in 1919. We get a glimpse, but only a tiny one, of the forces at play and the violence of the emotions involved: charges of "'temperamental idiosyncrasies'" on one side, accusations of "stacked" cards on the other (*Library Journal* Editors; Squires, "As").

Milden ties the early union movements "not only [to] the issues of economics and professionalism, but also the more volatile issues of sexual discrimination and the status of women in librarianship. It was these latter issues that sparked public library unionism and contributed to its speedy collapse" (150). We have seen the debacle enacted in the 1919 annual ALA meeting, in which women shot themselves in the foot, despite Maude Malone's absolutely on-the-mark, though strident, presentation of the state of the field. Time and time again, women have been sidetracked from seeing to their basic human rights by the decoys of gentility, ladylikeness, and self-sacrifice.

By 1940, there were six library unions, some including what would now be regarded as support staff. Unionization continued throughout the '40s, affecting mainly public libraries. Clopine drew up a chart in his thesis showing a total of twenty-four library unions which rose and, in some cases, fell, between 1916 and 1950. By 1950 only ten of these were left (175).

The first academic library to agitate for unionization, according to Clopine, was Howard University, whose librarians worked towards this end throughout the 1930s and finally in 1945 agreed to affiliate with the United

Federal Workers of America (112–14). Yale in 1946 convened a union meeting composed of thirty clerical and ten professional library workers. It was the first academic institution to have organized nonprofessionals as well as librarians (Clopine 116, 118). Most of these early union efforts were concentrated in large metropolitan areas of the Midwest and East, were affiliated with extant national unions, and suffered high "mortality" rates (Kusack 11). In the '50s and early '60s, the economy was strong enough that library workers saw no need to turn to unions for betterment, but in the late '60s and '70s clerical workers in libraries, mounting in number and incensed by "professional" snobberies and insultingly low pay, though their educational level and their job responsibilities were rising, again turned to labor unions for succor (Flanagan 491–2; Flexman 27–8).

Legislation in the '30s (the National Labor Relations Act), the '40s (the Taft-Hartley Act), the '50s (the Landrum-Griffin Act), the '60s (Executive Order 10988), and again in the '70s (the National Public Employment Relations Act) allowed disgruntled workers of all kinds—both private and public sector—the right to organize with the unions of their choice to redress grievances, which among library support staff were, in order of priority, in the areas of wages, benefits, pay equity, grievance procedures, and fair representation (Kusack 13; Lilore 6; Flanagan 492 & 499; "Collective" 18). Throughout the '50s, library employees, hampered perhaps by overly genteel notions of their status, had relied on "merit systems, civil service, and staff associations" to defuse problems with management (Flanagan 492).

Support staff turning to ALA for help found that body unwilling to do more than issue a policy statement. Its "Statement of Principles of Intellectual Freedom and Tenure for Non-Professional Employees," was, as Flanagan puts it, "never worth a cup of coffee to anyone but the printer" (493). ALA refused to assume a union function for any library worker despite the feeling of the "majority of librarians and library school students [that] the American Library Association should be the organization to work aggressively to better their economic and professional positions" (Rosenthal, "Impact" 54, citing Schlachter 194, 196).

Nor was this the first time serious observers had urged this function upon the ALA. Marjory Doud, in a 1920 article for *Library Journal*, compared the plight of librarians at all salary grades with that of teachers, who in their desperation for a "worthy" living wage were then contemplating affiliation with the American Federation of Labor, as were library workers. She suggested

> that the simplest and most natural form of organization for librarians would be local branches of the American Library Association. Units of this kind could have the independence of purely individual organizations and also the strength which comes from union.... The local units would gain by the experience and standing of the A.L.A. The A.L.A. would profit by having more general support of members from more parts of the country, undoubted sources for freshness of

ideas and plans for progress. To the average assistant, the A.L.A. is a far off thing, not directly concerned with any individual. It is politic to know the name of its president, but beyond that it has little of personal appeal. To arouse the interest of the A.L.A. in the library workers of all communities, and to arouse the interest of library workers of all communities in the A.L.A. is the direct and simple method of progressive and constructive organization [543].

This suggestion fell into a void. Thus Flanagan in 1974, as if continuing her train of thought, wrote:

Abandoned by the ALA, ... facing the open hostility of many "professionals" who could not define the word "professional," the support staffs of the country began to look inward and outward. Introspectively, they found they were far more numerous and skilled than they had ever been. It was becoming quite ordinary to find college graduates among them, with specializations in programming, AV technology, systems planning, personnel management, budgeting, and data processing. Many were, in fact, the "knowledge workers" George Berkley [had] predicted [would] number 50 percent of the working population by 1980 [493].

The '60s, '70s, and '80s, consequently, saw a spate of ivy league clerical and technical union drives.* Discussing this trend, Heller maintains that "universities attract strong-minded workers interested in bettering their own situations" (28). Dennis Blake, president of Local 680, United Stanford Workers, states that in university settings "'the white-collar worker tends to be a little more educated and a little less prone to be fearful of the employer'" (Heller 28). Specifically, more than one campus has found what administrators at Yale perceived: that of its clerical and technical workers, the library unit is both "a bellwether and a trouble spot" (Nyren, "Picket" 22). Harvard activist Kris Rondeau observes that "'The kinds of people who work at universities ... resent the divisions and hierarchies, and they speak up about it'" (Heller 28). In the 1980s, as in the late teens of the century, union drives at universities tended to rally around the truth "'that workers need a voice in the workplace,'" rather than around specific economic issues—the nagging voice of participative management again (Heller 28). By the mid–1980s, Lynden found, among ARL libraries, almost half with unions in their midst, and the number rising. For instance, from only ten institutions he counted more than 1,200 additional support-staff members seeking the protection of unions between 1980 and 1985 ("Unionization" 3).

The Directory of National and International Labor Unions shows that both academic and public library workers have (inappropriately, in my opinion) tended to join, first, AFSCME (the American Federation of State, County and

*And in 1974, 3,500 labor-union women collected themselves for another go at feministic trade unionism, as women in the WTUL had earlier in the century, establishing the Coalition for Labor Union Women (CLUW) (Wertheimer 372).

Municipal Employees) and, second, SEIU (the Service Employees International Union), often in units with custodial or other types of maintenance
workers (Lynden, "Unionization" 3). In public libraries, they are often in the
same units with librarians. Sometimes these often grudging alliances, called
"coordinate bargaining," have been fruitful (Flanagan 493). Roma Harris, however, claims, "In mixed units in which library workers are included with workers from a variety of different occupations, librarians often find that their interests are not particularly well looked after" (*Librarianship* 112). The same
experience has been true for many support-staff/blue-collar-worker coalitions,
where the blue-collar worker disdains women white-collar workers—"clerical
work ... [is] not seen as 'real work,' and clerical workers [are] not seen as 'real
workers'"—a proud tradition in the U.S.:

> If the prevailing social opinion of the day [1900–1930] was that women were not
> "real workers" and "shouldn't" organize, the view of organized labor seemed to add
> the element that women, and women clerical workers in particular, "wouldn't"
> organize, and that whether or not they tried made little difference to the labor
> movement [Feldberg 54, 61].*

However, in some coalitions this conservatism is absent, or there is greater
worker homogeneity. In coalitions in which all unionized units in an institution have worked together informally, in a sense of unmandated but fierce fel-
low-feeling and loyalty, rectification of grievances, unsurprisingly, occurs more
expeditiously than with isolated groups (T. Meyer). "Where library support
staffs and librarians have worked together in private institutions, their strength
has been [most] impressive" (Flanagan 496). Support staff, however, more frequently unionize than librarians ("Collective" 18).

Today, AFSCME continues to lead the list of the many unions enlisted
to aid library workers in their quest for higher pay and equity of every sort
(Kusack 17; Rosenthal, "Impact" 53; "Collective" 18). The Communications
Workers of America, the United Auto Workers, and even the Teamsters,
among the larger unions, also enlist increasing numbers of library clerical and
technical workers (M. Weber, "Support" 69 & 85). Even the American Federation of Teachers "decided [in the 1980s] to expand their organizing targets
to include nurses, librarians, and library workers" (M. Weber, "Support" 85).
Library of Congress workers, though largely represented by AFSCME's Local
2477 (2,000 members), also has a contingent represented by the Congressional Research Employees Association (CREA, 415 members), though neither local, because of federal regulations, can negotiate rates of pay (Harger,
"Talkin' Union" 11/1/89, 1250 & "Talkin' Union" 11/15/89, 22). Yale affiliated

---

*At Syracuse University, library workers learned this grim lesson with regret during, and in
the years following, their strike in 1973–74, when 120 "clerks" walked the picket lines for
58 days at the height of a bitter winter (Kusack 23).

with the Federation of University Employees, Local 34 (2,600 workers), and Harvard with AFSCME in 1988 (3,500 clerical and technical employees), thus becoming the "largest bargaining unit at any private institution in the U.S." (Heller 1; McClure).* Eleven hundred similar workers at Columbia organized in 1984 (Heller 1). By 1985, at Boston University all non-administrative library workers were organized, though support staff opted to be in a separate unit from librarians (Nyren, "Picket" 22). In November, 1991, 65 percent of Los Angeles Public Library's 1,500 employees, members of SEIU's Local 660—librarians and support staff alike—participated in a one-day strike to underscore a tentative agreement regarding health insurance parity and parking reached by union officials and county negotiators, an agreement which the county reneged upon several days after it was made. At issue, also, but to be resolved later, were salary and benefit issues for library support-staff workers (Goldberg, "One").

Kenady maintains that "[w]ith few exceptions, ... pay equity studies and adjustments ... have been the result of active union involvement" (60). Rosenthal maintained, in a secondary study of Minnesota unions, that unionized library workers enjoy better wages, fringe benefits (health coverage, average number of days off) and experience lower employee turnover than non-unionized employees ("Library"). In her study of 120 libraries and library systems in 1983, she declared unqualifiedly that unionized employees in both clerical and professional categories "received, on the average, substantially higher wages than did their nonunion counterparts" ("Union" 31).† Wozniak, as per the Bureau of Labor Statistics, claims union wages and benefits packages in 1994, averaged $23.26 per hour as compared to non-union wages, which were far lower: $16.04 per hour (6). Unions, even the most inert, still provide paraprofessional workers a hedge against arbitrary firings and some of the more blatant job inequities and humiliations, through grievance procedures (Tsang 6). Rosenthal found that the very presence of a union on-site, whether including the clerical group or not, was sufficient to provide enough "spillover" to boost library clerical salaries ("Impact" 56).

In providing support staff with job security, unions may also—but also may not—protect them against three insidious new management tactics: the contracting out of certain library services (like cataloging), the elimination of full-time jobs with the substitution of unbenefited part-time employment, and the mushrooming use of volunteers, for the most part affecting women workers all over the country (Judd & Morales Pope 88; Alvarez, *Library*; Schuurman; et al.).

*To understand how both unions and management can work together to make support staff's life pure misery, and to see how extremely effectively people must work to succeed against these odds, see Shostak.

†It is odd, in light of her finding, that although most unionized support staff are in the Northeast, wages are higher for them in the West, according to a 1994 support-staff salary survey in *Library Mosaics* (Martinez & Roney, "1993" 7).

On the down side, Lilore's contention that paraprofessional library workers have been regarded as weak groups hardly worth the organizing is borne out in Flanagan's findings: "In their diverse organizations and scattered libraries these staff unions apparently do not maintain communication with one another—and that certainly does not strengthen them" (Lilore 15–16; Flanagan 496). In fact,

> [s]upport staffs in private colleges and universities have ended up in many types of unions, no one of which is devoted to library workers. Even the union leaders themselves cannot calculate the number of clerical and technical locals having library support staffs as a portion of their membership,

maintains Flanagan, a fact true even today (496). Having written to the AFL-CIO/ALA Joint Committee on Library Service to Labor Groups, requesting information on how many units of workers were represented in the AFL-CIO (among other things), I received the following reply from Margaret Myers, in the ALA Office for Library Personnel Resources: "...there are no real current statistics that we have on number belonging to unions" [sic].

If support-staff membership seems feckless to unions, how much more so, overall, do unions to support staff, despite the success of organizing drives, and the initial successes of the large and conspicuous units at Yale and Harvard? After a lengthy comparison of the sparse literature on library support staff and labor unions, and study of the effects of collective bargaining on wages for union as opposed to non-union members, Kusack maintains,

> Most research seems to indicate that there is probably some wage advantage which can be attributed to collective bargaining, but the gains are not nearly as large as those enjoyed by workers in other occupations. The best guess may be that library support staff employees gain, on average, something like 4 to 8 percent wage improvements through unions—a figure low enough to bring into question whether improved compensation is adequate motivation to participate in collective bargaining [5, 21, 30 & 39].

G. Ruben, in 1989, discussing wage settlements for private industry, pointed out that

> [s]ettlements covering 1,000 workers or more ... reached between 1982 and 1987 provided wage adjustments averaging between 1.6 and 3.8 percent annually over their life; during the first 9 months of 1988, the average was 2.4 percent. By contrast, between 1972 and 1981, the over-the-life average was between 5.1 and 7.9 percent annually [25].

Perhaps the poor to moderate improvement in wages for library paraprofessionals is part of a larger disenchantment with labor unions which could account for the recent steadily declining percentage of union members nationwide and across all classes of work, as the number of workers increases, but the number of unionized workers decreases in proportion ("Collective" 17).

And the workers unions target above all others—blue-collar males and female white-collar clerical and technical workers—are the group the least well-off in the 1990s, despite women's having risen to constitute 37 percent of union membership in 1990 (D. Harris 26; Branan 32). "Among blue-collar workers," says Diane Harris, "hourly wages dropped 14.6% for men and 6.2% for women, while those for men and women in service jobs fell 10.8% and 4.2%, respectively"(26). Despite these foreboding figures, *New Republic's* John Judis sees a brighter day for unions: "'Although union membership steadily declined from 22 million in 1975 to 16.4 million in 1992, it actually grew last year, to 16.6 million—the first gain in fourteen years'" (Branan 30).

Nevertheless, unions have been most often responsible for the studies undertaken to aid library workers in attaining job equity. And they are usually not solicited for help unless a group feels real outrage with library administration. Mark Weber, himself a library director, writes matter-of-factly:

> In most library settings where management and staff have a good working relationship and where staff believe they are being treated fairly, union organizing campaigns do not even reach the stage of a representation election.... In most work environments where there is a union organizing effort, the union is there because employees honestly believe that there are significant problems surrounding pay, benefits, job security, or other issues. In most cases, these have been issues for some time, and an effort by the library administration to answer union charges after a formidable organizing drive has began [sic] will make almost no difference as to whether or not a union organizing drive will succeed [73].

Recently, for instance, the Albany Public Library felt such outrage—over unreasonable behavior on the part of the library director—and commenced a unionization drive ("Union"). By 1994, Local 3933 of AFSCME had won the vote of these disaffected workers and was filing an unfair labor practices charge against the still unregenerate director, William O'Connor ("Staffers"; "Union-Busting"). Is it an altogether positive comment on the integrity of unions that this man believes "managing [APL's] employees ... would 'be easier' once his workers have a contract" (Kotzin)? The much-discussed unionizing and striking Yale and Harvard employees had similar acrimonious experiences: 600 people were arrested during the Yale strike, for instance (T. Meyer).

Lilore, in her study of unions in libraries, prognosticates, "If the union runs a vindictive campaign, or if management interferes with the process at all, a negative relationship of distrust will begin which may never change" (26). I would go farther, and maintain that in *any* unionization which begins with hatred and mistrust of management, which most do, that "negative relationship" will persist, and if management then wages a war of union-busting consultant interference during organizing, the term "negative relationship" will become euphemistic at best. Weber claims, "[A]ggressive anti-union campaign[s], ... using the services of an outside consulting firm [are] ... generally a mistake.... The major effect of the anti-union campaign in these situations

[is] to further polarize the relationship between the union and the library administration" (72–3). By 1979, 31,167 accusations of consultant "involvement" in organizing campaigns had been leveled, and 159 labor disputes had erupted because of them, "a 127 percent increase since 1975" (Field 69). "Most bargaining [today] is still adversarial and rule-oriented," finds H. Lewis (19).

Lynden and Fark, musing on the evolution of unionization at Brown University, which at the time of union affiliation ranked seventy-third in support-staff salary level out of seventy-eight ARL libraries, found that

> [o]ne of the most interesting aspects of negotiating with a labor union was what it told us about our own management of the Brown Library…. The most crucial factor contributing to the origin of the union … was the lack of effective communication between the management and staff…. Many of the changes won in the first contract had been proposed previously by the library staff association, but slow reaction or inaction on the part of the administration contributed to the profound discontent [90–91].

Nor has the rancor which Lynden and Fark document abated over the years. In addition to the strikes called in the early years of unionization at Brown, in 1990 still another was underway, 95 support staff members having taken umbrage at inadequate salary and health-benefit coverage proposed for their most recent contract ("Brown Clerical Workers"; Harger & Rosenzweig). Further, SEIU's Local 134 indicated that "[t]he university is trying to use the library unit to kill an organizing drive of 750 other clerical and technical workers in a larger unit on campus. A good contract for the library workers could put the university in a bad position with that effort" (McCormick, "Clerical"). Obviously, management had not only failed to learn anything from the criticism of its tactics implicit in the original formation of a library unit in the 1970s, but had continued spitefully in its accustomed ways until it alienated yet another clerical group on campus.

Women library workers differ in degree of politicization. Thus, strikes can be undermined by timid souls who stay inside. From this, corrosive interpersonal relationships develop that persist for years once striking workers are back on the job (Nyren, "Picket" 22).

A further dismal truth also illustrated by the Brown case is that, in time, a union may become as hated and mistrusted as the management because of its questionable practices. One of the strikes conducted by Brown employees in the 1970s evidently was fostered by unscrupulous union leadership. The unionists involved had to resign their positions in response to unit outcry (Lynden & Fark 92–3). At Syracuse University an SEIU Local left similar abiding discontent among library workers in the wake of a disastrous strike waged in 1973, in a story not yet properly told.

Most unionized support staff are concentrated in the Northeast, but while "[f]orty-five percent of the labor force is female[,…] only 25 percent of union members are women," claimed Field in 1980, a percentage which undoubtedly carries over into considerations of support staff (Kusack 57; Field 95). Lynden and Fark found that Brown University's library unit was composed of "over 70 percent women members" (94). Because the overall strength of women in large trade unions is meager (ca. 37 percent), the strength of a mainly female bargaining unit will be meager as well, unless excessive ferocity characterizes the group—ferocity sufficient to intimidate both employer and union leadership. Women in large numbers are still reared to be not fierce, but ladylike. Unless American women as a group raise their consciousness to the point that they recognize ferocity as virtue, they will never thrive economically in the workplace—or indeed, anywhere.

In most unionized libraries, the impetus to organize has come from paraprofessionals; "'professionalism' [is] … a major obstacle to organizing women" (Kusack 4; Field 95). Lilore indicates, in addition, that units in which professional and paraprofessional staff mingle may not at first experience strain, but later experience "conflict," a finding in opposition to Flanagan's (29). Conflict is not a surprising development, considering that conflict is woven throughout the fabric of professional/paraprofessional history.

More than ever, in the face of conservative backlash, library workers need unions, or some strong body to advocate for them; yet their access to unionization is threatened today as it has not been for many years. Labor unions view the Republicans' "Teamwork for Employees and Managers Act of 1995" as the latest assault on employees' ability to unionize, since it attacks their right to choose their own bargaining units. "It would allow management to create, mold and terminate employee organizations and employee representation plans at will … [and] block worker attempts for a real voice through a collective bargaining agreement" (Parks). Isn't it time for ALA to take up a union function at last?

The ALA as Union

> I firmly believe that the root of all our evil is money. No calling in the modern world that doesn't pay well can attract the best men and women in sufficient numbers [Nyren in "Library Education" 1766, *anno* 1966].

In 1919, Clara Herbert urged, as Doud was to urge even more eloquently a year later, "[A]ny chance of getting adequate salaries depends upon united A.L.A. effort and not upon each city's wringing it from its reluctant appropriation body" (108). Doud, convinced that ALA needed to become the bargaining agency for its workers at all levels, argued, "When organized, the expressed opinion of the assistants as a body would carry more weight not only with the librarian and the library board, but with the public, in propaganda for raising taxes for library purposes and in any movement for progress in the library world" (543). Ranck suggested the ALA set minimum salary levels, mandate education requirements for different levels of work, and in general aspire to set salaries at levels enjoyed by other infant professions of his time, 1920 (127). But the ALA remained obdurately unresponsive to this form of activity, perhaps considering it too ungenteel. Had the ALA at this point, when the library field was distraught over its inability either to retain or recruit line workers of high quality, gone ahead with a politically aggressive agenda—had it taken the leap into shark-filled waters and bitten and slashed for adequate funding and working conditions for its constituency, instead of sitting on the shore, simpering, wishing, and issuing empty mandates—we might have had an entirely different kind of library field at the end of the twentieth century, instead of going over old ground again and again, discovering and rediscovering, with each new generation of library worker, that we are underpaid and underappreciated, and that our image needs revamping. A politically penetrative agenda, an effort to hire men and women—even non–MLS-holding men and women—who would lobby, lobby, lobby on behalf of libraries on Capitol Hill side by side with the most tenacious PACs, would have changed the whole history of libraries. Instead of pitiful institutions from which the citizenry took and took without feeling the need to give back, either in the form of respect or in taxes sufficient unto the libraries' needs; instead of library workers low on self-respect and living on a shoestring, we might have a profession proud of itself at all levels of employ, filled with people who never for a moment thought their calling needed defense. In short, if the ALA had espoused the American way—hungry and ruthless—long ago, or indeed if it would espouse it now, carrying on the impetus initiated by recent ALA presidents Martinez and Curley, we would be enjoying what a *Library Service* article in 1920 called, prettily, "'a reasonably care-free and worthy existence'" (A.L.A. Salaries Committee 66; Berry, "Who"; Curley; Schuman & Curley). We would have been able to do our work unapologetically. We would have learned what the most astute library literature long ago urged upon us: "*Esprit de corps*," "team spirit," and we would, perhaps, have been free not only from the attritive meanness of spirit and outlook poverty engenders, but from the "great divide" that, like a persistent low-grade infection, has kept us from functioning at full capacity for 100 years. "If you don't promote," writes David Drake succinctly, "you're doomed to defend" ("When" 153).

35. Contract Workers, Unbenefited Part-Time Workers, Volunteers, and Students

C. Berger and Company boasts,

> ...during a hiring freeze, a long illness, or at peak periods, libraries can reap the benefits of having additional trained professionals and paraprofessionals on board without incurring costly screening, training, overhead, or overtime charges ["Action" 920].

Across the nation, "contracting out" threatens established full-time salaried workers (Wozniak 5). But "contract workers" (used in libraries—really another sort of library paraprofessional), claim Judd and Morales Pope, "who may earn more per hour than salaried workers, aren't really better off. A long-term illness with no paid sick days, no medical insurance, and no guaranteed job to come back to will quickly wipe out the value of a few dollars more per hour" (88). Euster confirms this advantage, from the point of view of the library administration: "[L]ibrary service companies are offering nighttime reshelving.... Such agencies claim ... their work crews are quicker and more efficient than regular staff, and that the library escapes payment of employee benefits, thus saving even more. Other contractual services are likely to follow this trend" ([2]). Library director D'Andraia, at a 1994 COLT conference, confirmed that "out-sourcing" was an increasingly attractive option for libraries facing budget cuts (Gonzales et al. 25). What a dismal reward these contract services workers (other "paraprofessionals"?) face for being "quicker and more efficient."

A recent article in the *AFL-CIO News* maintained that "American businesses ... sought ... to ... push wages and benefits down to global rates, and continued expansion of part-time and contingent employment.... 'Personnel services' ... grew a whopping 20 percent. Manpower Inc. is now the nation's largest employer" (Wozniak 5). This trend, affecting workers nationwide, has also crept up on the hapless library clerical worker, from whom, as from other employees, workplaces have been demanding "concessions." The increasing utilization of unbenefited part-time help is a real threat to the full-time career paraprofessional. The part-timer herself may also suffer in the end, when she wants to procure a full-time job and finds that because of people like herself, there are none to be had. In addition, part-timers, at least according to one job satisfaction survey, enjoy far less contentment with benefits (since they have none), the "work itself," and "operational procedures" (Voelck 165).

As full-time, benefited workers leave their jobs, either for other jobs or for retirement, libraries, or larger governing agencies of which libraries are a small, insignificant part, "freeze" their positions. Then, at first as a stopgap measure, but then as an established practice, administrations hire a couple of temporary unbenefited part-time employees to cover the work previously done by the full-time employee, but, of course, at reduced rates, *sans* benefits, and *sans* job security. Unions often do absolutely nothing about this substitution.

"From 1980 to 1986," claimed Rubin, trying to flesh out the future of public-library support staff, "the part-time workforce grew by 20%" (21). He cited the increasing use of temporary workers as "a significant trend" (22). Growth in this category of worker "has been substantial ... 75% from 1980 to 1986," he went on. "[T]he employer has far fewer obligations towards [temporaries] in terms of benefits or conditions of employment," he warned. "As employers' costs rise as well as legal liabilities, they may well consider temporary workers as an effective substitute for regular employees" (22). Willy-nilly, the temptation to insert a couple of part-time housewives supplementing dwindling family incomes into previously full-time and better remunerated but vacated positions "frozen" by local governments will in the end be too strong for even well-intentioned administrators to resist.

Another, older threat to paraprofessionals needing secure, well-paid work, and to their sister librarians as well, is the abundant use of volunteer workers (Sgritta), which unions, by their very presence in a workplace, *should* deter, but all too often do nothing about ("Action" 919). Schuurman, covering a typical large public library system in Salt Lake City, offers,

> Many library directors are, for the first time, considering volunteer programs because of a nationwide pattern of shrinking library budgets or frozen budgets tied to inflated costs. One way to avoid curtailment of services or hours is to supplement the efforts of the paid staff with the efforts of a volunteer staff. Volunteers can be used to assume some job duties to relieve the pressures on paid staff [4].

Increasing use of volunteers, smiled upon by library directors from Will Manley to Robert Alvarez, is really, for library workers who cannot afford to volunteer, a very dangerous development (Manley, *Unprofessional* 168–9).

Student workers, like volunteers, are in themselves innocuous, yet in many libraries, especially academic, they are now the absolute backbone of off-hour, and indeed sometimes on-hour-, library service. So much a part of library life are they that in one document they became unionized as part of a teaching-assistants' unionization drive and subsequent strike (Tsang). Many of these people "self-identified" with library clerical staff when voting for an affiliation, choosing AFSCME rather than the more "professional" AFT (American Federation of Teachers) (8).

Therefore it is incumbent upon unions to stand fast against the encroachment of unpaid, or unbenefited, part-time labor on extant full-time benefited library jobs, or in time, they, too, may be out of work. In 1985, Alvarez averred,

> ...The Volunteer Program has been one of the fastest growing and most important developments in public libraries in the past ten years. The idea of enlisting unpaid "volunteers" for service in the library was almost unheard of before 1975, but now almost all public libraries have one or more volunteers. Some have the help of over 100 such workers and a few others have branches that are entirely staffed with volunteers [*Library* 217].

By 1986, he was remarking with satisfaction that in the Iowa Public Library, "241 service volunteers ... gave a total of 5,837 hours of work to the library last year. This represents the equivalent of 2.9 full-time employees" (220). Of another system, he contends, "York County, Pa., may well be the No. 1 county in the U.S. for library volunteers. 600 volunteers is a tremendous number of enlisted helpers for any library system ... [; the 43,000 hours they contribute] is equivalent to the work of almost 21 full-time employees" (222). OUCH!

"Paid workers," assures Schuurman, "should not feel threatened by the use of volunteers. The jobs of paid workers will be protected through the process of promotion and attrition" (4). But they *should* feel threatened. Here is another instance of the mirroring that haunts librarian/clerk relationships. Just as librarians have been increasingly replaced by paraprofessionals, paraprofessionals will increasingly be replaced by contract workers, unbenefited part-time workers, and volunteers (and MLS-holders who cannot get a job anywhere else). To the "profession" as a whole, all of this is quite damaging, because in effect substitution of these kinds of transient workers simply demonstrates that library work can be mastered by *anybody*. The powers that be—the writers in professional magazines, the library administrators governed by expedience, the ALA—should all be in a stew here, really. All of them can be replaced; all of them are guaranteeing endangerment to their own "class" down (or up) the line when they endanger any of the other groups. The notions of unity, teamwork, and participatory management cannot come quickly enough to the field of library science, if it is to survive as a paying profession for anybody into the twenty-first century, and its doing so has less to do with the granting or holding of the MLS than with library leaders' own shortsightedness in allowing—nay, engineering—the unfolding of these trends.

36. Paraprofessional Associations

> Paraprofessionals will continue to have problems that parallel those of professionals until they become strong enough to voice their own concerns [Gill 397].

The earliest staff associations were clubs formed by interested assistants to, in effect, "network" throughout their cities, for instance one in Providence in 1896, and another in Philadelphia in 1897. They appear to have been formed by librarians, but to have included lower-level employees. In these organizations, women heard speeches, sometimes gave talks on their professional readings, and generally bonded with each other (Foster; J. Thomson). Other informal groups met outside library hours to pursue in more depth subjects covered in apprentice classes (Wales).*

The earliest true association of "support staff"—i.e., non–library-school-educated workers—with political intent arose in 1920, as library-school graduates became the clearly favored employment candidates emerging out of the then-extant alternate routes to librarianship: apprenticeship, training classes held in the nation's larger libraries, and graduate-level library-school education (which was mainly clerical training despite its housing in a university setting). This group, the Library Workers' Association (LWA), objected to the almost trade-union-like status of library schools, to the clout they afforded their graduates in the job market: according them degrees, and then finding them jobs. The association, like many paraprofessional associations today,

---

*As an example of the extensiveness of apprentice-class training, Reese's "Training in Medium-Sized Libraries," 1924, is most interesting. As I read article after article like this one, I thought that if I had had training like this in library school, I would have been much better equipped to go forth into Libraryland. I believe that apprentice classes offered fully professional coverage of library work, and that women completing them were more entitled to be termed "professional" than many graduates of library schools today. In another article on training, Reese states, "Most libraries secure their lowest grade assistants by means of training classes, entrance to which is gained by means of educational qualifications and competitive examinations and which are *really elementary library schools* [emphasis added]" (Reese, "Facts" 311).

desired to upgrade non–MLS-holding employees' image, insisting that their competencies were equal to those of library-school graduates. Writing in support of its goals, C. S. Thompson cried,

> The profession ought no longer to recognize two bodies of librarians, trained and untrained.... I look to see the day when the phrase "trained librarian" will again not be synonymous with "library school graduate." ... [W]e need to insist that all professional members of our staffs should become trained librarians, either thru the easiest and best route of the library school or thru the thornier path of training class, experience, and hard work ... ["Hearty"].

The LWA sought to eradicate the unfortunate dichotomy between degreed and non-degreed workers which has always constituted less a modest division than a chasm: "[W]e desire to form an Association ... [w]hich shall not create any unfortunate distinctions between different groups of persons employed in library work" (Van Dyne, "Library" 451). It also tried to implement what we would call today "continuing education" for its constituency (Evans, "Evolution" 73 & 75). The LWA soon faded into obscurity, squeezed out by the influence of the Williamson Report, which accorded library schools greater prestige than ever, and played on librarians' fears over their professional status.

In February 1966, rankling from a slight received from a "professional" librarian, one vocal Special Library Association member warned witheringly:

> [T]here are a lot of members [of SLA] who are not professional librarians in the true sense of the word. Either from having been in SLA and the library field a long time, or having some special talent that brought them to professional status without benefit of formal education in library science, they have earned the title of "professional." If any further and derogatory comments are made about the "non-professional" librarians, it is quite likely that they may, en masse, start a move towards an organization of their own such as the Association of Assistant Librarians is in England. At which time—due to the falsely elevated levels of "professional" librarianship in the special library field—SLA may find itself short of a large section of its membership [Pfeil].

As if thus conjured, in May 1966 the Society of Library and Information Technicians (SOLIT) was organized in Washington, D.C. Though originally open only to "students and graduates of the Department of Agriculture's Graduate School Seminar in Library Techniques," it soon expanded membership to include all library workers employed as library technicians (Boelke [3]). It published a newsletter, and though it ultimately disappeared, it was still active as recently as 1981 (Gill 369).

In 1967, a more long-lived association, COLT, was being conceived. Participants in a Catonsville Community College conference on library technicians entertained the idea of forming a paraprofessional organization which could be allied to a larger library organization, e.g., via junior-college sections associated with either ALA or SLA (Nicholson et al. 8). Today known as the "Council on Library/Media Technicians," it was first realized as the "Council on Library Technology," then the "Council on Library Technical-Assistants," then the "Council on Library/Media Technical-Assistants," name changes all revealing the changing focus of the organization (Evans, "Evolution" 84–5). It grew out of ALA's initial refusal to support paraprofessional training programs, and in the face of organizations like CLOUT (Evans, "Evolution" 82; Dougherty, "Personnel" 107). Dougherty wrote, in the mid–1970s,

> The intent of COLT is unmistakable. Its hope is to work toward an expansion of membership and a revision of its constitution in order to allow annual meetings in conjunction with ALA. For a complex set of reasons, COLT will probably not succeed at organizing library assistants on a national scale ["Personnel" 112].

Initially an "organization of educators concerned only with one- and two-year training programs," it evolved into an association run, until 1987, by librarians, but concerned with every aspect of the paraprofessional dilemma (Evans, "Evolution" 85; B. Smith 14). Because it was at first taken up with the question of appropriate education for support staff, it inevitably encountered the opinions of an array of librarians and entered into formalized dialogue with members of ALA library-education divisions. In 1974, ALA "extended an olive branch" to COLT, in the form of affiliation, despite Dougherty's dire prognostications (Evans, "Evolution" 86). Though COLT did not come under paraprofessional control until the 1980s, it has been functioning with unbroken vitality for almost thirty years for the benefit of the library assistant and is considered today the oldest extant paraprofessional association in the United States.

COLT held its twenty-eighth annual conference in June 1995. Though its official membership hovers around 700, its yearly conference garners participants "from as far away as Bermuda, Canada and Hawaii" (*Encyclopedia of Associations* [28th ed.] 926; Verma 18).

The very first *National* Paraprofessional Conference was held in February 1993 in Florida; 179 paraprofessionals from 15 states and 57 institutions participated (Waltz 15). Though many of the state support-staff conferences draw more people (e.g., New Jersey, with 500 in 1993)—probably because of reduced travel time and expense—the national conference was significant because it might augur the establishment of a lobbying, standard-setting group comparable to the ALA, but independent of it, unlike COLT ("New Jersey"). Paraprofessionals need an umbrella organization (like the AFL-CIO) under which the more than thirty-eight state paraprofessional organizations could shelter and consolidate their concerns ("New Jersey" 10; Lechner, "Benefits").

The ALA presently offers paraprofessionals succor in the form of "round tables" dedicated to support-staff issues in twenty-two of fifty-two ALA chapters, and other peace offerings ("Making" 7). For instance, ACRL, a division of ALA, in 1991 strongly promoted inclusion of paraprofessionals in their association and their chapters, believing involvement would increase paraprofessional commitment to their parent academic institution ("ACRL Task Force" 6). Could it also be, as Padley pondered, "to manage the complainer" ("ALA's 112th" 617)?

But I believe any group of workers struggling for professional recognition does better for itself if it stands up alone on its own strengths, like the early "local" trade unions, which were composed of persons with very specific skills and a very specific agenda (Lilore 2–5). In addition, ALA has a long history of dragging its feet on important issues and is viewed by some members as "an association run by library administrators," which hardly suits it for the role of protector of support staff—more the fox set to guard the hen coop (Todd 285). It is unfortunate that an independent national support-staff organization did not emerge out of a meeting held in Davis, California, in 1968, which, though presided over by a librarian, E. A. Wight, was attended by over 100 library technicians with "a lot of gripes ... receptive to the idea of a separate organization to advance their lot" ("Nonprofessionals" 2410). At the time, paraprofessionals were barred from the Special Library Association, as well as the local California Library Association—ironic in light of the fact that the SLA was founded by John Cotton Dana, a librarian with no library-school education ("Nonprofessionals" 2410; Varlejs in *Education* 4). Perhaps meetings like these were instrumental in causing state library organizations to open their memberships to library assistants, not so much to embrace technicians as peers, but to co-opt their drive to institute their own organizations, which would have been formed over against librarians' groups and which would always have been in consequence, to a greater or lesser degree, over against librarians, rather than with them.

State associations, whose conferences are better attended than COLT's national conference, and whose memberships are proportionally larger, are close to the old "locals," although unfortunately most of them are allied with extant state organizations for librarians, which are in turn allied with the ALA, which is emphatically *not* a parent union.

The first state support-staff organization arose in the early 1970s, paralleling the great paraprofessional movement towards trade-union affiliation, in the state of Washington, when 241 "non-professionals" formed the Classified Library Employees of Washington State (Flanagan 495). Other states followed suit, including New York State at LeMoyne College, Syracuse, in 1988, with NYSLAA (New York State Library Assistants' Association), which numbers over 450 members (Selby; NYSLAA packet; Hanna). NYSLAA "is one of the few organizations not affiliated with existing associations for librarians" ("At"). The reason may lie in the difficulty support staff had in gaining entry to and a voice in the New York Library Association in the 1970s. They were put off and urged to accept the "established 'division of labor'" even as many, frustrated about the field's failure to address their concerns, seethed over the field's prevalent "master-slave mentality" ("NYLA").

The frequently updated *National Directory [of] Library Paraprofessional Associations*, put out by ALA's SSIRT, lists forty-four state paraprofessional organizations (some states enjoy more than one, e.g., New York, with eight). Happily, it is easier to note the states *not* having paraprofessional organizations than the ones which do. Currently without such organizations are Alaska, Idaho, Kentucky, Michigan, Mississippi, Montana, New Hampshire, New Mexico, North Dakota, Rhode Island, South Dakota, Vermont, Virginia (appears to be stirring), Wyoming (also seems to have some movement afoot) (Support Staff Interests). Maine is the most recent of the states to form a paraprofessional division, the Maine Library Support Staff Association, established in May 1995 as a section of the Maine Library Association.

PART VI:
WHY THE MLS?

37. Library Schools
Under Fire

It has been a long time since any university started a new library school [White, "Why" 51].

Many of the librarians around *Library Journal* agree that the greatest danger in an LIS program is that it may kill the enthusiasm that a new recruit brings to our field [Berry, "What"].

"Master's, schmasters... For what[?] to go in the back room and put stuff away?" Mayor Newton E. Miller [Gaughan, "Mayor"]

In 1923, when Williamson undertook his famous study of libraries, he advised, among other things, that the educational basis for professional librarianship be a baccalaureate degree plus at least a year of graduate study at an ALA-accredited library school. The ALA did not act on his recommendation until 1951, a hesitation of thirty years, during which time the stigma of excessive clericism encompassed the profession and degraded it almost past the point of redemption in the public eye, in the eyes of university administrators and scholars, and in the eyes of countless boards of directors, all of whom were able to see what Presthus stresses: that librarians as a group are people "with high dependency needs," uncomfortable with autonomy and sluggish in pursuit of intellectual advancement as well (30). Librarians, as we have seen, were slow—sometimes loath—to divest themselves of clerical duties in the '30s, '40s, and '50s, and in 1971 officially declared that they were unwilling to earn a master's other than the MLS in a specialty field as a prerequisite for attaining faculty status in academic libraries, an astonishing and inexplicable move underscoring the intellectual inanition that has characterized the majority of professional librarians for over sixty years (Bishop 5, 6, 18–20). Their "endorsement" of the master's as a prerequisite for professional library work in the 1950s was obviously a weak one, since they came to the same realization again in 1970, as though it were a new thought (Harris, *Librarianship* 114).

The first library school "was not an academic institution, despite its association with Columbia College," states Evans ("Evolution" 71). "It was a technical training program 'designed to produce the same kind of competence as apprenticeship by using more systematic methods,'" he goes on, quoting White. In other words, despite the hypotheses of Miksa that the maiden library program at Columbia sought to inculcate a certain degree of academic, or at least bibliographic, knowledge, in addition to pragmatic management skills, early library schools performed the same functions as the later—and present— LTA programs, except that their students were college educated. The tasks mastered in early library schools were in the main technical, clerical skills— cataloging rules, accessioning, the "library hand," and so on. By 1900, six library schools had evolved; by 1929, there were sixteen, all mimicking the apprenticeship and training-class programs prevalent in the large urban libraries of America, all clerical in emphasis (Bohannon 216; Evans, "Evolution" 74). Library schools arose, as noted, as auxiliary apprenticeship-like programs because the huge number of would-be librarians, responding to the huge numbers of libraries being endowed and built in the early twentieth century, could no longer be trained through extant apprenticeship programs. Library schools grew in number to 25 by 1934, to 32 in 1946, and to 34 by 1952 (Evans, "Evolution" 77; Danton 14; Bryan 21). By 1964, there were 36 accredited library schools in the United States; in 1968, 45; and in 1974, 62, facing crises prevalent today (Dougherty, "Personnel" 108).

Evans believed that the "dependence on library schools as the sole source of training ... forced those schools to give technical training that was not consistent with their ... graduate status" ("Evolution" 78). Perhaps their level of training was not consistent, even in the early days, with the intellectual attainments of many of its coeds, some of them graduates from Vassar, Barnard, and Wellesley, intelligent women versed in history, languages (Latin, Greek, French, German, Italian, Spanish, and Russian), mathematics, and philosophy ("Proceedings" 280). Asheim, in 1967, giving both the field and the library schools adequate early warning about one aspect of the problems which are now currently engulfing the profession, wrote, "[T]he majority of the schools, even accredited ones, are devoting their time to vocational training—partly because the educators themselves are not willing to face the challenge, and partly because the field demands more Indians and few chiefs" ("Manpower" 1797). He claimed, "[W]herever I go..., generally speaking, libraries want ... people with more educational background who could be trained in the skills on the job" (*ibid.* 1795). (Is this image not consistent with the profile of the paraprofessional worker emerging in the late '60s and throughout the '70s?) Library-school graduates themselves at this time were, though not unkind, firm about stressing that "[t]here is too great an attempt in library school to make academic what is practical, and, conversely, a failure to acknowledge that library science is not academic and that there is no shame in this" ("What's Wrong" 1774). Whitelock, a para turned pro, declared in 1975 of his professional education:

> I ... learned the hard way.... For many years I worked full time while taking my professional courses during spare time and at summer schools. Many times since then I have asked myself, "And what did you really learn?" I think I have proved time and time again that the best library school is the library itself, though no one, I expect, will disagree that the piece of paper one gets at the end of school is necessary for getting a good library job.

Today there are only fifty accredited library schools, and these are beleaguered with confusion (Zipkowitz, "1993" 28). This figure, while far lower than that of 1974, still does not accurately reflect the degree of the carnage. "The phenomenon that began in 1978 with the elimination of the graduate library education program at the University of Oregon continued into 1990, when it was announced that the venerable School of Library Service at Columbia University would close its doors" (Paris, "Dilemma" 23). By the end of 1993, a total of seventeen programs had been terminated, including two of the original university-affiliated American library schools, and two more were threatened with extinction, UC–Berkeley and, in Canada, Dalhousie (Berry, "Old" 54; Bohannon 217; "GSLIS"; Gaughan, "Proposal" 905). Since then, Northern Illinois University has "closed its doors" (Zipkowitz, "1993" 28). Yet the wholesale destruction of library-school programs should not have come as a surprise to anybody. In 1978, some 60 percent of deans and faculty responding to Martha Boaz's survey on the future of library studies predicted a 10 percent demise of accredited library programs (Mugnier, *Paraprofessional* 98). "During the seventies, organized challenges to the master's degree in librarianship as prerequisite to appointment to professional positions ... [were] mounted," wrote Mugnier in 1980. She pointed to a "trend among bellwether libraries to provide alternate means for attaining professional status, such as apprenticeship and examination or coursework outside degree programs" (*Paraprofessional* 36). Administrators today are sounding the death knell of the MLS as it presently exists: "As prognosticators, [library-school deans recently interviewed in *Library Journal*] foresaw the breakup of the monolithic MLS degree, touting specialization almost unanimously" ("Dean's" 60).

Pundits are alarmed by the rapidity of extinction and the many reasons behind it. Also, library schools not yet actually terminated are suffering diminution of services and funding, notably loss of extension-campus sites (Quinn & Rogers 16; "Library Schools: Groping" 12). Even distance-education programs offering library-science courses do not number more than the fingers on both hands, and those offering programs that lead to a library master's degree number less than the fingers on one: University of Arizona, Mind Extension University, and University of South Carolina (Burgess 21, 69; Gaughan, "Library" 215). Many of the other schools offering library distance-education programs are unaccredited. The disturbed paraprofessional, contemplating this devastation, questions the wisdom of seeking such a discredited degree.

Certain schools have sought to dissociate themselves from the dread concept of "library," renaming themselves with titles including either "information" or "science" ("Library Schools: Groping" 14; Quinn & Rogers 16; White, "Why" 52). One defensive administrator stated gruffly that his college of information studies was "not a library school" (Gaughan, "Taking (I)" 1020). Another shrieked, "Don't ghettoize us in libraries[!]" at the 1992 ALISE conference (Berry, "Old" 54). Griffiths, director of the University of Tennessee's School of Library and Information Science, recently oversaw the elision of "Library" from her school's name, because "'Library Science' did not fully reflect 'the nature of one's work in the modern library.'" "People can focus on libraries and librarianship and that whole aspect of it," she explained witheringly, "or they can focus on a broader field of systems and technology" (St. Lifer and Rogers, "Lib. School").

Digs at library schools have abounded since their inception. One commentator observed that the gist of "complaints haven't changed much in ... one hundred years" (Bohannon 216).* Williamson carped that instructors in twelve library schools of his time had proven to be "unfit" for their teaching responsibilities; half of them had not even graduated from college ([34]). He claimed that library schools were recruiting their professoriat "from a group which is not eligible for attractive positions in other fields" ([34]). He charged programs with retaining "the flavor of apprenticeship training" (36). "The schools ... must be put on a higher professional basis and ... instructors ... [must] make contributions to the scholarly or practical sides of library work," he adjured (38).

When *Library Journal* polled library administrators in the mid-'60s on their views of library education *vis-à-vis* the librarian shortage, one of them termed the master's and doctoral programs "esoteric"; another advised, "[T]hree-fourths of all work done in libraries requires something less than graduation from an accredited graduate library school" (R. Franklin and J. Orne in "Library Education" 1763). Charges today range from lack of "intellectual rigor" ("the profession's research base is suspect") to "institutional sexism" (White, "Your" 45; Dougherty, "Library"; Marchant 33; White, "Why" 52; Paris, "Why" 42; Paris, "Dilemma" 25). "Graying" of the faculty (in 1990, one-third of extant faculty was age fifty-five or over), library school "isolation" on campus, paucity of "dead Germans" in library education, intellectual inadequacy of published research, and inability of library school administrators to "define mission" are others (Daniel 100; Paris, "Dilemma" 26; White, "Why" 51; Paris, "Why" 40–2; Pierce; Bohannon 217; Paris, "Dilemma" 24). Many universities housing library schools ("weak sisters") have evidently merely been "tolerating" their presence (Paris, "Why" 40–1).

---

*J. P. Danton's litany of complaints about the library schools of his time offers amusing corroboration of this statement.

In no case was budget constraint in the parent institution the sole reason for closure (Paris, "Dilemma" 23 and "Why" 39; White, "Grapes" 46). Embattled library educators claimed they had been framed, in effect: "criteria established by administrators were fabricated to ensure that the library school could not meet them"; "administrators' minds were made up in advance" (Paris, "Why" 42; Marchant 33). Also, more legitimately, library schools' incursion into "valuable" information territory has been viewed as a reason for attack (Paris, "Why" 41).

Accreditation or lack of it usually has had nothing to do with the survival or failure of a library school. In fact, the "Big Ten" library schools are in favor of jettisoning accreditation, as a way of lessening pressure on still-surviving programs; the accreditation process is time-consuming, expensive, and laborious, and there is much dispute in this area (e.g., Gaughan, "Taking (II)" 25; Berry, "Old" 54; White, "Grapes" 46).

"[T]he list of new scholarly books in the *Chronicle of Higher Education* does not include books on library science," moans Marchant (36). "What can we do?" queries Dougherty.

> If foundations and federal agencies, who have been traditional sources of dollars for support, could be convinced to give more, we could pursue our research agenda more aggressively. The Title IIB program, which is only marginally funded, is the most logical governmental source at present. This year, only four out of forty applications were funded—a very unhealthy situation ("Library").

But even back in 1966, the brighter commentators were taking the lack of scholarly attainment among library-school personnel very seriously. Edward Montgomery was scathing in his denunciation of library schools comprising a mere "sub-class of the community of scholars" (4897). Disaffection with library workers' intellectual capabilities made its way into library publications as early as 1917, when Adam Strohm mused, "I fear that the library profession is not laboring under a very heavy weight of scholarship" ("Being" 135).

"Student satisfaction" is another problem bound into consideration of the morbidity of library schools (Gaughan, "Taking (II)" 24 and "Best" 924). Plaiss charges that library-school classes and professors are for the most part "inane and insipid" (589). Biggs, more politely, notes that the undemanding level of most graduate-level library courses "is one reason why some of our brightest students complain so much, why they become frustrated to the point of discouragement" ("Undergraduate" 36). Mugnier's sample population of entry-level librarians pronounced individual professors "inspiring," but found "few total faculties ... [to be] strong"; certain courses were deemed "intellectually demanding," but many found "the total experience poor" (*Paraprofessional* 74). One professional librarian, content with librarianship's being a "vocation," rather than a "profession," observes calmly that she "endured" library school to "[get] the seal upon my forehead so that the 'profession' would take me seriously" (Welton). "Not much energy in the department," lamented one master's candidate at the University of Rhode Island, worried that the library-science department might "stifle" her before she could ever become the kind of practicing librarian she had so admired before she applied for the program (Bartlett). Hansel suggested that "professionals aren't as motivated to attend continuing education activities because library school is so deadly that it kills our enthusiasm for such things" (Burgin and Hansel 67). One library-school enrollee mourned, "[I]n the last six months, my interest has waned for anything to do with libraries. Maybe my feelings are burnout after working and doing homework nearly every day for the last four years..." (Anderson-Story). One horrified paraprofessional—who, despite her paraprofessional status, holds a four-year bachelor's degree in Business in Information and Library Management from an Australian school—contemplated her disillusioned MLS-seeking husband and exclaimed, "My husband began to realize that the one thing his master's (MLS) degree had taught him was that he did not want to work in libraries" (Laws).

Bohannon maintained that "library students are older than the norm ... and ... tend to be a more cynical group" (218). New college graduates do not regard librarianship as a "cherry" career. It is a field usually entered late in life, now, as ever, after other options have been explored and rejected or children raised. In the 1970s, 53.5 percent of paras interviewed by Mugnier on whether they would go for the MLS "were not interested in the professional credential"; the reason given most frequently for this lack of interest was "lack of respect for library master's degree" (*Paraprofessional* 78). Herbert White in 1994 perused the *Chronicle of Higher Education*'s annual statistical listings for evidence of librarianship's status. "[T]he percentage of college undergraduates who express a desire to enter what *CHE* calls 'library and archival science' is a consistent 0.0 percent," he notes shortly ("What" 50).

Not only are MLS candidates older, but they tend to be ex-support-staff members: "In 1988, a study of students in ALA-accredited master's programs found that over fifty percent of those enrolled had library employment prior to matriculation" (Heim et al. 156). Anderson-Story writes,

> Many of us consider an MLS degree because we have a passion for our work and a high degree of dedication to our libraries as institutions. We want the responsibilities and recognition that appear to go with an MLS degree as the current support staff structure does not reward or recognize our dedication.... [But m]any of us report that we are not fully satisfied with our schools' curriculums.... [On a Libsup-l survey of support staff on the MLS track o]ne concern repeatedly expressed was about the program's usefulness: "For those of us with experience, it is a waste of time and money."

Mugnier asked her respondents—library associates, or paraprofessionals—who had gone on through library school, "Was your library school experience essentially a positive one?"

Of the thirty-two librarians responding to this question, 28 percent said that their library school experience had been positive, 37.5 percent rated their experience negatively, and 34.4 percent rated it as fair.... Among the positive reactions, only five respondents revealed any real enthusiasm. The prevailing attitudes were either that "going to library school" was the means by which one became a professional with little expected or gained, or that an eagerly anticipated experience had turned out to be disappointing. A typical comment: "Library school was a means toward an end—no personal satisfaction but a promise of advancement" (73)... One-third said that their library educations provided them with substantial professional advantages, one-third felt that they had gained little advantage, and the final third believed that the advantages were not as great as they had hoped for or expected [72].

Presthus, querying librarians in both Canada and the United States in 1970, found that 66 percent of his subjects would not have chosen librarianship as a career if they had it to do over again (69). He found, interestingly, that only 57 percent of clericals would not have entered the field if they had it to do over again, probably because of a quite understandable "low job involvement" (69). This dissatisfaction is an echo of a larger truth: that "less than half of all white-collar workers and blue-collar workers in America would choose their same jobs if given the opportunity to backtrack and re-enter the work force" (Freeman & Roney 21). Donald Welch sorrows,

> [T]he duties performed by most workers in libraries do not require a masters. By and large, the majority of tasks performed by "librarians" (and I mean ones with degrees, too) are redundant physically and mentally and can be learned easily with on-the-job-training.... I believe the profession has created a monster that beckons victims into a maw of dissatisfaction with a lure (*the* masters) that is an over-achievement.

"The complaint is voiced frequently at practitioner gatherings that the quality of graduates of library educational programs is not what it should be or even what it used to be 'in the good old days,'" wrote White and Paris frankly. "That argument has a reverse side because sometimes graduates complain that their work assignments underutilize both their intellectual and professional preparation" (22; see also Van Oosbree). How bitter, then, to have proceeded from unrewarding nonprofessional jobs through the MLS program, hoping to escape disillusionment and poverty, only to come away with reactions like these.

Just as there is a problem with finding a library school to attend in many parts of the United States, there is the related one of facing probable relocation if one does live close enough to a library school to have attended one. Michelle Laws describes the catch:

> The University of Texas at Austin has 50,000 students enrolled in it. They need to work while they are there, and when they are finished, often decide to stay here to get that first job and experience, or for good. This results in a constant willing

workforce. It pushes up the difficulty of getting any job and pushes down the pay levels. Getting into a job in which you have experience is difficult enough, let alone one in which you have none.

Another facet of the problem is, as Laws noted of her library in Austin, that "[q]ualified masters degreed librarians working as library assistants is not uncommon here." Other Libsup-l posters have abundantly confirmed this trend. Gillen, in a special issue of *JELIS* devoted to paras, charged, "A growing category of LAs are those who have obtained an M.L.S. but have yet to find jobs as librarians" ("To" 7). Oberg and colleagues worried about this problem in 1992: "Another phenomenon [warranting investigation] ... is the effect of hiring candidates with graduate library degrees into paraprofessional positions" ("Role" 234). Zipkowitz calls the exploitation of MLS-holding paras "distressing," and claims the number of part-time and nonprofessional placements have doubled since her last survey. Thus 20 percent of the 1993 graduating classes are "working at the margins of the profession" ("1993" 26).

The glut of extant MLSs causes problems for non–MLS paraprofessionals. Institutions favor hiring overqualified people desperate for work; their additional training becomes a desirable freebie. "The unfortunate aspect of this all is that there are many deserving, and dedicated employees of the library who are denied job promotions because of the large pool of MLS candidates also vying for the upper-level library assistant positions" (Pat Nelson, Libsup-l poster). Nor is this a new habit in Libraryland: we have seen the cunning E. E. Williams back in 1945 giving a sly nod to hiring library-school graduates as clerks (307). In 1974 UC–Berkeley was rebuked by AFSCME for hiring professional librarians to fill nonprofessional posts, thus "open[ing] the flood gates to further exploitation of overqualified employees" and "clos[ing] off the already severely limited opportunities for promotion of ... nonprofessionals" ("Librarians &"). In 1977, Bayless was protesting "the increasing practice of hiring degreed professionals for library assistant positions, assigning them professional duties, and paying them a library assistant salary" (1716). Writing in May 1995, a Libsup-l paraprofessional supports Laws' observation:

> Have you ... observed that at your library MLS positions are reclassed to staff positions? ... This situation is particularly prevalent in academic libraries in areas with MLS programs. Although BYU [Brigham Young University] closed its library school in August 1993, not all of the graduates have yet found professional level positions. Several are working in part-time positions, others in full time no–MLS positions, and some are *volunteering* [emphasis added] to get enough experience to compete for MLS or no–MLS positions [Debra Lords].

Another poster concurs, noting at her university at least twelve MLS-holders in staff positions. One contended that many MLSers work in shops, sell insurance, because the field cannot offer them paying positions which would support life. Glass adds,

Some support staff would like reassurance of professional level jobs at their present libraries if they acquire the MLS, but this is an unrealistic expectation. Many position vacancies, under the scrutiny of state or federal guidelines, are subject to national searches for candidates. Local residents with MLS degrees, who are unwilling or unable to risk relocating for positions elsewhere, often are unable to match the qualifications of applicants from a national pool. The geographically-restricted MLS-holders then find themselves trapped in nonprofessional positions, and their level of frustration can only be imagined [11–12].

Net support staff confirm this trend: "[E]ven if I do earn the MLS," mopes one, "there are many other staff at paraprofessional levels who have already done so, and they are still stuck!" (Kentfield 19).

And there is the highly insidious "caste"-related problem to be reckoned with, having to do with librarians' tendency to typecast character inflexibly and unimaginatively according to job title. This tendency forces many MLS recipients to look for professional work elsewhere than where they currently hold a position, despite the statement in segment 16 of *LEPU* which mandated "eligibility for promotion, upon completion of the master's degree, to positions of professional responsibility and attendant reclassification to the professional category" (American…, *Library Education*). The wording of this statement strongly implies that this reclassification should take place in the library for which one already works, yet informal observation of feedback from the Libsup-l listserv is that many more people are recruited from outside a home library than are promoted from within. Hard-working, capable individuals are insultingly passed over, often in preference to less experienced outsiders who must then be taught by the incumbent. Libsup-l communicants worry that outside applicants seem to have the edge in obtaining faculty positions. One federal ILL and serials technician, queried on Libsup-l about her feelings about the MLS, answered:

> I personally see no reason to get an MLS. First of all I would have a three-four hour commute each day—the expense and the effort and time is not worth pounding the pavement to look for a librarian's job elsewhere, because I would never be hired here as a librarian. My boss views me as competent, but not a librarian. If a job opening came up, she would hire for the "new blood" from outside—not within. It's a feudal world we live in, and if you ain't a blue blood, they don't want you marrying the king's son [anonymous respondent].

A poster on the "Soaring to Excellence" listserv wrote,

> I'm a Library Assistant at the University of California in Berkeley, and I got my MLS in 1985. When I began to look at librarian jobs, I quickly realized that 1) it would be virtually impossible to get a job at UC Berkeley, since the "once an LA always an LA, and go prove yourself elsewhere" rule seemed to apply, and 2) that most of the local (California) Librarian jobs were part-time, temporary, or required experience as an MLS. Because of my academic library experience, I was not considered for public library jobs. In addition, as a Library Assistant V with

almost 20 years experience, I was making more, by 5–10 thousand dollars a year, than most entry-level librarians. As a single mother, I could not afford that kind of pay cut for the sake of a "professional" career [Aija Kanbergs, February 28, 1995].

Larry Oberg and his colleagues rightly question "whether the abrupt rupture of forced relocation is an appropriate entry requirement into the profession" ("Role" 234).

Enrollments are down in library schools, and, given the shortage of professional—and paraprofessional—jobs, this is as it should be, despite the yammering of library-school proponents. Students, among them the hapless paraprofessional, require "programs that offer some prospects of future employment" (Gaughan, "Best"). Dougherty perceived in the 1970s, when a spate of library programs were generated against an insufficiency of jobs for graduates, that "the profession did not give evidence of a capability to control the juggernaut it had helped to create" ("Personnel" 109). Now, again, complaints of an insufficiency of jobs lodge in the letter columns of *American Libraries* (Frieburger; G. Sandler). In addition to MLS candidates' being unable to find employment, the employment they do find will be paid at a rate not only inadequate, but rising, as of 1993, at a lower percentage rate than comparable civilian jobs: 1.2 percent (Lynch).

Given all of the problems noted above, it is tempting to inquire what one of the ten deans of library schools recently interviewed in *Library Journal* could have been thinking, in these days of the sunset of library affluence and the telescoping of opportunity, when she said, "I think ALA must address the question of how to educate library support staff. They should ask how ALA can deliver—using distance education methods—programs to educate support staff. There are thousands of them, and there is real money in it" (Robbins in "Dean's" 61). (Hers is no novel observation; Kinzer in 1961 griped, "[G]raduate library schools ... are doing nothing about the fact that over half of the members of the library profession are ... without any formal library training" [221].) Other than to receive specialized technological training, which computer departments are more qualified to deliver than the average library school, why would support-staff members be recruited to a library school, other than for the money? They already know how to do not only their own jobs—a whole generation of them is now approaching retirement, for heaven's sake—but often a sizable portion of the supervising librarians' as well. So we could have more underemployed librarians? More clerks with MLSs? A higher level of professional and personal frustration? More money misspent? To raise the gross national income?

With a less mercenary emphasis, Berry charges that library schools

now give only lip service to library practice. They withdraw from off-campus programs located where working library people can attend. They neglect continuing library education, even for their own alumni. They almost completely ignore the huge education and training needs of that great majority of people and jobs in libraries, the work done by so-called "nonprofessionals." ... [W]e cannot depend on the library schools to recruit the new librarians, nor can we continue to neglect that most fruitful reservoir of recruits, the people who already work with us. We desperately need ... continuing education ... particularly for the older librarians both on our front lines and in our upper echelons, many of whom are information technology illiterates ["Two Crises"].

But the field has always averted its eyes from paras as among its "gifted and talented." And library-school professors, no less than practicing librarians, have conformed to this custom as resolutely as if it were a divine commandment: "At my library school no one mentioned support staff yet over 50% of the people working in libraries I've worked in are in this classification. This astounds me,'" commented one interviewee in the ALA/SCOLE *World Book* project ("Issue Paper #4").

Library schools at their peak in 1974 graduated 6,370 students (Dougherty, "Personnel" 108). *Library Journal*'s 1992 "Placements & Salaries" survey showed a total of 3,625 graduates, almost half that number (Zipkowitz, "Fewer" 30). In 1993, it is true, the number rose to over 4,754, but Zipkowitz claims a great number of them are "'still out [there] looking'" for work ("1993" 32).

On the one hand, as Paris shows, "the number of library schools in the United States greatly outstrips student demand...," perhaps because they are concentrated in certain parts of the country and thus saturate the market ("Why" 40). On the other, "[i]t has not been demonstrated that when a library school closes, enrollment increases at the remaining schools. Rather, would-be applicants choose graduate programs other than library and information studies," Paris concludes ("Dilemma" 24). In addition, beyond the drop in MLS aspirants, there is a "dearth of Ph.D.-holding professors available to replace an aging professoriat" (Gaughan, "Taking (II)" 25). Robbins claims a decrease in full-time faculty, high turnover among those remaining, and a drop in the number of doctoral degrees awarded: from 123 in 1974–5 to 42 in 1990 (*Education* 13).

Behind the dearth of Ph.D.s, however, lies the problem of the calibre of library-school candidates themselves:

> Library directors who complain about the quality of the graduates of our schools might have to pay salaries that would allow the libraries to recruit the quality of graduates they say they want, but for whom they are clearly unwilling to pay. Why would a person with 1300 GRE scores and a cum laude degree spend a year and a half in graduate school in order to get a job that might pay $25,000 a year? [B. Boyce 258]

Will Manley, debunker of librarial posturing and pomposity, quotes a hypothetical prospective library-school candidate, Nancy Rae Studebaker:

Sure I wanted to be a librarian, and yes I even looked forward to going to library science classes, but when I found out that the closest route to becoming a librarian ran through Berkeley, Denton, Tucson, or Emporia, I began looking for another profession. At the time I was thirty years old, the mother of a five year old son and a seven year old daughter, and the wife of an aerospace engineer. Did I want to pay $20,000 for the privilege of moving away and ruining my family, in hopes of eventually getting a job as a reference librarian that would probably pay me $26,000? I hope I don't look that retarded ["Manley" *Art* 182].

In addition, the group most likely to be bound for library school—women— will find, according to Murgai, that it is harder for them to obtain financial aid than it is for men. In a survey consisting of 82 percent women and 18 percent men, men went to library school full-time more often than women, and male full-time students found it easier to get scholarships and fellowships than female full-time students (638–9).

The schools which do survive have a power base made up of younger faculty; they have a strong publishing record; they are active in their respective universities; they accommodate the high technology requirements of today's information providers, only one of which is the library (Berry, "Old" 53; Fialkoff). Debunkers of the COA (Committee on Accreditation) see the dropping of the accrediting process, or its thorough revision, as a way of "liberating and unburdening" schools so they can "find a variety of innovative and creative entrepreneurial and experimental mergers and niches to gain the respect and enrollment they need to compete in an increasingly hostile academic marketplace" (Berry, "Old" 53).

Rutgers, in the interests of survival and of keeping pace with deep technology, has merged its library school with programs in "communicative disorders, and communication and information studies." It commands "six technology labs, including its own minicomputer for integrated library systems and a new cutting-edge multimedia lab" (Fialkoff). It is in sync with the necessity to utilize all the high technologies set forth by Budd: "PCs, CD-ROMs, interactive video, videotext, parallel processing—coupled with the uses to which these innovations have been put—online databases, E-mail, synchronous and asynchronous communications networks, international telecommunications networks, computer imaging, desktop publishing, facsimile transmission," and more (44). University of Kentucky's library school followed Rutgers' course, merging in 1992 with its College of Communications (St. Lifer and Rogers, "U.").

In the "educating" vs. "training" debate, Rutgers has opted to train, which seems very sound; people can become educated at any time (Dougherty, "Are"). Many, as MLS candidates and already previously quite well-educated people, would have preferred, as required course work, a plethora of systematic, hands-on technological training modules, rather than the general offering of often vague and haphazardly presented material. Where I have worked, slight

training is offered piecemeal to selected people, while others languish in ignorance. If one knows enough to ask, one may be released to be trained on company time for job-related skills, and often not. Those who are curious but not
adjudged to have a "need to know" must often take courses on their own time,
and often at their own expense. Adequate and fairly proffered formal on-site
training is almost totally unknown, cross-training is nil, and a lot of unnec-
essary ill will is generated when largesse is extended to some people and departments, but not others. The people who teach the day- or days-long courses
are not particularly good teachers. Half the class is soon whispering queries
to near neighbors. Everything goes by quickly, notes are taken, instructors
depart; back on the job, the questions begin.

    Thus, despite or perhaps because of the meager training most workers,
librarian or clerk, are given, a lot of wondering and bungling occurs on a daily
basis. The jargon is unfamiliar; there is not time to learn from manuals on the
job. One has the feeling of being left utterly in the dust. A lot of one's training comes, in the end, from oneself, at the cost of many tears and false starts—
a pure waste of work time and a source of extreme aggravation. The need for
intensive on-site training, like that offered by Line and Robertson, is palpable. In school, too, I had the feeling that technological reality was a ghostly
presence hovering beyond my grasp. The courses I was required to take and
could take (I was a commuter, and time, schedule, and money constraints ruled
my life) in the MLS program were nowhere near as relevant to current library
needs as hardcore technical training courses would have been. I would preferred
to concentrate on the technological aspects of librarianship, rather than on,
for instance, rare books, interesting as rare books are. But to have taken the
programming courses, as a commuter, I would have had to own a computer
(so the word went around the department: even people on site were lost without a home computer). For me, at that time, a computer was far too expensive
to purchase. In one course, the class was given bootlegged copies of an indexing program on which to do a term project. Some of these copies were defec-
tive. When I discovered mine was one of them, I was far away, restricted to
using public-library computers for an hour at a time, and with no one to ask
for help. It seemed to me that the "haves" in this program would be rewarded,
and the have-nots could stew. In addition, with only a couple of exceptions, I
received more useful and gracious help from the department secretary than
from the majority of the professors.

    In moving away from the clerical stigma that adhered to library schools
into the '70s, library schools appear to have drifted into an irrelevant hash of
semi-clerical, quasi-theoretical maunderings, which insult the intelligence of
many library-school graduates (many of whom have extensive post-graduate
training in other areas) and do not prepare them to hit the ground running
when they emerge from library school and enter the work force as putative
experts in the field. Though I am a person with a short fuse, I saw many more

students with shorter fuses than mine driven to frothing at the mouth over a professor's antics and statements in class.

But in fact, practicing librarians of many years' standing, with a conspiratorial laugh and a confidential aside, assure the agonizing MLS candidate that it was ever so, and that they learned most of what they know on the job. A minority have found their MLS training sufficient. And today, only the newest graduate from the most technologically advanced and adapted schools in the country would really be prepared to take on the immensity of electronic library reality.

> Approximately one hundred years ago five percent of the work force was engaged in the information sector. This proportion grew to about one-third in the early 1950s and is estimated to be about 43 percent at the present time in the U. S. This is truly a phenomenal occurrence with substantial implications for our general economy, employment structure, social behavior and our general well-being,

wrote Griffiths and King in 1986, in a tome on the direction of "information science" education (11). Doubtless the percentage is even higher now. In library schools we are taught, in theory, what "information" is, but not a whole lot about the actual way people in the real world access it and spew it out again (I never once heard the term "Internet" breathed in any class, though the Net has been in existence, in a quiet, immanent way, since circa 1968; it was a military creation contemporaneous with Woodstock [L. Larocca]). In 1974, Jestes cautioned,

> [W]hile ... librarians are dickering about how to tell people where the bathroom is, computer terminals are being used in private offices to elicit instant bibliographies; companies are establishing bibliographic searching and document delivery services; and media centers ... are being set up outside the jurisdiction of libraries.... [L]et's ... get on with being the foremost guides to recorded human knowledge [15–6].

Recent tocsin-sounders like Seavey, in "A Failure of Vision: Librarians Are Losing the War for Electronic Professional Turf," are correct when they warn, "If we don't enter the realm of data, we are going to be relegated to low-paying custodial jobs in giant buildings full of unused paper..." (944).

On the other hand, there is no shame in keeping the "liber" (book) in "library." It is strange that people see the need to dichotomize technology and books. Why does a school need to be ashamed to call itself a "library" school, as well as a technological school? Books, in their day, constituted a bright new technology, too; nothing has since been invented to excel them. Modern-day libraries are as much in need of their books as their technologies. Books are well-loved by millions, and a feat of engineering not to be sneered at, though I recently learned of a campus built without library—some planner obviously suffering from Gorman's "techno-lust" or short-sighted Internet infatuation.

(How, I wonder, could I ever have researched and written this book just utilizing the Internet? Must we always throw the baby out with the bath?)

But it does seem, in MLS programs, as if each constituency is served
short. De La Peña McCook writes, "Virtual reality has captured our attention. We forget, however, that the same effect is gained by skillful readers each
time they engage the printed word.... [B]ooks [and] reading [are] ... thriv-
ing today as never before amidst the enveloping cyberspace" (626). She continues, "New technologies do not replace old. They coexist and sustain each
other"; she argues that technology facilitates our access to all sorts of information in every format (627). Martell tells a wonderful tale of how he
described the powers of the computer to his skeptical mother, yet sustained a
sense of the power of the book:

> [M]y eyes focused on the first letter on the page, the letter "y." "See that letter?
> You can't do anything with it. It's fixed. It's static.... Let me put that letter 'y' in
> a computer and I will return it to you in a thousand different ways.... There is
> probably a software program that can give you the letter 'y' in every known type-
> face that London printers have used since the invention of moveable type. I can
> send this letter to people throughout the world.... What color would you like it
> to be?... Let's move into hypertext.... Letters, images, and sounds can be com-
> bined in nanoseconds, transmitted to the moon, and rearranged quicker than you
> can blink.... By the way," I said, "I'm reading a wonderful book by Alice Walker.
> How about you?" ["Letter"].

Yet in library schools, one rarely hears books—the sorts of books both academic and public library users require—discussed as objects of love, except in
the odd collection-development or children's literature course, if the instructor is so inclined, or discussed at all, except as information-bearing formats or
as rare books. Library schools seem to have lost the loving feeling about the
contents of books. We have seen how the early library practitioners stressed
love of books and reading as paramount job qualifications. Even later, in the
mid-'60s, for instance, books and all of the psychological lambency that plays
about the very idea of them, when they are loved dearly enough, were still valued. Both library administrators and library-school graduates stringently condemned non-readers. E. Gaines writes, "The one thing I wish library schools
would do is weed out the nonreader" ("Library Education" 1779). Echoing him,
the students write, "It is appalling to observe the large number of people
enrolled who do not love books and reading..." ("What's Wrong" 1774).

Also, in addition to a dearth of relevant technological courses and the lack
of emphasis on love of bookish pursuits, ultra-practical programs like the ones
facetiously delineated by Donna Cole are all but absent in library schools:
"LS104. Photocopiers"; "LS105–106. Deviant Behavior I & II"; "LS107. Ejec-
tion Etiquette" [certainly as essential as any library management course];
"LS205. Environmental Hazards. Participants will be prepared to deal with
sick building syndrome, inadequate lighting, malfunctioning equipment, and

foul-smelling patrons"; etc. ("Library" 57–8). The ongoing tension between practice-vs.-theory proponents in the library-school tussles, the inability of library schools to strike a balance between practical coursework geared toward the working environments of the real world and a substantial, challenging intellectual basis at the graduate level, is also a source of library-school enervation (White; Paris).

A larger problem is limned by Hildenbrand, discussing the erosion of librarianship:

> The low esteem in which librarianship is held ... derives from America's distaste for things cultural, as reflected in the lack of support and reliance on volunteers that libraries have in common with museums and the Philharmonic ["Not" 628].

The sense that America is filled with philistines is not new: in 1914 Sarah Askew suspected, "[I]f the free public library is the highest effort of democracy to crown itself, democracy doesn't know it" (194). Maack concurs, citing Hofstadter, pointing out that "public libraries could hardly expect to reach a majority of the population in a country whose culture was characterized by a strong, persistent strain of anti-intellectualism" (165). Scheppke points out that in mid-century America, public library users were mainly the white, well-educated middle class; today, although the ethnic base has broadened somewhat, the average user is still likely to present this profile (35–6). Most of the nation does not care a fig for the library.

Proponents of the sooner-death-than-lack-of-accreditation school (White, "Grapes") perhaps need to temper their idealism with realization that in some areas, this belief in the magic of accreditation enacted would not only lead to no library schools, but to no local libraries, either. Then even fewer people would be library users. We live in a time which sees the flourishing not only of extreme technology (as outlined by Budd), but of profound poverty and backwardness as well.

In Waitsburg, Washington State, the local library "installed its first telephone just prior to buying a PC" (R. Sass 15). In communities like this one, library services are offered on a shoestring. Library workers are trained through correspondence courses offered, in this instance, by the RLTP (Rural Library Training Project), created by the Southern Alberta Institute of Technology. Classes are conducted by mail and phone, with finals offered by "a professional person" in students' respective home towns. Nine courses of six to eight modules yield a "Certificate in Small Library Operations" sponsored by the Washington State Library and the Institute, neither of which, according to *Library and Book Trade Almanac*, is accredited. (For that matter, "20 percent of American library, information science, and school media graduate programs are not accredited [13 of 65 schools]" [Harris, *Librarianship* 114].) Fourteen courses are offered overall. Their contents might not be equivalent to what students now receive from accredited library "science" and "information" schools—or again, they might. The RLTP offers rudimentary training for dedicated rural aficionados of books and public service. Is it one of White's "[l]ittle two-bit programs" ("Grapes" 45)? Probably, but Washington State's SMILE (Small Municipal Independent Libraries for Excellence) network would not exist without it.

One of the major problems facing rural library workers is the scarcity of educational programs within feasible commuting distance. The ALA's Committee on Accreditation considered distance education one of the most "important" issues in its 1993 revision of *Standards for Accreditation of Master's Programs in Library & Information Studies* (26). In 1990, LISDEC (Library and Information Science Distance Education Consortium), also referred to as CLIS, was developed to address the problem of providing access to accredited master's programs for people facing unfeasible commuting distances to extant schools. Based in South Carolina, it was planned with the aim of offering courses developed by ALA-accredited schools nationally through Mind Extension University, which functions out of Engelwood, Colorado (Daniel 100–1; Burgess 68; Barron 33). CLIS in 1992 commenced a three-year cycle designed to offer an accredited master's degree to students in South Carolina, West Virginia, and Georgia. It operates via pretaped videocassettes, live interactive televised classes, and live weekend sessions. "This is the first time in the history of the profession," boasts Sykes, "that an entire MLIS degree program has been offered through live, interactive television and on-site delivery" (60).

> Conceptually, this promises the student ... the ability to take course work from any accredited school in the country through the Jones Intercable Network.... Its beauty rests on a simple concept[:] each school accepts the credits of all other members of the consortium. The student would matriculate into one program and receive a degree from that institution by following all of the parent school's requirements. However, [she/he] could choose course offerings from the other accredited schools regardless of [her/his] geographical location. LISDEC is one of the important ideas of the 1990s [Vavrek, "Educating" 8].

LISDEC is also credited with "[encouraging] experimentation with network organization and new information technologies in instructional delivery"; it is designed not only for LTAs, but for master's candidates (Daniel 101).

The University of Wisconsin–Madison School of Library and Information Studies Continuing Education Services offers a semester-long "Public Librarians" course through a telecommunications network that covers 200 sites over every county in Wisconsin. A similar service is offered by UPLIFT (Utah Public Library Institute for Training), which offers five-day workshops to supply the rudiments of library training to rural "indigenous" librarians. West Virginia, Kentucky, and Vermont—in fact, most states—seek to reach, with similar training programs, the 76 percent of "nondegreed librarians" (as of 1988) running libraries in communities with under 25,000 inhabitants

(Stanke 80). Arizona, working with the Western Interstate Commission for Higher Education (WICHE) and Jones Intercable, is seeking to provide wider access to programs in the West (Barron 33). St. Lifer and Rogers report that at least one library is willing to host distance-learning programs on television or video for interested individuals willing to form a class. One of Palms Springs Public Library's first offerings will be a Master of Arts in Library Science from the University of Arizona ("Library").

In addition, from the earliest days of librarianship and on into the 1950s state extension agencies existed, at least theoretically, to offer untrained but earnest librarians, who by 1951 ran no fewer than 5,000 village libraries—"65 percent of the public libraries in the United States"—the opportunity to augment their experience and intuitiveness with traveling workshops and courses held from campuses nearby the students' home libraries (e.g., Dixson; Leigh quoted by L. Martin 133). Alas, even in those days, extension programs had been largely eviscerated. In 1939, Munn rated only eight of the state agencies as "highly developed"; by 1951, only two programs were regarded as having "importance in the conduct of ... library business," despite budget increases in nineteen state library agencies (L. Martin, quoting Garceau, 133). Yet in 1988, as noted, a plethora of "extension" courses was again in place, in a return to the early training methods of the modern library field (Stanke). And the number of nondegreed librarians is within a few percentage points of being as high as it ever was, and perhaps, if the non-respondents to Lynch and Lance's recent survey of public libraries were rural, higher.*

Sometimes, perhaps, dedication is worth a ton of accreditation. In one accredited library school (Syracuse), the cataloging instructor informed her class that she had never worked with LC cataloging, that the books were in the hall, and that the class should go look at them and see what it could make of them. Surely students could not have received less professional instruction in the RLTP, or any of the myriad other distance-training programs.

Mugnier proclaimed as early as 1980 that "[t]he credibility of the master's degree in librarianship as *the* determinant of who is professional is being challenged, and the right of the national professional organization (through its accrediting program) to determine professional status among librarians is on the verge of shifting into the hands of other organizations and agencies, many of them entirely outside the profession" (*Paraprofessional* 99). "[T]he profession must take the blame," claims B. Boyce in a recent *American Libraries* editorial, for its failure to establish its research base and academic credentials, for being unwilling to "pay" for the calibre of graduate student that would draw the respect of the working world. And what of libraries' dismissive attitude towards library schools and their curricula, despite their frequent insistence

---

*For example, Brenda Hawley maintains that in Colorado, in the Pikes Peak District, a full *80 percent* of staff are non-degreed (10).

on the MLS as a prerequisite for professional work? In 1993, Shirley Rais recounted the experience of an "aspiring librarian who was told by her supervisor to 'Cut the library school crap'" (819). A speaker at the Chicago Library Club recently predicted the demise of the library profession by 2004, because of failure "to create a more striking concept of what it is they are about" (A. Jones). It may well be, as J. Campbell and Bohannon, in separate articles, surmise, that traditional library education, eschewing change and remaining intellectually static, will ensure that the MLS ceases to be a "viable credential" and will itself become "a dinosaur of the 20th century" (562; 219).

38. LTA Programs and the Issue of Certification

One of the earliest proposals for college-based "junior-library-assistant" training came from O. R. Howard Thomson in 1925. While in general "library assistant" was a term applied to all sorts of lower echelon workers—both grade-school only and college-educated—the "junior" library assistant was unquestionably high-school educated only, much like the target population of LTA training courses in the 1960s and 1970s. Thomson's concerns for such people echoed the concerns of later advocates of LTA training: "safeguarding" employment futures for these youngsters, and allowing them access to higher-level positions as they grew in library work. He said, simply,

> The human mind recognizes no limit. There must be no iron-studded barrier barring advance to higher positions should they fit themselves to occupy them. Make the door formidable if you please; make it heavy to move and hard to pass; but see to it that the hinges do not rust beyond possibility of use.

"Opportunity and America are synonyms," he pronounced, utterly without irony (296).

Twelve years later, in September 1937, Los Angeles City College offered the earliest two-year, or junior-college, library clerical training program, the Clerical Library Aides course, to cover training for the more than 300 clerical positions then extant in Los Angeles (Martinez, "In" 7; Pidduck 406). It offered no certification, but assumed that students would be taking—and passing—civil service examinations to qualify for work in the city system. The next two were offered by the U.S. Department of Agriculture Graduate School (Washington, D.C.) and the Ballard School of the YWCA (New York), in 1948 and 1949, respectively (Evans, "Evolution" 82–3). Others sprang up throughout the '50s and '60s. Although these programs were sprinkled throughout the country, in their heyday schools on the West Coast (California alone, with 27 programs, accounted for over half of the national LTA placements) and East North Central regions placed the greatest number of graduates at the highest salaries (according to John James, in Christianson 17–18).

295

In 1961, there were 31 junior colleges offering library technician courses (Martinez, "In" 7). In 1965, John Martinson, impelled by a concern over the adequacy of "medical communication" and funded by the U.S. Office of Education, undertook what is still considered a landmark study on library technician courses in the two-year college setting (Martinson *vii*). He found 24 junior colleges (out of the 719 extant schools) offering LTA programs (1, 4). In 1967, writing of the proliferation of inadequate "hybrid" community college courses (still "at least 30 … in the U.S. and Canada") attempting to fill the need for trained paraprofessional—then "technical"—staff, Samuel Sass flew into a frenzy of derogation (2123). Basically, he feared that incompetent staff would be teaching even more incompetent applicants; at the base of his irritation is a larger, quite legitimate, question about the quality of community college faculty and community college students ("Library" 2124–5). Nyren jeered at the courses themselves:

> As for watering down library education to produce "technicians" or "library aides," no one in his right mind is going to pay for education that will enable him to run a charging machine, paste pockets, or type library cards. It just doesn't pay enough and none of it is that difficult to learn. I can't imagine what advocates of a program like this are thinking of—unless it is training the mentally retarded [Nyren in "Library Education" 1766]. *anno* 1966

Perhaps because of scorn like theirs, certification programs were forced to become more responsible. Perhaps not.

Despite alarums and misgivings, by 1968 seventy programs had burgeoned, according to Lorena Garloch, in the U.S. and Canada (Bebbington). By 1969, there were "90 or more" (Steele 47). By 1973, Christianson, utilizing COLT's *Directory of Institutions Offering or Planning Programs for the Training of Library Technical Assistants* and the *North American Library Education Directory and Statistics* (NALED) and noting that "the mortality rate for the newer programs is high [i.e., 1 in 4]," counted 118 LTA programs in 1971 (*iii*, 20, 7).

These programs were characterized by a high rate of attrition (twenty-nine collapsed between 1968 and 1971), though others sprang up constantly to take their places (8). Thus, statistics were protean. Moreover, that perennial critic of LTAs and LTA education, Samuel Sass, proved correct in charging shoddy planning and execution of junior-college programs (Christianson 8). Many faculty were part-time, often recruited from the colleges' library staff, and, according to Billy Hensley in a 1971 master's thesis, schools attempting LTA programs were not well equipped to initiate programs, having no advisory boards, little information on the waiting job market for graduates, and a paucity of instructors (Christianson 13, 8).* Fewer than half offered certificates;

---

*Robert Booth posed this conundrum to the Second Annual COLT Conference attendees: "Well qualified faculty are hard to find and keep, even in the American Library Association most offered two-year degrees (*ibid.* 13). As to graduates, of 7,300 enrollees from the inception of the LTA programs to 1971, only 1,319 had graduated; few of the schools kept records of placement or of starting salaries after graduation (*ibid.* 15). A substantial number of graduates could not find jobs as LTAs, and many, when placed, were simply categorized as "clerks," though others were more appropriately titled "library technicians" or "library assistants" (*ibid.* 17, 18).

The majority of paraprofessionals is still comprised of those trained on the job. The problem is how to validate these people on paper, so they can garner the salaries and recognition they feel should be theirs. Certification has seemed, for many, to be a step in the direction of validation, and has been much discussed on Libsup-l. Many are hot to see certification implemented nationally; others claim that, for the salaries support staff make, tests and courses would be a deterrent, rather than a stimulant. Many of them would never have gone into library work, they claimed, had they had to jump through hoops to do so, primarily because salaries are so dismal and prospects for advancement so few.

Weibel points out that there is no nationally or professionally mandated certification program for support staff ("Certification" 15). There are certificates awarded for participation in workshops, extension courses, two-year college programs, community colleges, and the like, but no systematized state or federally mandated program which outlines standards or basic requirements for employment of support staff, in its many manifestations. The *Library Technician Series*, GS-1411 (1966), and the *Library Education and Personnel Utilization Policy* (1970) only detail various paraprofessional job descriptions and suggest entry-level requirements, respectively (Weibel, "Certification" 15; Evans, "Evolution" 86). Beyond authorizing committees and papers on support-staff issues, the ALA, which one imagines would be concerned in this matter, really does not involve itself with this aspect of library management, or quality-control.

In the end, it may not matter whether the ALA or any other body believes there should be rigid employment standards for paraprofessionals, because the same problems which beset librarians (and library schools) also beset support staff, usually even more severely. Low salary and low respect are female problems: librarian and clerk alike are mainly female. Earth is no woman's world. High-minded idealism about training for clerks and other paraprofessionals is otiose: most paraprofessionals cannot afford to pay for or commute to the programs that would train them. Their lack of formal preparation for work in

(cont.)   accredited library schools. That being the case, who that is qualified will be willing to teach in a library technical assistant program? If the Library Technical Aide programs are getting the kind of people they should have, then they are competing with the professional library schools" (*Progress* 10).

libraries has nothing to do with "lack of commitment to the profession" (Bayless 1716). Libraries are loath to send support staff to training sessions at their own expense; they mind less training people on site. They are loath to pay a grander salary to someone bearing a technician's certificate than to a bright person off the street, no matter what institution or state or federal department issued it. Many drives for pay equity are bound to founder on these sad truths, as well.

Rural libraries constitute 43 percent of the nation's public libraries, and only 4 percent of the staff in these libraries bear even the MLS. In 1987 a survey of librarians (both with and without the MLS) working in small and rural libraries found the largest single concentration of respondents (24 percent) making between $5,000 and $9,999 per year; half made between $10,000 and $24,999. Only 26 percent made $25,000 or higher (Vavrek, "Small"). Thus in tiny libraries, 74 percent were making less than the starting salary for urban librarians. In some libraries, director and clerk may be one and the same person, with an annual salary hovering around $15,000, although one fervid researcher (N. Busch) claims it is higher, around $21,600 (Vavrek, "Educating" 7). In any case, such ill-funded libraries—almost half the libraries in the United States—are not going to be able to afford certified paraprofessionals, if they cannot even afford to pay the average national starting salary to their librarians or directors.

Indeed, unsurprisingly, over the past ten years the popularity of LTA— or ILT (Information Library Technician)—programs has declined, paralleling the decline in library schools, and many have ceased to exist (Veihman 12). There are only about 60 LTA programs in America, most in two-year community colleges, whereas in 1969, there were over 90, and in 1977, throughout Canada and the United States, there were 157 (Few 9; Martinez, "In" 7; Evans, *Paraprofessional* 6). These typically grant either a certificate to students completing the course work for the library technician module, or an associate's degree, if the student has completed other coursework in addition to LTA courses in fulfillment of the college's graduation requirement.

Certainly it is true that "dependence upon the library/media technician will increase as the twentieth century comes to a rapid close," but on-the-job training and the odd workshop seem to be as close as most paraprofessional library workers will ever come to formal education, unless they opt to go for the MLS (Few 9). In a hortatory article about future opportunities for aspiring but "plateaued" LTAs, O'Brien and Cowans urge a "can do" mindset, almost willfully overlooking the widespread and accurate perception that paraprofessionalism is "dead end" (20–1; Mort 91). They urge seeking additional education, mentoring, volunteering, but the reality is that to progress out of the economic and spiritual cul-de-sac of support-staff employment, one must become a librarian, or leave the field to do related work in other information-geared industries. O'Brien and Cowans state flatly and redundantly, "If you want to be a librarian, get an MLS" (20). But of course, in pursuing this route to advancement, one ceases altogether to be a paraprofessional; it is no answer to the multitude of "captive" paras Oberg and colleagues note to urge attendance at library school ("Role" 234). "Perhaps some consider this route [the MLS] to be the traditional continuing education path for paraprofessionals, but in fact this is education for librarianship and a way out of a paraprofessional career," Younger accurately states (59).

Unfortunately, the odd workshops suffer, first, because "some libraries do not participate in the paraprofessional workshops," and, second, because "there has been no coordinated attempt at on-the-job training to either complement, or even implement, what might have been learned during the workshops" (J. Boyce 180).

Chiefly, however, most libraries will neither pay to train existing non-professional staff, nor go to extra lengths (viz., offer salary commensurate with training) to obtain certificate-holding support staff; support staff typically are constrained, not so much by lack of native ability, but by lack of money—"On $6,061.00/year, it is difficult to save a great deal of money unless the individual lives in a tent and eats peanut butter"—or inability to commute to locations offering LTA courses (Toolis 21: *anno* 1976).

Despite the depression of the 1990s, certification is still a concern for support staff—as evidenced by renewed concern over the issue on the Net. And extant distance-education programs are still providing library education to willing but unable library workers, desiring to do the most professional job they can on limited resources. In addition to LISDEC, RLTP, and SMILE, there are electronically transmitted distance-education programs for library workers running out of University of Arizona's VideoCampus, the Mind Extension University (mentioned above), the University of Idaho, the University of New Hampshire, Ohio University, and the University of Hawaii (SLIS) (Burgess; Gaughan, "Library"). Offering state certification is Iowa's program developed by the University of Iowa's library school. It is delivered to participants via the college's telecommunications network at twenty-two sites (Stanke 80–1).

But the future of certification is as dim as the future of LTA programs. In 1986, Pikes Peak Community College proudly unveiled its first LTA course (Bueno, "Paralibrarian Education"). By 1991, the program was defunct: "The last library technician course offered at Pikes Peak Community College had less than five registered for the course." Queried Oreada Mitchell despondently, "Did support staff not know about these courses, or choose not to make the effort?" ("Focus Group Afterthoughts"). Most likely paras simply did not see a payoff down the line for them in either career prospects or salary, and decided not to throw their money away.

39. Non-MLS-Holding Heads of Libraries

...60% of directors in 9,000 public libraries nationwide do not have MLS degrees ... [Wakefield & Martin, citing Weibel 9].

Because there were 14,948 public libraries (with over 500 volumes) in the U.S. as of 1992, perhaps the figure quoted above is not as startling as it looks. Nevertheless, *any* percentage of library directors without the MLS is startling, when one considers the ruckus that has been made in the last seventy-five years over graduate library education as a *sine qua non* for library "professionalism" (*Library and Book Trade Almanac*, 1992). Consider the fury in recent years over Daniel Boorstin or James Billington heading the Library of Congress, and Vartan Gregorian, Timothy Healy, and Paul LeClerc heading the New York Public Library: "We are in large part to blame for our low perception by allowing nonlibrarians to administer our library education programs and our libraries," frets White ("Your" 45).

> Whereas only doctors are appointed Surgeon General and only lawyers are appointed to the Supreme Court, it is only the library profession that is constantly insulted by having non-librarians appointed to major library positions such as the Librarian of Congress, the dean of the Pratt Library School, and the president of the New York Public Library,

fumes Fursa in a letter to *American Libraries*, quite sensibly pointing out the inconsistency of the New York State Department of Education proposing that all libraries in the state be administered by MLS holders only and then making an exception for the New York Public Library. In fact, however, it has made other exceptions for rural libraries and their directors, as well it might, since "[m]ore than half of the public libraries in New York state are managed by librarians without advanced degrees" ("Libraries and the M.L.S." 4). The Board of Regents proclaimed in 1989 that "rural librarians in New York will not have to have professional master's degrees," but will perhaps be subject to "new training and certification procedures" instead ("Country").

300

Appointment of non–MLS-holding directors of libraries is hardly a new problem. Jerrold Orne in 1955 agonized that he was

> increasingly alarmed at the steady progression of major academic library appointments of non-librarians.... [I]s there something wrong with us, academic librarians as a type, that causes us to fall short of the requirements of the job? ... Where are the deans of the library schools on this question? ... [w]here are our organizations...? We serve and support large central professional organizations, yet not since MacLeish has there been a direct action taken on this subject. Can you now conceive of an appointment of a history professor to the headship of a mathematics department going unnoticed by the A.A.U.P.?

In 1973, Christianson noted: "One research study, using the requirement of a master's degree in library science as the only criteria for professionals, ended up with a large category of nonprofessional chief librarians, many of whom had advanced degrees in other subjects" (2). "Imperfect definition and imperfect recognition of professional requirements exist and complicate analysis of the nonprofessional," she continues. "Strict application of an educational requirement will artificially place into the nonprofessional category personnel who are operating at a professional level" (*ibid.* 2).

"Why should a prestigious library, or any library, be run by an individual who has no library experience? I find ALA's lack of criticism, and its lack of leadership on this issue, disappointing," writes a distressed ALA member (Pollakoff). But ALA has hardly ever been noted for strong, timely, or controversial stands on behalf of the field. And behold the Canadian Library Association, barely better, which in 1992 inaugurated its "first nonlibrarian president" (Dowding 551). But Healy calmly observes that "[h]aving a scholar head the library is a tradition at the Bodleian"; besides, a scholar can hardly be accused of lacking library experience, immersed in study as he must constantly be (Kniffel, "NYPL's"). With indignation, a less famous and more typical library director wrote *Library Journal* in response to its "Dean's List" article:

> What makes [Cronin] so sure a degree has any correlation at all with quality of leadership?
> Ask my trustees. After wading through more than 20 applications from MLS-qualified candidates for a directorship, they hired me. I do not hold an MLS. However, in my favor I have almost 17 years of library experience, a level head, a professional outlook, an attitude of open-mindedness, and a bona fide love for the job. In a small library setting, I would match my collection development skills, managerial ability, and programming experience with anyone's and would not be found wanting [Beales].

Dr. Garceau, in 1951, ventured, "There are cases ... of small, middle-sized, and very large libraries being excellently administered by people with only very rudimentary specific professional training, or with none at all" (L. Martin 134–5).

Nonetheless, Pollakoff's observation must stand, after all the smoke has cleared, as unanswerable and clear as the child's candid voice in "The Emperor's New Clothes": "If he [Healy] doesn't need an MLS, why does any individual in the field need one?"

Conclusion

The MLS has been regarded as a "ticket punch," or a "union card" (Bohannon 218; Para 12).

"When we pay our support staffs as well as other municipal agencies and the local private sector pay them, and when we treat the requirement for work in the evening and on weekend as these needs are generally remunerated, the problem of training and motivating our clerical staff will disappear, particularly once the library budget funds training," claims White ("Your" 46). Larry Oberg asserts, "[W]e librarians may fail to resolve our own long-standing identity problems if we are unwilling or unable to help paraprofessionals resolve theirs" ("Paraprofessionals: Shaping" 4).

Veaner, writing of professionalism and the problem of paraprofessionals, insists that the "issue of [paraprofessionals'] capacity [to perform professional work] is irrelevant" ("Continuity" 12). He goes on, "[I]t is far better that work remain *undone* in order that position justifications remain valid and recruiting be justified" (13). He discusses two options, the "discontinuous" and the "continuous," the discontinuous model basically being a perpetuation of the "class" system in libraries, and the continuous model predicating

> that librarianship is an art, trade, craft or vocation rather than a profession. Implement an apprenticeship system: all skills to be learned on the job and imparted by training and oral instruction. Library to be managed by a professional administrator and perhaps half a dozen professional deputies or coordinators who may or may not be librarians [9].

The "continuous" is the model he condemns, yet it accurately describes the practical reality of what transpires in many libraries in the United States today. As Mary Kalnin et al. remark, "We do not dispute his analysis; it is our position the theory is already out of date" (17). I believe the "continuity model" is the only one offering any hope for today's libraries and today's library workers, with the proviso that ongoing continuing education, beyond what the employee is hired with, be required and provided for by the workplace for all levels of staff. Mark Sandler, in his extremely interesting "Workers Must Read..." article, cites the Commonwealth College Library as a "library remarkable for its stability and linear progress ... characterized not by factionalism but by consensus..." (47). In addition, "the fact that the Commonwealth library staff had no formal training raises tantalizing questions about the wisdom of current approaches to library education," he ventures (48). "That the Commonwealth College Library flourished, or for that matter maintained any level of service, presents a powerful argument for the import of staff commitment as opposed to staff training or expertise" (50–1).

It is precisely the "capacity" Veaner deprecates and the ardor Sandler describes which need to be both sought and allowed for, as Joseph Wheeler did in the 1920s and 1930s in the Enoch Pratt Free Library, which he thus made into "one of the finest public libraries in the world." He "[studied his] staff for latent talent," recruiting people, regardless of credentials, for positions in which he sensed they would excel, and they did. He instituted on-site training courses, which were "[s]o comprehensive and well-run ... that they were said to equal some accredited library schools in effectiveness" (Coplan 266–7).

True professionalism consists of talent and intelligence combined with dedication and a love of learning. "Autodidacticism" is the operative concept. I believe a truly professional library worker must be committed to her own ongoing education. She must *want* to read, *want* to be trained in new technologies, *want* to indulge her curiosities and those of others. Too many clerks and too many librarians are complacent, incurious, unintelligent, uneducated, unenthusiastic, and unmilitant on behalf of libraries. This perceivable reality, and not the possession or non-possession of the MLS or any other form of certification, damns libraries.

The whole squabble between "professional" (MLS-bearing) and "non-professional" (non–MLS-bearing) is totally beside the point. Library workers' and library managers' energies and "capacities" need to be concentrated elsewhere. Arthur Curley, recent president of ALA, believes libraries need advocacy, that "the public perception of the importance of libraries has been altered," that "we [by whom I hope he means all library workers] must assert the importance of libraries to the most fundamental informational needs of virtually all citizens" (McCormick, "President-elect").

What becomes of the *children* in a society without free public libraries and the library workers within them who enable children to open their minds to new visions of the world? What becomes of immigrant populations, inveterately poor and culturally dazed, seeking literacy and advancement in an alien land, if libraries fail because of lack of funding, because of lack of advocacy? These are the lacks that will make libraries founder, not the lack of an MLS. The time for librarians and paraprofessionals to be "passive, reactive" people is over (Veaner & Ackerman, "1985 [I]" 215). Militancy is going to have to raise its ugly head—militancy on the part of librarians and paraprofessionals, both in the interests of their own survival and in the interests of their constituency. Politeness about mistreatment and neglect has proven to be largely self-defeating in America. I believe library workers have the right to a sharp edge in their tone, and that the militancy which other oppressed groups in this country have had to assume to gain even a modicum of respect and wealth must become ours. It is not a vain exercise to see ourselves as a sort of "minority" group; we are *all* of us a "disadvantaged majority."

We need to stop squabbling about who is professional and who is not; in the context of sheer survival, the MLS is totally irrelevant. The intelligent, those with "capacity" in every library, should be merging into one militant force to ensure survival of their institutions, with participatory government the norm, and promotion based on skill and vision—nothing more. If that means return to apprenticeship, even if it means military training (consider the number of library workers who have been shot or attacked in the last two or three years), who cares?

Libraries are under attack by sociopaths, politicians, thieving patrons, increasing societal ignorance, and their own internal dissensions and snobberies. All these distractions cripple the right of the ordinary citizen of modest means and earnest intent to enjoy the privileges of democracy, one of which is indubitably the right to enter the library and find there people who burn to help him. Evans, as long ago as 1977, maintained that insistence on the MLS as the sole valid credential for employment in librarianship "implicitly denied that learning could take place elsewhere than in an academic program—an attitude that is remarkable in a profession that prides itself on being a source of help in independent, self-guided education" ("Evolution" 81).

Wherever they go, to whomever will listen, all library workers must speak up for libraries. They must also speak up for their right to be adequately paid for the work they do. It is time to lobby, to form strong associations of all kinds to push for the survival of America's embattled library systems. Today libraries are closing in record numbers (one candidate is the entire city of Troy, New York [Kristi]). Peter Jennings recently announced on television that "even during the Great Depression, there is no record of a branch library closing its doors." (This is a stirring statement, though not quite true; Clopine (60–1) and Fetty (29) both discuss branch closings in the 1930s.) Elliott Skelkrot, director of the Free Library of Philadelphia, stated on the same program: "'Democracy depends on an informed society. Goodness is its own reward in heaven. Here on earth we lobby'" ("On the Agenda").

Speaking at the 1992 ALISE Conference, "[f]ormer San Antonio Mayor Henry Cisneros ... saw libraries as a center of community in a divided society" (Berry, "Old" 54). Would that more public figures were persuaded to view libraries this way. The free public library is one of democracy's greatest concepts, something it can proudly and without reservation offer to a chaotic, greed-ridden world profoundly in need of reform and redemption. It would be tragic to watch its demise. And the Internet is no substitute for it.

Where there is inequity, there cannot be harmony. Where there is no harmony, there is no unity: "United we stand, divided we fall." Gubert reflects that "[b]oth the Greeks and Romans associated medicine with reading, the Greeks inscribing over library doors, 'Place of Healing for the Soul'" (129). The transmuted saw which springs to mind here is "Librarian, heal thyself." Berry wrote of library paraprofessionals in a controversial editorial,

> Here is a large group of talented, experienced people who want to work in libraries. We are already exploiting their readiness to help us fill the vacant jobs in this time of a shortage of library school graduates [1989]. We must do no less than welcome them to the fold and meet their needs for career growth and meaningful recognition ["Other"].

Heim et al., pulling even fewer punches, state,

> If, in times of shortages, capable support personnel can assume responsibilities that would be assigned to librarians, there are fundamental problems with the structure that now exists. Such problems make librarianship vulnerable to legal action or to challenges of the meaningfulness of the extant degree (152).

Veaner, also, points to the possibility of "class action litigation in the area of equal pay for equal work" ("Continuity" 2). Will support-staff members have to resort to such stratagems, in addition to having had to unionize, to gain their rightful places in unreconstructed library hierarchies? It would be devastating to realize too late that the energy wasted on enforcing protocols based on the having or not having of the MLS, a dubious achievement, could have been better expended on the battle to save the Library.

Appendix A:
Interview with
a Grade-1 Library Clerk

How old are you? 27

Are you married? No.

What are your current living arrangements? Why are they necessary? I am currently living with my parents. This is because I am not paid enough money to rent a halfway decent apartment in a *safe* neighborhood.

How long have you worked at your library? Six years full-time.

What positions have you held? Started as a page (part-time); later became a Library Clerk I.

What position do you hold now? For how long? Have the conditions under which you were hired altered since you started? Current position Library Clerk I for eight years. Conditions altered in the following ways: a) Raises are non-existent, or so small that they are swallowed up by increases in health or dental insurance. No cost-of-living adjustment; b) Substantial increase in circulation and other library duties in general. Less staff, however, due to hiring freeze and budget cuts; c) Increase in rude, abusive behavior from patrons, from people who are just belligerent or unappreciative to people who are *physically* abusive. We've had numerous seminars and meetings recently regarding "problem" or "violent" patrons. Our safety is definitely threatened and not to be taken for granted anymore.

What is your salary? Any hope of an increase? Are you paid according to merit? Salary approximately $8/hour. Next increase in January, 1993 at 4% (*great* for people with salaries $30,000 and up!) Salary is *not* according to merit. My work is not only increasingly frustrating and demanding, but has grown in such proportions I have no hope of *ever* catching up as long as things continue this way; my work alone should be divided among three people.

Any hope of a promotion? Do you believe that the people promoted in your system are the most suitable, or the brightest, or the hardest-working? My hope of a promotion is no more. There are far too few positions to promote to within the library and too many employees in competition. People are promoted according to test scores [civil service] which in actuality don't count for much—tests are seldom accurate regarding job duties. People with more seniority also have an edge. However, because of job security, people are rarely fired and it is quite easy to maintain a position here for a number of years—or even until retirement. People who promote are usually "sheep"—easily led, won't make waves, good followers, and will loyally stay with the system (usually because they can't make it anywhere else). People who are bright, hard-working, and are capable of making their own decisions, even developing more logical procedures, or novel ideas, are usually not promoted. It is *very* discouraging.

Do you find your job responsibilities exceeding your job description? How specific is your job description? My responsibilities seem to be exceeding my job description in that I am now doing the clerical work for departments other than my own.

What other job experiences have you had? Previous employment experience includes work in an animal hospital, a non-profit agency, a nursing home, housekeeping, and sales.

How far did you go in school? I have a high school diploma and 6 college credits.

How much do you work with the public? Do you find this part of your job more stressful than the other parts? I work with the public every day, sometimes only a couple of hours, other times 4-5 hours. This is the *most* stressful part of the job by far. The public has become (over the years) increasingly demanding, rude, unappreciative and verbally (and sometimes physically) abusive. That's not to say we don't get any polite, friendly patrons—there are still quite a few. Unfortunately, the majority treats us as though we are stupid, incompetent public "servants" and no matter what we do, it's never enough, and any fines or other problems that they have become *our* fault because we apparently don't know what we're doing. There are many street people and mentally ill who "use" (and I use the term loosely) our facilities and can become violent at the least, or without any, provocation. Many are drunk. We've had people (in the past few months) spit at us and other patrons while making sexual remarks, a man who sneaks into the ladies room when female *employees* are in there, a man who follows female employees around the stacks and tries to look up their dresses, a man who attacked other patrons and knocked a fiche reader to the floor after ripping up a book, a man who (without any reason) attacked and injured a male librarian, and a rash of purse thefts. These are only a handful of the incidents that have occurred.

What kind of a schedule do you have? Do you find it stressful? My schedule is basically 9-5, one night a week (1-9) and every third Saturday. Day to day, I spend one hour (either 12-1, or 1-2) on the registration desk, and either three hours in the morning or afternoon on registration or circulation. The remaining time is spent returning [books]. A couple of times a week I have a few hours to work on labels, known as my "indirect" task (a *very* important job)—and every couple of weeks I'll have a whole day to work on them. However, with 500-600 bar code labels coming in per week, and the increasing volume of circulation and returns, I don't see how I can ever catch up: it will always be backed up. Stressful? Yes!

Do you enjoy your work? I enjoyed my work when I was first hired. Now, however, it discourages and depresses me. Oftentimes I am very angry and find it very difficult to be courteous to the public.

Do you bring any special (and unrewarded) talents to your job? The only talents I've brought to my job have been dependability, hard work, organization, and good problem-solving skills. Sometimes these, and other things, are recognized and appreciated, but not, in my opinion, often enough.

In this year of fiscal crisis, have you been asked to assume extra jobs, in addition to enduring an increased amount of the sort of work you have always performed? Have you ever been asked to assume jobs not normally thought of as "clerk-work"? Because of the economy, we have a hiring freeze. Whenever anyone leaves, their position is nullified. To date we've lost approximately 22 positions in my library alone, so everyone (especially clerks) is overworked and burned out. The library I worked in previously had a display that was up too long. I offered to change it (when asked to). To make a long story short, I ended up doing one adult and one juvenile display per month. Briefly, I also supervised and prepared schedules for pages, as the librarian who had this job duty was not performing it.

How easy is it to transfer to another job in another location? It is *impossible* to laterally transfer at this point because of the hiring freeze (we can't afford to lose any more people), and there are hardly any positions to promote to.

Have you ever trained a librarian? Supervised other workers? Answered reference questions in a pinch? What is your library's policy on clerks answering questions? Yes, at times the librarians need training on the circulation terminal and also on registration procedures. There was one librarian in particular who knew almost nothing and I spent many a time training her and watching her at the desk. Oftentimes I was interrupted on lunch hours because she was "stuck" and needed help. I also spent a great deal of time both training and supervising a fellow clerk because this same librarian apparently didn't have the time. Unfortunately I was placed in an awkward situation when I was asked to take an active part in his evaluation and recommend whether he would remain employed or be terminated. Obviously clerks neither have the authority, and, most important, the salary, to make these decisions. While the library's policy is to only have librarians answer reference questions and find books, there were numerous instances where I had to do these things either because of a shortage in staff or because of the librarian's being involved in a program or meeting without adequate coverage.

You belong to a union. What protection do you think it affords you? The union makes sure once you are permanent (one year), it is next to impossible for you to be fired. While it's comforting to have job security, a lot of incompetents slip through. The union hasn't been able to protect us from working on Sundays, against rising insurance costs, or from hiring freezes, and no raises. Even if you choose not to belong to the union, dues are *still* deducted from the paycheck.

How effective are you in remedying insufferable situations? In an intolerable situation, I try both to use my judgement and firmly stick to the rules—which is what we're told to do. It's discouraging and embarrassing, therefore, when, after firmly stating policy to a disgruntled patron, a librarian comes along and on a whim decides to undo it all and side with the patron. This makes us look like unyielding, bitchy, incompetent idiots. It would be nice if the librarians backed us up more often.

Have you ever had to supplement your income with a second job? I've had to find a second job *three* times to supplement my income—which is considered poverty level, by the way.

Are you seeking other employment? Why? I am seeking other employment because I need a better salary to support myself and would also like to find a job where I am respected and my work appreciated. I also intend to go back to college. Clerking is a dead-end job.

Do you think of yourself as a "professional?" Yes, I consider myself a professional not only because of the quality of my work, but also my attitude and ability to deal favorably with all kinds of people.

Have you ever contemplated going to library school? I would never attend library school. Librarians are not well paid, work bad hours, deal with a rude and unappreciative public, and lack the chances for significant advancement that other "professionals" enjoy.

Do you find that librarians patronize you? Yes. Librarians automatically think that because they have a degree, they are smarter, more qualified, and have better judgment than clerks; we are treated as though the only thing we're probably capable of doing is running a light pen over a bar-code. We are treated like mindless idiots.

How much do you respect librarians and the work they do? There are a few librarians I do respect—those who not only know their job inside and out, but who also understand and respect the clerical positions. However, most aren't doing anything that a person of average intelligence and some common sense couldn't accomplish *without* all the years of library school; their job isn't as demanding—especially *mentally*—as the clerk's job.

Do you believe that your work is more arduous than the librarians' work? Yes, a clerk's work is certainly more arduous, both physically and emotionally, than a librarian's. We handle *all* the acquisitions after the librarian places a checkmark next to the titles in the catalogue—from the processing to the label data entry and keeping track of its due cards, statistical reports, patron card registration (and *all* the assorted problems with patrons!), ordering supplies, etc, etc. It is most emotionally arduous when we have to deal with "problem" patrons. We are the front line—all the bad news (fines, rules) come from us, though we do not formulate policy. Many patrons look down upon us and resent us.

Please give any opinion you like on being a library clerk. I intend to use this interview verbatim. Do you object to my using your name? I think I've summed up just about everything involving the clerk's job and feelings that go along with it in the previous questions. Basically, it's an emotionally demanding, financially unrewarding, and *thankless* job—and it's about time we got some respect and recognition, dammit! [*Interview conducted in 1992. Respondent preferred anonymity. She has since resigned her position.*]

Appendix B:
Interview with
a Paraprofessional
Library Worker at a
Four-Year University Library

How old are you? 44

Are you married? Yes.

Where do you work? At an academic institution (I would prefer that neither my name nor institution appear in the interview, because I believe that whatever problems exist here are typical of those which can be found in any major academic institution. Furthermore, if I thought the problems here were unique to this institution, there would be little point in taking part in this interview; I would simply look for another job).

How many years have you worked at this institution? 24

What formal training did you have for this job (workshops, courses)? Has your employer paid for these, or have you? In 1989 I attended Columbia University's Rare Book School for a course: "Integrated Descriptive Systems for Manuscripts and Archives" at employer's expense, including air fare, tuition, room and board, and compensatory time.

Was a B.A. required for your job? Job requirements: Bachelor's degree or equivalent combination of education and experience; 3–5 years library experience in cataloging; Knowledge of MARC format used with either OCLC or RLIN, 3–5 years experience necessary;Knowledge of cataloging principles and systems; Knowledge of library material preservation principles; Supervisory skills; ability to set priorities, manage time, monitor work flow; Supervisory experience, 1–2 years desirable.

What is your educational background (major, minor)? 3.5 years of college toward a B.A. in English.

How many positions have you held at your Institution? What were they and what were you expected to do? Oct. 1989–date—Archives/Manuscripts Supervisor, Department of Special Collections: Train support staff in processing archival/ manuscript collections and in cataloging those collections using the national on-line bibliographic utility RLIN (Research Libraries Information Network)*; assign work for processing unit; determine appropriate arrangement and description criteria for collections requiring processing; revise and edit inventories, name-index entries, and other finding aids prepared by library specialists to assure quality control, specifically adherence to local practices and national standards; revise online RLIN catalog entries for manuscript and archival collections; participate in selection of collections for priority processing; serve as resource person for processing questions relating to the organization and description of collections; participate in decisions concerning preservation issues; participate in review of processing procedures and recommend improvements; maintain system documentation; participate in evaluating staff performance; provide reference service through mail and to those who visit the Library for selected collections or groups of collections; interact with donors by mail and in person to solicit their assistance in the identification of their materials; provide reference service to donors for their own collections and for other library materials. I should mention that all cataloging records for Special Collections manuscript materials using the AMC format on RLIN are essentially original input. The upgrading of existing records, when such exist, involves the conversion and expansion of machine-loaded minimum-level records (part of Cornell University's SPINDEX project) to AACR2 format, and includes the addition of biographical information, contents notes, and subject headings, as well as verification and/or addition of all access points in the record.

Aug. 1984–Sept. 1989—Library Specialist, Department of Special Collections: Organize and process the Library's manuscript collections; produce finding aids, inventories, and indexes for collections; produce original cataloging for manuscript collections using the RLIN AMC Format; upgrade and standardize through RLIN online system the SPINDEX records which were tape loaded by the New York State Historical Resources Center at Cornell University; provide reference service to manuscript collections both through the mail and for patrons who visit the library; supervise and train three to five work-study students during the school year in a variety of clerical tasks, and supervise and train one or two full-time summer employees in processing manuscript materials; use OCLC for authority work in processing and cataloging.

Mar. 1988–Sept. 1989—Serials OCLC Cataloger, Dept. of Special Collections: Worked 20–25 hours per week under the supervision of the Serials
Librarian to catalog the serial holdings in Special Collections. Search NUC,
OCLC and RLIN to find catalog copy; input and/or update OCLC record,
enhancing access points for use by Special Collections; prepare holdings cards
for the general and special collections; prepare local data record (LDR) work
sheet for input into OCLC union list sub-system.

Jan. 1980–July 1984—Serials OCLC Cataloger, Technical Services: Catalog
and search new serials titles using Serials Format on OCLC; re-catalog and
close serials titles, and catalog title changes; use local database to identify and
report conflicts in number assignments for serial titles; report catalog information to Serials Acquisitions and Book Preparation Unit.

Feb. 1974–Dec. 1980—Central Serials Records Editor, Technical Services: Produce and maintain authority file for series titles; maintain consistency of manual file, reconciling conflicts between Library of Congress decisions and local
practice; transfer and code manual-file data for input into online Series Authority File; edit Series Authority File print-outs; use OCLC for searching.

July 1972–Jan.1974—Monographic searcher and LC-copy Cataloger: Manually search NUC and prepare catalog cards for typist

Sept. 1970–June 1972—Bindery Supervisor: Maintain library's bindery records
for serials and periodicals; prepare paperback books for bindery; supervise and
train two full-time employees.

Nov. 1969–Aug. 1970—Monographic LC-copy Cataloger: Manually catalog
monographs using LC copy; edit online shelflist print-out.

*Did the job you actually did conform to the University's formal written job descrip-
tion? Was your salary adequate at any of these jobs? Do you think you could live as
a single person on your present salary or any of your previous salaries? What is your
present salary?* Salary assessment: It's probably simplistic, and certainly predictable, to say that I feel that, commensurate with my responsibilities and
experience, my salary has been inadequate for all positions I've held in the
library. I believe however that it's inarguable that for those positions which
were non-exempt, my wage was not merely inadequate, but a less-than-living
wage (below $15,000 for the highest paying paraprofessional non-exempt posi-
tion in the library). It has always been difficult for me to accept the market
reality that the person who empties my trash is compensated more than I for
doing a job which is perceivably less technical, and requires less education and
training, but I suppose this is capitalism at work. One cannot help but wonder how universities can place so low a value on the products of their own institution. If I were a single person, I could not survive on this or any of my previous wages without a very drastic drop in my standard of living. Present salary
[in 1992]: $21,900

Did you ever have to work a second job/overtime to make a living wage? I was offered several opportunities over the years as a non-exempt employee to work overtime. I always took full advantage of them, sometimes working overtime as many as 25 hours per week. It was never a matter of "having" to work that number of hours; I simply availed myself of the opportunities whenever they presented themselves, because I was grateful for the chance to earn extra money, knowing that those occasions were rare and would not last indefinitely.

Are you a member of any union? Were you in the past? Please give your views on unions, or the specific union you were in, vis-à-vis paraprofessional/clerical library workers. I am presently not a member of a union, but was for many years. I was working at the library when the staff organized itself, and at the time, it seemed necessary because the University showed no evidence of willingness to recognize the conditions under which people were working (as a full-time employee in 1972, I earned less than $4,000), and the library administration itself appeared corrupt, in that it arbitrarily paid individuals different wages for doing the same job, with no regard to competence or years of service as a measurement on which to base those higher wages. Also, it was a common practice to appoint individuals to supervisory positions who had no training in either librarianship or supervision, in some cases creating positions where none had existed before with no advance notice to those employees already working in the department. This created terrible morale problems within departments, especially when competent employees were routinely overlooked for advancement, and often were forced to train their new supervisors, many of whom were "friends of friends" of administrators. It was really quite scandalous. It was my belief then, and, if anything, more my belief now, that employees do not consider unionizing if they perceive that they are being treated fairly by their employers. In this case, the library administration did not even bother to project the appearance of fairness in dealing with its staff. Unfortunately, although the union did stop some of the more blatant abuses of the then library administration by at least giving individuals a chance to move up within the library, it also encouraged a minimum standard of competency for any job, such that those who excelled in their work were held back from advancement, and often felt resentful of being lumped together with those who brought a slovenly approach to their jobs to the workplace. (I hasten to add however that it has never been demonstrated to me in either the unionized or non-unionized situation that there is any relationship between the degree of competence one brings to one's job and financial remuneration. I have no reason to believe that the library administration would have chosen to reward more competent individuals, had it been able to do so. The presence of a union within the library merely permitted the administration to use that as an excuse for its failure to recognize and reward a superior performance.) I do believe that the unionization of the staff brought a certain "factory" mentality to the library, and I believe that this was the result of the collaborative, if tacit, agreement between the library and the union hierarchy. It worked to both their advantages to view the staff as an undifferentiated group. In retrospect, I found it a very demeaning experience to be part of a group with whom I felt I had little in common, and to be represented by union representatives for whom I not only had no respect, but also real contempt. I feel that the library administration and the union hierarchy shared a mutual interest (keeping employees in their place) which worked to the disadvantage of the workers. There were no heroes in this situation, merely two evils.

Do you think being in a union might protect you against a possible layoff this year [this University has been asked to cut approximately $800,000 from the library budget]? In tough financial times, I don't believe that one can ever be safe enough. While I don't believe that competence is protection from being caught in the wrong job at the wrong time (departments of Special Collections seem more vulnerable than other areas of the library), I don't feel particularly threatened. If the library administration is forced to make personnel cuts, I don't believe that positions will be evaluated on an individual basis. I think it more likely that the Department will disappear altogether than that I will be singled out to lose my job. There is however no evidence for the moment that that is likely to occur. The present library administration seems kindly disposed toward Special Collections and would (I hope) only dissolve the department under very dire circumstances.

Do you enjoy your job? I feel very lucky to be in a job situation which brings so much personal satisfaction to me. In other library positions, I felt that beyond a certain point, while I brought increasing experience to the job, the work didn't reciprocate by teaching me anything. This job brings to me as much as I bring to it, and it actually enriches my life. I don't feel that I'll ever stop learning. It also allows for a certain degree of creativity—for the first time in my life, I no longer think of myself as a Clerk. I stopped thinking of myself as one as soon as I moved to the job as manuscripts processor ... and that in itself felt wonderful. Workers in Special Collections are treated as responsible individuals and reciprocate by fulfilling that expectation. I don't feel that all areas of the library have discovered that basic mechanism of human behavior.

What special talents do you bring to your job which you think are not adequately credited, in the form of salary, merit pay, etc.? This is difficult to talk about, as I don't believe we are capable of seeing ourselves as others see us. I think that I bring to this job a high level of organizational skills, depth of experience in cataloging and all related technical service activities, strong oral and written communication skills, the motivation to generate a high quality product for our users, and enthusiasm for my work which allows me to train others thoroughly. I believe that I'm credited for these skills by having earned the respect of my colleagues, but this hasn't translated into the salary I believe I'm worth.

Do you ever take work home? Are you on call? Are you recompensed for any of this?
I routinely take work home: revision of inventories (even prior to my assumption of present responsibilities) has always been done on my time, as it requires a degree of concentration which is rarely possible during the work day. I often stay at work late, come in early, take a short or no lunch, all without compensation. The Special Collections Library has its own alarm system. When it signals University Security for whatever reason, I am called to re-set it. This is a practical matter of my proximity to the University, not a measure of my level of responsibility in terms of the Library.

Have you ever published articles pertaining to your work? How does your publishing record compare with that of professional librarians in your area? I've published two articles based on our collections in the library's scholarly publication for its Library Associates; another is currently in preparation. I believe my publishing history compares favorably with that of my professional colleagues.

Do you think your workload exceeds that of professional librarians in your area? The Special Collections department is a library within a library, encompassing both bibliographic and public service. Although my strong background in cataloging and manuscripts processing suggests an almost exclusive orientation toward bibliographic services, I often interact with many of the most demanding and prestigious users of the library's collections, as well as a number of donors. While I have great respect for my colleagues from whom I've learned a great deal, I don't believe that anyone else in the department offers the degree of flexibility in terms of experience in both bibliographic and public service. I hasten to add that I'm grateful for the freedom to move between my technical and public service roles, allowing me at once to both specialize and diversify. Our curator is fortunately more concerned with producing the best processing products and offering the best public service than with protecting the territorial boundaries of office politics.

Judging from what you've seen of professional librarians in your tenure at the library, do you think the MLS has qualified them uniquely to do work you do, or could do, sans MLS? I have never recognized the usefulness of an MLS. Certainly at this time in my work career, it would, I believe, be a waste of my time. I am best able to do my job by reading on my own, and thus providing a context in which to view the materials with which I am in contact every day, I deal almost exclusively with literary manuscripts and am an avid reader of contemporary fiction and poetry. However, that sort of subject specialization is what makes the library work: each person brings to our varied collections a knowledge of one or more areas: art, architecture, photography, European history, languages, religion, journalism, literature, the book arts, and industrial design. From my point of view, it is the combined subject knowledge of the staff, not the accumulation of MLS degrees, which makes this library function as well as it does.

This is not to say that I have nothing to learn. I very much enjoyed and benefited from the course I attended at Columbia University's Rare Book School. I found it useful to speak with and learn from others who work with manuscript materials—it is an isolating job, and there are not many individuals with whom one is able to compare experiences. The course had a practical application, enabling me to incorporate many of its suggestions into the manuscript processing procedures here. Had I been a student with no prior experience of manuscript processing but with a desire to explore that avenue of librarianship as a professional, I don't believe that the course would have been nearly as useful. I think that for courses of this sort to be productive, one must have some context in which to evaluate the issues under discussion.

Do you consider yourself a "professional"? I consider myself every bit as "professional" as many of the librarians with whom I've worked over the years. There is certainly no donor or researcher who has ever interacted with me in the library who would consider me other than professional. I would like to believe that my colleagues would agree.

With "professionalism" in mind, please comment on the whole issue of MLS- vs. non–MLS-bearing library workers. I believe that, as with many occupations, librarianship is learned through experience. When I view my colleagues, I find it difficult to identify any single hallmark of Professionalism. For some, it may be defined in terms of their supervisory roles, although within our library, some librarians have no such responsibilities, while some paraprofessionals do. To others, Professionalism may be said to consist of involvement in committee work; however, it seems to me that when such activities leave the paraprofessional to deal with students, faculty, shelving, cataloging, preservation, reference, circulation, and supervision of student assistants, in short, keeping the Library functioning, then who is to say who is more visibly involved in the professional work of librarianship? Others point to a willingness to work unpaid overtime as a mark of Professionalism; however many librarians seem as unwilling to work uncompensated hours as their paraprofessional counterparts.

I believe that the barrier between professional librarian and paraprofessional is in large part artificial, and that the insistence on such a hierarchy jeopardizes the quality of service to our patrons. It certainly undermines the morale of the workforce for paraprofessionals to understand that they're not only paid less than librarians, but also that the work they perform isn't valued or respected. At a time of fiscal belt-tightening, there has been a growing awareness in the library administration that such a caste system is counter-productive to the goals of the institution. It's my hope that eventually the support for "professional" development will be extended to the entire library staff in recognition that in our fast-paced world of technological change, libraries cannot afford to leave anyone behind.

To most patrons, the person to whom they go for help in the library is the "librarian." They do not differentiate, nor are they much interested in, the hierarchy which sets librarians and paraprofessionals apart. I believe that Professionalism is best exemplified by those who take their jobs seriously and who work tirelessly and often without adequate compensation in service to their users. These are the individuals with whom I identify and whom I'm proud to call my colleagues, and they are as easily to be found among those with or without MLS degrees.

I intend to use this interview verbatim in a dissertation paper which will be accessible to the public. Do you object to my using your name? [*Interviewee preferred anonymity, for reasons stated above. This interview transpired in 1992. She is still employed at this institution doing the same work. She was still making under $25,000 per annum, as of September 1995.*]

Bibliography

"ACRL Personnel Officers Discuss Professional and Support Staff Roles," *Library Personnel News* 7(3):3 & 5 (May-June 1993).

"ACRL Task Force Recommends Increased Paraprofessional Participation," *Library Mosaics* 2(4):6–7 (Mar./Apr. 1991).

A. D. L. "A Word to Assistants," *Public Libraries* 21(7):307–308 (July 1916).

A. K. "The Cat Is Out of the Bag," *Public Libraries* 21(2):72–73 (Feb. 1916).

"A.L.A. Meetings in Chicago. A.L.A. Council Meeting. First Session," *Public Libraries* 19(2):75–79 (Feb. 1914).

A.L.A. Salaries Committee. "Minimum Salaries for Library Assistants," *Library Journal* 48(2):63–68 (Jan. 15, 1923).

"ALA Seeks Critiques of Manpower Policy," *Library Journal* 100(10):908 (May 15, 1975).

"ALA's 112th Annual Conference: Upbeat and Hopeful in New Orleans," *American Libraries* 24(7):613–625 (July/Aug. 1993).

Abalos, Patricia A. "A Paraprofessional's Plea." Letter. *American Libraries* 20(6):523–524 (June 1989).

"Academic Librarians Discuss Nonprofessionals," *Library Journal* 92(1):40–41 (Jan. 1, 1967).

"Action Exchange." Letters. *American Libraries* 24(10):919–920 (Nov. 1993).

Agg, Rachel. "Over the Loan Desk," *Public Libraries* 24(9):355–357 (Nov. 1919).

Ahern, Mary Eileen. "The Day's Wage," *Public Libraries* 25(6):316 (June 1920).

_____. "Demand for Trained Workers," *Public Libraries* 15(10):426–427 (Dec. 1910).

_____. "The Duty of the Hour," *Public Libraries* 22(6):227–228 (June 1917).

_____. "Editorial. [Desk Assistants]," *Public Libraries* 4(10):449 (Dec. 1899).

_____. "Editorial. [Desk Attendants]," *Public Libraries* 6(9):538 (Nov. 1901).

_____. "Editorial. [Library Assistants]," *Public Libraries* 1(7):270–271 (Nov. 1896).

_____. "Editorial. [Training for Assistants]," *Public Libraries* 2(6):270–271 (June 1897).

_____. "For the Library Assistant," *Public Libraries* 21(2):68 (Feb. 1916).

_____. "Library Salaries," *Public Libraries* 23(6):271–272 (June 1918).

_____. "The Library's Place," *Public Libraries* 22(7):279 (July 1917).

_____. "The Living Wage," *Public Libraries* 22(4):142–143 (Apr. 1917).

_____. "Man or Woman," *Public Libraries* 22(7):278 (July 1917).

_____. "Meager Salaries," *Public Libraries* 24(1):11–12 (Jan. 1919).

_____. "Mutual Obligations," *Public Libraries* 25(7):372–373 (July 1920).

_____. "Reclassification of Government Service," *Public Libraries* 26(2):68–69 (Feb. 1921).

*Other items of interest not cited in text.

_____. "Refined Cruelty," *Public Libraries* 19(2 [3]):106–107 (Mar. 1914).

_____. "Trade Unions for Libraries," *Public Libraries* 23(8):371–372 (Oct. 1918).

_____. "Where Is the Staff?" *Public Libraries* 22(3):103 (Mar. 1917).

* Alire, Camila A. "Information Library Technician Curriculum for Library Paraprofessionals at Pikes Peak Community College," *Colorado Libraries* 13(2):13–14 (June 1987).

Allen, Evelyn H. "Are Librarians Good Employers?" *Wilson Library Bulletin* 22(7):518–519 (Mar. 1948).

* Aluri, Rao, and Jeffrey W. St. Clair. "Academic Reference Librarians: An Endangered Species?" *Journal of Academic Librarianship* 4(2):82–84 (May 1978).

Alvarez, Robert S. "Let's Start Recruiting," *Wilson Library Bulletin* 15(5):367–369, 371 (Jan. 1941).

_____. *Library Boss: Thoughts on Library Personnel.* San Francisco: Administrator's Digest Press, 1987.

"American Library Association. Council Meeting," *Public Libraries* 18(2):73–78 (Feb. 1913).

* American Library Association. Council of the American Library Association. *Library Education and Manpower: A Statement of Policy Adopted by the Council of the American Library Association, June 30, 1970.* [Chicago]: ALA, 1970.

American Library Association. *Library Education and Personnel Utilization.* Chicago: American Library Association, 1976.

American Library Association. Office for Accreditation. *Standards for Accreditation of Master's Programs in Library & Information Studies.* Chicago: American Library Association, 1992.

American Library Association. Office for Library Personnel Resources. Standing Committee on Library Education. *World Book–ALA Goal Award Project on Library Support Staff* [?Chicago: ALA, 1993].

America's Top 300 Jobs: A Complete Career Handbook [Based on the U.S. Department of Labor's *Occupational Outlook Handbook*, Bulletin 2450]. Indianapolis IN: JIST Works, 1994.

Anderson, A. J. "Latchkey Adults," *Library Journal* 119(12):58 (July 1994).

Anderson, Byron, and Samuel T. Huang. "Impact of New Library Technology on Training Paraprofessional Staff," *The Reference Librarian* 39:21–29 (1993).

Anderson-Story, Janet. "An MLS Degree: Is It the Right Thing to Do?" *Associates* 1(1):unpaged (July 1994).

Andrew, Judith, and Ed Gillen. "Mary Kalnin and the LIBSUP-L," *Library Mosaics* 5(4):8–11 (July/Aug. 1994).

Andrews, Virginia Lee, and Carol Marie Kelley. "Changing Staffing Patterns in Technical Services since the 1970s: A Study in Change," *Journal of Library Administration* 9(1):55–70 (1988).

Anonymous. "A Librarian. By His Assistant. From the Library." [Reprint, *LJ*, Jan. 1894.] *Library Journal* 118(17):88 (Oct. 15, 1993).

Another Librarian. "[Library School Graduates]" Letter. *Public Libraries* 21(6):261–262 (June 1916).

Anxious. "Sick Librarians." Letter. *Public Libraries* 22(3):100–101 (Mar. 1917).

"Applicants for Civil Service Examination," *Public Libraries* 22(8):303 (Oct. 1917).

"Arolana Meissner," *Library Mosaics* 6(3):9 (May/June 1995).

Aron, Cindy S. "'To Barter Their Souls for Gold': Female Clerks in Federal Government Offices, 1862–1890," *Journal of American History* 67(4):835–853 (Mar. 1981).

Asheim, Lester E. "The Core Curriculum," *Journal of Education for Librarianship* 19(2):152–158 (Fall 1978).

_____. "Education and Manpower for Librarianship," *ALA Bulletin* 62(9):1096–1118 (Oct. 1968).
_____. "Education of Future Academic Librarians." In *Academic Libraries by the Year 2000: Essays Honoring Jerrold Orne*, Herbert Poole, ed. New York: Bowker, 1977, pp. 128–138.
*_____. "Implications of the Policy of Library Education and Manpower," *Tennessee Librarian* 24:7–12 (Wint. 1972).
_____. "Manpower: A Call for Action." *Library Journal* 92(9):1795–7 (May 1967).
Ashwell, Elizabeth. "Clerical Work in Public Libraries," *PNLA [Pacific Northwest Library Association] Quarterly* 8:98–99 (Apr. 1944).
Askew, Sarah B. "Library Heresies," *Public Libraries* 19(5):191–196 (May 1914).
Assistant. "How It Was Received." Letter. *Public Libraries* 21(4):173 (Apr. 1916).
Assistant. "Progressive Progress." Letter. *Public Libraries* 21(4):167–168 (Apr. 1916).
Assistant Librarian. "Will They Consent to Do This?" Letter. *Public Libraries* 22(2):59 (Feb. 1917).
Aston, Jacquie, and John Lavery. "The Health of Women in Paid Employment: Effects of Quality of Work Role, Social Support and Cynicism on Psychological and Physical Well-Being," *Women & Health* 20(3):1–25 (1993).
"At SUNY Health and Science Center Library Assistant Leads Statewide Group," *The Public Sector* [CSEA] 16(1):19 (Jan. 1993).
Ayala, John L. "Equivalency Scheme." Letter. *Library Journal* 101(7):842–843 (Apr. 1, 1976).
Azad, Asadollah. *Job Satisfaction of Paraprofessional Librarians: A Comparative Study of Public and Technical Services Departments in Selected University Libraries*. Unpubl. Ph.D. dissertation. University of Pittsburgh, 1978.
Bacon, Corinne. "A Library That's Alive," *Public Libraries* 18(2):50–55 (Feb. 1913).
_____. "The Present Tendency of Public Library Service," *Public Libraries* 20(6):241–247 (June 1915).
_____. "Relation of the Library School to the School and College Library," *Public Libraries* 19(10):396–398 (Nov. 1914).
Bagley, Helen A. "Books for Men," *Public Libraries* 22(9):355–358 (Nov. 1917).
Bailey, Louis J. "Qualifications of Librarians," *Public Libraries* 17(5):172–173 (May 1912).
Baker, Mary E. "The Reasons Anent Cataloging," *Public Libraries* 22(4):138–140 (Apr. 1917).
* Baker, Roger. "The One Person Librarian and His Staff, Or, Solitary Pleasures," *Colorado Libraries* 15(3):10–11 (Sep. 1989).
Baker, Sharon M. "Managing Resistance to Change," *Library Trends* 38(1):53–61 (Sum. 1989).
* Barnes, Melvyn. "Organizing Your Library: Lessons from 1974–1978," in *Profiting from the Cuts: Papers Read ... 10 May, 1978*, Vaughan Whibley, ed. London: The Library Association, 1978, pp. 19–32.
Barron, Daniel. "Expanding Access to Accredited MLS Programs," in *Education for the Library/Information Profession*, Patricia Reeling, ed. Jefferson NC: McFarland, 1993, pp. 29–40.
Bartlett, Karol. Letter. *WLW Journal* 9(1–2):1 (Jan.–June 1984).
Bauer, Harry C. "Low Man on an Organization Chart," *ALA Bulletin* 47(1):18, 37–38 (Jan. 1953).
Baum, Christina D. *Feminist Thought in American Librarianship*. Jefferson NC: McFarland, 1992.
Bayless, Sandy. "Librarianship Is a Discipline," *Library Journal* 102(15):1715–1717 (Sep. 1, 1977).

Bayne, Pauline S., et al. "Implementing Computer-Based Training for Library Staff," *Library Administration & Management* 8(2):78–81 (Spr. 1994).

Beales, Donna. "Educating Support Staff," *Library Journal* 119(9):8 (May 15, 1994).

Beard, William Randall. "Staff Development and Training: A Model," *Journal of Education for Library and Information Service* 36(1):35–37 (Wint. 1995).

Bebbington, Marguerite. "Library Technicians: A Welcome." Letter. *Special Libraries* 59(6):457 (July/Aug. 1968).

Bellany, Carolyn R., et al. "Scullery Maids Unite!" Letter. *Library Journal* 114(17):6 (Oct. 15, 1989).

Bement, Constance. "The Library Worker Speaks," *Library Journal* 51(19):961–962 (Nov. 1, 1926).

Bénaud, Claire-Lise. "The Academic Paraprofessional Cataloger: Underappreciated?" *Cataloging & Classification Quarterly* 15(3):81–92 (1992).

Benjamin, Selma. "Workers in Wonderland (Hazards of the Workplace)," *Unabashed Librarian* #41:5–6 (1981).

Berelson, Bernard. "Library Unionization," *Library Quarterly* 9(4):477–510 (Oct. 1939).

Berman, Sanford. *Prejudices and Antipathies: A Tract on the LC Subject Heads Concerning People.* Jefferson NC: McFarland, 1993 [rev. ed.].

Berry, John N., III. "Brown County Library, Green Bay, Wisconsin," *Library Journal* 119(11):30–33 (June 15, 1994).

_____. "Maybe Less, But Not Bad Government," *Library Journal* 120(1):6 (Jan. 1995).

_____. "Old Fears and New Targets," *Library Journal* 117(4):53–54 (Mar. 1, 1992).

_____. "The Other 'Librarians,'" *Library Journal* 114(2):4 (July 1989).

_____. "'Professional' Is Only a Label," *Library Journal* 120(12):6 (July 1995).

_____. [Profile of Elizabeth Beere], *Library Journal* 119(17):28 (Oct. 15, 1994).

_____. "The Two Crises in Library Education," *Library Journal* 118(14):102 (Sep. 1, 1993).

_____. "The Two Professions," *Library Journal* 102(15):1699 (Sep. 1, 1977).

_____. "What Should We Tell Corinne?" *Library Journal* 119(5):6 (Apr. 1, 1994).

_____. "Who Ya Gonna Call? ALA!" *Library Journal* 120(3):98 (Feb. 15, 1995).

* "Better Recognition, Salaries for Pennsylvania LTAs Urged," *Library Journal* 103(15):1554–1555 (Sep. 1, 1978).

Betts, Mitch. "VDT Vision Problems May Affect 10 Million," *Computerworld* 27(6):31 (Feb. 8, 1993).

Bianco, Susan A. "Tri-State College Library Cooperative Support Staff Interest Group (TCLC-SSIG), Pennsylvania," *Library Mosaics* 5(5):11 (Sep./Oct. 1994).

Biggs, Mary. "Librarians and the 'Woman Question': An Inquiry into Conservatism," *Journal of Library History* 17(4):409–428 (Fall 1982).

_____. "Undergraduate Library Education: Time to Sell an Old Idea in a New Bottle," *Journal of Academic Librarianship* 18(1):36 (Mar. 1992).

* Bihon, Connie S. "Paraprofessionals: Yes, But." Letter. *Library Journal* 114(16):6, 9 (Oct. 1, 1989).

Billings, Carol D., and Betty Kern. "Sources of Satisfaction and Dissatisfaction among Library Paraprofessionals: A Study Based on Fifty Interviews," *LLA Bulletin* 52:171–178 (Spr. 1990).

Bishop, Olga B. *The Use of Professional Staff in Libraries: A Review 1923–1971.* Ottawa: Canadian Library Association, 1973.

Bixby, A. F., and A. Howell. "Historical Sketches of the Ladies' Library Associations of the State of Michigan," reprinted in *The Role of Women in Librarianship 1876–1976*, K. Weibel and K. Heim, eds. Phoenix AZ: Oryx, 1979, pp. 3–4.

Black, Mary J.L. "Concerning Some Library Fallacies," *Public Libraries* 23(5):199–204 (May 1918).

* Black, William K. "...They Are Not Librarians." Letter. *Library Journal* 114(18):8 (Nov. 1, 1989).

Blackwelder, Paul. Letter. *Public Libraries* 18(5):193–194 (May 1913).

Bloomberg, Marty. *Introduction to Public Services for Library Technicians.* Littleton CO: Libraries Unlimited, 1977.

Bluman, Ethel. "Keepers of Books: Some Thoughts for the Future for Public Libraries," *Wilson Library Bulletin* 19(4):274–275, 277 (Dec. 1944).

* Bock, Joleen, et al. "Criteria for Programs to Prepare Library Technical Assistants," *Special Libraries* 60(4):253–258 (Apr. 1969).

Boelke, Joanne. *Library Technicians: A Survey of Current Developments.* Minneapolis MN: ERIC Clearinghouse, Sep. 1968. ERIC # ED 019 530.

Bohannan, April. "Library Education: Struggling to Meet the Needs of the Profession," *Journal of Academic Librarianship* 17(4):216–219 (Sep. 1991).

Bolton, Charles Knowles. "The Librarian's Duty as a Citizen," *Library Journal* 21(5):219–222 (May 1896).

Borda, Owen M. "It Takes More Than Credentials," *Library Journal* 102(15):1727 (Sep. 1, 1977).

Bostwick, Arthur E. "The Carnegie Corporation Report on Library Training," *Public Libraries* 28(9):496–497 (Nov. 1923).

_____. "The Internal Working of a Public Library," *Public Libraries* 21(2):56–57 (Feb. 1916).

_____. "System in the Library," *Library Journal* 34(11):476–482 (Nov. 1909).

_____. "Three Kinds of Librarians [Pt. 1]," *Public Libraries* 20(1):1–4 (Jan. 1915)

Bowerman, George F. "Library Personnel Administration: Some Experiences," *Library Journal* 66(14):644–648 (Aug. 1941).

Bowker, R. R. "Libraries and the Century in America: Retrospect and Prospect," *Library Journal* 26:5–7 (Jan. 1901).

Boyce, Bert R. "The Death of Library Education," *American Libraries* 25(3):257–259 (Mar. 1994).

Boyce, Judith I. "Continuing Education for Paraprofessionals," *LLA Bulletin* 52:179–184 (Spr. 1990).

Boyer, Ann. [Letter to the Editor]. *College & Research Libraries* 54(1):74 (Jan. 1993).

Boyer, Laura M., and William C. Theimer, Jr. "The Use and Training of Nonprofessional Personnel at Reference Desks in Selected College and University Libraries," *College & Research Libraries* 36(3):193–199 (May 1975).

Braden, Sally, et al. "Utilization of Personnel and Bibliographic Resources for Cataloging by OCLC Participating Libraries," *Library Resources and Technical Services* 24(2):135–154 (Spr. 1980).

Branan, Brad. "State of the Unions: Improving," *Utne Reader* # 65:30, 32 (Sep./Oct. 1994).

Brand, Barbara E. "Librarianship and Other Female-Intensive Professions," *Journal of Library History* 18(4):391–406 (Fall 1983).

* Bratton, Phyllis Ann K. "Or Too Difficult to Achieve?" [Letter]. *College & Research Libraries News* 53(6):411 (June 1992).

Brewitt, Theodora R., and Mary Duncan Carter. "Professional and Non-Professional Work: A Work Analysis," *Library Journal* 63(18):773–775 (Oct. 15, 1938).

Brigham, Harold F. "The Point of View of the Administration," *American Library Association Bulletin* 31(11):790–791 (Oct. 15, 1937).

* Brigham, Herbert O. "Classification of Librarians by U.S. Census Bureau." Letter. *Library Journal* 45(15):699 (Sep. 1, 1920).

Briscoe, Judy. "The Cost of Child Abuse and Neglect," *Corrections Today* 56(7):26, 28 (Dec. 1994).

Brooklyn Public Library (Staff). "Petition for Adequate Remuneration," *Public Libraries* 22(4):140–141 (Apr. 1917).
* Brown, Elizabeth. "To Recommend or Not to Recommend." Letter. *Special Libraries* 56(7):532 (Sep. 1965).
Brown, Karl. "Page Help in the Library," *Library Journal* 67(15):722–723 (Sep. 1, 1942).
Brown, Martha J. "The Trials and Tribulations of an Assistant," *Public Libraries* 21(2):76–77 (Feb. 1916).
Brown, Phyllis. [Autobiographical interview in] *Library Mosaics* 1(6):19–20 (July/Aug. 1990).
"Brown Clerical Workers Back at Work," *American Libraries* 22(2):126–127 (Feb. 1991)
Bryan, Alice Isabel. *The Public Librarian*. New York: Columbia University Press, 1952.
Budd, Richard W. "A New Library School of Thought," *Library Journal* 117(8):44–47 (May 1, 1992).
Bueno, Jo. "Paralibrarian Education: The Information/Library Technician Curriculum at Pikes Peak Community College," *Colorado Libraries* 14:17 (Sep. 1988).
*_____. "Paralibrarians—A Celebration," *Colorado Libraries* 13(2):9 (June 1987).
*_____. "Paralibrarians in Colorado," *Colorado Libraries* 13(2):18 (June 1987).
* Buller, Katie. "'Us Versus Them': An Unscientific Assessment of Union and Nonunion Educational Benefits in Libraries," *Journal of Education for Library and Information Science* 36(1):42–45 (Wint. 1995).
* Bunge, Charles A. "Reference Desk Staffing Patterns," *RQ* 26:171–179 (Wint. 1986).
_____. "Stress in the Library Workplace," *Library Trends* 38(1):92–102 (Sum. 1989).
Burgess, William E. *The Oryx Guide to Distance Education*. Phoenix AZ: Oryx, 1994.
Burgin, Robert, and Patsy Hansel. "Library Management: A Dialogue," *Wilson Library Bulletin* 66(1):66–68 (Sep. 1991).
* Burgoyne, Elizabeth. "Made to Feel Important." Letter. *Wilson Library Bulletin* 54(10):614 (June 1980).
Butcher, John E. "Handling Aggressive Patrons," *NYSLAA Network Connection* 7(2):2 (Fall 1994).
Buthod, Craig. "No More Waiting." Letter. *Library Journal* 119(7):8 (Apr. 15, 1994).
* "COLT Says the LTA Needs Certification," *Library Journal* 103(15):1555 (Sep. 1, 1978).
"Calif. Librarians Unite Against Nonpro Threat," *Library Journal* 101(4):572 (Feb. 15, 1976).
"Calif. Meet Pegs Dichotomy Between Pros & LTAs," *Library Journal* 101(12):1369 (June 15, 1976).
* Campbell, Corinne. "Rational Is as Rational Does." Letter. *Special Libraries* 60(4):251 (Apr. 1969).
Campbell, Jerry D. "Choosing to Have a Future," *American Libraries* 24(6):560–566 (June 1993).
Canon, E. T. "How to Get the Best Books Read," *Public Libraries* 19(2 [3]):96–98 (Mar. 1914).
"Career Development: Defining the 'Issues of the Nineties,'" *Library Journal* 114(2):52–55 (July 1989).
Carmichael, James V., Jr. "Gender Issues in the Workplace: Male Librarians Tell Their Side," *American Libraries* 24(9):227–230 (Mar. 1994).
Carrier, Esther Jane. *Fiction in Public Libraries, 1900–1950*. Littleton CO: Libraries Unlimited, 1985.
Cart, Michael. "Here There Be Sanctuary: The Public Library as Refuge and Retreat," *Public Library Quarterly* 12(4):5–23 (1992).
Castelyn, Mary. "Paraprofessionals or Assistants or Technicians—or What?" *Library Association Record* 92(3):159–160 (Mar. 1990).

"Certification of Librarians," *Library Journal* 46(19):891–892 (Nov. 1, 1921).

Chase, Frank H. "The Librarian's Leisure Hour Reading," *Public Libraries* 28(9): 494–497 (Nov. 1923).

Chicago Tribune. "Gary Library Attendant Wins $50 Prize," *Public Libraries* 26(3): 141–142 (Mar. 1921).

* "Choosing a Librarian," *Public Libraries* 16(9):374–375 (Nov. 1911).

Christensen, John O., et al. "An Evaluation of Reference Desk Service," *College & Research Libraries* 50(4):468–483 (July 1989).

Christianson, Elin. *Paraprofessional and Nonprofessional Staff in Special Libraries.* [N.A.]: Special Libraries Association, 1973.

* "Civil Service in Libraries," *Public Libraries* 24(8):301–302 (Oct. 1919).

Clark, Elizabeth D. "The Faithful Library Employee," *Library Journal* 58(6):264–266 (Mar. 15, 1933).

"Cleveland Offers Pro Status Via Job Experience," *Library Journal* 100(19):1965 (Nov. 1, 1975).

Clopine, John J. *A History of Library Unions in the United States.* Master's dissertation. Graduate School of Arts and Sciences of the Catholic University of America, June 1951.

Cole, Donna L. "Killed in the Line of Duty." Letter. *Library Journal* 120(2):8 (Feb. 1, 1995).

_____. "Library School: The Alternative Curriculum," *Wilson Library Bulletin* 67(8):57–59 (Apr. 1993).

Coleman, Kathleen, and Elizabeth Margutti. "Training Nonprofessionals for Reference Service," *RQ* 16(3):217–219 (Spr. 1977).

"Collective Bargaining in the 1980s," *Library Personnel News* 3(2):[17]–26 (Spr. 1989).

"Colorado Library Association," *Public Libraries* 18(1):23–27 (Jan. 1913).

Connolly, Louise. "Women as Employees," *Public Libraries* 19(5):196 (May 1914).

Conroy, Barbara. "The Human Element: Staff Development in the Electronic Library," *Drexel Library Quarterly* 17(4):91–106 (Fall 1981).

Cook, Winifred A. "The First Woman's Club in U.S.," *Public Libraries* 19(3):153–154 (Apr. 1914).

Cooper, Elizabeth. "An Open Letter to Librarians," *Oklahoma Librarian* 14:128 (Oct. 1964).

Coplan, Kate M. "Memories of Enoch Pratt Free Library," *American Libraries* 24(3):266–270 (Mar. 1993).

Corwin, Margaret Ann. "An Investigation of Female Leadership in Regional, State, and Local Library Associations, 1876–1923," *Library Quarterly* 44(2):133–144 (Apr. 1974).

"Country Librarians," *Women in Libraries* 18(3):5 (Feb. 1989).

Countryman, Gratia. "Contact with the Public," *Public Libraries* 4(9):397–399 (Nov. 1899).

* Courtois, Martin P. and Lori A. Goetsch. [Letter to the Editor]. *College & Research Libraries* 51(3):282 (May 1990).

_____. "Use of Nonprofessionals at Reference Desks," *College & Research Libraries* 45(5):385–391 (Sep. 1984).

Cox, Frances. "Professional Straitjacket," *Library Journal* 85(6):1058–1060 (Mar. 15, 1960).

Cravey, Pamela J. "Occupational Role Identity of Women Academic Librarians," *College & Research Libraries* 52(2):150–164 (Mar. 1991).

Cromer, Donna L. ["Supporting Cast"]. [Autobiographical interview in] *Library Mosaics* 6(1):27 (Jan./Feb. 1995).

Crowley, Terence. "Half-Right Reference: Is It True?" *RQ* 25(1):59–68 (Fall 1985).

Curley, Arthur. "Library Advocacy Now!" *American Libraries* 25(8):784 (Sep. 1994).

Curran, Charles. "Down with Slogans," *American Libraries* 24(11): 999–1000 (Dec. 1993).

Dana, John Cotton. "Women in Library Work," *The Independent* 71:244–250 (Aug. 3, 1911).

* Dane, Chase. "Speaking for Clerical Help," *LLA Bulletin* 129:46–47, 74 (Sum. 1966).

Daniel, Evelyn H. "Education for Library and Information Science." In *Libraries and Information Services Today: The Yearly Chronicle*, June Lester, ed. Chicago: ALA, 1991, pp. 97–103.

Daniels, Jane W. "Aid Through Aides," *Library Journal* 88(11):2194–2197 (June 1, 1963).

Danton, J. Periam. *Education for Librarianship: Criticism, Dilemmas, and Proposals.* [NY]: School of Library Service, Columbia University, 1946.

Davis, R. L. "Some Library Reminiscences," *Public Libraries* 22(5):180–182 (May 1917).

Davis, Robert, and Sam Vincent Meddis. "Random Killings Hit a High," *USA Today*: 1–2(sec. A) (Dec. 5, 1994).

Dawson, John M. "Not Too Academic," *College & Research Libraries* 27(1):37–39, 55 (Jan. 1966).

"Dean's List: 10 School Heads Debate the Future of Library Education," *Library Journal* 119(6):60–64 (April 1, 1994).

Deeney, Kay. "The Role of Paraprofessionals at the Reference Desk," *Bulletin of the Medical Library Association* 78(2):191–193 (Apr. 1990).

* Defa, Dennis R. "Position Analysis of Library Assistants," *Library Administration & Management* 9(2):88–93 (Spr. 1995).

De Gennaro, Richard. "MLS Irrelevant for NYPL Boss." Letter. *American Libraries* 21(3):192 (Mar. 1990).

Deiss, Kathryn J. "Staff-Based Policy Building," *College & Research Libraries News* 55(11):730, 733 (Dec. 1994).

De La Peña McCook, Kathleen. "The First Virtual Reality," *American Libraries* 24(7):626–628 (July/Aug. 1993).

"The Desk Assistant: An Imaginary Conversation," *Library Journal* 27(5):251–254 (May 1902).

Detlefsen, Ellen G. "Specialists as Professionals in Research Libraries: An Overview of Trends and an Analysis of Job Announcements," *Library Trends* 41(2):187–197 (Fall 1992).

Dewey, Melvil. "Women in Libraries: How They Are Handicapped," *Library Notes*:89–90 (Oct. 1886).

Distressed Librarian. "Where Did He Come From?" *Public Libraries* 19(1):11 (Jan. 1914).

Ditzion, Sidney Herbert. *Arsenals of a Democratic Culture.* Chicago: American Library Association, 1947.

Dixson, Zella Allen. "Teaching Library Science by University Extension Methods," *Public Libraries* 2(6):285–289 (June 1897).

* Doherty, Teresa J., et al. "The Subprofessional or Technical Assistant," *Special Libraries* 60(3):179–184 (Mar. 1969).

Donahugh, Robert H. "The Apprentices Are Coming!" *Ohio Library Association Bulletin* 38:9–11 (Jan. 1968).

* Dorsett, Cora Matheny. *Library Technical Assistants: A Survey of Training Programs and Employment in Selected Libraries.* Ph.D. dissertation. University of Mississippi, 1972. Ann Arbor MI: University Microfilms, 1975.

Doud, Marjory. "The Inarticulate Library Assistant," *Library Journal* 45(12):540–543 (June 15, 1920).

Doughan, David. "Conference Report: International Symposium of Women's Libraries held at the Women's Library and Information Centre, Istanbul, 8–9 October, 1991," *Women's Studies International Forum* 15(1):I–III (1992).

Dougherty, Richard M. "Are We Educating or Training?" *Journal of Academic Librarianship* 16(3):139 (July 1990).

_____. "Library Education: The 1990s," *Journal of Academic Librarianship* 17(3):138 (July 1991).

_____. "Personnel Needs for Librarianship's Uncertain Future." In *Academic Libraries by the Year 2000: Essays Honoring Jerrold Orne*, Herbert Poole, ed. New York: Bowker, 1977, pp. 107–117.

Dowd, Frances Smardo. "Latchkey Children: A Community and Public Library Phenomenon," *Public Library Quarterly* 10(1):7–22 (1990).

Dowding, Martin R. "Canadian Librarians Confront Tough Financial Times in Winnipeg," *American Libraries* 23(7):551, 608 (Jul./Aug. 1992).

Downs, Robert B., and Robert F. Delzell. "Professional Duties in University Libraries," *College & Research Libraries* 26(1):30–39, 69 (Jan. 1965).

Drake, David. "The 'A' Factor: Altruism and Career Satisfaction," *American Libraries* 24(10):922, 924 (Nov. 1993).

_____. "When Your Boss Isn't a Librarian," *American Libraries* 21(2):152–153 (Feb. 1990).

Duchac, Kenneth F. "Manpower: A Proposal," *Library Journal* 92(9):1797–1798 (May 1, 1967).

Dudgeon, Matthew S. "Extensive Extension and Intensive Extension," *Public Libraries* 20(6):247–251 (June 1915).

Dumars, Denise. "Peeved at Professionals." Letter. *American Libraries* 22(7):619 (July/Aug. 1991).

*_____. "Support Staff in Public Library Reference Services," *Library Mosaics* 4(3):12–13 (May/June 1993).

_____. "*Women Library Workers Journal*," *Library Mosaics* 3(1):14 (Jan./Feb. 1992).

Dwyer, William G. "End of an Experiment," *Library Journal* 87(18):3619–3622 (Oct. 15, 1962).

Dyckman, A. Ann. "Library Assistants in the Year 2000," *Journal of Library Administration* 17(1):77–90 (1992).

Eaglen, Audrey. "A Note from the Editor," *WLW Journal* 14(4):2 (Sum. 1991).

Eastman, Linda A. "Holding the Library Workers." Letter. *Public Libraries* 25(5):251 (May 1920).

Education for the Library/Information Profession: Strategies for the Mid-1990s, Patricia G. Reeling, ed. Jefferson NC: McFarland, 1993.

Elliott, Anna. "Melvil Dewey: A Singular and Contentious Life," *Wilson Library Bulletin* 55(9):666–671 (May 1981).

Elliott, Julia E. "The Relation of the Librarian to the Assistant," *Public Libraries* 10(9):463–465 (Nov. 1905).

Elmendorf, H. L. "American Library Association. Large Library Section. Library Organization. Friday. [Assistants]," *Public Libraries* 4(6):289–290 (June 1899).

* Elsom, Ruth B. [Letter to the Editor]. *Special Libraries* 60(6):414 (July/Aug. 1969).

*_____. "Volunteers Establish Special Library Seek Advice." Letter. *Special Libraries* 60(3):175 (Mar. 1969).

Emmick, Nancy J. "Nonprofessionals on Reference Desks in Academic Libraries," *The Reference Librarian* 12:149–160 (Spr./Sum. 1985).

"Erasing Dissatisfaction," *Wilson Bulletin for Librarians* 12(9):590 (May 1938).

Eskoz, Patricia A. "The Catalog Librarian—Change or Status Quo? Results of a Survey of Academic Libraries," *Library Resources & Technical Services* 34(3):380–392 (July 1990).

Estabrook, Leigh, et al. "Managing the Work of Support Staff," *Library Trends* 41(2):231–249 (Fall 1992).

* Estes, Rice. "Let's Make More Ripples." Letter. *Special Libraries* 60(4):250–251 (Apr. 1969).

Euster, Joanne R. "Changing Staffing Patterns in Academic Libraries," *Library Issues* 7(1):[1]–[3] (Sep. 1986).

Evans, Charles. "The Evolution of Paraprofessional Library Employees." In *Advances in Librarianship* 9, Michael H. Harris, ed. New York: Academic Press, 1979, pp. 63–101.

_____. "Library Technicians in Kentucky," *Kentucky Library Association Bulletin* 35:17–23 (Apr. 1971).

_____. *Paraprofessional Library Employees.* [Waterville, OH]: COLT, [1977?].

Ex-Librarian. "Hours of Labor in the Library," *Public Libraries* 22(3):109 (Mar. 1917).

"Experience of a Library Apprentice," *Public Libraries* 6(3):155–156 (Mar. 1901).

* F. B. R. "Misnamed Educational," *Public Libraries* 20(2):62 (Feb. 1915).

"Fair Pay Act Endorsed by ALA: Lift for Library Pay?" *Wilson Library Bulletin* 69(1):17 (Sep. 1994).

Fairchild, Salome Cutler. "Women in American Libraries," *Library Journal* 29(12): 157–162 (Dec. 1904).

"Fairy Gold," *Public Libraries* 22(5):182–184 (May 1917).

Faludi, Susan. *Backlash: The Undeclared War against American Women.* New York: Anchor/Doubleday, 1991.

Fatzer, Jill B. "Paraprofessionals in the Academic Library," *LLA Bulletin* 52(4):159–162 (Spr. 1990).

Fehlman, Sheila, and Dhani Verma. "Support Staff and Paraprofessionals in Online Catalog Management: The Expanding Role of Cataloging Assistants at Boston College," *Library Mosaics* 4(6):20–21 (Nov./Dec. 1993).

Feldberg, Roslyn L. "'Union Fever': Organizing Among Clerical Workers, 1900–1930," *Radical America* 14(3):53–67 (May-June 1980).

"Female Library Assistants," *Library Journal* 14(4):128–129 (Apr. 1889).

Fennell, Janice Clinedinst. *A Career Profile of Women Directors of the Largest Academic Libraries in the United States: An Analysis and Description of Determinants.* Ph.D. dissertation. Ann Arbor MI: U.M.I. Microfilms International, 1978.

* Ferguson, Elizabeth. "Subprofessional Training," *Wilson Library Bulletin* 24(1):70–72 (Sep. 1949).

_____. "Through the Pre-professional Training Maze," *Special Libraries* 60(2):93–94 (Feb. 1969).

Fernberg, Patricia. "Is Your Terminal Ill?" *Health* 23(2):36, 38 (Mar. 1991).

Fetty, Irene. "Conservation of Personnel," *Wilson Library Bulletin* 18(1):29, 33 (Sep. 1943).

Few, John. "Current Educational Programs for Library Media Technicians," *Library Mosaics* 1(5):8–10 (May/June 1990).

"A Few Brickbats from a Layman," *Public Libraries* 18(7):277–279 (July 1913).

"A Few Gleams from the Assistants' Side," *Public Libraries* 21(2):78–79 (Feb. 1916).

Fialkoff, Francine. "Rutgers Does It Right," *Library Journal* 117(8):46 (May 1, 1992).

Fidell, L. S. "Empirical Verification of Sex Discrimination in Hiring Practices in Psychology," *American Psychologist* 25(12):1094–1098 (Dec. 1970).

Field, Anne. "'Pinkertons' in Pinstripes Wage War on Women," *Working Woman* 5(12):68–72, 94–95 (Dec. 1980).

Figura, Theodore. "Pros & Parapros—Arm in Arm." Letter. *Library Journal* **101**(21):2403 (Dec. 1, 1976).

Files, Kathy. [Autobiographical interview in] *Library Mosaics* **1**(4):22 (Mar./Apr. 1990).

Fitch, Donna K. "Job Satisfaction among Library Support Staff in Alabama Academic Libraries," *College & Research Libraries* **51**(4):313–320 (July 1990).

Fitch, Donna K., et al. "Turning the Library Upside Down: Reorganization Using Total Quality Management Principles," *Journal of Academic Librarianship* **19**(5):294–299 (Nov. 1993).

Flagg, Charles A. "A Librarian to His Assistants," *Public Libraries* **25**(9):516 (Nov. 1920).

Flagg, Gordon. "Gunman Opens Fire at Cleveland Public Library," *American Libraries* **25**(2):135 (Feb. 1994).

_____. "Insurer Settles Kreimer Claim without Morristown Library Ok," *American Libraries* **23**(4):270 (Apr. 1992).

_____. "Las Vegas Library Changes Policy Following Lawsuit by Homeless," *American Libraries* **23**(2):127 (Feb. 1992).

Flagg, Gordon, et al. "In Hot Miami Beach: More Reports from Annual Conference," *American Libraries* **25**(8):716–733 (Sep. 1994).

_____. "Issues of Reach and Grasp: ALA Faces Up to Success. States Compare Notes in Minimum-Salary Struggle," *American Libraries* **21**(3):252–261 (Mar. 1990).

_____. "Midwinter by the Numbers," *American Libraries* **24**(3):222–230, 259–265 (Mar. 1993).

Flanagan, Leo Nelson. "A Sleeping Giant Awakens: The Unionization of Library Support Staffs," *Wilson Library Bulletin* **48**(6):491–499 (Feb. 1974).

Flexman, Ellen. "Library Unionization and Its Ties to the Public Sector: History, Issues, and Trends," *Indiana Libraries* **10**:27–44 (1991).

Flexner, Jennie M. "Choosing a Librarian from the Viewpoint of the Assistant," *Public Libraries* **25**(8):429–432 (Oct. 1920).

_____. "The Essential Qualities of a Good Assistant," *Public Libraries* **24**(10):405–410 (Dec. 1919).

* Forsyth, Kenna, and Mary Y. Parr. "Library Technicians at Drexel," *College & Research Libraries* **27**(2):120–122 (Mar. 1966).

Foster, William F. "Staff Meetings," *Public Libraries* **1**(8–10):312–313 (Dec. 1896).

* Frank, Dennis. "Librarianship Too Attractive?" Letter. *College & Research Libraries News* **53**(6):411 (June 1992).

Franklin, Grace A. "Paraprofessionals at the Reference Desk," *Ohio Libraries* **4**:6, 8, 9 (May/June 1991).

Franklin, Robert D. "Personnel Primer," *Library Journal* **90**(16):3542–3549 (Sep. 15, 1965).

Freeman, Marilla W. "Conditions and Requirements for Public Library Assistants," *Public Libraries* **21**(2):80–81 (Feb. 1916).

Freeman, Pamela W., and Robert K. Roney. "The Neglected Majority: Non-Faculty Employees in Higher Education," *Journal of the College & University Personnel Association* **29**:21–29 (Fall 1978).

Freides, Thelma. "Current Trends in Academic Libraries," *Library Trends* **31**(3):457–475 (Wint. 1983).

Frieburger, William. "Beating The Dead MLS Horse." Letter. *American Libraries* **24**(11):985 (Dec. 1993).

Fursa, Edmond. "...But Not For All." Letter. *American Libraries* **20**(1):28 (Jan. 1989).

"GSLIS 'Disestablished' at UCLA; Task Force Acts to Save MLS, ph.D.," *American Libraries* **24**(7):508 (July/Aug. 1993).

Gale, Peggy. "Wanted—A Professional Position," *Unabashed Librarian* #63:13–14 (1987).
Galen, Michele, et al. "Repetitive Stress: The Pain Has Just Begun," *Business Week* (#3274):142, [144–145] (July 13, 1992).
Garbacz, Gerald G. "Library Politics: A Manifesto for Change," *Library Journal* 118(15):46 (Sep. 15, 1993).
Garrison, Dee. *Apostles of Culture: The American Public Librarian and American Society, 1876–1920.* New York NY: Free Press, 1979.
_____. "The Tender Technicians: The Feminization of Public Librarianship, 1876–1905," *Journal of Social History* 6(2):131–159 (Wint. 1972-73).
Garten, Edward D. *Motivational Properties of Support Staff Tasks in the Face of Automation.* July, 1981. ERIC # ED 217 830.
Gaughan, Thomas M. "The Best of Times, the Worst of Times," *American Libraries* 22(10):924 (Nov. 1991).
_____. "Georgia Librarian Murdered While Working Alone," *American Libraries* 24(10):902 (Nov. 1993).
_____. "Librarian Raped, Murdered in Arizona Public Library," *American Libraries* 24(1):7 (Jan. 1993).
*_____. "Librarianship Out, Information Studies in at Chicago's Graduate Library School," *American Libraries* 20(3):182 (Mar. 1989).
_____. "Library Teleducation: Live and Interactive," *American Libraries* 24(3):214–215 (Mar. 1993).
_____. "A Long Distance Call from a Homeless Man," *American Libraries* 21(2):92 (Feb. 1990).
_____. "Mayor Ends Campaign to Fire Letter-writing Library Staffer," *American Libraries* 24(3):214 (Mar. 1993).
_____. "Prison Librarian Freed Unharmed after Being Held Hostage," *American Libraries* 23(6):431 (June 1992).
_____. "Proposal: Remove the L from SLIS at Dalhousie," *American Libraries* 24(10):905 (Nov. 1993).
_____. "Taking the Pulse of Library Education, Part One," *American Libraries* 22(11):1020–1021, 1072 (Dec. 1991).
_____. "Taking the Pulse of Library Education, Part Two," *American Libraries* 23(1):24–25, 120 (Jan. 1992).
Gavryck, Jacquelyn. "Library Instruction for Clerical Staff: The Rest of the Iceberg," *Journal of Academic Librarianship* 11(6):343–345 (Jan. 1986).
Gebhard, Patricia. "School for Ninety-Day Wonders," *Library Journal* 88(11):2198–2200 (June 1, 1963).
Giesecke, Joan R. "Reorganizations: An Interview with Staff from the University of Arizona Libraries," *Library Administration & Management* 8(4):196–199 (Fall 1994).
Gill, Suzanne. "New Directions for Library Paraprofessionals," *Wilson Library Bulletin* 55(5):368–370 (Jan. 1981).
Gillen, Ed. "Challenges of the Future," *Associates* 1(1):unpaged (July 1994).
_____. "To Live and Die an LA: Career Paths and Professional Development of the Library Assistant," *Journal of Education for Library and Information Science* 36(1):5–11 (Wint. 1995).
Glass, Betty J. "Scenes from Academic Libraryland," *WLW Journal* 15(4):11–12 (Wint. 1992/93),
* Glazer, Adam. "It's About Time." Letter. *Associates* 1(1):unpaged (July 1994).
Goldberg, Beverly. "Colo. Library Workers' Malaise Traced to Sick Building Syndrome," *American Libraries* 23(10):824, 826 (Nov. 1992).

_____. "Endowment on Welcome Mat for New Miami Librarian," *American Libraries* 20(9):839, 841 (Oct. 1989).
_____. "One-Day Strike Closes Most L.A. County Libraries," *American Libraries* 22(11):1016 (Dec. 1991).
Goldhor, Herbert. "Democracy and the Library," *Wilson Library Bulletin* 15(1):30–31, 33 (Sep. 1940).
Gonzales, Laura, et al. "1994 COLT Annual Conference Miami Beach, Florida," *Library Mosaics* 5(5):24–25 (Sep./Oct. 1994).
* Gordon, Ruth. "A Savannah Ricochet." Letter. *Special Libraries* 60(6):414 (July/Aug. 1969).
Gorman, Michael. "A Bogus and Dismal Science, or, The Eggplant That Ate Library Schools," *American Libraries* 21(5):462–463 (May 1990).
Goss, Theresa C. "The Status of Paraprofessionals as Perceived by Community/Junior College Library Directors and Librarians," *Community & Junior College Libraries* 3(3):47–50 (Spr. 1985).
Gould, Dana Grove. *A Study of the Current Role and Status of the Paraprofessional as Perceived by Selected Academic and Public Library Administrators.* Ph.D. dissertation. University of Southern Mississippi. Ann Arbor MI: Xerox University Microfilms, 1974.
Gould, Donald P. "Measuring Levels of Work in Academic Libraries: A Time-Based Approach," *College & Research Libraries* 46(3):236–248 (May 1985).
Goulding, Anne. "Managing the Job Satisfaction of Public Library Paraprofessionals in a Changing Climate," *Public Library Journal* 6(4):93–99 (July/Aug. 1991).
Grady, Ruth Ellen. "Library Work Without an MLS," *Library Journal* 102(15):1726 (Sep. 1, 1977).
Gramer, Robert, et al. "Nonpro Credentials." Letter. *Library Journal* 101(13):1467 (July 1976).
Green, Denise. [Letter to the Editor]. *College & Research Libraries* 51(3):282 (May 1990).
Greer, Agnes F. P. "Professional Ethics for the Library Worker," *Library Journal* 42(11):891–892 (Nov. 1917).
Greiner, Ann Claire. "Terminal Hazards," *Technology Review* 94(2):16–17 (Feb.-Mar. 1991).
Greiner, Joy M. "A Comparative Study of the Career Development Patterns of Male and Female Library Administrators in Large Public Libraries," *Library Trends* 34(2):259–289 (Fall 1985).
_____. "Non-M.L.S. Professionals in the Library," *Public Libraries* 29:209–214 (Jul./Aug. 1990).
_____. "The Role of Nonprofessionals in Small Public Libraries," *Public Libraries* 27(2):76–78 (Sum. 1988).
Griffiths, José-Marie, and Donald W. King. *New Directions in Library and Information Science Education.* White Plains NY: Knowledge Industries Publications, 1986.
Gross, Dean C. "Training the Non-Professional," *Library Journal* 82(12):1622–1625 (June 15, 1957).
Grundt, Leonard. "Equivalency Scheme." Letter. *Library Journal* 101(7):842 (Apr. 1, 1976).
Gubert, Betty K. "Sadie Peterson Delaney: Pioneer Bibliotherapist," *American Libraries* 24(2):124–130 (Feb. 1993).
Hadley, Chalmers. "The A.L.A. and the Library Worker," *Public Libraries* 25(7):357–362 (July 1920).
_____. "The Internal Affairs of a Library," *Public Libraries* 21(2):57–59 (Feb. 1916).

_____. "The Library School and Its Work for Libraries," *Public Libraries* 17(10):401–405 (Dec. 1912).

_____. "Outside of Working Hours," *Public Libraries* 28(1):1–4 (Jan. 1923).

_____. "State Library Associations," *Public Libraries* 17(2):37–39 (Feb. 1912).

Hall, Rosalind. "Pro vs. Parapro." Letter. *Library Journal* 100(10):896 (May 15, 1975).

Halldorsson, Egill A., and Marjorie E. Murfin. "The Performance of Professionals and Nonprofessionals in the Reference Interview," *College & Research Libraries* 38(5):385–395 (Sep. 1977).

Halsted, Deborah D., and Dana M. Neeley. "The Importance of the Library Technician," *Library Journal* 115(4):62–63 (Mar. 1, 1990).

Hamill, Harold L. "Selection, Training, and Staffing for Branch Libraries," *Library Trends* 14(4):407–421 (Apr. 1966).

Hammond, Carol. "Information and Research Support Services: The Reference Librarian and the Information Paraprofessional," *The Reference Librarian* 17(37):91–107 (1992).

Hanna, Donna. "Membership Update," *NYSLAA Network Connection* 7(3):2 (Wint. 1995).

Hardesty, Rex. "Survey: Workers Want Bigger Role, Don't Get It," *AFL-CIO News* 39(26):2 (Dec. 12, 1994).

Harger, Elaine. "Talkin' Union," *Library Journal* 114(18):24–26 (Nov. 1, 1989).

_____. "Talkin' Union," *Library Journal* 114(19):20, 22 (Nov. 15, 1989).

Harger, Elaine, and Mark Rosenzweig. "Talkin' Union: Strikes at Bridgeport and Brown," *Library Journal* 116(1):31 (Jan. 1991).

* Harlow, Neal. "Misused Librarians," *Library Journal* 90(7):1597–1599 (Apr. 1, 1965).

Harrelson, Larry E. "Large Libraries and Information Desks," *College & Research Libraries* 35(1):21–27 (Jan. 1974).

Harrington, Jan. "Human Relations in Management During Periods of Economic Uncertainty," *Drexel Library Quarterly* 17(2):16–26 (1982).

Harris, Diane. "Salary Survey 1995," *Working Woman* 20(1):25–27 (Jan. 1995).

Harris, Roma M. "Gender, Power, and the Dangerous Pursuit of Professionalism," *American Libraries* 2(9):874–76 (Oct. 1993).

_____. *Librarianship: The Erosion of a Woman's Profession.* Norwood NJ: Ablex, 1992.

_____. "The Mentoring Trap," *Library Journal* 118(17):37–39 (Oct. 15, 1993).

Hart, E. D., and W. J. Griffith. "Professional or Clerical," *Library Journal* 86(15):2758–2759 (Sep. 1, 1961).

Hawley, Brenda G. "Paralibrarians—A Celebration," *Colorado Libraries* 13(2):10–11 (June 1987).

Hawley, Frances B. "Some Non-Technical Qualifications for Library Work," *Library Journal* 29(7):360–362 (July 1904).

Hazeltine, Mary Imogene. "Keep Them Profitably Busy—These New Assistants," *Library Journal* 65(20):943–946 (Nov. 15, 1940).

Head Librarian. "[Thank you...]." Letter. *Public Libraries* 21(6):262 (June 1916).

Heathcote, Lesley M. "Men Librarians." Letter. *Library Journal* 75(7):518, 520 (Apr. 1, 1950).

Heim, Kathleen M., et al. "Staff Utilization in Libraries: The Historical and Environmental Context for Renewed Attention to Education, Role Definition, and Articulation with Special Consideration of Medicine and Law," *LLA Bulletin* 52(4):149–157 (Spr. 1990).

Held, Charles Holborn. *The Status of Library Technicians in the United States.* Ph.D. dissertation. Wayne State University. Ann Arbor MI: University Microfilms, 1969.

Heller, Scott. "Clerical Workers Gaining Attention Through Unions," *Chronicle of Higher Education* 29(19):1, 28 (Jan. 23, 1985).
* Henerey, Eleanora M. "A Direct Answer, Please." Letter. *Special Libraries* 60(3):174 (Mar. 1969).
Henry, Elizabeth G. "Staff Rotation and Exchange," *Wilson Bulletin for Librarians* 12(5):307–308, 313 (Jan. 1938).
Henry, William E. "Living Salaries for Good Service," *Library Journal* 44(5):282–284 (May 1919).
_____. "The Salary Question," *Public Libraries* 25(3):121–123 (Mar. 1920).
Herbert, Clara W. "Recruiting a Training Class: An Experience and Some Reflections Thereon," *Library Journal* 44(2):107–109 (Feb. 1, 1919).
Hermelin, Francine G. "Legislating Fair Pay," *Working Woman* 20(1):34 (Jan. 1995).
Hernon, Peter, and Charles R. McClure. "Unobtrusive Reference Testing: The 55 Percent Rule," *Library Journal* 111(7):37–41 (Apr. 15, 1986).
Herrman, Jennie. "An Assistant's View of the A.L.A. Meeting," *Public Libraries* 11(8):458 (Oct. 1906).
Herself. "The Case of the Desk Assistant," *Library Journal* 27(10):876–878 (Oct. 1902).
Hewins, Caroline M. "Library Work for Women," *Library Journal* 16(9):273–274 (Sep. 1891).
Heyneman, Alan L. "Librarian Trainee Program," *Library Journal* 84(4):557–560 (Feb. 15, 1959).
Hiatt, Robert M. "Education and Training of Cataloging Staff at the Library of Congress," *Cataloging & Classification Quarterly* 7(4):121–129 (Sum. 1987).
Hiebing, Dottie. "Current Trends in the Continuing Education and Training of Reference Staff," *The Reference Librarian* 30:5–15 (1990).
Hilbert, Rita. [Autobiographical interview in] *Library Mosaics* 2(2):19–20 (Nov./Dec. 1990).
Hildenbrand, Suzanne. "Some Theoretical Considerations on Women in Library History," *Journal of Library History* 18(4):382–390 (Fall 1983).
Hill, Frank P. "Organization and Management of a Library Staff," *Library Journal* 22(8):381–383 (Aug. 1897).
Hitchler, Theresa. "Library School Training Versus Practical Experience," *Library Journal* 42(12):931–938 (Dec. 1917).
_____. "The Successful Loan-Desk Assistant," *Library Journal* 32(12):554–559 (Dec. 1907).
Hoage, Annette L. "Resignations in Two University Libraries," *College & Research Libraries* 11(2):28–32, 39 (Jan. 1950).
Hobson, Charles J., et al. "Circulation/Reserve Desk Personnel Effectiveness," *Journal of Academic Librarianship* 13(2):93–98 (May 1987).
Hodges, Julie E. "Stress in the Library," *Library Association Bulletin* 92(10):751, 753–754 (Oct. 1990).
Hoerr, John. "The Payoff from Teamwork," *Business Week* (#3114):56–62 (July 10, 1989).
Hoffman, Shannon L. "Who Is a Librarian?" *Library Mosaics* 4(4):8–11 (July/Aug. 1993).
Holley, Robert P. "The Future of Catalogers and Cataloging," *Journal of Academic Librarianship* 7(2):90–93 (May 1981).
"Homeless Man Claims Harassment," *Wilson Library Bulletin* 65(3):12 (Nov. 1990).
Horton, Marion. "Library Schools. Los Angeles Public Library," *Public Libraries* 27(5):300 (May 1922).
Hosmer, James Kendall. "The Library Assistant: His Title, Duties, and Relation to His Chief," *Library Journal* 24(7):54–57 (July 1899).

Hostetter, Anita M. "Shortage of Librarians," *ALA Bulletin* 36(6):384–386 (June 1942).
* Houston, Julianne, and Judy Orahood. "We Are All *Professionals*," *Library Mosaics* 1(3):8–11 (Jan./Feb. 1990).
Howard, Paul. "Library Personnel in the Depression," *Library Journal* 64(6):219–222 (Mar. 15, 1939).
Hudson, Judith. "On-the-Job Training for Cataloging and Classification," *Cataloging & Classification Quarterly* 7(4):69–78 (Sum. 1987).
* Huston, Esther. "Alternate' Career Ladders." Letter. *Library Journal* 99(18):2550 (Oct. 15, 1974).
Hyde, Dorsey W., Jr. "Reorganizing the Library Personnel System of the Federal Government," *Public Libraries* 28(5):287–290 (May 1923).
Hyman, Karen. "Dignity in Work?" *Unabashed Librarian* [orig. pub. in *Libraries Unlimited (NJ) Newsletter*] #39:5 (1981).
* Iazzetta, Muriel. "Made to Feel Important." Letter. *Wilson Library Bulletin* 54(10):614, 686 (June 1980).
"Idaho State University Awards Professional Leave to Library Staff Member," *Library Mosaics* 1(5):6 (May/June 1990).
"Illinois Library Association Notes," *Public Libraries* 22(2):73 (Feb. 1917).
Imm, Eumie. "Ask ARLIS IV: Training Paraprofessionals and Support Staff for Reference Work in the Art Library," *Art Documentation* 11(2):78–79 (Sum. 1992).
"Impressions of a Cub Librarian Based on Inexperience," *Public Libraries* 21(2):71–72 (Feb. 1916).
"Indiana's Thirtieth Anniversary. Library Assistants," *Public Libraries* 26(10):620–622 (Dec. 1921).
"Indoor Air Pollution: Foot-Dragging on Solutions," *The Office* 115(3):24 (Mar. 1992).
* "An Interesting Questionnaire," *Public Libraries* 27(4):233 (Apr. 1922).
Intner, Sheila S. "The Education of Copy Catalogers," *Technicalities* 11(3):4–7 (Mar. 1991).
* Isenhart, Deborah. "It's as If I Invaded Their Territory." Letter. *Library Journal* 114(18):6 (Nov. 1, 1989).
"It's Not Fair," *Commonweal* 121(16):3–5 (Sep. 23, 1994).
J. C. D. "Staff Examinations," *Public Libraries* 17(1):8–9 (Jan. 1912).
J. F. "The Over Zealous Library Worker," *Public Libraries* 23(10):466–467 (Dec. 1918).
Jackson, Jim. "In-Service Training," *Associates* 1(2):unpaged (Dec. 1994).
* Jackson, Sidney L. "Gray Manpower Areas." Letter. *Library Journal* 92(12):2311 (June 15, 1967).
Jacobs, Margaret L. "Supervisor-Assistant Relationships," *Wilson Library Bulletin* 19(5):336–337 (Jan. 1945).
Jahoda, Gerald, and Frank Bonney. "The Use of Paraprofessionals in Public Libraries for Answering Reference Questions," *RQ* 29(3):328–331 (Spr. 1990).
Jankowitz, Rachel. "[Investigation narrative]." Letter from NY State's Division of Health and Safety, Sep. 19, 1994.
Jennings, Jennie Thornburg. "Of Good Report." Letter. *Public Libraries* 28(4):186 (Apr. 1923).
Jestes, Edward. "Why Waste Professional Time on Directional Questions?" *RQ* 14(1):13–16 (Fall 1974).
Jones, Adrian. "In Defense of Librarians." Letter. *Internet World* 5(4):8 (June 1994).
Jones, Clara S. "Women in the Inspiration of Librarianship." In *Women in the Library Profession: Leadership Roles and Contributions*, Michigan. University School of Library Science, 1971, pp.16–19.
Jones, Dorothy E. "Library Support Staff and Technology: Perceptions and Opinions," *Library Trends* 37(4):432–456 (Spr. 1989).

Jones, Noragh, and Peter Jordan. *Staff Management in Library and Information Work.* 2nd ed. Brookfield VT: Gower, 1982, 1987.

Josephson, Aksel G.S. "Preparation for Librarianship," *Library Journal* 25(5):226–228 (May 1900).

Joyce, Charles. "The Suppliant Maidens," *Library Journal* 66(22):4247–4249 (Dec. 15, 1961).

Judd, Karen, and Sandy Morales Pope. "The New Job Squeeze," *Ms.* 4(6):86–90 (May/June 1994).

Jurow, Susan. "Preparing for Library Leadership," *Journal of Library Administration* 12(2):57–73 (1990).

* Kalnin, Mary T. "The Case for the Conference: One Paraprofessional's View," *Journal of Education for Library and Information Science* 36(1):22–25 (Wint. 1995).

Kalnin, Mary T., et al. "The Paraprofessional in Today's Libraries," *Library Mosaics* 5(3):16–18 (May/June 1994).

Kamm, Sue. "Take Advantage of the Situation," *Library Journal* 119(12):58–59 (July 1994).

Kao, Mary. "An Open Letter to H. W. Wilson Company, Publisher of *Library Literature,*" *Library Mosaics* 2(1):6 (Sep./Oct. 1990).

Kaplan, Louis. "On the Road to Participative Management: The American Academic Library, 1934–1970," *Libri* 38(4):314–320 (Dec. 1988).

Karpin, Molly. "Sick Building Makes Reader Ill." Letter. *American Libraries* 22(9):842–843 (Oct. 1991).

Kartman, Jon. "Demonstrators Rail Against Enoch Pratt Railings," *American Libraries* 25(8):708–709 (Sep. 1994).

_____. "'Sick Building Syndrome' Shutters Library," *American Libraries* 25(11):979–980 (Dec. 1994).

Kathman, Michael D., and Lenore Felix. "A Library Paraprofessional Pay System," *Library Administration & Management* 4(4):202–204 (Fall 1990).

Katz, Bill. "Magazines: *Library Mosaics,*" *Library Journal* 116(2):112 (Feb. 1, 1991).

Kaufman, Paula T. "Professional Diversity in Libraries," *Library Trends* 41(2):214–230 (Fall 1992).

* Kelley, Grace. "Library Staff Associations," *Public Libraries* 29(10):416–417 (Dec. 1919).

Kemp, Jan. "Reevaluating Support Staff Positions," *Library Administration & Management Association* 9(1):37–43 (Wint. 1995).

Kenady, Carolyn. *Pay Equity: An Action Manual for Library Workers.* Chicago: ALA, 1989.

Kentfield, Kathie. "Public Library Support Staff Survey," *Library Mosaics* 6(2):18–19 (Mar./Apr. 1995).

Kerr, Willie H. "Psychology for Librarians," *Public Libraries* 16(10):425–431 (Dec. 1911).

Kinzer, Rose W. "A Discussion of the Library Aide or Clerk: His Status and Training," *Junior College Journal* 32(4):217–224 (Dec. 1961).

Kirkpatrick, L. N. "Girls as Pages." Letter. *Library Journal* 67(19):918–919 (Nov. 1, 1942).

* Klein, Regina. "Who's Behind the Help Desk?" *Database* 11:15–20 (Aug. 1988).

Kleiner, Kurt. "Seattle's Homeless Surf the Internet," *New Scientist* 143(1938):6 (Aug. 13, 1994).

* Knapp, Patricia B. "Division of Responsibility," *Library Journal* 91(18):4889–4891 (Oct. 15, 1966).

"Knife-Wielding Youth Slays Public Staff Member," *American Libraries* 14(4):174 (Apr. 1983).

Kniffel, Leonard. "Bomb Blast Jolts Library at Michigan's Oakland U.," *American Libraries* 21(3):180-181 (Mar. 1990).

_____. "First Woman to Serve as ALA Executive Director—Linda Crismond Envisions 'the Association of the World,'" *American Libraries* 20(7):622-623 (July/ Aug. 1989).

_____. "NYPL's Healy to AL Readers: 'I will work for you, ... learn "people's library" aspect of job,'" *American Libraries* 20(5):384 (May 1989).

_____. "Two Librarians Slain by Gunman at Sacramento PL," *American Libraries* 24(6):462 (June 1993).

Knight, Hattie M. "Library Technician—A Definition and an Invitation," *Utah Libraries* 7:4-6 (Spr. 1964).

Knowlton, John D. "Headlines Tell Story of LC's History," *Library of Congress Information Bulletin* 50(7):120-122 (Apr. 8, 1991).

Koopman, Harry Lyman. "Vacations and Holidays," *Public Libraries* 21(2):64–65 (Feb. 1916).

Kopp, Gary. "The People Making It Happen." Letter. *Library Journal* 117(3):102 (Feb. 15, 1992).

Kotzin, Mark M. "CSEA Participates in Library Conference," *The Public Sector* [CSEA] 18(2):9 (Feb. 1995).

Kozsely, Marianne Gabriella. *Support Staff in Academic Decision Making.* Master's thesis. Kent State University, Aug. 1991. ERIC # ED 343 587.

Kranick, Frank G. "Librarians Should Stress Personality in Selecting Staff," *Library Journal* 70(2):60–61 (Jan. 15, 1945).

Kranz, Jack. "Paraprofessional Involvement in Music Cataloging: A Case Study," *Cataloging & Classification Quarterly* 10(4):89–98 (1990).

"Kreimer Decides to Appeal," *American Libraries* 23(7):550 (July/Aug. 1992).

Kreiss, Kathleen. "The Sick Building Syndrome in Office Buildings—A Breath of Fresh Air," *New England Journal of Medicine* 328(12):877–878 (Mar. 25, 1993).

Kreitz, Patricia A. "Recruitment and Retention in Your Own Backyard," *College & Research Libraries News* 53(4):237–240 (Apr. 1992).

Kreitz, Patricia A., and Annegret Ogden. "Job Responsibilities and Job Satisfaction at the University of California Libraries," *College & Research Libraries* 51(4):297–312 (July 1990).

Kristi, Carol. "Troy, N.Y., Library May Close as City, County Cut All Funds," *American Libraries* 25(9):808, 810 (Oct. 1994).

Kulp, James, and Edith McCormick. "Librarian Stabbed at Desk," *American Libraries* 6(4):213–214 (Apr. 1975).

Kusack, James M. *Unions for Academic Library Support Staff: Impact on Workers and the Workplace.* New York: Greenwood, 1986.

"LED [Library Education Division, ALA] Statement of Policy: Criteria for Programs to Prepare Library Technical Assistants," *ALA Bulletin* 63(6):787–794 (June 1969).

"LTAs in Medical Libraries: Survey Pegs Their Roles," *Library Journal* 103(10):1016 (May 15, 1978).

* "LTA's Role in Libraries Debated at Arizona Meet," *Library Journal* 103(1):12 (Jan. 1, 1978).

LTA's_____Their Teachers, Their Training: Proceedings of the Council on Library Technology (COLT) Central Region Workshop Held February 5 and 6, 1971, Richard L. Taylor, ed. Chicago: Council on Library Technology, 1971.

"Labor Unions and Libraries," *Public Libraries* 24(8):304–305 (Oct. 1919).

Lamb, Geo. H. "Progress." Letter. *Public Libraries* 19(2 [3]):103 (Mar. 1914).
Lamont, Sylvia. "Non-pros = Low Status for Some...." Letter. *American Libraries* 20(1):28 (Jan. 1989).
Landram, Christina, "A Test for Applicants for Paraprofessional Cataloging Positions," *Cataloging & Classification Quarterly* 4(1):73–79 (Fall 1983).
Laurence, Andrew. "Support Staff and the Law Libraries," *Library Mosaics* 4(1):8–10 (Jan./Feb. 1993).
Laws, Michele. "A Matter of Degrees," *Associates* 1(2):unpaged (Dec. 1994).
Lawson, V. Lonnie, and Larry Dorrell. "Library Directors: Leadership and Staff Loyalty," *Library Administration & Management* 6(4):187–191 (Fall 1992).
Lechner, Carol. "Benefits of a Paraprofessional Section," *Nebraska Library Association Quarterly* 23:11 (Fall 1992).
_____. "An Idea Blossoms: The Paraprofessional Roundtable," *Nebraska Library Association Quarterly* 23:22–23 (Spr. 1992).
Leek, Max. "Confusion in the Staff Lounge," *Library Journal* 119(12):59 (July 1994).
* Lentini, Allan A. "Paraprofessional Position and Classification Review by Librarians at Cornell University Libraries," *Journal of Academic Librarianship* 11(2): 154–158 (July 1985).
Lewis, Eleanor F. "An Experiment in Self-Government," *Public Libraries* 12(8):304–306 (Oct. 1907).
Lewis, Helen. "Beyond Bread and Butter: Professional Unionism," *Library Personnel News* 3 (2):18–20 (Spr. 1989).
Lewis, Ralph W. "Miss Fibblesworth, Doctors, Bedpans and Such," *Special Libraries* 60(9):606–608 (Nov. 1969).
Librarian. "The Antagonized Public Again," *Public Libraries* 11(7):373 (July 1906).
_____. "Ill-Health Among Library Workers," *Public Libraries* 12(1):11 (Jan. 1907).
_____. "Like a Burden or Refrain." Letter. *Public Libraries* 20(1):11 (Jan. 1915).
_____. "A Wail of Despair." Letter. *Public Libraries* 21(5):215–216 (May 1916).
"Librarian Explains New Security Measures: Letters Sent to Scholarly Societies," *Library of Congress Information Bulletin* 51(11):230 (June 1, 1992).
"Librarians & Low-Level Jobs: An Issue at UC Campuses," *Library Journal* 99(10):1350 (May 15, 1974).
"Librarians' Image," *Unabashed Librarian* #39:4 (1981).
"Libraries and the M.L.S." *Women in Libraries* 18(2):4–5 (Nov./Dec. 1988).
The Library and Its Workers: Reprints of Articles and Addresses, Jessie Sargent McNiece, ed. New York: Wilson, 1929.
Library Assistant. "Antagonism between the Public and Library Assistants." Letter. *Public Libraries* 11(5):256 (May 1906).
"Library Assistants: Shortcomings and Desirable Qualifications," *Library Journal* 29(7):349–359 (July 1904).
"Library Education and the Talent Shortage," *Library Journal* 91(7):1761–1773 (Apr. 1, 1966).
"Library Employment vs. the Library Profession," *Library Notes* 1:50–51 (June 1886).
Library Journal Editors. [Editorial on Adelaide Hasse's removal from directorship of NYPL]. *Library Journal* 44(8):488 (Aug. 1919).
Library Literature. New York: H. W. Wilson Co., 1990 & 1992.
"Library Meeting: Massachusetts. Reference Work," *Public Libraries* 19(2 [3]):117–119 (Mar. 1914).
"Library Meetings. Indiana," *Public Libraries* 20(1):21–24 (Jan. 1915).
* "Library Meetings. New York," *Public Libraries* 22(6):235–236 (June 1917).

Library of Congress Subject Headings. 17th ed. Washington DC: Library of Congress Cataloging Distribution Service, 1994. Vol. 3.

"Library Schools. New York State Library," *Public Libraries* 22(8):343 (Oct. 1917).

"Library Schools. Riverside Instruction in Library Service," *Public Libraries* 30(3): 91–93, 141–142 (Mar. 1915).

"Library Schools: Groping, Going, Gone," *School Library Journal* 38(2):12, 14 (May 1992).

"Library Work as an Occupation," *Public Libraries* 25(8):444 (Oct. 1920).

* Liedorff, Marilyn. "Interview: 'From Paraprofessional to Librarian,'" *Nebraska Library Association Quarterly* 23:36–43 (Spr. 1992).

Lilore, Doreen. *The Local Union in Public Libraries*. Hamden CT: Library Professional Publications/Shoestring, 1984.

Line, Maurice, and Keith Robertson. "Staff Development in Libraries," *British Journal of Academic Librarianship* 4(3):161–175 (1989).

* Lipow, Anne Grodzins. "Training for Change: Staff Development in a New Age," *Journal of Library Administration* 10(4):87–97 (Dec. 1989).

Lipow, Anne, et al. *A Report on the Status of Women Employed in the Library of the University of California, Berkeley, with Recommendations for Affirmative Action*. Berkeley: Library Affirmative Action Program for Women Committee, Dec. 1971. ERIC # ED 066 163.

* Liptak, Stephany. "Grassroots Movement," *Library Mosaics* 4(4):17 (July/Aug. 1993).

*_____. "Grassroots Movements," *Colorado Libraries* 18:38–39 (Dec. 1992).

_____. "Lucy Schweers on Paralibrarians and CLA," *Colorado Libraries* 13(2):11–12 (June 1987).

_____. "Paralibrarians and the Colorado Library Association," *Colorado Libraries* 16:51 (Dec. 1990).

Liverpool, E. "Oxygen for Libraries." Letter. *Public Libraries* 22(2):59 (Feb. 1917).

"Local Press Defends Ann Arbor PL Behavior Rules Banning Problem Patrons," *American Libraries* 16(1):7 (Jan. 1985).

Longland, Jean R. "Library Technicians: Strong Convictions." Letter. *Special Libraries* 59(7):535 (Sep. 1968).

Longsworth, Eileen B. "A School Too Far." Letter. *American Libraries* 22(9):841–842 (Oct. 1991).

Lowry, Charles B. "Managing Technology: Perspectives and Prospects for a New Paradigm," *Journal of Academic Librarianship* 19(4):237–238, 246 (Sept. 1993).

Luke, Robert A. "Technical Training for Nonprofessional Assistants," *Library Journal* 67(5):201–203 (Mar. 1, 1942).

Lynch, Beverly P., and Jo Ann Verdin. "Job Satisfaction in Libraries: Relationships of the Work Itself, Age, Sex, Occupational Group, Tenure, Supervisory Level, Career Commitment, and Library Department," *Library Quarterly* 53(4):434–447 (Oct. 1983).

_____. "Job Satisfaction in Libraries: A Replication," *Library Quarterly* 57(2):190–202 (April 1987).

Lynch, Mary Jo. "Librarians' Salaries: Increasing at a Decreasing Rate," *American Libraries* 24(10):945 (Nov. 1993).

Lynch, Mary Jo, and Keith Curry Lance. "M.L.S. Librarians in Public Libraries: Where They Are and Why It Matters," *Public Libraries* 32(4):204–207 (July/Aug. 1993).

Lynden, Frederick C. *Unionization in ARL Libraries. SPEC Kit 118*. Washington DC: Systems and Procedures Exchange Center, Office of Management Studies, Association of Research Libraries, Oct. 1985. ERIC # ED 264 881.

Lynden, Frederick C., and Ronald K. Fark. "Management Lessons from Negotiations with Support Staff." In *Options for the 80s: Proceedings of the Second National Conference of the Association of College and Research Libraries*, Michael D. Kathman and Virgil F. Massman, eds. Greenwich CT: JAI, 1982, pp. 89–98.

Maack, Mary Niles. "Toward a History of Women in Librarianship: A Critical Analysis with Suggestions for Further Research," *Journal of Library History* 17(2): 164–185 (Spr. 1982).

* McBride, Patricia. "Pro vs. Parapro." Letter. *Library Journal* 100(10):896 (May 15, 1975).

MacCampbell, James C. "Better Utilization of Personnel," *Library Journal* 102(15): 1718–1720 (Sep. 1, 1977).

McCaslin, Sharon. "The Displacement of Mary Jones," *American Libraries* 21(3): 186–191 (Mar. 1990).

McClure, Laura. "Harvard Workers Form New Union," *New Directions for Women* 17(4):3 (Sep./Oct. 1988).

McCollough, Ethel F. "The Power of Choice," *Public Libraries* 28(1):4–6 (Jan. 1923).

McCormick, Edith. "Clerical Workers Strike at Brown Universities," *American Libraries* 22(1):13 (Jan. 1991).

_____. "President-elect Says ALA Must Forcefully Address the Problem of Underfunding," *American Libraries* 24(7):668 (July/Aug. 1993).

* McCoy, Ralph E. "Personnel in Circulation Service," *Library Trends* 6(1):42–51 (July 1957).

_____. "Personnel Policies and Problems in Public Libraries," *Illinois Libraries* 48:492–496 (June 1966).

McCulley, Lucretia, and Dan Ream. "From the Editors," *Virginia Librarian* 41:3 (Apr./June 1995).

McCune, Bonnie. "Leading Technology by the Nose: Denver Public's Booktech 2000," *Wilson Library Bulletin* 68(3):33–35 (Nov. 1993).

McDaniel, Julie Ann, and Judith K. Ohles. *Training Paraprofessionals for Reference Service*. New York: Neal-Schuman, 1993.

McDiarmid, Errett W. "Training of Clerical and Subprofessional Workers," in *Education for Librarianship: Papers Presented at the Library Conference, University of Chicago, August 16–21, 1948*, Bernard Berelson, ed. Chicago: American Library Association, 1949, pp. 232–253.

Mace, Janis M. "Creighton University's Reference Paraprofessionals," *Library Mosaics* 4(3):15–16 (May/June 1993).

*_____. "A Paraprofessional Jesuit College Wage Survey," *Library Mosaics* 3(4):8–9 (July/Aug. 1992).

McLane, Susan A. "A College Desk Assistant Looks at Her Job," *Wilson Library Bulletin* 23(4):308–309 (Dec. 1948).

McMillan, Mary. "Some Causes of Ill Health Among Library Workers," *Public Libraries* 8(9):412–414 (Nov. 1903). [Macmillan, Mary. "The Relation of Librarian and Assistants," *Library Journal* 28(10):717–718 (Oct. 1903), is a condensed version of this same speech, which was given at Lake Placid.]

McMullen, Haynes. "The Very Slow Decline of the American Social Library," *Library Quarterly* 55(2):207–225 (Apr. 1985).

McNair, Jeanene. "Merit Pay for Librarians: The Florida Academic Model," *Library Personnel News*, 3(2):21–24 (Spr. 1989).

McNeal, Archie I. "Ratio of Clerical to Professional Staff," *College & Research Libraries* 17(3):219–223 (May 1956).

McReynolds, Rosalee. "The Sexual Politics of Illness in Turn of the Century Libraries," *Libraries & Culture* 25(2):194–217 (Spr. 1990).

Maddox, Lucy J. "Collegiate Training for Library Technicians," *Special Libraries* 51(6):293–294 (July/Aug. 1960).

Maguire, Constance J. "New Students Need New Schools." Letter. *Library Journal* 118(3):106 (Feb. 15, 1993).

Makinen, Ruth H., and Susan Speer. "Paraprofessional Staff: A Review and Report on Current Duty Assignment in Academic Health Sciences Libraries in North America," *Bulletin of the Medical Library Association* 81(2):135–140 (Apr. 1993).

"Making the ALA, COLT and Techniques Work," *Library Mosaics* 1(2):6–8 (Nov./Dec. 1989).

* Malia, Elizabeth. "What's in a Name? It Depends," *Colorado Libraries* 13(2):16–17 (June 1987).

* Manley, Marian C. "The Library Workers' Association." Letter. *Library Journal* 45(9):424 (May 1, 1920).

Manley, Will. "Facing the Public," *Wilson Library Bulletin* 63(3):82–83 (Nov. 1988).

_____. *The Manley Art of Librarianship.* Jefferson NC: McFarland, 1993.

_____. *Unprofessional Behavior: Confessions of a Public Librarian.* Jefferson NC: McFarland, 1992.

_____. "Why Do Librarians Want to Be Animals?" *American Libraries* 25(8):771 (Sep. 1994).

Marchant, Maurice P. "The Closing of the Library School at Brigham Young University," *American Libraries* 23(1):32–33, 36 (Jan. 1992).

Marcum, Deanna B. "The Rural Library in America at the Turn of the Century," *Libraries & Culture* 26(1):87–99 (Wint. 1991).

Mark, Linda. "Trouble with a Capital T: Teens in Troubled Times," *Wilson Library Bulletin* 69(3):11 (Nov. 1994).

Marot, Helen. *American Labor Unions.* New York: Holt, 1914.

Martell, Charles. "The Letter 'Y'," *Journal of Academic Librarianship* 19(3):139 (July 1993).

_____. "The Nature of Authority and Employee Participation in the Management of Academic Libraries," *College & Research Libraries* 48(2):110–122 (Mar. 1987).

Martin, Kathleen M. "Finding Our Voice: Support Staff in Professional Organizations," *Journal of Education for Library and Information Science* 36(1):26–28 (Wint. 1995).

Martin, Laura K. "Let's Start with People," *ALA Bulletin* 45(4):133–135 (Apr. 1951).

* Martin, Sara. "Ethics and the Paraprofessional," *Library Mosaics* 3(4):17 (July/Aug. 1992).

* Martinez, Edward B. "Certification of Library Support Staff," *Library Mosaics* 2(6):7–10 (Nov./Dec. 1991).

_____. "Give Us Five," *Library Mosaics* 5(5):5 (Sep./Oct. 1994).

_____. "In the Beginning, There Was Support Staff...," *Library Mosaics* 1(1):6–8 (Sep./Oct. 1989).

_____. "MIG Shines Golden at the ALA," *Library Mosaics* 3(4):15 (Sep./Oct. 1992).

_____. "Of Horns and Lambs and Lessons Learned," *Library Mosaics* 2(7):5 (Sep./Oct. 1991).

*_____. "Preference for Reference," *Library Mosaics* 4(3):5 (May/June 1993).

_____. "Say Hey!" *Library Mosaics* 1(4):5 (Mar./Apr. 1990).

_____. "What's Professionalism Got to Do with It?" *Library Mosaics* 1(3):5 (Jan./Feb. 1990).

_____. "Writing the Support Staff Story," *Journal of Education for Library and Information Science* 36(1):38–41 (Wint. 1995).

* Martinez, Ed, et al. "Library Support Staff Salary Survey 1989," *Library Mosaics* 1(6):8–14 (July/Aug. 1990).

Martinez, Ed, and Raymond Roney. "Library Support Staff Salary Survey 1990," *Library Mosaics* 2(6):8–12 (July/Aug. 1991).

_____. "1993 Library Support Staff Salary Survey," *Library Mosaics* 5(3):6–10 (May/June 1994).

Martinson, John. *Vocational Training for Library Technicians: A Survey of Experience to Date.* Washington DC: Communication Service Corp., 1965.

Masek, Doris. Letter. *American Libraries* 22(3):218 (Mar. 1991).

* Massey, Tinker. "Educating Support Staff: A Continuous Programming for the Future," *Journal of Education for Library and Information Science* 36(1):3–4 (Wint. 1995).

_____. "Mentoring: A Means to Learning," *Journal of Education for Library and Information Science* 36(1):52–54 (Wint. 1995).

Mayo, Elna Ann. "You've Come a Long Way, Paraprofessionals!" *Virginia Librarian* 39:17–18 (Jan.-Mar. 1993).

"Md. Library Clerks Seek Parity with Liquor Clerks," *Library Journal* 101(6):770 (Mar. 15, 1976).

[Meeting]. "American Library Association, July 5–9, 1898 (Lakewood, N.Y.)," *Public Libraries* 3(8):294–319 (Oct. 1898).

"Meeting of the A.L.A. at Louisville. Lending Department Round Table," *Public Libraries* 22(8):321 (Oct. 1917).

Meiseles, Linda, and Sue Feller. "Training Serials Specialists: Internships as an Option," *Library Administration & Management* 8(2):83–86 (Spr. 1994).

Melum, Verna V. "Training Clerical Aides," *Wilson Library Bulletin* 23(9):692–696 (May 1949).

Mentges, Mark. "Library Paraprofessionals in Academic Libraries—Where to Now?" *Library Mosaics* 2(4):14–15 (Mar./Apr. 1991).

Menzies, Richard, et al. "The Effect of Varying Levels of Outdoor-Air Supply on the Symptoms of Sick Building Syndrome," *New England Journal of Medicine* 328(12):821–827 (Mar. 25, 1993).

Meyer, Robert S. "Library Technician Training Programs and Special Libraries," *Special Libraries* 59(6):453–456 (July-Aug. 1968).

Meyer, Thomas J. "Clerical and Technical Workers at Yale U. Approve Contract, End 4-Month Dispute," *Chronicle of Higher Education* 29(20):27 (Jan. 30, 1985).

"Mid-Winter Meeting of A.L.A.," *Public Libraries* 28(2):75–85 (Feb. 1923).

Miksa, Francis L. "The Columbia School of Library Economy," *Libraries & Culture* 23(3):249–280 (Sum. 1988).

Milden, James W. "Women, Public Libraries, and Library Unions: The Formative Years," *Journal of Library History* 12(2):150–158 (Spr. 1977).

Miletich, L. N. "Pulling Together: A 21st Century Management Primer for the Befuddled, Benumbed & Bewildered," *Journal of Library Administration* 14(1):35–49 (1991).

Miller, Lynn, et al. "A Long Way to Go: Feminist Personnel Issues," *New Jersey Libraries* 16:1–8 (Fall 1983).

Miller, Rosanna. "The Paraprofessional," *Library Journal* 100(6):551–554 (March 15, 1975).

Miller, Rush. "Support Staffs in Academic Libraries: The Dilemma and the Challenge," *Journal of Educational Media & Library Sciences* 25(4):355–366 (1988).

Miller, Ruth H., and H. Scott Davis. *Support Staff Involvement in Library Planning: A Staff Development Activity.* 1990. ERIC ED # 322 923.

Mitchell, Oreada. "Focus Group Afterthoughts," *Colorado Libraries* 17(2):32 (June 1991).

Mixer, Charles W. [Re: Calling "assistants" "librarians"]. *Wilson Bulletin for Librarians* 13(4):266 (Dec. 1938).

Molyneux, Robert E. "Staffing Patterns and Library Growth at ARL Libraries, 1962/63 to 1983/84," *Journal of Academic Librarianship* 12(5):292–297 (Nov. 1986).

Montag, John. "Choosing How to Staff the Reference Desk," *The Reference Librarian* 14:31–37 (Spr./Sum. 1986).

Montgomery, Edward B. "Accept the Shortcomings," *Library Journal* 91(18):4897–4898 (Oct. 15, 1966).

Morse, Anna L. "Credit for Staff Members." Letter. *Public Libraries* 12(3):93 (Mar. 1907).

Mort, Sarah Louise. *Toward Effective Motivation of Academic Library Support Staff: Identifying and Correlating Motivators Valued with Demographic Attributes.* Ph.D. dissertation. Indiana University. Ann Arbor MI: U.M.I., 1992.

* Mosebauer, Geraldine C. "Knowledge from an Experienced Guide." Letter. *Special Libraries* 60(3):174–175 (Mar. 1969).

Mosher, William E. "Implications of an Enlightened Personnel Policy," *Library Journal* 62(20):849–852 (Nov. 15, 1937).

Mourer, Lyle E. [Autobiographical interview in] *Library Mosaics* 5(3):27 (May/June 1994).

Muesser, Emilie. "An Interesting Experiment," *Public Libraries* 23(10):483 (Dec. 1918).

Mugnier, Charlotte Marie. *The Library Assistant: High Level Paraprofessional.* Ph.D. dissertation. Columbia University. Ann Arbor MI: Xerox University Microfilms, 1976.

_____. *The Paraprofessional and the Professional Job Structure.* Chicago: ALA, 1980.

Mulcahy, Fred. "No Free Rides for Dumb Students," *Newsweek* 124(7):12 (Aug. 15, 1994).

Muller, Robert H. "Principles Governing the Employment of Nonprofessional Personnel in University Libraries," *College & Research Libraries* 26(3):225–226 (May 1965).

Munn, Ralph Russell. "It Is a Mistake to Recruit Men," *Library Journal* 118(19):S10 (Nov. 15, 1993—Reprint, orig. Nov. 1, 1949).

_____. "Morale Improves Thru Belonging," *Library Journal* 74(5):515–518 (Apr. 1, 1949).

Murfin, Marjorie, and Charles Albert Bunge. "Paraprofessionals at the Reference Desk," *Journal of Academic Librarianship* 14(1):10–14 (Mar. 1988).

Murgai, Saria R. "Attitudes Toward Women as Managers in Library and Information Science," *Sex Roles* 24(11/12):681–700 (June 1991).

Myers, Marcia J., and Paula T. Kaufman. "ARL Directors: Two Decades of Changes," *College & Research Libraries* 52(3):241–254 (May 1991).

Myers, Margaret. Letter. [March 24, 1992].

"NYLA Nonpros Urge Creation of Support Staff Unit," *Library Journal* 101(2):301 (Jan. 15, 1976).

NYSLAA membership packet, 1994.

* Nagel, Mary, and Jeanne Molloy. "In Praise of Students as Supervisors," *College & Research Libraries News* 52(9):577–578 (Oct. 1991).

Nahl, Diane, et al. "Effectiveness of Fieldwork at an Information Desk: A Prototype for Academic Library-Library School Collaboration," *Journal of Academic Librarianship* 20(5/6):291–294 (Nov. 1994).

Napoli, Maryann. "Decoding the Clinton Health Care Plan," *Ms* 4(5):58–62 (Mar./Apr. 1994).

Nauratil, Marcia J. *The Alienated Librarian.* Westport CT: Greenwood, 1989.

Neal, James G. "Staff Turnover and the Academic Library." In *Options for the 80s: Proceedings of the Second National Conference of the Association of College and Research Libraries*, Michael D. Kathman and Virgil F. Massman, eds. Greenwich CT: JAI, 1982, pp. 99–106.

Nettlefold, Brian A. "Paraprofessionalism in Librarianship," *International Library Review* 21(4):519–531 (Oct. 1989).

Neville, Sandra H. "Job Stress and Burnout: Occupational Hazards for Services Staff," *College & Research Libraries* 42(3):242–247 (May 1981).

Nevin, Susanne. "Minnesota Opportunities for Technical Services Excellence (MOTSE): An Innovative CE Program for Technical Services Staff," *Library Resources & Technical Services* 38(2):195–198 (Apr. 1994).

"New Career 'Ladders' Pose Status Threat to Librarians," *Library Journal* 99(13):1746 (July 1974).

New England Parts. "Another Side of the Struggle." Letter. *Public Libraries* 25(5):251 (May 1920).

"New Jersey Association of Library Assistants," *Library Mosaics* 2(7):10 (Sep./Oct. 1991).

"The New President of the A.L.A.," *Public Libraries* 16(6):249 (June 1911).

"New York State Library Association [meeting]. Tuesday. The Desk Assistant," *Public Libraries* 6(9):560–563 (Nov. 1901).

Nicholson, John B., et al. *Library Technicians—A New Kind of Needed Library Worker: A Report of a Conference on Library Technology Sponsored by Catonsville Community College (Chicago, May 26–27, 1967).* Catonsville Community College MD: June 1967. ERIC # ED 017 277.

* "Nonpro Library Supervisors: COLT Takes a Stand," *Library Journal* 100(10):908 (May 15, 1975).

"Nonprofessionals Organize in Greater Phoenix," *Library Journal* 95(8):1428 (Apr. 15, 1970).

"Nonprofessionals Ponder Separate Organization," *Library Journal* 93(12):2410, 2414 (June 15, 1968).

Norris, Helen L. "We Insist on a Third Classification!" *Library Journal* 76(5):392–394 (May 1, 1951).

"Not the Big One II," *American Libraries* 23(8):628–636 (Sep. 1992).

* Nourse, Jimmie Anne, and Patricia C. Profeta. "Indian River Community College's LTA Program: A Model," *Journal of Education for Library and Information Science* 36(1):16–21 (Wint. 1995).

Nourse, Louis M. "Speaking for the Dissatisfied Young Assistant," *American Library Association Bulletin* 31(10):629–634 (Oct. 1, 1937).

Nyren, Karl. "Libraries and Labor Unions," *Library Journal* 92(11):2115–2121 (June 1, 1967).

_____. "Picket Lines and Paradises," *Library Journal* 110(20):20, 22, 24 (Dec. 1985).

Oberg, Larry R. "The Emergence of the Paraprofessional in Academic Libraries: Perceptions and Realities," *College & Research Libraries* 53(2):99–112 (Mar. 1992).

_____. "Paraprofessionals and the Future of Librarianship: An Interview with Larry R. Oberg," *Library Mosaics* 4(6):8–10 (Nov./Dec. 1993).

_____. "Paraprofessionals: Shaping the New Reality," *College & Research Libraries* 52(1):3–4 (Jan. 1991).

_____. "*Response* to Hammond: 'Paraprofessionals at the Reference Desk: The End of the Debate,'" *The Reference Librarian* 17(37):105–107 (1992).

* _____. "Rethinking Reference: Smashing Icons at Berkeley," *College & Research Libraries News* 54(5):265–266 (May 1993).

Oberg, Larry R., et al. "Faculty Perceptions of Librarians at Albion College: Status, Role, Contribution, and Contacts," *College & Research Libraries* 50(2):215–230 (Mar. 1989).

_____. "Rethinking Ring and Shapiro: Some Responses," *College & Research Libraries News* 55(3):145–148 (Mar. 1994).

_____. "The Role, Status, and Working Conditions of Paraprofessionals: A National Survey of Academic Libraries," *College & Research Libraries* 53(3):215–238 (May 1992).

O'Brien, Jane, and Joseph A. Cowans. "LTA World! The Next Generation," *Library Administration & Management* 9(1):19–22 (Wint. 1995).

O'Connell, Kay. "Indecent Exposure: Sex Offenses in the Library," *ALKI* 9(2):17–18 (July 1993).

An Old Librarian. "Library Needs," *Public Libraries* 27(7):400–401 (July 1922).

"On the Agenda," *American Libraries* 24(11):979 (Dec. 1993).

One Who Has Been There. "The Assistant—Why Anonymous?" *Library Journal* 20(8):266 (Aug. 1895).

One Who Isn't. "The Anonymous Assistant," *Library Journal* 20(7):241–242 (July 1895).

Orahood, Judy A. "Library Classified Staff Issues," *Library Personnel News* 3:41 (Sum. 1989).

Orne, Jerrold. "Why Non-Librarians to Academic Library Posts?" Letter. *Library Journal* 80(14):1618–1620 (Aug. 1955).

"'Other Compensations': A Story," *Public Libraries* 16(10):431–432 (Dec. 1911).

"Pacific Northwest Library Association. Library Assistants," *Public Libraries* 25(10):594–595 (Dec. 1920).

Palmini, Cathleen C. "The Impact of Computerization on Library Support Staff: A Study of Support Staff in Academic Libraries in Wisconsin," *College & Research Libraries* 55(2):119–127 (Mar. 1994).

"Papers and Proceedings. Ottawa Convention, A.L.A., 1912," *Public Libraries* 17(10):419–420 (Dec. 1912).

Para, A. [pseud.] "Thanks for the Invitation," *Colorado Libraries* 15:12–13 (Mar. 1989).

Paris, Marion. "The Dilemma of Library School Closings." In *Libraries and Information Services Today*, June Lester, ed. Chicago: ALA, 1991, pp. 23–27.

_____. "Why Library Schools Fail," *Library Journal* 115(16):38–42 (Oct. 1, 1990).

Parks, James B. "Sham Union Bill Assaults Worker Rights," *AFL-CIO News* 40(3):1, 3 (Feb. 6, 1995).

Parmer, Coleen, and Dennis East. "Job Satisfaction among Support Staff in Twelve Ohio Academic Libraries," *College & Research Libraries* 54(1):43–57 (Jan. 1993).

Parsons, Jerry L. "Characteristics of Research Library Directors, 1958 and 1973," *Wilson Library Bulletin* 50(8):613–617 (Apr. 1976).

Passet, Joanne Ellen. "Men in a Feminized Profession: The Male Librarian, 1887–1921," *Libraries & Culture* 28(4):385–402 (Fall 1993).

_____. "Reaching the Rural Reader: Travelling Libraries in America, 1892–1920," *Libraries & Culture* 26(1):100–118 (Wint. 1991).

Pearson, Adona. "'Respect Library Technicians." Letter. *Library Journal* 115(9):8 (May 15, 1990).

Peelle, Linda. "What It's Like to Work for a Dying Library," *Library Mosaics* 3(1):10–12 (Jan./Feb. 1992).

* Person, James E. "Technician Training." Letter. *Library Journal* 92(18):3571 (Oct. 15, 1967).

"A Personnel Formula," *Library Journal* 80(6):600–605 (Mar. 15, 1955).

Pesek, James G., and Joseph P. Grunenwald. "An Analysis of the Use and Effectiveness of Various Recruitment Sources at Public Libraries," *Public Library Quarterly* 10(3):45–56 (1990).

Pettee, Julia E. "The Library Assistant Once More: A Plea for Our Professional Ideal," *Library Journal* 29(11):584–587 (Nov. 1904).

Pfeil, Dorothea Sanderson. "More Thoughts on Professionalism." Letter. *Special Libraries* 57(2):124 (Feb. 1966).

Phillips, Edna. "Staff Progress Measurement." Letter. *Wilson Library Bulletin* 17(4):330 (Dec. 1942).

Phinney, Eleanor. "About Library Training." Letter. *Library Journal* 72(3):208 (Feb. 1, 1947).

Pidduck, Janice. "A Curriculum for Library Clerical Aides," *Journal of Secondary Education* 13(7):406–409 (Nov. 1938).

Pierce, Sydney J. "Dead Germans and the Theory of Librarianship," *American Libraries* 23(8):641–643 (Sep. 1992).

Plaiss, Mark. "Libraryland: Pseudo-Intellectuals and Semi-Dullards," *American Libraries* 21(6):588–589 (June 1990).

Plummer, Mary Wright. "Campaign of Library Publicity in the General Magazines," *Public Libraries* 19(2):41–42 (Feb. 1914).

Podolsky, Arthur. *Public Libraries in 50 States and the District of Columbia: 1989.* [Washington, DC]: U.S. Department of Education, Office of Educational Research and Improvement, National Center for Education Statistics, Apr. 1991.

Pollakoff, Stanley R. "Hostile to Healy." Letter. *American Libraries* 20(6):524 (June 1989).

"Portland Conference. Fifth Session," *Library Journal* 30(9):163–178 (Sep. 1905).

"Positions, Salaries and Conditions," *Public Libraries* 22(3):122 (Mar. 1917).

Pratt Institute Monthly. "Salaries, Hours, and Vacations of Library Graduates," *Library Journal* 24(8):481–482 (Aug. 1899).

_____. "Some Grievances as Viewed from the Other Side," *Public Libraries* 2(3):92–93 (Mar. 1897).

Preece, Barbara G. "Paraprofessional Training in Technical Services," *Illinois Libraries* 72(6):503–505 (Sep. 1990).

"The Preprofessional Program from Three Points of View," *Library Journal* 82(20):2942–2944 (Nov. 15, 1957).

Presley, Roger L., and Carolyn L. Robison. "Changing Roles of Support Staff in an Online Environment," *Technical Services Quarterly* 4(1):25–39 (Fall 1986).

Presthus, Robert. *Technological Change and Occupational Response: A Study of Librarians. Final Report.* Washington DC: Office of Education, Bureau of Research, June 1970.

"Proceedings of the Conference of Librarians, London, October 2nd, 3rd, 4th, and 5th, 1877. Sixth Sitting: Friday Morning, Oct. 5th, at 10," *Library Journal* 2(5–6):272–282 (Jan./Feb. 1878).

Progress and Prospect: A Summary of the Proceedings of the Second Annual Conference of the Council on Library Technology, May 23–25, 1968. COLT, 1968.

Prybil, Lawrence D. "Job Satisfaction in Relation to Job Performance and Occupational Level," *Personnel Journal* 52(2):94–100 (Feb. 1973).

Quigley, Eileen. "The Homeless," *CQ Researcher* 2(29):665–688 (Aug. 7, 1992).

Quinn, Judy, and Michael Rogers. "Library Schools: Confusion and Threat Remain," *Library Journal* 17(6):16–17 (Apr. 1, 1992).

Rader, Hannelore B. "Teamwork and Entrepreneurship," *Journal of Library Administration* 10(2/3):159–168 (1989).

Rais, Shirley. "Managing Your Support Staff: An Insider's View," *American Libraries* 24(9):819–20 (Oct. 1993).

Ranck, Samuel H. "The Welfare of Librarians," *Public Libraries* 25(3):127–130 (Mar. 1920).

Ratcliff, Linda. "California Library Employees Association," *Wilson Library Bulletin* 54(7):447–448 (Mar. 1980).

Rathbone, Josephine Adams. "The Opportunity of the Library Assistant," *Public Libraries* 14(9):[333]–338 (Nov. 1909).

_____. "Requests Sent to One Library School," *Public Libraries* 20(3):116–118 (Mar. 1915).

_____. "Salaries of Library School Graduates," *Library Journal* 39(3):188–190 (Mar. 1914).

_____. "Some Aspects of Our Personal Life," *Public Libraries* 21(2):53–56 (Feb. 1916).

_____. "Standardization in Library Service," *Public Libraries* 27(10):585–590 (Dec. 1922).

Ravdin, Susan B. [Autobiographical interview in] *Library Mosaics* 4(3):22 (May/June 1993).

"Reading the Indicator," *Public Libraries* 22(7):268–273 (July 1917).

Reed, Sarah R. "Library Education Report," *Journal of Education for Librarianship* 7(1):43–47 (Sum. 1966).

Reese, Rena. "The Facts in the Case." Letter. *Public Libraries* 25(6):311–312 (June 1920).

_____. "Training in Medium-Sized Libraries," *Public Libraries* 29(2):53–59 (Feb. 1924).

_____. "Training the Library Assistant," *Public Libraries* 29(8):391–396 (Oct. 1924).

"Report of the Library Employees' Union No. 15590 Greater New York, 1917 to 1919," *Library Journal* 44(8):512–513 (Aug. 1919).

Rich, Lora. "How Can the Beneficence of Libraries Be More Successfully Directed Toward Their Assistants?" *Public Libraries* 25(7):365–368 (July 1920).

Riechel, Rosemarie. *Personnel Needs and Changing Reference Service.* Hamden CT: Library Professional Publications/Shoestring, 1989.

Ring, Daniel F. "Carnegie Libraries as Symbols for an Age: Montana as a Test Case," *Libraries & Culture* 27(1):1–19 (Wint. 1992).

_____. "The Origins of the Butte Public Library: Some Further Thoughts on Public Library Development in the State of Montana," *Libraries & Culture* 28(4):430–444 (Fall 1993).

Robbins, Jane B. "1992: The State of Library and Information Education: An Essay," in *Education for the Library/Information Profession*, Patricia G. Reeling, ed. Jefferson NC: McFarland, 1993, pp. 11–21.

Robbins-Carter, Jane B., et al. "Reactions to '1985 to 1995: The Next Decade in Academic Librarianship,' Parts I and II," *College & Research Libraries* 46(4):309–319 (July 1985).

Robert, James. "Against 'Alternate Ladders.'" Letter. *Library Journal* 99(22):3157 (Dec. 15, 1974).

Robinson, Charles W. "The Electronic Library & BCPL." Letter. *Library Journal* 118(12):8 (July 1993).

_____. "Promise and Fulfillment (More or Less)," *Library Journal* 93(18):3756–3759 (Oct. 15, 1968).

Rocky Mt. Region. "Commitment vs. Struggle," *Public Libraries* 25(4):186–187 (Apr. 1920).

Roden, Carl B. "On a Certain Reticence or Inarticulateness Among Librarians," *Public Libraries* 28(9):489–494 (Nov. 1923).

* Rogers, Sam L. [Reply to Herbert O. Brigham's letter]. *Library Journal* 45(15):699 (Sep. 1, 1920).
Romine-Weyandt, Leah, and Scott C. Weyandt. "Career Challenges for the Paraprofessional," *Library Mosaics* 6(4):17 (July/Aug. 1995).
* Roney, Raymond G. "Changing Job Scene for Support Staff," *Library Personnel News* 2(1):2–3 (Wint. 1988).
Rosenberg, Jane A. "Patronage and Professionals: The Transformation of the Library of Congress Staff, 1890–1907," *Libraries & Culture* 26(2):251–268 (Spr. 1991).
Rosenthal, Joseph A. "Nonprofessionals and Cataloging: A Survey of Five Libraries," *Library Resources & Technical Services* 13(3):321–331 (Sum. 1969).
* Rosenthal, Mary. "Collective Bargaining and Pay Equity," *Library Personnel News* 3(2):24 (Spr. 1989).
_____. "The Impact of Unions on Salaries in Public Libraries," *Library Quarterly* 55(1):52–70 (Jan. 1985).
_____. "Library Unions in Minnesota," *Minnesota Libraries*:102–109 (Wint. 1982).
_____. "Union/Nonunion Wage Differentials in Public Library," *Public Library Quarterly* 6(4);27–41 (Wint. 1985/86).
Rosier, Sharolyn A. "Assaults at the Workplace," *AFL-CIO News* 39(26):5 (Dec. 12. 1994).
*_____. "Working Women Count on Unions, Survey Finds," *AFL-CIO News* 39(23):12 (Oct. 31, 1994).
* Ross, Janet. "Sending a Message: Marketing Your Library for Maximum Impact," *Library Mosaics* 6(2):16 (Mar./Apr. 1995).
Rothstein, Samuel. "Why People Really Hate Library Schools," *Library Journal* 110(6):41–48 (Apr. 1, 1985).
*_____. "Williamson's Message," *Library Journal* 91(18):4884–4885 (Oct. 15, 1966).
Ruben, George. "Collective Bargaining and Labor-Management Relations, 1988," *Monthly Labor Review* 112(1):25–39 (Jan. 1989).
Rubin, Richard. "The Future of Public Library Support Staff," *Public Library Quarterly* 12(1):17–29 (1992).
* Rudnik, Mary Chrysantha. "What Every Librarian Should Know About Library Technical Assistants," *Wilson Library Bulletin* 46(1):67–72 (Sep. 1971).
* Russell, Norman J. *The Job Satisfaction of Non-Professional Library Staff*. Leeds Polytechnic. Department of Library and Information Studies, 1986.
*_____. [Letter to the Editor]. *College & Research Libraries* 46(2):179 (Mar. 1985).
_____. "Professional and Non-Professional in Libraries: The Need for a New Relationship," *Journal of Librarianship* 17(4):293–310 (Oct. 1985).
"Ruth Tolbert," *Library Mosaics* 6(3):8 (May/June 1995).
* Ryan, Susan. "Staff Committees: A Voice for the Paraprofessional," *Library Mosaics* 4(6):16–19 (Nov./Dec. 1993).
Rymer, Anne J. "An Analysis of Work in a Small Public Library," *Wilson Library Bulletin* 13(6):392–4 (Feb. 1939).
"Sacramento Librarians Oppose Non-Pro Mobility," *Library Journal* 99(15):2024–2025 (Sep. 1, 1974).
"Sacramento Proceeds with Exams for Pro Status," *Library Journal* 100(8):716 (Apr. 15, 1975).
Sager, Donald J. *Participatory Management in Libraries*. Metuchen NJ: Scarecrow, 1982.
Sager, Harvey. "Training Online Catalog Assistants: Creating a Friendly Interface," *College & Research Libraries News* 47(11):721–723 (Dec. 1986).
St. Clair, Jeffrey W., and Rao Aluri. "Staffing the Reference Desk: Professionals or Non-Professionals," *Journal of Academic Librarianship* 3(3):149–153 (July 1977).

St. Lifer, Evan. "Are You Happy in Your Job? LJ's Exclusive Report," *Library Journal* 19(18):44–49 (Nov. 1, 1994).

_____. "Bomber Holds Librarian and Patrons Hostage at Utah PL," *Library Journal* 119(6):17 (Apr. 1, 1994).

_____. "How Safe Are Our Libraries?" *Library Journal* 119(13):35–39 (Aug. 1994).

St. Lifer, Evan, and Michael Rogers. "Lib. School Changes Name," *Library Journal* 119(14):126 (Sep. 1, 1994).

_____. "Library Offers Master's Degrees," *Library Journal* 119(15):16, 18 (Sep. 15, 1994).

_____. "U. of KY Schools Merge," *Library Journal* 118(14):124 (Sep. 1, 1993).

_____. "ULC Study Finds Libs. Invest Little in Staff Development," *Library Journal* 118(14):112–113 (Sep. 1, 1993).

_____. "Urban Library Directors: Public Must Perceive Libraries as Safe," *Library Journal* 120(3):107 (Feb. 15, 1995).

Sakers, Don. "Brokering without a License." Letter. *Library Journal* 119(16):10 (Oct. 1, 1994).

"Salaries, Hours, and Vacations in Indiana Libraries," *Library Journal* 39(3):196–198 (Mar. 1914).

* "Salary Increases," *Public Libraries* 25(1):17–19 (Jan. 1920).

Sallee, Denise. "Reconceptualizing Women's History: Anne Hadden and the California County Library System," *Libraries & Culture* 27(4):351–377 (Fall 1992).

* Salmon, Eugene N. "Clerical Aptitude in Library Employment," *College & Research Libraries* 23(4):311–314, 322 (July 1962).

Salter, Charles A., and Jeffrey L. Salter. *On The Frontlines: Coping with the Library's Problem Patrons*. Englewood CO: Libraries Unlimited, 1988.

Sandler, Gary. "One Fewer Librarian." Letter. *American Libraries* 24(10):912 (Nov. 1993).

Sandler, Mark. "Workers Must Read: The Commonwealth College Library, 1925–1940," *Journal of Library History* 20(1):46–67 (Wint. 1985).

Sargent, Dorothy W. "Professional or Clerical?" *Wilson Library Bulletin* 25(1):61–64 (Sep. 1950).

Sarkodie-Mensah, Kwasi. "Paraprofessionals in Reference Services: An Untapped Goldmine," *Library Mosaics* 4(3):8–10 (May/June 1993).

Sass, Rivkah. "The Evolution of Small Libraries in Washington State: Something to SMILE About," *Library Mosaics* 3(1):15–16 (Jan./Feb. 1992).

Sass, Samuel. "After the Afterthoughts." Letter. *Special Libraries* 60(8):565 (Oct. 1969).

* _____. "Librarians Must Be Educated." Letter. *Library Journal* 114(17):6 (Oct. 15, 1989).

* _____. "Library Technicians: A Caution." Letter. *Special Libraries* 59(6):457 (July-Aug. 1968).

_____. "Library Technicians—'Instant Librarians'?" *Library Journal* 92(11):2122–2126 (June 1, 1967).

* _____. "Ranking Librarianship as a Career." Letter. *Special Libraries* 57(9):662 (Nov. 1966).

* _____. "Sauk Squawk." Letter. *Special Libraries* 60(3):177 (Mar. 1969).

* _____. "Vs. Nonpro Mobility." Letter. *Library Journal* 100(5):420 (Mar. 1, 1975).

* Saunders, Carol Stoak, and Russell Saunders. "Effects of Flexitime on Sick Leave, Vacation Leave, Anxiety, Performance, and Satisfaction in a Library Setting," *Library Quarterly* 55(1):71–88 (Jan. 1985).

Sawyer, Ethel R. "How Much Do Imponderables Weigh?" *Public Libraries* 28(8):413–420 (Oct. 1923).

Scanlon, James J. "How to Mix Oil and Water: or, Getting Librarians to Work with Programmers," *College & Research Libraries News* 51(4):320–322 (Apr. 1990).

Scheppke, Jim. "Who's Using the Public Library?" *Library Journal* 119(17):35–37 (Oct. 15, 1994).

Schiller, Anita R. "The Disadvantaged Majority," *American Libraries* 1(4):345–349 (Apr. 1970).

_____. "Women in Librarianship," reprinted in *The Role of Women in Librarianship 1876–1976*, K. Weibel and K. Heim, eds. Phoenix AZ: Oryx, 1979, pp. 222–256.

Schlachter, Gail. "Quasi Unions and Organizational Hegemony within the Library Field," *Library Quarterly* 43(3):185–198 (July 1973).

Schneider, Margaret S. "Stress and Job Satisfaction among Employees in a Public Library System with a Focus on Public Service," *Library & Information Science Research* 13(4):385–404 (Oct.-Dec. 1991).

Schuman, Patricia Glass. "Librarians and Support Staff: We All Make It Happen," *American Libraries* 23(5):415 (May 1992).

Schuman, Patricia Glass, and Arthur Curley. "The Bucks Start Here: ALA Kicks Off Library Funding Campaign," *Library Journal* 119(18):38–40 (Nov. 1, 1994).

* Schuneman, Anita, and Deborah A. Mohr. "Team Cataloging in Academic Libraries: An Exploratory Survey," *Library Resources & Technical Services* 38(3):257–266 (July 1994).

Schuurman, Guy. "Salt Lake County Library System Takes Stock," *Unabashed Librarian* #41:3–4 (1981).

Schwarz, Narda L. "The Professional Attitude," *Library Journal* 102(15):1729–1731 (Sep. 1, 1977).

* Scull, Judy. "A Leg Up to the Light Switch." Letter. *Special Libraries* 60(6):414–415 (July/Aug. 1969).

* "Seattle Zeroes in on Staff Development," *Library Journal* 102(15):1701 (Sep. 1, 1977).

Seavey, Charles A. "A Failure of Vision: Librarians Are Losing the War for Electronic Professional Turf," *American Libraries* 24(10):943–944 (Nov. 1993).

Selby, Janet. "Networking—New York Style," *Library Mosaics* 2(3):14–15 (Jan./Feb. 1991).

Selfe, Glenn. "I'm Not a 'Nonprofessional.'" Letter. *Library Journal* 119(13):8 (Aug. 1994).

* Sellers, Rose Z. "Differences of Opinion." Letter. *Library Journal* 92(14):2685 (Aug. 1967).

Selth, Jefferson P. *Ambition, Discrimination, and Censorship in Libraries*. Jefferson NC: McFarland, 1993.

Sgritta, Verna L. "Recruiting for Stability," *Public Library Quarterly* 12(1):31–39 (1992).

* Shapiro, Lillian L. "We Must Be Doing Something Wrong: Recruiting Young Blood for School Libraries," *Library Journal* 92(10):1992–1994 (May 15, 1967).

* Shea, Frances C. "Recruits from Within." Letter. *Library Journal* 114(17):8 (Oct. 15, 1989).

Sherrer, Johannah. "Job Satisfaction Among Colorado Library Workers," *Colorado Libraries* 11:17–21 (Sum. 1985).

Shields, Gerald R. "Editor's Choice," *ALA Bulletin* 62(9):1063 (Oct. 1968).

Shores, Louis. "Library Technician: A Professional Opportunity," *Special Libraries* 59(4):240–245 (Apr. 1968).

Shostak, Arthur B. *Robust Unionism: Innovations in the Labor Movement*. Ithaca: ILR, 1991.

Shuman, Bruce A. "Problem Patrons in Libraries," *Library & Archival Security* 9(2):3–19 (1989).

"A Significant But Not Unusual Situation." Letter. *Public Libraries* 17(6):212–213 (June 1912).

Simmons, Kendall. "Editorial," *Associates* 1(2):unpaged (Dec. 1994).

_____. "Editorial: Welcome to *Associates*," *Associates* 1(1):unpaged (July 1994).

_____. "From the Editor," *Associates* 2(1):unpaged (July 1995).

_____. "Support Staff Journal," *NYSLAA Network Connection* 7(4):5 (Spr. 1995).

* Slade, Kent. "Certification of Support Staff: What Is It, What Does It Do?" *Journal of Education for Library and Information Science* 36(1):12–15 (Wint. 1995).

* Slavens, Thomas P., and Jean Legg. "Experimenting in Education for Library Associates," *Journal of Education for Librarianship* 11(2):182–185 (Fall 1970).

Slocum, Grace. "Bachelor Librarians: An Interim Training Program," *Library Journal* 93(18):3754–3755 (Oct. 15, 1968).

Smith, Bettye. "A Look into the Role and Purpose of COLT," *Library Mosaics* 1(2):14–15 (Nov./Dec. 1989).

* Smith, Duncan F., and Robert Burgin. "The Motivations of Professional and Paraprofessional Librarians for Participating in Continuing Education Programs," *Library & Information Science Research* 13:405–429 (Oct.-Dec. 1991).

Smith, Sidney B. "A Co-operative Team," *Library Journal* 79(19):2043–2048 (Nov. 1, 1954).

South-Cliffe, Mabel. "A Protest—'Subordinates' vs. 'Assistants,'" *Library Journal* 39(3):198 (Mar. 1914).

"Speaking Right Out." Letter. *Public Libraries* 21(6):262 (June 1916).

Squires, Tilloah. "As the Library Union Sees Things." Letter. *Library Journal* 44(10):672 (Oct. 1919).

_____. "Masculine vs. Feminine Librarians." Letter. *Public Libraries* 25(8):435–436 (Oct. 1920).

"Staffers Claim Albany PL Director Is Trying to Break Their Union," *Library Journal* 119(16):13 (Oct. 1, 1994).

Stanke, Nicky. "Training the Nondegreed Library Worker: How It Is and How It Should Be," *Public Libraries* 27(2):79–81 (Sum. 1988).

"Status of Trained Librarians at Washington," *Public Libraries* 23(9):430–431 (Nov. 1918).

Stearns, Lutie E. "The Question of Library Training," *Library Journal* 30(9):68–71 (Sep. 1905).

Steele, Carl L. "Library Technicians—The Big Controversy," *Special Libraries* 60(1):45–49 (Jan. 1969).

Stephens, Annabel K. "Staff Involvement and the Public Library Planning Process," *Public Libraries* 28:175–181 (May/June 1989).

Sterling, Thomas. "Reclassification: What Good Will It Do Librarians?" *Public Libraries* 28(2):62–64 (Feb. 1923).

Stewart, Nathaniel. "Library In-Service Training, [Pt. I]," *Library Journal* 72(1):16–18 (Jan. 1, 1947).

* Stoddard, Judie. "The North Carolina Library Paraprofessional Association: A Force at Work for the Nineties," *North Carolina Libraries* 48:280–282 (Wint. 1990).

Stone, Elizabeth W. "Introduction," in *New Directions in Staff Development: Moving from Ideas to Action.* Chicago: American Library Association, 1971, pp. 1–5.

Stoops, Louise. "Is This a Problem?" *Special Libraries* 56(5):323 (May-June 1965).

Strohm, Adam. "Being Fit," *Public Libraries* 22(4):135–138 (Apr. 1917).

_____. "The Efficiency of the Library Staff and Scientific Management," *Public Libraries* 17(8):303–306 (Oct. 1912).

Strout, Donald E., and Ruth B. Strout. "Salaries Stronger[,] More Positions," *Library Journal* 82(12):1597–1604 (June 15, 1957).

* Stuart, Margaret. "Profession of Library Science and Trade of Library Science." Letter. *Special Libraries* 59(8):647 (Oct. 1968).
* Sudar, Dan D. "Three Levels of Education," *Library Journal* 91(18):4899–4903 (Oct. 15, 1966).
"Support Staff by Any Other Name...," *Library Mosaics* 1(1):10–12 (Sep./Oct. 1989).
Support Staff Interest[s] Round Table, American Library Association. *National Directory [of] Library Paraprofessional Associations.* [Chicago?]: SSIRT, ALA, Feb. 1995.
Svorenick, Maria. "To Recommend or Not to Recommend." Letter. *Special Libraries* 56(7):531–532 (Sep. 1965).
Sykes, Gayle D. "The MLIS Program Via Distance Education at the College of Library and Information Sciences, University of South Carolina," *Journal of Education for Library and Information Science* 36(1):60–62 (Wint. 1995).
Symmers, Nora. [Autobiographical interview in] *Library Mosaics* 6(4):27 (July/Aug. 1995).
Syracuse University. Graduate Study. Syracuse University School of Information Studies. "Master Program in Library Science, 1992–93."
_____. "Master's Program in Library Science 1994–95."
"Task Force to Address Paraprofessionals Continuing Education Needs," *Library Mosaics* 5(2):7 (Mar./Apr. 1994).
Taylor, Jackie. "The Lowest of the Low: Library Assistants in Public Libraries," *Librarians for Social Change* 9(1):14–15 (1981).
* "Tech Assistant Survey Reveals New Trends," *Library Journal* 94(14):2714, 2717 (Aug. 1969).
"Technicians Seen Emerging as 'Traditional' Librarians," *Library Journal* 93(13):2594 (July 1968).
Teiger, Catherine, and Colette Bernier. "Ergonomic Analysis of Work Activity of Data Entry Clerks in the Computerized Service Sector Can Reveal Unrecognized Skills," *Women & Health* 18(3):67–77 (1992).
["Thank you for the opportunity..."], *Public Libraries* 21(4):173–174 (Apr. 1916).
Thapisa, A. P. N. "The Burden of Mundane Tasks," *British Journal of Academic Librarianship* 4(3):137–160 (1989).
* _____. "The Motivation Syndrome: Job Satisfaction Through the Pay Nexus," *International Library Review* 23(2):141–158 (June 1991).
_____. "Work, Its Significance, Meaning, and Challenges Among Library Assistants," *Journal of Library Administration* 16(4):19–43 (1992).
Thompson, C. Seymour. "'Hearty Support and Approval' of the L. W. A." Letter. *Library Journal* 45(15):712 (Sep. 1, 1920).
Thomson, John. "An Assistants' Club," *Public Libraries* 2(4):147 (Apr. 1897).
Thomson, O. R. Howard. "What the Librarian Has a Right to Expect from the Library School Graduate," *Public Libraries* 30(5):293–296 (May 1925).
Thornton, Mary Helen. "These New Assistants," *Library Journal* 66(20):965–968 (Nov. 15, 1941).
Timberlake, Phoebe. "Paraprofessionals in Louisiana Libraries," *LLA Bulletin* 52(4):147 (Spr. 1990).
Timberlake, Phoebe, and Sybil A. Boudreaux. "Louisiana Libraries and the Role of the Paraprofessional," *LLA Bulletin* 52(4):163–171 (Spr. 1990).
Todd, Katherine. "Collective Bargaining and Professional Associations in the Library Field," *Library Quarterly* 55(3):284–299 (July 1985).
Toolis, Lorna. "Invisible People: Library Assistants," *Emergency Librarian* 4(1):19–21 (1976).
* "Training the LTA: Programs on the Upswing," *Library Journal* 103(10):1015–1016 (May 15, 1978).

Traveler. "Inconsistencies." Letter. *Public Libraries* 22(2):57 (Feb. 1917).
Trumpeter, Margo. "Non-librarians in the Academic Library," *College & Research Libraries* 29(6):461–465 (Nov. 1968).
Tsang, Daniel C. *Collective Bargaining and Academic Libraries: Staff Assistants at Michigan.* Dec. 1976. ERIC # ED 145 809.
* Tuchmayer, H. "Supporting the Support Staff," *North Carolina Libraries* 48:24–52 (Wint. 1990).
* Turner, Anne M. "Appraising Support Staff: Not Just a Silly Paper Ritual," *Library Administration & Management* 4(4):181–183 (Fall 1990).
_____. *It Comes with the Territory: Handling Problem Situations in Libraries.* Jefferson NC: McFarland, 1993.
Turner, Brenda G. "Nonprofessional Staff in Libraries: A Mismanaged Resource," *Journal of Library Administration* 16(4):57–66 (1992).
Turner, Diane J. "The Professional/Paraprofessional Gap: Are There Any Solutions?" *Library Mosaics* 3(4):13 (July/Aug. 1992).
"U.S. Civil Service Examination," *Public Libraries* 20(8):364–365 (Oct. 1915).
* Ulveling, Ralph A. "To What Extent Is It Possible to Segregate Professional from Non-professional Work in a Public Library," *Bulletin of the American Library Association* 30(8):761–762 (Aug. 1936).
"Under Thirty." "The Salary Question Is Not the Only One." Letter. *Library Journal* 45(15):712 (Sep. 1, 1920).
"Union-Busting Charged in Albany," *American Libraries* 25(9):813 (Oct. 1994).
"Union Vote Is Blizzard Fallout," *American Libraries* 24(11):980 (Dec. 1993).
* United States Civil Service Commission. *Position-Classification Standards. Librarian Series GS-1410.* [Washington, DC: Government Printing Office], Feb. 1966.
*_____. *Position-Classification Standards. Technical Information Services Series GS-1412.* [Washington, DC: Government Printing Office], Feb. 1966.
United States Department of Labor. Women's Bureau. *Working Women Count!* Washington, DC: Government Printing Office, 1994.
Ury, Connie. [Autobiographical interview in] *Library Mosaics* 5(5):27 (Sep./Oct. 1994).
"Users Give High Marks to Library Service; Want More," *American Libraries* 25(8):782 (Sep. 1994).
Utley, George B. "Resolution on Salaries Adopted by the American Library Association June 27, 1919," *Public Libraries* 24(10):461 (Dec. 1919).
Valentine, Patrick M. "The Struggle to Establish Public Library Service in Wilson, North Carolina, 1900–1940," *Libraries & Culture* 28(3):294–306 (Sum. 1993).
Van Allen, Neil. "After the Afterthoughts." Letter. *Special Libraries* 60(8):565–566 (Oct. 1969).
Van Buren, Maud. "The Librarian and Her Apprentices," *Public Libraries* 15(9): 369–372 (Nov. 1910).
Van Dyne, Catherine. "The Library Workers' Association: Draft of Organization Adopted at Atlantic City, April 30, 1920," *Library Journal* 45(10):451–452 (May 15, 1920).
* Van Fleet, Connie. "Career Changing: Options and Strategies for Library Paraprofessionals," *LLA Bulletin* 52(4):184–188 (Spr. 1990).
Vann, Sarah K. *Training for Librarianship before 1923.* Chicago: American Library Association, 1961.
Van Oosbree, Charlotte. "I'm Typing as Fast as I Can—" [orig. pub. in *Show Me Libraries*], *Unabashed Librarian* #48:5–6 (1983).
Varlejs, Jana. "Preface: Practitioners and Educators Talking Together—A Crucial Conversation," in *Education for the Library/Information Profession,* Patricia G. Reeling, ed. Jefferson NC: McFarland, 1993, pp. 1–4.

Vaughn, William J., and J. D. Dunn. "A Study of Job Satisfaction in Six University Libraries," *College & Research Libraries* 35(3):163–177 (May 1974).

Vavrek, Bernard. "Educating Rural Library Staff," *Library Mosaics* 3(1):7–9 (Jan./Feb. 1992).

_____. "Small Libraries = Small Salaries," *American Libraries* 20(2):124 (Feb. 1989).

Veaner, Allen B. "Continuity or Discontinuity—A Persistent Personnel Issue in Academic Librarianship." In *Advances in Library Administration & Organization* 1. Greenwich CT: JAI, 1982, pp. 1–20.

_____. "1985–1995: The Next Decade in Academic Librarianship, Part II," *College & Research Libraries* 46(4):295–308 (July 1985).

_____. "Paradigm Lost, Paradigm Regained? A Persistent Personnel Issue in Academic Librarianship, II," *College & Research Libraries* 55(5):389–402 (Sept. 1994).

Veaner, Allen B., and Page Ackerman. "1985 to 1995: The Next Decade in Academic Librarianship, Part I," *College & Research Libraries* 46(3):209–229 (May 1985).

Veihman, Robert A. "A Library Technical Assistant Program Designed to Meet the Needs of Today's Students," *Library Mosaics* 1(5):12–14 (May/June 1990).

Verma, Dhani. "Report on the 1993 New Orleans COLT Conference," *Library Mosaics* 4(5):18–19 (Sep./Oct. 1993).

Vincent, Ida. "Staff's Perceptions of Public Library Goals: A Case Study of an Australian Public Library," *Library Quarterly* 54(4):396–411 (Oct. 1984).

Visitor. "A Plea for the Assistant Librarian," *Public Libraries* 22(3):100 (Mar. 1917).

Voelck, Julie. "Job Satisfaction Among Support Staff in Michigan Academic Libraries," *College & Research Libraries* 56(2):157–170 (Mar. 1995).

Wakefield, Kate, and Sara Martin. "Nebraska Library Association Paraprofessional Roundtable," *Library Mosaics* 2(7):8–10 (Sep./Oct. 1991).

Wald, Lillian D. "Organization Amongst Working Women," *Annals of the American Academy of Political & Social Science* 27:638–643 [176–183] (1906).

Wales, Elizabeth B. "The Assistants' Class at Braddock (Pa.)," *Public Libraries* 3(1):8 (Jan. 1898).

Walker, H. Thomas. "In-Service Training for Subprofessionals," *ALA Bulletin* 59(2):134–138 (Feb. 1965).

Wallace, Linda. "The Image—and What You Can Do About It in the Year of the Librarian," *American Libraries* 20(1):22–25 (Jan. 1989).

Wallace, Ruth. "Staff Meetings," *Public Libraries* 21(2):60–63 (Feb. 1916).

* Walters, Corky. "Librarian Wanted," *Unabashed Librarian* #59:6 (1986).

Walton, Carol G., and Cecilia Botero. "Offloading or Staff Development? Team Cataloging at the University of Florida," *Cataloging & Classification Quarterly* 15(1):49–73 (1992).

Waltz, Marianne. "First Annual Paraprofessional Conference," *Library Mosaics* 4(5):15 (Sep./Oct. 1993).

Wanden, Joy A. "Alternative Education Options for Library Staff," *Journal of Education for Library and Information Science* 36(1):29–32 (Wint. 1995).

Watson, Paula D. "Founding Mothers: The Contribution of Women's Organizations to Public Library Development in the United States," *Library Quarterly* 64(3): 233–269 (July 1994).

Watstein, Sarah Barbara, and Rosalyn Wilcots. "Disturbances in the Field: Sexual Harassment Part III: Policies and Procedures of Selected National Organizations," *Wilson Library Bulletin* 69(1):26–29 (Sep. 1994).

Weaver, Maggie. "Library Technicians and Information Technology Go Hand in Hand," *Canadian Library Journal* 46(3):149–150 (June 1989).

Webb, Gisela M. "Educating Librarians and Support Staff for Technical Services," *Journal of Library Administration* 9(1):111–120 (1988).

_____. "Preparing Staff for Participative Management," *Wilson Library Bulletin* 62(9):50–52 (May 1988).

* Webb, Josephine. "The Non-professional in the Academic Library: Education for Paraprofessionalism," *Personnel Training & Education* 7(2):21–30 (1990).

Webber, Nigel. "Prospect and Prejudice: Women and Librarianship," *Library History* 6:153–162 (1984).

Weber, Dorothy. "The Clerical Staff," *Library Trends* 3(1):52–58 (July 1954).

Weber, Mark. "Support Staff Unions in Academic and Public Libraries: Some Suggestions for Managers with Reference to the Ohio Experience, 1984–1990," *Journal of Library Administration* 17(3):65–86 (1992).

Weibel, Kathleen. "Certification for Support Staff," *Library Mosaics* 2(6):15–16 (Nov./Dec. 1991).

_____. "I Work in a Library But I'm Not a Librarian," *Library Personnel News* 2:8 (Wint. 1988).

Weil, Carol. "Support Staff in Bibliographic Instruction," *Library Mosaics* 4(3):17 (May/June 1993).

* Weingand, Darlene E. "I Work in a Library, But..." *Journal of Education for Library and Information Science* 33(4):338–339 (Fall 1992).

*_____. "Support Staff: An Important 'New' Market," *Journal of Education for Library and Information Science* 33(2):148–150 (Spr. 1992).

* Weintraub, Benjamin. "The Chain of Causation," *Library Journal* 91(18):4892–4893 (Oct. 15, 1966).

Weissenborn, Lenore. "What an Assistant Expects of a Librarian," *Public Libraries* 21(2):73–75 (Feb. 1916).

Welch, Donald A. "Strike Idea 'Impetuous.'" Letter. *American Libraries* 20(5):441 (May 1989).

Welker, Peggie. [Autobiographical interview in] *Library Mosaics* 2(3):20–21 (Jan./Feb. 1991).

Wells, Sharon B. *The Feminization of the American Library Profession, 1876 to 1923.* Master's dissertation. Chicago: University of Chicago, 1967.

* Welsh, Janet. "The Key Is Flexibility: The Role of the Paralibrarian in a Small Academic Library," *Colorado Libraries* 13(2):17 (June 1987).

Welton, Ann. "A Vocation, Not a Profession." Letter. *American Libraries* 21(8):717 (Sep. 1990).

Wertheimer, Barbara Mayer. *We Were There: The Story of Working Women in America.* New York: Pantheon, 1977.

"What's Wrong with Our Library Schools?" *Library Journal* 91(7):1773–1775 (Apr. 1, 1966).

* Wheeler, Helen Rippier. "The Technician Level of Library Staffing: A Bibliography with Annotations," *Special Libraries* 60(8):527–534 (Oct. 1969).

White, Herbert S. "Differences of Opinion." Letter. *Library Journal* 92(14):2685 (Aug. 1967).

_____. "The Grapes Were Probably Sour, Anyway," *Library Journal* 117(17):45–46 (Oct. 15, 1992).

_____. "Lead Me Not into Temptation to Do Good," *Library Journal* 119(15):47–48 (Sep. 15, 1994).

_____. "Our Goals and Our Programs: We're Better at Caring Than at Getting Others to Care," *Library Journal* 119(17):38–39 (Oct. 15, 1994).

_____. "Our Retreat to Moscow, and Beyond," *Library Journal* 119(3):54–55 (Aug. 1994).

_____. "Pseudo-Libraries and Semi-Teachers, Part 1," *American Libraries* 21(2):103–106 (Feb. 1990).

_____. "Pseudo-Libraries and Semi-Teachers. Part 2," *American Libraries* 21(3):262–266 (March 1990).

_____. "Small Public Libraries—Challenges, Opportunities, and Irrelevancies," *Library Journal* 119(7):53–54 (Apr. 15, 1994).

_____. "To Recommend or Not to Recommend." Letter. *Special Libraries* 56(7):532 (Sep. 1965).

_____. "Tough Times Make Bad Managers Worse," *Library Journal* 119(3):132, 134 (Feb. 15, 1994).

_____. "What Do We Want to Be When We Grow Up?' *Library Journal* 119(9):50–51 (May 15, 1994).

_____. "Why Do 'They' Close Library Schools?" *Library Journal* 117(19):51–52 (Nov. 15, 1992).

_____. "Your Half of the Boat Is Sinking," *Library Journal* 118(17):45–46 (Oct. 15, 1993).

White, Herbert S., and Marion Paris. "Employer Preferences and the Library Education Curriculum," *Library Quarterly* 55(1):1–33 (Jan. 1985).

White, Neva. "'Goodwill' in the Library," *Library Journal* 84(4):567–568 (Feb. 15, 1959).

Whitelock, Alfred T. "Para & Pro." Letter. *Library Journal* 100(20):2082 (Nov. 15, 1975).

Whitmore, Frank H. "A Library Interpreter," *Public Libraries* 21(1):16–17 (Jan. 1916).

Wiegand, Wayne A. "The Development of Librarianship in the United States," *Libraries & Culture* 24(1):99–109 (Wint. 1989).

Wiener, Paul B. "Whose Fight Is It anyway?" Letter. *Library Journal* 114(16):6 (Oct. 1, 1989).

Wight, Edward A. "Separation of Professional and Nonprofessional Work in Public Libraries," *California Librarian* 14(1):29–32, 54 (Sep. 1952).

Wilcox, Almira R. "A Mistaken Judgement." Letter. *Public Libraries* 22(9):366–367 (Nov. 1917).

Williams, Edwin E. "Who Does What: Unprofessional Personnel Policies," *College & Research Libraries* 6(4):301–310 (Sep. 1945).

Williams, Karen. *Implementing an Information Desk: Avenues Toward Increased Quality of Reference and Loan Services. Summary and Evaluation of the Information Desk Experiment.* [Paper presented to ALA], 1987. ERIC ED # 290 496.

* Williams, Laurie. "Paralibrarian and Proud," *Colorado Libraries* 13(2):15 (June 1987).

* Williams, Leslie Joann. "Professional Development at UCI: The Administrators Speak," *Library Mosaics* 2(4):8–11 (Mar./Apr. 1991).

Williamson, Charles Clarence. *The Williamson Reports of 1921 and 1923: Including Training for Library Work (1921) and Training for Library Service (1923).* Metuchen NJ: Scarecrow, 1971.

Wilson, Pauline. *Stereotype and Status: Librarians in the United States.* Westport CT: Greenwood, 1982.

Windsor, Phineas L. "Statement of the Committee on Standardization of Libraries and Certification of Librarians," *Library Journal* 42(9):719–724 (Sep. 1917).

Winkler, Judith A. "Support Staff Classification in Academic Libraries," *Library Mosaics* 4(6):11–13 (Nov./Dec. 1993).

Winstead, Elizabeth B. "Staff Reactions to Automation," *Computers in Libraries* 14(4):18–21 (Apr. 1994).

Wittingslow, G. E., and Mitcheson, B. "Job Satisfaction Among Library Staff," *Journal of Library Administration* 5(4):61–69 (1984).

Wolcott, Debbie. [Autobiographical interview in] *Library Mosaics* 2(5):25 (May/June 1991).
Women in Librarianship: Melvil's Rib Symposium. Margaret Myers and Mayra Scarborough, eds. New Brunswick NJ: Bureau of Library & Information Science Research, Rutgers University Graduate School of Library Service, 1975.
Woodard, Beth S. "The Effectiveness of an Information Desk Staffed by Graduate Students and Nonprofessionals," *College & Research Libraries* 50(4):455–467 (July 1989).
Woodard, Beth S., and Sharon J. Van Der Laan. "Training Preprofessionals for Reference Service," *The Reference Librarian* 16:233–254 (1986/87).
Woolf, Virginia. *A Room of One's Own.* New York: Harcourt, Brace & World, 1929.
_____. *Three Guineas.* New York: Harcourt, Brace & World, 1938.
Woolson, Barbara. "'Small' from the Inside." Letter. *Library Journal* 119(11):8 (June 15, 1994).
* "Working Women Count!" *AFSCME: The Public Employee Magazine* 60(1):28 (Jan./Feb. 1995).
Wozniak, Robert. "Bargaining: Settlements Lag Despite Economic Growth," *AFL-CIO News* 40(6):5–8 (Mar. 20, 1995).
Wright, Carroll D. *The Working Girls of Boston.* Boston: Wright & Potter, 1889 [Reprinted by Arno, 1969].
Wyer, James I. "Women in College Libraries," *School and Society* 29(738):227–228 (Feb. 16 1929).
"The Year in Library Circles," *Public Libraries* 17(1):13–14 (Jan. 1912).
York State. "An Amateur View of How to Do It," *Public Libraries* 20(6):258–259 (June 1915).
Younger, Jennifer. "Continuing Education: A Focus on Paraprofessionals," *ALCTS Newsletter* 2(6):57–59 (1991).
Zipkowitz, Fay. "Placements & Salaries 1990: Losing Ground in the Recession," *Library Journal* 116(18):44–50 (Nov. 1, 1991).
_____. "Placements & Salaries 1992: Fewer Graduates but Salaries Climb," *Library Journal* 118 (17):30–36 (Oct. 15, 1993).
_____. "Placements & Salaries 1993, Part 1: 1993 Placements Up, But Full-Time Jobs Are Scarce," *Library Journal* 119(17):26–29 (Oct. 15, 1994).

Index